Surviving Hitler and Mussolini

Occupation in Europe Series

Surviving Hitler and Mussolini is part of the European Science Foundation (ESF) programme 'Occupation in Europe: The Impact of National Socialist and Fascist Rule'.

The ESF acts as a catalyst for the development of science by bringing together leading scientists and funding agencies to debate, plan and implement pan-European scientific and science policy initiatives. It is also responsible for the management of COST (European Cooperation in the field of Scientific and Technical Research).

ESF is the European association of seventy-seven major national funding agencies devoted to scientific research in thirty countries. It represents all scientific disciplines: physical and engineering sciences, life, earth and environmental sciences, medical sciences, humanities and social sciences. The Foundation assists its Member Organizations in two main ways. It brings scientists together in its Scientific Forward Looks, Exploratory Workshops, Programmes, Networks, EUROCORES, and ESF Research Conferences, to work on topics of common concern including Research Infrastructures. It also conducts the joint studies of issues of strategic importance in European science policy and manages, on behalf of its Member Organizations, grant schemes, such as EURYI (European Young Investigator Awards).

It maintains close relations with other scientific institutions within and outside Europe. By its activities, the ESF adds value by cooperation and coordination across national frontiers and endeavours, offers expert scientific advice on strategic issues, and provides the European forum for science.

Surviving Hitler and Mussolini

Daily Life in Occupied Europe

Edited by
Robert Gildea, Olivier Wieviorka and Anette Warring

Oxford • New York

English edition
First published in 2006 by
Berg
Editorial offices:
1st Floor, Angel Court, 81 St Clements Street, Oxford OX4 1AW, UK
175 Fifth Avenue, New York, NY 10010, USA

© ESF 2006

Paperback edition published in 2007

Berg is the imprint of Oxford International Publishers Ltd.

Library of Congress Cataloging-in-Publication Data
Surviving Hitler and Mussolini : daily life in occupied Europe / edited by
Robert Gildea, Olivier Wieviorka and Anette Warring.—English ed.
    p. cm.—(Occupation in Europe series)
    Includes bibliographical references and index.
    ISBN-13: 978-1-84520-181-4 (pbk.)
    ISBN-10: 1-84520-181-7 (pbk.)
    ISBN-13: 978-1-84520-180-7
    ISBN-10: 1-84520-180-9
  1. World War, 1939-1945—Occupied territories. 2. Europe—Social
conditions—20th century. 3. Europe—Economic conditions—1918-1945.
4. Military occupation—Social aspects. 5. Military occupation—
Economic aspects. I. Gildea, Robert. II. Wieviorka, Olivier, 1960-
III. Warring, Anette, 1958- IV. Series.

    D802.E9S87 2006
    940.53'37—dc22

                                                            2006007829

British Library Cataloguing-in-Publication Data
A catalogue record for this book is available from the British Library.

ISBN 978 1 84520 180 7 (Cloth)
      978 1 84520 181 4 (Paper)

Typeset by JS Typesetting Ltd, Porthcawl, Mid Glamorgan
Printed in the United Kingdom by Biddles Ltd, King's Lynn

www.bergpublishers.com

Contents

Acknowledgements

We are indebted first and foremost to the European Science Foundation (ESF), which funded the project on *Occupation in Europe: The Impact of National Socialist and Fascist Rule* (INSFO) of which this volume is one of six parts, and to Hans Blom of the Netherlands Institute for War Documentation (NIOD) and Wolfgang Benz of the Technical University, Berlin, who directed the project. We would like to thank Madelise Blumenroeder of the ESF, and Johannes Houwink ten Cate and Conny Kristel of NIOD, successively research co-ordinators of the INSFO project, for their skill and diplomacy in managing the project.

The Daily Life team would like to thank those institutions which hosted their workshops, notably Gustavo Corni of the University of Trento and Italian-German Historical Institute, the Warden and Fellows of Merton College, Oxford, Brigitte Marin and Catherine Garbin of the French School at Rome, Gérard Chastagnaret and Jean-Paul Brutus of the Casa Velázquez, the French School at Madrid, and the staff of the NIOD in Amsterdam.

We would like to thank those who contributed to the research and writing of this book who do not appear in the final list of contributors. Most especially these include Lidia Santarelli, Lutz Klinkhammer, Davide Rodogno, Agnieszka Cieślikowa and Tatiana Maksimova. Their support over the years of the project was invaluable.

Lastly, thanks are due to Iain Chadwick of Oxford University, who compiled the bibliography and index with great professionalism.

Notes on Contributors

Geraldien von Frijtag Drabbe Künzel is a lecturer at the Faculty of Arts, University of Utrecht. She is the author of *Het recht van de sterkste. Duitse strafrechtspleging in bezet Nederland* (Amsterdam, Bert Bakker, 1999) and *Kamp Amersfoort* (Amsterdam, Mets & Schilt, 2003)

Juliane Fürst is a junior research fellow at St John's College, Oxford. She is editing a book on *Late Stalinism: Society between Reconstruction and Reinvention* and preparing a monograph entitled *Stalin's Last Generation: Youth, Culture and Identity in the Post-war Soviet Union 1945–1956*.

Robert Gildea is Professor of Modern French History at the University of Oxford. His books include *Marianne in Chains: In Search of the German Occupation, 1940–1944* (London, Macmillan, 2002) and *The Past in French History* (Yale University Press, 1994). He is currently working on 1968 in European perspective.

Dirk Luyten is a researcher at the Centre d'Études et Documentation Guerre et Sociétés Contemporaines (CEGESOMA), Brussels. He has written *Burgers boven elke verdenking? Vervolging van economische collaboratie in België na de Tweede Wereldoorlog* (Brussel, VUB-Press, 1996) and co-written *België tijdens de Tweede Wereldoorlog* (Antwerp, Standaard Uitgeverij, 2004).

Bénédicte Rochet is a researcher at the Centre d'Études et Documentation Guerre et Sociétés Contemporaines, Brussels. Her publications include *Les Universités belges pendant la Seconde Guerre mondiale* (Université Catholique de Louvains, 1998).

Jacek Tebinka is a lecturer in the Department of Contemporary History, Institute of Political Sciences, University of Gdansk. He has written *Polityka brytyjska wobec problemu granicy polsko-brytyjskiej 1939–1945* (Warsaw, Neriton, 1998) and edited *Na najwyzszym szczeblu. Spotkania premierow Rzeczypospolitej Polskiej i Wielkiej Brytanii podczas II wojny swiatowej* (Warsaw, Wydawnictwo LTW, 1999).

Polymeris Voglis is a lecturer at the University of Thessaly. He has written *Becoming a Subject: Political Prisoners during the Greek Civil War* (New York and London, Berghahn, 2002).

Pavla Vošahlíková is a professor at the Institute of History, Academy of Sciences, Prague. She has written *Jak se žilo za časů Františka Josefa I* (Prague, Nakladetelství Svoboda, 1996) and *Auf der Walz. Erinnerungen böhmischer Handwerksgesellen* (Vienna, Böhlau, 1994).

Anette Warring is Professor of History in the Department of History and Social Theory, University of Roskilde. Among her publications are *Tyskerpiger – under besættelse og retsopgør* (Copenhagen, Gyldendal, 1994, 1998) and *Historie, magt og identitet – grundlovsfejringer gennem 150 år* (Århus, Aarhus Universitetsforlag). She is currently directing a project on alternative culture in Denmark in the 1960s and 1970s.

Fabrice Weiss is a doctoral student at the University of Metz. He is completing a doctorate on education in Luxemburg and the Moselle under the German occupation.

Olivier Wieviorka is Professor of History at the École Normale Supérieure de Cachan, Paris. Among his publications are *Une certaine idée de la Résistance. Défense de la France, 1940–1949* (Paris, Seuil, 1995) and *Les orphelins de la République. Destinées des députés et sénateurs français, 1940–1945* (Paris, Seuil, 2001). He is currently writing a book on D-Day.

Abbreviations

AK – Armia Krajowa – Polish Home Army
AL – Armia Ludowa – Polish People's Army (communist)
BCh – Bataliony Chłopskie – Polish Peasant Battalions
BSV – Bratskoe Sotrudchestvo Voennoplennikh – Brotherly Collection of Soviet POWs
CCI – Comité Central Industriel – employers' organization (Belgium)
CGT – Confédération Générale du Travail – French trade-union federation
CGPF – Confédération Générale du Patronat Français – employers' federation (France)
CIEEs – Comité interprofessionel d'épuration d'entreprise – Interprofessional Business Purge Committees (France)
CLS – Comités de Lutte Syndicale – underground communist trade-union movement (Belgium)
COBTB – Comité d'Organisation du Bâtiment et des Travaux Publics – Building and Public Works Cartel under Vichy
COS – Comités d'Organisation – industrial cartels under Vichy
EAM – Ethniko Apeleutherotiko Metopo – National Liberation Front
ELAS – Ethnikos Laikos Apeleutherotikos Stratos – National People's Liberation Army
FLAK – Flieger Abwehr Kanone – Anti-aircraft artillery
FNDIR – Fédération nationale des déportés et internés de la résistance – National Federation of Deportees and Internees of the Resistance (France)
IMIs – Italian Military Internees
KAJ – Katholieke Arbeidersjeugd – Catholic Workers Youth (Belgium)
KKE – Kommounistiko Komma Elladas (Communist Party of Greece)
MNPGD – Mouvement national des prisonniers de guerre et déportés – National Association of Prisoners of War and Deportees (France)
MSU – Mouvement Syndical Unifié – underground communist trade-union movement (Belgium)
MVC – Militärverwaltungschef – Chief military administrator
NKVD – Narodny Komissariat Vnutrennikh Del – Soviet People's Commissariat for Internal Affairs
NS – Nasjonal Samling – Norwegian Nazi Party
NSB – Nationaal Socialistische Beweging – Dutch National Socialist Movement
NSDAP – Nationalsozialistische Deutsche Arbeiterpartei – Nazi Party

NSLB – Nationalsozialistischer Lehrerbund – National Socialist Teachers' Union
NSUF – Nasjonal Samlings Ungdoms Fylking – Norwegian Youth Organization
NSV – Nationalsozialistische Volkswohlfahrt – Nazi People's Welfare Organization
NVV – Nederlands Vakverbond – Netherlands Socialist Trade Union
OKW – Oberkommando der Wehrmacht
ORA – Organisation de Résistance de l'Armée
OSE – Organisation pour le Sauvetage des Enfants – Organization for Rescuing Children (France)
POB – Parti Ouvrier Belge – Belgian Socialist Party
SMERSH – Smert' Shpionam – Soviet counter-intelligence department
SNCASO – Société Nationale de Construction Aéronautique du Sud-Ouest – aeroplane factory at Nantes-Bouguenais
SOE – Special Operations Executive
STO – Service du Travail Obligatoire – Forced labour (France)
UTMI – Union des Travailleurs Manuels et Intellectuels – German-sponsored trade union in Belgium
VdB – Volkdeutsche Bewegung – Pro-German movement (Luxemburg)
ZWZ – Związek Walki Zbrojnej – Union For Armed Struggle (Poland)

Source: Peter Calvocoressi, Guy Wint, John Pritchard, *Total War: Causes and Consequences of the Second World War* (Viking, 1989)

Introduction

Robert Gildea and the Team

Is everyday life possible in a situation of total war, foreign occupation and subjection to a Nazi or Fascist political order? Europe, between 1939 and 1945, was in the grip of a war of ideology, extermination and genocide which resulted in as many casualties among civilians as among combatants. While combatants engaged in battles with immense fire-power from Stalingrad to Normandy, and over 3 million out of 5 million captured Russian soldiers died in German prisoner of war camps, civilians bore the brunt of bombing by Axis and Allied planes alike and the scorched-earth policy of both Soviets and Germans. Civilian populations were displaced in their millions, whether fleeing before invading armies, fearful of atrocities, evacuated from bombed cities, or moved by the Soviet authorities as unreliable ethnic minorities away from the front line. The economies and labour forces of occupied Europe were riveted to the needs of the German war machine, with over eight million people brought to work in Germany. In the absence of their menfolk, whether as soldiers or as deported workers, women were frequently the main breadwinners as well as heads of the family, and were liable to seduction or rape by invading or occupying forces. Occupying forces purged or exterminated target groups that were seen as a menace to their war effort, the Germans in occupied Poland getting rid first of intellectuals, then of Jews. In the heart of occupied Europe Nazi and fascist ideology was imposed by propaganda, schooling, youth movements and the persecution of churches. Food was generally in short supply, and famine stalked the land from Greece to Russia. Where civilians took up arms against the occupying forces as partisans or *maquisards*, regular armies having dwindled away, they found themselves fighting an unequal battle, sustaining heavy losses and subjected to torture to betray their comrades. Where resistance fighters struck, then the occupying forces resorted to collective reprisals against civilians suspected of harbouring them, from the execution of hostages to the torching of villages.

Estimates of casualties are contested, but it is clear that some parts of Europe suffered much more sharply than others from war and occupation. Stalin's admission of 7 million Soviet dead was revised up to 20 million by Khrushchev and to 27–28 million in 1990, or 16 per cent of the 1939 population.[1] Poland lost 450,000 battle casualties but 6 million people altogether, among whom were 3 million Jews, or 19 per cent of her population. Germany itself lost between 4 and 7 million people, including 125,000 Jews, or between 6 and 10 per cent of her population. The Yugoslavs lost about 1.7 million people, most of them civilians, or 12 per cent of the population, while Greece lost perhaps 300,000, or 3.4 per cent of the population, including 60,000 Jews and 140,000 deaths from famine. Other countries were more fortunate. Czechoslovakia lost about 415,000 or 2.8 per cent of its population. In western Europe, the Netherlands was worst off, with 200,000 deaths, or 2.2 per cent of the population, while France lost 600,000 or 1.5 per cent, Italy 410,000 or 0.95 per cent, Belgium 60,000 or 0.7 per cent, and Denmark only 4400 or 0.1 per cent.[2]

The steep gradient between the impact of the war in the east and that in the west can be explained by three factors: the nature of the war in the region, the presence or absence of governmental or administrative structures in occupied Europe, which could mediate between the occupying authorities and the local population, and the extent to which occupation was accompanied by policies of Germanization or Nazification. In some sense there were two very different wars in Europe, a *Blitzkrieg* in the west, which brought about the rapid surrender of the Netherlands, Belgium, Luxemburg and France in May and June 1940, while Denmark was occupied with scarcely a shot being fired, and wars of attrition in the Balkans and on the eastern front, in which the occupying forces never fully imposed control and opposition was kept up by partisans in the Balkans and regular armies with partisan involvement in the east. It should not be forgotten, however, that the impact of war was not only the responsibility of the Axis powers. Famine in Greece in 1941–2 and in the Netherlands in 1944–5 were as much the result of Allied blockade, while towns and cities in continental Europe were bombed in the latter stages of the war not by the Luftwaffe but by the British and American air forces, seeking in theory at least to destroy the Axis war economy and break civilian morale.

The nature of the occupation arrangements was the second factor shaping daily life. Denmark, for example, enjoyed a so-called peace-occupation, its sovereignty recognized, the monarchy in place and government functioning until August 1943 and its administrative institutions in place after that.[3] In the case of the Netherlands, the Queen and the government went into exile, but the Dutch administration continued under the authority of the secretaries-general of government departments who assumed the position of ministers, under the German civil administration of the Austrian Dr Arthur Seyss-Inquart.[4] Occupied Belgium and northern France were placed under a German military administration, the Militärbefehlshaber at Brussels von Falkenhausen and at Paris Otto von Stülpnagel, but the Belgian and French administrations remained intact under them.[5] Under the Armistice of June 1940 the French government of Marshal Pétain at Vichy was formally sovereign over the whole of France, given what was on the face of things a temporary military occupation of the north, but effective only in the centre and south of France, and that only until November 1942.

Occupation regimes were much more severe in central, southern and eastern Europe. The predominantly German-speaking part of Czechoslovakia, the Sudetenland, was annexed directly to the Reich in October 1938 as the Sudetengau, and Slovakia became an independent satellite state, while Bohemia-Moravia became a protectorate under the south German diplomat Konstantin von Neurath, with responsibility for defence and foreign affairs, although under him were a Czech president, Hácha, and prime minister, Eliáš. Conditions became much more brutal, however, with the arrival of a new Protector, Hitler's security chief Reinhard Heydrich, in September 1941, with Eliáš one of hundreds to be tried and executed, and terror reached even greater intensity after the assassination of Heydrich in June 1942.[6] Poland was again partitioned under the Nazi–Soviet pact, with eastern territory around Lvov going to the Soviets. The German part was not given the luxury of its own government: the areas around Posen and the free city of Danzig were annexed to the Reich under the Gauleiters of Warthegau and West Prussia respectively, while the General Government of a rump Poland at Warsaw was little more than a German dictatorship under the lawyer Dr Hans Frank and a dumping ground for Poles and Jews.[7] The Italian attack on Greece in October 1940 was repulsed by the Greeks, but in April 1941 the Germans invaded Yugoslavia, destroying its government, set up Croatia as an independent satellite state and partitioned the country into German and Italian zones of occupation.[8] Greece was likewise defeated by the Germans and partitioned between Germany, Italy and Bulgaria, but a government under the 'Greek Pétain' General Tsolakoglu managed a degree of autonomy until November 1942.[9] When the Germans invaded the Soviet Union in June 1941, Soviet rule evaporated in the zones they occupied. An Ostministerium under Alfred Rosenberg oversaw two civilian Reichskommissariats, one for Ukraine, the other for the Baltic Republics and White Russia/Belorussia (Ostland), although in practice the German military were reluctant to let go of territories under their control. Russian authority was limited to the local level – mayors and village elders or *starosty*, together with local police forces – who were not in a strong position to protect the local population.[10]

A third factor which shaped daily life was the degree to which an area was integrated into the Greater German Reich, undergoing a process of Germanization and Nazification. Areas that had been part of the German Empire before 1918, such as Alsace and the Moselle, the Warthegau and West Prussia, together with areas with a heavy concentration of ethnic Germans, such as the Sudetengau, were subjected to a full process of Germanization by means of propaganda, education and ideological conformity through recruitment to organizations such as the Hitler Youth. Areas just outside the core, such as the Protectorate of Bohemia-Moravia and the General Government of Poland, suffered the destruction of their educated class and national culture rather than being Germanized, and were not seen fit to collaborate in the Nazi project. Further afield, countries were subjected to economic exploitation, military order and police security, so that any form of opposition was ruthlessly dealt with. There daily life faced the same challenges of survival, but not the additional offensive of conformity to German nationalism or Nazi ideology.

Occupation was experienced as highly disruptive, but how so depended on what had been experienced before. Thousands of Belgians and French people fled before the invader in May–June 1940, fearing a repetition of the atrocities committed by the

Germans in 1914–18, but were relieved to find the behaviour of the German soldiers 'correct'. As German forces entered Nantes, recorded a local schoolmaster, 'civilians surrounded the soldiers and tried to question them, showing no animosity, while the Germans took photos of them'.[11] When they crossed the borderlands of Russia a year later, older people remembered the German occupation of the First World War as relatively benevolent. Since then they had endured a violent sovietization, with the elimination of national culture, the closure of churches, forced collectivization and a famine in 1932–4 that had cost the lives of seven million Soviets, five million of them Ukrainian. Not surprisingly, Ukrainian women blessed German soldiers with crucifixes and offered them bread with salt.[12]

Although occupied countries were under enormous pressure, this did not mean that they were literally enslaved or that civil society was entirely extinguished. People faced more than a clear-cut choice between collaboration with the occupying forces or resistance. Survival in fact tended to suggest finding ways towards a *modus vivendi* with the occupier, towards forms of 'accommodation' or 'cohabitation'.[13] The demands of the German war economy created opportunities for profit and employment as well as the risk of being drafted forcibly into the labour force. Shortages and rationing on the official market gave rise to black and grey markets where prices were more flexible and supply more available, if at higher prices. Churches that had been persecuted by the French Third Republic or closed by the Soviet authorities enjoyed renewed independence, while populations in need of temporal salvation turned in greater numbers to religion. National cultures were sometimes allowed to flourish under an official policy of divide and rule, or were sustained by clandestine schools and associations functioning in parallel to the official ones. Occupied populations were guaranteed protection of their lives, property and religion so long as they admitted defeat, obeyed the occupying authorities and offered no resistance. Resistance by non-combatants was not the same as war by soldiers: it was regarded as violating the laws of war and was punished under martial law.[14] Collective punishments such as hostage-taking, which were formally outlawed under the laws of war, were widely used by the Germans in order to maintain order, but with different weight according to the context. While 33,000 Jews were massacred in the ravine of Babi Yar outside Kiev on 29–30 September 1941 after explosives left by the retreating Soviet army greeted the German forces who had just occupied the city, the Germans refrained from executing a second batch of fifty hostages in response to the assassination of the Feldkommandant of Nantes on 20 October 1941, because the military governor Otto von Stülpnagel did not want to alienate the French population by the 'use of Polish methods in France'.[15] Of course suffering increased as the war drew to its bloody end, but even in the most extreme of circumstances people's instinct for survival was manifest: after the German Sixth Army surrendered at Stalingrad on 2 February 1943, after months of fighting with Soviet forces, nearly ten thousand civilians, including a thousand children, emerged from the rubble of the city.[16]

Although all these dimensions of the experience of occupation are representative of 'daily life', 'daily life' has not until now been a favoured subject for historians studying the Second World War. Three reasons may be suggested for this relative neglect: conceptual, political and professional. In the first place, it is not clear what daily life is as a concept of use to historians. Is it purely private life with the politics left out? Is it history 'from the bottom up' rather than that of high politics and great men? Does it deal with the silent majority, the grey mass of anonymous, ordinary people who are the victims of events but do not influence them? Is it habit or routine, a material culture outside the sweep of historical trends? Is it essentially local rather than national or global, or *petite histoire*, anecdotal and descriptive, defying meaningful analysis?

Secondly, politically, the study of civilian life during the Second World War has been heavily politicized, if not moralized, because the identity, solidarity and honour of nations and groups challenging for power has been at stake. Ideologically inspired narratives have been constructed to legitimate one group or to delegitimate another. In many countries a myth of resistance to Nazism or fascism has been elaborated to wipe away the shame of defeat and occupation and the guilt of collaboration in what Pieter Lagrou has called 'a desperate need for patriotic memories'.[17] In Italy, despite its fascist moment, the emphasis was on resistance to Nazism after 1943 until Claudio Pavone's *Una guerra civile* (1991) suggested an alternative paradigm of a civil war between fascists and anti-fascists and class war cutting across the familiar patriotic war against the Germans.[18] In Greece a pervasive Cold War anti-communism portrayed the resistance as a communist plot masterminded by Moscow, a dominant view that was not challenged until after the end of military rule in 1974.

The only escape from the labelling of resister or collaborator has been to be recognized as a victim, even a martyr. The Holocaust has set an alternative agenda by which other groups which suffered in the Second World War, from gypsies to gays and from forced labourers to POWs, have laid claim to the blessing of victimhood.[19] But the political model is still dominant, and roles have been hierarchized, not least by resistance organizations, according to the degree of resistance they manifested. Thus Italian soldiers taken prisoner by the Germans after Italy surrendered to the Allies in September 1943 have preferred to fight for their honour as soldiers rather than seek sympathy as victims, French forced labourers have continually campaigned for the status of 'deportee' denied them by resistance organizations who regard this as denoting political resistance, while Jewish groups have been keen to highlight cases of Jewish resistance to Nazism.[20]

Thirdly, professionally, daily life has been regarded unfavourably as a subject of study by academic historians. For long it was seen as the territory of local historians, right-wing historians, amateur historians, or historians outside the dominant schools in the universities. In France, for example, Hachette launched a series on *la vie quotidienne* in the late 1930s. The flagship volume was *Daily Life in Ancient Rome*

(1939) by Jerôme Carcopino, who went on to blot his career by becoming education minister in the Vichy government. Jean Robiquet's *Daily Life in the French Revolution* (1938) is not cited in the standard works on the Revolution by Georges Lefebvre, Albert Soboul or François Furet. The multivolume history of daily life under the German occupation by Henri Amouroux is marginalized by academic historians on the grounds that it is based on testimonies sent in by the public rather than on official archives, and written by an amateur historian or with a right-wing bias.[21]

Much more effective in the early days was the work of sociologists who did not labour under the institutional snobbery aimed at daily life. The Polish sociologist Florian Znaniecki, who emigrated to the USA in 1913, and an American sociologist, William Thomas, produced a study of how migrant Poles coped with the daily life challenges of their new country in *The Polish Peasant in Europe and America* (1913–20). For western Europe, the seminal work was the study by the Belgian sociologist Guillaume Jacquemyns, undertaken during the war itself and published soon after, on the standard of living and mentality of workers in the industrialized Walloon part of Belgium, *La Société belge sous l'occupation allemande, 1940–1944*. Commissioned by the governor of the Société Générale, Alexandre Galopin, who had a keen practical interest in wartime industrial relations, it was not followed by any Belgian historical study of daily life until the 1980s. Around that time the American sociologist and anthropologist James C. Scott used the case study of a Malaysian village to explore ways in which the peasantry resisted those demanding taxes, rent, labour and food not by political resistance, which was 'suicidal', but by 'everyday forms of resistance … the ordinary weapons of relatively powerless groups', such as foot-dragging, desertion, pilfering, arson and sabotage. What he called the 'weapons of the weak' offered an insightful way of understanding the ways in which ordinary communities adopted survival strategies that defied categorization either as heroic resistance or as victimhood.[22]

Despite these handicaps, the history of everyday life has been rescued in recent years as a fruitful, inventive and increasingly central historical approach. Both a practice and a theory of everyday life have been elaborated in France, Britain and above all Germany. Broadly speaking, this can be traced back to the intellectual ferment created by 1968, and the emergence of libertarianism, feminism, ecology and so on. It rescued for historical study groups that had been considered marginal to mainstream history, and their efforts to find a place and an identity. That historical study was conducted not from ivory towers but democratically, involving as participants those who themselves were the objects of study. Everyday life was redefined in an enabling way, not as habit or routine but as the tactics of the weak against the strong, to turn unpromising situations to their advantage.

The first theoretical steps were taken in France. The Marxist Henri Lefebvre, writing in 1967, saw everyday life as grasping for autonomy but manipulated by what he called the Bureaucratic Society of Controlled Consumption, using such tools as advertising, fashion and tourism. He saw signs of resistance in yearnings for the traditional, the communitarian, the natural and sacred, but was not convinced by their stamina to ward off modern, technocratic and consumerist society.[23] Much more positively, taking into the account developments in the 1980s, Michel de Certeau published *The Practice of Everyday Life* (1984). He saw everyone at the mercy of productivist and consumerist culture as marginal, so that 'marginality is becoming universal. A marginal group has now become a silent majority'. He did not, however, see that majority as powerless since through the practices of everyday life they were able to seize opportunities to turn the tables on the powerful. Where Foucault in *Discipline and Punish* (1977) had concentrated on the 'micro-physics' of power, the way the tentacles of power operate most effectively in the schoolroom, workshop or hospital, de Certeau highlighted the 'everyday creativity' of individuals, their skill in subverting rules in small ways, and their forging of a 'network of antidiscipline, which is the subject of this book'.[24]

A second volume of *The Practice of Everyday Life*, written by Pierre Mayol and Luce Giard, on community life and cooking in the Croix-Rousse quarter of Lyon, indicating exciting ways forward, was not taken up in French academic circles. At virtually the same time Fernand Braudel brought out his *Civilization and Capitalism*, a three-volume study of the pre-industrial world on which he had been working on and off since 1950.[25] Its first volume, *The Structures of Everyday Life*, presented an inflexible view of daily life as 'habit or, better yet, routine... I think that mankind is more than waist-deep in routine'.[26] This 'material life' of constraints on population growth, the struggle for 'daily bread', habitat, clothing, traditional modes of production and exchange, were considered by Braudel to be outside the 'history' he dealt with in the last volume of the expansion of international capitalism. This monument of the *Annales* school, casing everyday life in iron, was a road leading nowhere.

In Britain, the main breakthrough came with the history workshop that started at Ruskin College, Oxford, whose students were adults mainly drawn from the labour movement, under the guidance of Raphael Samuel, in 1967. Designed as 'an attack on the examination system, and the humiliations ... imposed on adult students' by the Oxford academic establishment, it drew on the experiences of the students themselves and their local and workplace milieux as a democratic route into historical study. Concentrating mainly on labour and people's history in the nineteenth and twentieth centuries, it was a history of ordinary people by ordinary people for ordinary people. Self-consciously socialist, but in a libertarian way, it intersected with the emerging feminist movement and the Oral History Society, founded in 1971.[27] Of course it could not eschew academic history altogether, and enjoyed the patronage of the likes of Gareth Stedman Jones, Tim Mason, Christopher Hill, E.P. Thompson and Eric Hobsbawm. In 1976 it launched its own journal, *History Workshop*, in which studies of the working class and popular culture, women and gender, local and oral history had pride of place. Although 'everyday life' was not explicitly used as a category of analysis, it was without doubt the unspoken territory of the journal.

More explicit about its terminology was the movement of *Geschichtswerkstätten* or history workshops which sprang up in West Germany in the 1980s. Democratic like their British counterpart, they involved professional historians with active members of local communities and lay people who wanted to share memories about the past. They argued that history was public property and not just the concern of university departments and in particular wished to explore the phenomenon of Nazism in the experience of ordinary people and from the angle of everyday life.[28] The movement intersected with a vogue for documentaries and fact-based films on ordinary lives under Nazism, from *Holocaust* in 1979 to *Heimat* in 1984 and *Das schreckliche Mädchen* in 1990. Local history and oral history were central to the enterprise and formed the basis of Lutz Niethammer's study of the experience of the working population of the Ruhr between 1930 and 1950.[29] Clear also was a generational war in the universities, with younger historians opposed to the 'historical social-science' or *Gesellschaftsgeschichte* of the so-called 'guild' of Hans-Ulrich Wehler, Heinrich-August Winkler and Jürgen Kocka, who saw the nineteenth and twentieth centuries in terms of macro-historical modernizing processes such as industrialization, urbanization, bureaucratization and the development of the nation-state, and dealt with large social groups, championing instead an *Alltagsgeschichte*, which set out to put everyday, ordinary people back at the centre of history. Their mouthpiece was a journal, *Geschichtswerkstatt*, animated by the likes of Michael Wildt, Thomas Lindenberger, Alf Lüdtke, Ina Merkel and Dorothee Wierling. Very influential in this respect was the Bavaria Project of Munich's Institute of Contemporary History, directed by Martin Broszat, which studied the impact of Nazism on everyday life in Bavaria, exploring how far ordinary people had accommodated to it and how far they had been able to criticize, oppose or resist. In particular it promoted the concept of *Resistenz*, which gave credit to everyday gestures of opposition to a regime that aspired to be totalitarian, such as refusing to say 'Heil Hitler' or criticizing the Nazi persecution of the Catholic Church and putting obstacles in the way of the regime's ambition to control the whole of economic, social and cultural life.[30]

Highly influential outside Germany was the work of former Marxists, such as Detlev Peukert's *Inside Nazi Germany. Conformity, Opposition and Racism in Everyday Life* (1989), which acknowledged the work of Tim Mason on working-class opposition to Nazism and explored youth movements hostile to the Hitler Youth, such as the Edelweiss pirates.[31] Most important, Alf Lüdtke edited a manifesto volume on *The History of Everyday Life* (1995), which echoed Michel de Certeau by placing 'human social practice' at the centre of its analysis, looking at how ordinary people experienced events, responded to them and, in small but creative ways, were able to influence them. One of the contributions, by Hans Medick, explicitly harnessed anthropological methods in the study 'the other', 'not in the so-called primitive societies, but in our own history', exploring the social practices by which groups marginalized by the process of modernization were able to re-appropriate the world as their own.[32]

There is now, therefore, a historiography of everyday life which, in the German case, developed precisely as what Peukert called 'everyday life under a state of emergency'.[33] One of its most recent manifestations is Andrew Bergerson, *Ordinary Germans in Extraordinary Times. The Nazi Revolution in Hildesheim* (2005).[34] The concept has been taken up by Sheila Fitzpatrick to explore Stalinist Russia, if not during the war then during the crisis of the 1930s. Her *Everyday Stalinism* (1999) is a study of 'ordinary people' in a situation of 'extraordinary everydayness', putting under the microscope 'forms of behaviour and strategies of survival and advancement that people develop to cope with particular social and political situations'.[35] The study of everyday life in fascist Italy has now also been explored by Richard Bosworth in his *Mussolini's Italy. Life under the Dictatorship.*[36]

The present work is guided by these powerful contributions but also seeks to make its own mark on the understanding of the social experience of ordinary people in occupied Europe, and in particular their strategies of survival. Its approach is fivefold. First, it is resolutely comparative, looking at societies under German occupation from France to Russia and also at those occupied jointly by the Germans and Italians, in particular Greece. Second, it develops as far as possible a 'bottom-up' approach which puts the emphasis on the lived experience of ordinary people rather than a 'top-down' approach dealing with German or Italian policy. It may be presented as a revenge of social history which explores the limits of the so-called totalitarian state rather than assuming that all totalitarian policies were unproblematically carried out. Third, it highlights the subjective experience of those people and how they made sense of the occupation, privileging where possible sources such as memoirs, police reports or oral testimony which allow access to 'voices from below'. Fourth, it starts not from 'hard' categories such as class, gender or nation but regards society as a 'soft wax' put under pressure by occupation. It begins with individual choices and works towards the social relations and networks formed in order to increase chances of survival. It explores how the occupation altered some social relations and balances while confirming or consolidating others. Fifth, it seeks to avoid judging individuals' actions in terms of legitimacy, praising 'good' resistance and condemning 'bad' collaboration, but starts from the perspective that individuals and communities generated their own norms and rules about what constituted acceptable and what unacceptable behaviour under occupation. As nation-states were put under pressure or collapsed, rules about what was acceptable were often conditioned less by what was good for the nation than by what was good for the family, factory, church or local community.

The contributors are all professional historians or researchers, but have presented their own ideas and confronted each other's at a series of workshops in Trento (2000), Oxford (2001), Rome (2002), Warsaw (2003), Madrid (2004) and Amsterdam (2005). Their project, dedicated to daily life, is one of six within the framework of a project entitled *Occupation in Europe: The Impact of National Socialist and Fascist Rule*, directed by Hans Blom of the Netherlands Institute for War Documentation and

Wolfgang Benz of the Technical University, Berlin, and sponsored by the European Science Foundation. Each chapter is comparative and has been written by one, two or three scholars, with additional input from the wider team.

The first chapter, 'Surviving Hunger', written by Polymeris Voglis, examines the problem of hunger under occupation as a result of German requisitions, Allied blockade, the collapse of state power and inadequate relief measures. There were severe shortages and famines, as in Athens in 1941–2, but people experimented with many kinds of survival strategies. New social relations were constructed in order to alleviate hunger. Urban populations rediscovered gardening and made new links with rural suppliers who enjoyed a new economic and social leverage. In many ways this was a golden age for the peasantry. Black marketeers sprang up, some with local connections, others more organized and with far more wide-ranging significance. Some did business with indigenous populations, others with occupying forces who had a great appetite for luxuries and considerable purchasing power. A class of new rich emerged on the back of the black economy. State and occupying authorities intensified efforts to extract resources from the countryside, but this only sharpened 'passive resistance': hoarding, poaching, theft, banditry, and the emergence of local bands who claimed to protect (but also exploited) local populations.

The second chapter, 'To Work or Not to Work', by Robert Gildea, Dirk Luyten and Juliane Fürst, looks at the choices that were open to producers, traders and workers under the occupation. On the one hand, the German war economy set up a huge demand for foodstuffs, manufactured goods and labour, creating opportunities for profit or employment, and the demand was often accompanied by various forms of pressure or force. On the other, they were constrained by their local or national communities, which were critical of collaboration with the Germans, including economic collaboration. Survival and patriotism regularly came into conflict. Ways were found, however, to reach compromises between the defence of economic interests and retaining a patriotic profile, which was important during the war and essential at the liberation. The chapter examines both working for the Germans at home, including what protection, if any, was secured for workers by employers and the state, and working for the Germans in Germany, in particular the experience of forced labourers in Germany, drawn from all parts of Europe. Using untapped diary records, for instance, in the case of Dutch and Belgian workers, and the records of filtration committees which processed forced labourers returning to the USSR, a picture is built up of how workers coped with the rigours of work in Germany and managed to keep body and soul together.

Chapter 3, by Anette Warring, examines intimate and sexual relations under the occupation, which radically changed relationships between men and women. With hundreds of thousands of men absent from home, whether as POWs, forced labourers, deportees or soldiers in the Wehrmacht or Waffen-SS, women assumed new roles as heads of household and breadwinners, running farms, shops and workshops. They also enjoyed greater sexual freedom than had been available in their patriarchal or provincial environments. They had many opportunities to fraternize with soldiers of occupying armies – working for them as cooks, cleaners, waitresses and secretaries, meeting them socially in bars, cafés and restaurants, or even forced into intimacy at home when German officers and soldiers were billeted on them. At the same time, local populations also had strict rules about what was permitted and what was not in the matter of fraternization. Women's bodies were 'combat zones', regarded less as their own than as the property of men, the family, the local community or even the nation. Opportunities for new relationships and demands for loyalty to traditional groups both increased and pulled in opposite directions. After liberation the ownership of women's bodies provoked even more conflict, with head-shaving and rape, as men, the family, communities and countries reasserted their ownership of women's bodies. Where fraternization had led to denunciation, much heavier sanctions were also applied.

Chapter 4, on 'Schooling as a Cultural Interface', by Pavla Vošahlíková, Bénédicte Rochet and Fabrice Weiss, examines the school as a site of struggle between on the one hand occupiers trying to manipulate education systems in their own interests in occupied areas, and even to Germanize or Italianize local populations in territories they annexed, and on the other families, local communities, churches and the teaching profession itself, which sought ways to preserve their own interests and autonomous culture. What these strategies were and how successful they were is explored. They ranged from the flight of students and teachers to safer havens, boycotting of official schools and the development of clandestine schools paralleling or supplementing them, opposition by teachers to programmes of retraining or indoctrination, foot-dragging by public officials over the introduction of new textbooks, and the steadfastness of the Catholic Church in the protection of its own schools and values.

The fifth chapter, 'Resisters: from Everyday Life to Counter-state', by Olivier Wieviorka and Jacek Tebinka, challenges the view that resisters were full-time heroes divorced from everyday life. Nothing is further from the truth. Resisters required papers, jobs, colleagues and families in order to engage in subversive activities, and tended to live a double life, both open and secret. The classic resister has often been imagined as a male, because of the assumption that he was a fighter, but resistance has to be re-imagined in a much broader way to bring in notions of the home as a base for resistance, or of the 'woman at the door' with her watchful eye, thus collapsing the distinction between public and private life. People did not just 'get on with their lives' in order to survive; rather the problems of daily life, such as hunger, work conditions or forced labour, often mobilized and politicized individuals and groups for resistance. Resistance might take traditional forms such as hoarding, poaching or strikes, that emerged directly from daily life. It might also be symbolic, such as raising the (banned) national flag, attending the funeral of an Allied airman shot down, commemorating a national hero, or demonstrating on a national day. In this way, for a moment, people escaped from the local and everyday and recognized themselves as part of a patriotic community. In some cases, however, where the authority of the occupier collapsed, proto-states were established in which resistance organizations defended the local population but also imposed their own rules and even raised their own taxes.

Chapter 6, 'Resistance, Reprisals, Reactions', by Geraldien von Frijtag Drabbe Künzel, explores resistance in a local, everyday context through the prism of collective reprisals. Popular resistance was an extremely risky business, given the German view of all taking up of arms by civilians as illegitimate – no different from terrorism, in fact. The practice of collectively punishing local communities for harbouring or supporting 'terrorists' provides a powerful way of tracing the relationship between armed resistance and the local community, which might react in a variety of ways. In some places, as in Greece, people responded positively, on the grounds that armed resisters provided protection from the brutality of the occupying forces. Proto-states emerged from the debris of the end of the occupation which had the support of local people, although their authority was heavily contested. Elsewhere, as in France and the Netherlands, where the transition from one regime to the next was more peaceful, local communities were more ambivalent. On the one hand, they supported armed resistance as the way to liberation; on the other, they resented the fact that innocent local people bore the brunt of German reprisals. This study deals with the reaction of local communities not only at the time but also subsequently, as they came to terms with or revised their views of violent resistance and its cost. It becomes clear that violent resistance which, from the perspective of national myths, was heroic and redemptive, from the perspective of the everyday life of the local community might be irresponsible and catastrophic.

Notes

1. John Barber and Mark Harrison, *The Soviet Home Front, 1941–1945* (Harlow, Longman, 1991), pp. 40–2.
2. Gordon Wright, *The Ordeal of Total War, 1939–1945* (New York and London, Harper Torchbooks, 1968), pp. 263–4; Peter Calvocoressi and Guy Wint, *Total War. Causes and Consequences of the Second World War* (London, Allen Lane, 1972), pp. 551–3; R.A.C. Parker, *Struggle for Survival. The History of the Second World War* (Oxford and New York, Oxford University Press, 1990), pp. 281–4.
3. Claus Bundgård Christensen, Joachim Lund, Niels Wium Olesen and Jakob Sørensen, *Danmark Besat. Krig og Hverdag, 1940–45* (Copenhagen, Høst & Søn, 2005).
4. Werner Warmbrunn, *The Dutch under German Occupation* (Stanford, Stanford University Press, 1963).

5. H.A.M. Klemann, *Nederland 1938–1948* (Amsterdam, Boom, 2002); Jules Gérard-Libois, José Gotovitch, *L'an 40. La Belgique occupée* (Brussels, CRISP, 1971); Hans Umbreit, *Der Militärbefehlshaber in Frankreich, 1940–1944* (Boppard-am-Rhein, Harald Boldt Verlag, 1968); Rita Thalmann, *La Mise au Pas. Idéologie et stratégie sécuritaire dans la France occupée* (Paris, Fayard, 1991); Philippe Burrin, *Living with Defeat. France under the German Occupation, 1940–1944* (London, Arnold, 1996).

6. Vojtech Mastny, *The Czechs under Nazi Rule. The Failure of National Resistance, 1939–1942* (New York and London, Columbia University Press, 1971); Y. Jelineck, *The Parish Republic. Hlinka's Slovak People's Party, 1939–1945* (Boulder and New York, Columbia University Press, 1976).

7. Jan Tomasz Gross, *Polish Society under German Occupation. The General-gouvernement, 1939–1944* (Princeton, Princeton University Press, 1979).

8. MacGregor Knox, *Mussolini Unleashed, 1939–1941. Politics and Strategy in Fascist Italy's Last War* (Cambridge, Cambridge University Press, 1982); Fred Singleton, *A Short History of the Yugoslav Peoples* (Cambridge, Cambridge University Press, 1985), ch. 9.

9. Mark Mazower, *Inside Hitler's Greece. The Experience of Occupation, 1941–1944* (New Haven and London, Yale University Press, 1993); John O. Iatrides (ed.), *Greece in the 1940s. A Nation in Crisis* (Hanover NH and London, University Press of New England, 1981).

10. Alexander Dallin, *German Rule in Russia, 1941–1945. A Study in Occupation Politics* (London, Macmillan, 1957/1981); Karel C. Berkhoff, *Harvest of Despair. Life and Death in Ukraine under Nazi Rule* (Cambridge, MA, Belknap Press of Harvard University Press, 2004); Bernhard Chiari, *Alltag hinter dem Front. Besatzung, Kollaboration und Widerstand in Weissrussland, 1941–1944* (Düsseldorf, Droste Verlag, 1998).

11. Edmond Duméril, *Journal d'un honnête homme pendant l'occupation, juin 1940–août 1944* (Thonon-les-Bains, L'Albaron, 1990), p. 28. See John Horne and Alan Kramer, *German Atrocities, 1914. A History of Denial* (New Haven and London: Yale University Press, 2001).

12. Robert Conquest, *The Harvest of Sorrow. Soviet Collectivization and the Terror-Famine* (London, Melbourne etc., Hutchinson, 1986), p. 303; Karel Berkhoff, *Harvest of Despair*, p. 20; Alexander Hill, *The War behind the Eastern Front. The Soviet Partisan Movement in North-West Russia, 1941–1944* (New York and London, Frank Cass, 2004), pp. 55–9.

13. Philippe Burrin, *Living with Defeat*, pp. 1–3 and Part II; Robert Gildea, *Marianne in Chains. In Search of the German Occupation, 1940–1945* (London, Macmillan, 2002), ch. 3.

14. Gerhard von Glahn, *The Occupation of Enemy Territory* (Minneapolis, University of Minnesota Press, 1957); Karma Nabulsi, *Traditions of War. Occupation, Resistance and the Law* (Oxford, Oxford University Press, 1999); Manfred

Messerschmidt, 'Völkerrecht und 'Kriegsnotwendigkeit' in der deutschen militärischen Tradition', in W. Wette (ed.), *Was damals Recht war. NS-Militär- und Strafjustiz im Vernichtungskrieg* (Essen, Klartext, 1996), pp. 91–230; Serge Klarsfeld, *Le Livre des otages. La politique des otages menée par les autorités allemands d'occupation en France de 1941 à 1943* (Paris, Les Éditeurs réunis, 1979).

15. Bundesarchiv-Militärarchiv, Freiburg RW 35/1, von Stülpnagel to Major General Wagner, 24 Oct. 1941. See also E. Jäckel, *Frankreich in Hitlers Europa. Die deutsche Frankreichpolitik im Zweiten Weltkrieg* (Stuttgart, 1966), pp. 192–4.

16. Antony Beevor, *Stalingrad* (London, 1998), p. 407.

17. Pieter Lagrou, 'Victims of Genocide and National Memory: Belgium, France and the Netherlands 1945–65', *Past & Present*, 154 (1997), pp. 220–1.

18. Claudio Pavone, *Una guerra civile. Saggio storico sulla moralità nella Resistenza* (Turin, Bollati Boringheri, 1991).

19. Jean-Michel Chaumont, *La Concurrence des victimes. Génocide, identité, reconnaissance* (Paris, La Découverte, 2002).

20. Raul Hilberg, *The Politics of Memory. The journey of a Holocaust* (Chicago, Dee, 1996).

21. Henri Amouroux, *La Grande Histoire des Français sous l'occupation* (8 vols, Paris, R. Laffont, 1976–88).

22. William Thomas and Florian Znaniecki, *The Polish Peasant in Europe and America* (5 vols, Richard G. Badger, 1918–20); Guillaume Jacquemyns, *La Société belge sous l'occupation allemande, 1940–1944* (3 vols, Brussels, Nicolson & Watson, 1950). It was not echoed until the catalogue of an exhibition in 1984, R. Gobyn, 'Het dagelijks leven tijdens de tweede wereldoorlog : een vreemd mengsel van individualisme en solidariteit', in *1940–1945. Het dagelijkse leven in België. 21 december 1984–3 maart 1985* (Brussels, 1984), pp. 17–107; James C. Scott, *Weapons of the Weak. Everyday Forms of Peasant Resistance* (New Haven and London, Yale University Press, 1985), pp. xv–xvi, 29.

23. Henri Lefebvre, *Everyday Life in the Modern World* (New Brunswick and London, Transaction Books, 1984/1999). The French edition was published in 1968.

24. Michel de Certeau, *The Practice of Everyday Life* (Berkeley and Los Angeles, University of California Press, 1984), pp. xi–xxiv. Originally published as *L'Invention du quotidien* (Paris, Union générale d'édition, 1980).

25. Fernand Braudel, *Civilization and Capitalism, 15th–18th Century. I. The Structures of Everyday Life. The Limits of the Possible. II. The Wheels of Commerce. III. The Perspective of the World* (London, Collins, 1981–3). Originally published as *Civilisation matérielle, économie et capitalisme, XVe – XVIIIe siècles. I. Les Structures du Quotidien. Le Possible et l'Impossible. II. Les Jeux de l'Échange. III. Le Temps du Monde* (Paris, 1979).

26. Fernand Braudel, *Afterthoughts on Material Civilisation and Capitalism* (Baltimore and London, Johns Hopkins University Press, 1977), p. 7.

27. Editorial, *History Workshop. A Journal of Socialist Historians,* I (1976); Raphael Samuel, 'On the Methods of History Workshop: a Reply', *History Workshop* (1980), pp. 162–76.

28. Thomas Lindenberger and Michael Wildt, 'Radical Plurality: History Workshops as a Practical Critique of Knowledge', *History Workshop,* 33 (1992), pp. 73–99

29. Lutz Niethammer, *Lebensgeschichte und Sozialkultur im Ruhrgebiet, 1930–1960* (3 vols, Berlin–Bonn, Dietz, 1983–5).

30. Martin Broszat (ed.), *Bayern in der N-S Zeit* (Munich–Vienna, Oldenbourg, 1977–83).

31. Detlev Peukert, *Inside Nazi Germany. Conformity, Opposition and Racism in Everyday Life* (London, Batsford, 1989). Originally published as *Volksgenossen und Gemeinschaftsfremde. Anpassung, Ausmerze und Aufbegehren unter dem Nationalsozialismus* (Cologne, Bund Verlag, 1982).

32. Alf Lüdtke, 'What Is the History of Everyday Life?', and Hans Medick, 'Missionaries in the rowboat': Ethnological Ways of Knowing as a Challenge to Social History', in Lüdtke (ed.), *The History of Everyday Life. Reconstructing Social Experiences and Ways of Life* (Princeton, NJ, Princeton University Press, 1995).

33. Peukert, *Inside Nazi Germany*, p. 19.

34. Andrew Bergerson, *Ordinary Germans in Extraordinary Times. The Nazi Revolution in Hildesheim* (Blomington, Indiana University Press, 2005).

35. Sheila Fitzpatrick, *Everyday Stalinism. Ordinary Life in Extraordinary Times: Soviet Russia in the 1930s* (New York and Oxford, Oxford University Press, 1999), pp. 1–12.

36. Richard Bosworth, *Mussolini's Italy: Life under the Dictatorship* (London, Allen Lane, 2005).

–1–

Surviving Hunger
Life in the Cities and the Countryside during the Occupation
Polymeris Voglis

With successive campaigns and within a year and a half after the invasion of Poland all but the few neutral European countries had succumbed to the German war machine. After 1941 the German objectives were on the one hand the campaign against the Soviet Union and, on the other, the reorganization of the economy and resources of the occupied countries with a view to supporting the German offensive in the east. The reorganization of the European economies in the direction of the establishment of a *Grossraumwirtschaft* and the pooling of resources from the different conquered countries had an impact not only on the individual economies but also on the everyday life of millions of people.

The foreign occupation constituted a new experience for the societies of continental Europe. The experience of occupation was not the same for all the people across Europe; in fact it varied greatly. It depended on the Nazi war aims and the level of development of each country but also on whether someone lived in the city or the countryside, was Jewish or not, was involved in the resistance or profited from the black market, worked in a factory of importance for the Germans or was unemployed. However, the experience of occupation was also unique because in many aspects it transformed everyday life. Food shortages, queues, the black market, ersatz products and rationing changed habits, affected mentalities, created new needs, transferred wealth, drove thousands of civilians to death from starvation, and reconfigured prewar social relations and hierarchies. The state machinery addressed some of the problems created by food shortages, but citizens had to rely on themselves to cope with the new situation. First came individual solutions but these were seldom adequate, so people often took advantage of family ties and networks. Collective responses were more difficult since political activities were banned. However, trade unions found ways to express their demands, and later, when the resistance emerged, food shortages and dire living conditions were high on the agenda of the anti-Nazi propaganda.

The food shortage was one of the main concerns of the people in occupied countries throughout the years of the Second World War. The question of food, as we shall see, was multifaceted. It was related to the policy of the occupation forces, the level of agricultural production, and the efficiency of rationing schemes in combating the black market. This chapter will discuss how and to what extent food shortages had an impact on the living conditions in occupied Europe and will focus on the western and southern European countries. It will begin by outlining the general aims of the Nazi economic policy and the impact of occupation on the agriculture of the conquered countries. It will then turn to the examination of the consequences of the food shortages, namely famine, rationing and the black market. Finally, it will discuss the impact of food shortages on everyday life and the ways in which people in the cities and the countryside coped with the new realities they faced.

The Nazi Policy in Occupied Europe

Even though daily life in occupied countries can be seen more as a result of an unequal negotiation between occupiers and occupied, there are two fundamental general principles regarding the occupation. The first is that occupation is a power relation. The occupier sets the rules, and decisions concerning major aspects of social life originate from the occupier or must have the occupier's consent. The second principle, following from the first, is that the goal of the occupier is to exploit the resources of the occupied country to its advantage.[1] The labour, assets, agricultural products, raw materials and industry of the conquered country are geared to the benefit of the occupier. The German plans regarding the administration of the economy in occupied countries were conditioned by three factors: the kind of economic development in each individual occupied country, the Nazi ideology, and the course of the Second World War.

The German economic policy depended on the structural characteristics of each occupied country. There were significant differences between the industrially developed economies of western Europe and the agrarian economies of eastern and southeastern Europe. In the first the high productivity of agriculture, the specialized division of labour, the concentration of production in large industrial areas and the effective organization and management of production made the administration of the occupied economy easier, in the sense that it could be centrally managed by Nazi agencies and, without major disruptions, adjusted to the needs of the Germans. In the agrarian countries of eastern and southeastern Europe the economic structures were different. In those countries the low mechanization and productivity of agriculture, the fragmentation of the arable land into small plots (save the Soviet Union), the low level of industrialization and the incompetence of the state bureaucracy made more difficult the control and the exploitation of production by the occupiers.[2] Thus, in western Europe the German policy aimed at the maintenance and adjustment of the prewar structures to the new needs with a view to rationally exploiting the resources, whereas in eastern and southeastern Europe the Nazi policy consisted of requisitions of the agricultural production and raw materials.

The Nazi policy in occupied countries was shaped not only by economic considerations but also by the Nazi ideology and war aims. There was no definite plan for the organization of New Europe, but the Nazis' racial ideas and social engineering were manifest in the policies that were followed in the different occupied countries. The war in the east was to provide Germany with *Lebensraum*, that is territories for the settlement of the German race and (human and material) resources for exploitation. Eastern territories were to be colonized by *Volksdeutsche* and their Polish and Jewish inhabitants were to be concentrated under the General Government or further east. Soviet Russia was to be colonized as well but also 'agrarianized' in order to provide the Reich with the necessary foodstuffs; Russians gradually were to be removed east of the Urals. These broad war aims were underpinned by Nazi ideology and the deep hatred of Jews, Poles, Slavs and Bolsheviks and resonated with the policy of confiscations, requisitions and maximum exploitation that the Nazis followed in eastern Europe.[3] In fact racial ideas and war aims were mirrored in the conduct of warfare. It would not be an exaggeration to argue that to a certain extent there were two wars in Europe. On the western front the Nazis after their quick victories sought the collaboration of the indigenous elites and population for the fulfilment of their economic and political goals, whereas on the eastern front there was a ruthless campaign of terror and extermination.

German economic policy in the occupied countries was also directly influenced by developments on the battlefield. The quick victories of the German army in the first year and a half created the impression that the war would be short. German policy until the offensive against the Soviet Union was that of requisitioning the industrial and agricultural goods necessary for the immediate support of the German army. When at the beginning of 1942 the German offensive stalled and the possibility of a long war arose, then the German economic strategy changed. The initial policy of requisitions and plundering was abandoned and replaced by an effort to organize the long-term rational exploitation of the resources of the occupied countries and to integrate them in an overall economic plan with a view to supporting the German economy in the war effort.[4] Moreover, the relative stability in western Europe (at least until D-Day) was in sharp contrast with the continuous war on the eastern front and the guerrilla warfare in southeastern Europe. War and guerrilla warfare created an altogether different social and economic setting and conditioned Nazi policy in the occupied countries (reprisals, counter-insurgency campaigns, mass executions, razing of villages).

The unsuccessful campaign against the Soviet Union had other consequences as well. In the German planning the reorganization of agriculture in occupied Europe the Ukrainian territories were of strategic importance. Ukraine was destined to become the breadbasket of Nazi Europe. Germans saw the Soviet food resources as almost unlimited. The reasoning was that Soviet agricultural production would feed not only the German troops on the eastern front and the Germans back home but also compensate for food deficiencies in western occupied countries like Belgium and Norway. What that policy entailed was a drastic reduction in food consumption in European Russia itself to levels equal to bare existence, which was in accordance with the racial Nazi world-view. However, German plans for the exploitation of Soviet agriculture foundered. For most of Ukraine the Nazi occupation lasted two years (from summer 1941 until summer 1943), so the Germans did not have enough time to fully materialize their plans. The grain collection of 1941–1942 was well below German expectations; a violent drive with combing-out operations to improve collection brought better results in terms of the quantities of grain but it provoked the hostility of the farmers. Moreover the Nazis, despite their anti-Bolshevik rhetoric, did not abolish the kolkhoz system to gain the support of the populace but left it in place because it made it easier to supervise the large-scale farm enterprises and was suited to the 'servant' mentality of Slav peasants.[5] The policy of 'scorched earth', the resistance of the farmers, who were not eager to deliver their crop to the occupier, the decline in productivity and continuous war forced the Germans to lower their expectations. The Soviet contribution to the food policy of the Reich was undoubtedly significant although much lower than originally anticipated. Overall, 9.1 million tons of (bread and feed) grain were collected from the occupied Soviet territories; most of it was consumed locally by the Wehrmacht and only 800,000 tons of bread grain were exported to the Reich.[6] These imports fell short of the German needs. The total value of agricultural and animal products imported to Germany between 1940 and 1944 amounted to 12,215 million Reichsmarks; the value of imports from the Soviet Union constituted only 751 million Reichsmarks or 6.1 per cent.[7] Germany had to rely on western and southeastern Europe rather than the Soviet Union to feed its civilian population and the population of occupied countries. This fact had serious and sometimes tragic consequences for the nutrition and the living standards of the peoples in western and southeastern Europe.

Food Policy and Agricultural Production

In the first period of war and occupation, when the Wehrmacht seemed invincible and the conquest of continental Europe imminent, the Germans followed an economic strategy suitable to the requirements of a short war, that is to provide the army with the foodstuffs, raw materials and industrial products that were necessary in order to support either the occupation army or the German war machine that was ready to unleash a total war on the eastern front. This policy was adaptable according to the conditions prevailing in each occupied country and the general plans for the New Europe. However, one has to point out the major difference between eastern and western Europe. The Nazis saw the Polish territories of the General Government as a source of raw materials and cheap labour. Colonial methods were adopted, large estates were confiscated and administered by a German agency and during the war agricultural production steadily declined due to the resettlement projects and the drafting of workers for the Reich. The policy of ruthless exploitation and looting was captured in a Goering directive: 'Enterprises which are not absolutely essential for the maintenance at a low level of the bare existence of the inhabitants must be transferred to Germany.'[8] The Germans followed a different policy in the annexed Polish territories (Wartheland, Danzig and West Prussia), designated for the settlement of *Volksdeutsche*. The Germans tried to develop these areas and supplied the farmers with fertilizers, farm machinery and seed, built warehouses and silos, established farm schools, and invested in food processing industries.[9]

In the occupied countries of western Europe the occupiers tried to adjust preexisting mechanisms and structures to the German war effort. The Germans thought highly of the organization and productivity of the Dutch and the administration was left intact after the occupation. In respect of other countries with which Germany had good diplomatic and trade relations before the war, like Denmark, the Germans sought to make a deal through negotiations. The first of these trade agreements was signed on 7 November 1940 and provided fixed export quantities for Danish butter and pork to Germany. The same path of trade negotiations was followed in subsequent years although the German demands were year by year increased to the dismay of the Danish government.[10] Sometimes, however, political aims clashed with economic considerations. The part of France that the Germans occupied directly was the most developed. The occupied zone contained the greater part of urban centres and of industrial production. That territory accounted for 76 per cent of coal production, 95 per cent of steel production, and the half of the textile and metallurgical production. The occupied zone also provided three quarters of the French production of cereals, milk, sugar and meat.[11] But at the same time the division of France into five different 'regimes', i.e. occupied, Vichy France, *Zone interdit*, the north-eastern *départements* (under the jurisdiction of the Military Governor of Belgium and the annexed departments of Alsace-Moselle, hampered the transportation of goods, fragmented the market, created labour shortages, and generated hostility among the local population.

In the first months of the occupation the German army requisitioned foodstuffs and industrial products, fixed prices and 'bought' the surplus production, set extremely high occupation costs in order to cover the expenses of the occupying forces, confiscated overseas assets, and in some countries disassembled factories to transfer them to Germany. The policy of requisition had a serious impact on the occupied economies and generally speaking the military defeat was followed by a more or less severe economic crisis. There was a fall in production because war mobilization had deprived fields and factories of peasants and workers, the naval blockade meant that the occupied countries were cut off from overseas imports of foodstuffs and raw materials, and the war had damaged part of the road and communications network. Thus, the first year of the occupation, until the occupied economy could adapt to the new conditions, was a year of shortages and deprivations for thousands of people in occupied Europe.

In the first year of German occupation there was a dramatic drop in agricultural production in occupied countries. The French production of grain between 1939 and

1940 fell from 7.3 to 5.1 million tons, of potatoes from 14.4 to 10.3 million tons (to be further decreased in 1941 to 6.9 million tons), of meat from 1.5 to 1 million tons.[12] Several factors contributed to that fall but the most important seemed to be the shortage of labour. Peasants left their fields to go to the front. Many of them did not return because they were either killed or became prisoners of war. In France alone 450,000 prisoners of war were peasants. After the dramatic fall in the first year of the occupation agricultural production increased in subsequent years and more or less stabilized, without however reaching the prewar levels (with the exception of Denmark and the Netherlands where agricultural production and productivity remained stable from the beginning of the occupation until 1943).

The record of the Nazi policy towards the agriculture of occupied countries was dismal. In France the land cultivated with grain had been reduced by 1943 by 1.4 million hectares in comparison with the prewar years. In the general decline of French agricultural production there was one exception, vegetable oil, which was destined to cover the nutritional needs of the German population. Belgium also experienced a decline in agricultural production although less dramatic than that of France. In 1944 grain production fell by 8 per cent in comparison with the prewar years and potato production was reduced by 35 per cent.[13] Belgium, however, also faced food shortages especially in bread. The reason was that before the war Belgium imported 1.2 million tons of cereals from overseas (80 per cent from the United States, Canada and Argentina). After the outbreak of the war, because of the naval blockade, imports of cereals were reduced drastically. During the war imports were 17 per cent of the prewar imports, and for the entire period of occupation Belgium imported 849 thousand tons of cereals.[14] In the Netherlands, the 'agriculture-model' for the Nazi policy makers, the area cultivated with potatoes and the yield were increased between 1939 and 1943, but the same did not happen for grain. In eastern and southeastern Europe war and occupation gravely dislocated the agrarian economies. The yearly average prewar grain production in Romania of 2.59 million tons fell to 1.4 million tons in 1940–2; in Hungary it fell from 2.22 to 1.8 million tons, while in Bulgaria it fell from 1.65 to 1.1 million tons.[15] In the territories of the General Government in Poland the grain area was reduced by 750,000 hectares; the yield of the grain harvest fell from an average of 4.8 million tons in the prewar years to 3.9 million tons in 1943; the potato crop showed a more drastic drop: from 14.1 million tons in the prewar years to 8.9 million tons in 1943.[16]

The occupation authorities tried to counter the problem of the fall in agricultural production and the resulting food shortages (especially grain) with a series of measures. The first measure, very common in war economies, was to centralize the control of agriculture with the purpose of maximizing collection and regulating consumption. Delivery quotas were set for farmers and the occupiers introduced rationing schemes. The second measure was the reduction of livestock so that feed crops (grain, barley, rye, etc.) could be diverted to human consumption. Practically this policy meant the expansion of crop production for direct food consumption at the expense of fodder crops, the ploughing up of grassland, the cultivation of grain and potatoes, strict control of the marketing of cattle and rationing of animal feed. The third measure was the improvization of a bonus system to stimulate farmers' productivity in occupied countries. When deliveries exceeded the quotas, the farmers received tokens to buy bonus goods, such as matches, tobacco, salt, sugar and similar commodities. Although this measure seemed to be popular among the farmers at the beginning, in the long run it was not very successful because the farmers quickly realized that an increase in production would lead to an increase in delivery quotas. In any event, from late 1942, when the Russian campaign began to falter, the occupation authorities arbitrarily raised the quotas and demanded increased food exports to the Reich, putting the burden on the population of the occupied countries.

Famine

The years of Nazi rule brought hardship for millions of people in the occupied countries. The problem of food became acute on the continent. The cessation of imports due to naval blockade deprived many countries of the necessary foodstuffs. Agricultural production on the continent fell in 1943–4 by 15–20 per cent in comparison with the prewar years due to the lack of manpower, fertilizers and draught animals. Some areas and countries suffered more than others but in general people escaped starvation, except in some places and for certain periods. Collaborationist governments and occupation authorities solved the problem of food shortages by rationing food and introducing changes in the diet during the occupation. The German policy of decreasing animal production and consumption led to wartime rations that consisted of more vegetables and less animal produce.[17] On the other hand, since regular trade between countries had ceased, it was up to the occupation authorities to supply the market with the necessary foodstuffs once food shortages became acute. In this case there was again a question of priorities in German economic policy in occupied Europe. Both Belgium and Greece depended on grain imports to cover the nutritional needs of their populations. The occupation authorities, however, responded in different ways. Belgium was supplied with fertilizers and seed and 596,000 tons of agricultural products imported from Germany during the occupation because the country was highly industrialized and therefore of particular importance for the Nazis. Greece, as we shall see below, had a very different fate.

Famine, in general, did not strike the continent, except in Greece and the Netherlands. The famine in the Netherlands was not a result of economic dislocation but rather of the course of the war. Between September 1944 and early 1945 the northern and eastern part of the Netherlands was cut off from the rest of the country because German forces stopped the advance of the Allies, and so no food supplies could be delivered with the consequence that thousands of people in urban centres (especially in Amsterdam) starved to death. It is estimated that 22,000 people succumbed to famine and cold during the Dutch Hunger Winter.[18] More space will be given to the case of Greece because it provides the opportunity to examine the several interrelated factors that caused the famine.

Greece capitulated in April 1941 and in the first winter under the Axis occupation famine hit the capital and other big cities. The famine of 1941–2 illustrated the impact of the occupation on a small agrarian country. In the prewar years domestic agricultural production had never been sufficient to cover the needs of the population. The average prewar grain and other cereals production was about 800,000 tons; 450,000 tons of wheat were imported, mainly from the United States, Canada and Australia. The extraordinary war circumstances, and especially the war mobilization and the requisition of draught animals, caused a dramatic drop in domestic production. Domestic production of wheat fell by one-third in 1940–1 to about 500,000 tons.[19] The net effect of the drop in domestic production and the cessation of imports, given all the other impediments (inefficient collection, plundering by the invaders, lack of means of transportation, etc.), was that the big cities and the capital were cut off from agricultural production in the provinces. The famine was also related to the fragmentation of the market because the three occupying powers (Germany, Italy and Bulgaria) divided the country into three zones of occupation with internal borders, which inhibited the free circulation of people and commodities. Moreover, the Bulgarians prohibited any transport of grain out of Eastern Macedonia and Thrace, where 30 per cent of the prewar grain was produced. The three occupation authorities issued their own currencies, which created monetary chaos. Moreover, the already poor communication network was damaged during the war, and the occupation forces confiscated all vehicles. As a result, agricultural products remained in the producing areas and did not reach the cities. The population of Athens could only be fed with imported foodstuffs. The numerous and urgent appeals to the United States for wheat were to no avail because the British were reluctant to lift the naval blockade. The collaborationist government repeatedly requested permission from the occupation authorities to import grain before the winter but again to no avail. Germany sent only 5,000 tons of grain, Italy about 10,000 tons, while Bulgaria did not bother at all. Bread consumption fell drastically from 500 g per capita per day in 1939 to 150 g in the winter of 1941–2. The few public soup kitchens organized by the Church and the Red Cross could not meet the needs of the starving population. Rationing did not help because the quantities were inadequate and the distribution erratic: 160 g of bread and a little sugar, but no oil, meat or vegetables for instance.[20]

The food shortage became a famine crisis that reached its climax in the winter of 1941–2. People who lived in the cities literally starved to death. In Athens the average calorie intake dropped to 930 calories. More than 40,000 people died in Athens and Piraeus within a year after October 1941, and it was estimated that the total population of Greece after the war was 300,000 less than it should have been because of famine or malnutrition.[21] The sight of dead people in the streets became commonplace. Even in Salonica, where famine was less severe, accounts were harrowing. 'Starvation', began a letter in January 1942, 'stalks the streets of Salonica. Famished men and women collapsed on the pavements and their bodies are later trundled away on open carts drawn by gaunt horses staggering in their traces from the effects of hunger. Subsequent burials are carried out without coffins, owing to lack of wood.'[22]

In the meantime, domestic and international pressures for a partial lift of the blockade so that imported foodstuffs could reach Greece had their first successes. Initially, the shipment of foodstuffs from Turkey, which was neutral and within the blockade zone, were permitted. The first ship with 1,100 tons of foodstuffs left Turkey for Greece in October 1941; it made five trips to Greece until January 1942, when it foundered and sank. One ship was not enough to alleviate the grave situation, and in February 1942 the British reconsidered their position and discussions were initiated between Britain and the United States to work out a plan of regular shipments of foodstuffs from North America through the blockade. The plan was that the aid would be under the auspices of the International Red Cross, the Swedish government would offer the vessels for the transportation of 15,000 tons of Canadian wheat per month (plus other foodstuffs that brought the average total to 18,600 in 1943), and the storage and distribution of aid would be under the supervision of a Swedish–Swiss committee. The first group of three vessels left Canada for Greece on 7 August 1942.

The purpose of the relief aid was to help the starving population in Greece. But the question then arose: who were the people in need? The commission responsible for handling the relief identified the categories of citizens eligible for relief. These were the city dwellers, especially in the area of the capital. The commission wanted to avoid a second famine in Athens, so the capital was prioritized in the distribution of the relief. Greece had a population of 7.3 million people in 1941 and of these 2.5 million persons received relief aid. Half the relief recipients (1,236,286) lived in the capital. If we take into account that the population of Athens was approximately 1.5 million people, then almost all Athenians received relief aid. The rest of the aid was distributed to the provinces. There the distribution of relief aid was based on the distinction between producing and non-producing areas, in terms of agricultural production. Producers of food of any kind (either farmers or cattle-breeders) and persons owning a quarter of an acre of cultivated land were classified as producers and were not entitled to any relief. On the other hand, refugees, vulnerable people (elderly, orphans, widows, etc.), civil servants and private employees in the provinces also received relief.[23]

Rationing and the Black Market

In occupied Europe the authorities implemented rationing and price controls to counter the problems created by food shortages and the emergence of a black market.

Although rationing and the black market appeared to complement each other, they were in fact based on antagonistic principles. Rationing was a welfare measure designed to reduce inequalities and guarantee the subsistence of the population. The black market on the contrary was socially unjust because it was based on the law of supply and demand in times of scarcity of foodstuffs and the ability of someone to pay the highest price.[24] In most occupied countries the allocation of foodstuffs was a mixture of rationing, price controls and the black market. Whether the black market or rationing would finally prevail in the supply was a complicated question; the government in order to fight against the black market had to guarantee regular supply of the market, enforce strict controls and command the support of the population for its cause.[25] Rationing required a highly effective administrative machine, and governments that had experimented before the war with rationing systems, like the Netherlands, which implemented rationing already in the 1930s due to the world economic crisis, were better capable of coping with the new situation.

Table 1.1 Calorific Value of Normal Rations, January 1941–44[26]

Country	1941	1942	1943	1944
Germany	1,990	1,750	1,980	1,930
Italy	1,010	950	990	1,065
Belgium	1,360	1,365	1,320	1,555
Protectorate	1,690	1,785	1,920	1,740
France	1,365	1,115	1,080	1,115
Baltic countries	–	1,305	1,305	1,420
Netherlands	2,050	1,825	1,765	1,580
Norway	1,620	1,385	1,430	1,480
Poland	845	1,070	853	1,200

As the table shows, rations remained stable in Germany throughout the war and were well above the rations of the occupied countries, which, generally speaking, declined during the occupation. The decline in rations as well as the very low rations of some countries in the above table may be attributed to several factors, such as the fall of agricultural production after 1941 (Italy and France), the inefficient system of distribution (Italy) and the predominantly agrarian character of the country (Poland).

Rationing was organized along similar lines throughout occupied Europe, that is ration stamps were distributed to the populace that entitled consumers to buy specific quantities of foodstuffs from specific traders, bakers and groceries. The quantities of food varied, as well as the timing and the kind of foodstuffs. In the Netherlands in 1939 only sugar was rationed, then in 1940 bread, butter, meat, cheese, eggs and coffee, in 1941 milk, potatoes and coffee substitute, and in 1942 oranges, apples and chocolate.[27] In France adults were entitled to 350 g of bread per day, 300 g of meat and 50 g of cheese per week, and 500 g of sugar, 200 g of butter, 200 g of margarine and 50 g of rice per month.[28] In Belgium rations were 250 g of butter, 1 kg of sugar, 1 kg of meat and 15 kg of potatoes per month and 225 g of bread per day.[29] Denmark introduced one of the most comprehensive and successful rationing and price control schemes because there was a regular supply of the market. It covered all the basic categories of foodstuffs, except meat. The measure of its success was that it remained in force until 1950–2, the prices in the black market remained stable throughout the 1940s and one of the most common offences was the illegal trade or theft of ration stamps.[30]

Table 1.2 Weekly Rations at the Beginning of 1942 (in Grams)[31]

Country	Bread	Meat	Fat
German Reich	2,000	300	206
Occupied France	1,925	250	105
'Free' France	1,925	180	100
Belgium	1,575	245	105
Netherlands	1,800	250	200
Denmark	2,275	Not rationed	315
Norway	1,900	100	210
Greece	1,260	Not provided	Not rationed
Protectorate	2,250	400	169
Baltic countries	1,700	250	180
Serbia (April 1943)	2,240	125	80

The population was also divided into different categories with different food entitlements: children, adults and manual workers. There were significant differences between normal rations and rations for manual and industrial workers. The much higher rations for industrial workers highlighted the interest of the occupation authorities in maintaining industrial production in order to sustain the German war effort.

Table 1.3 Calories of Rations for Different Categories of Consumers in 1944[32]

Country	Normal Consumer	Worker	Heavy Worker
Germany	2,000	2,760	3,500
Belgium	1,550	2,080	2,370
Czechoslovakia	1,760	2,520	3,270
Finland	1,346	1,955	2,140
France	1,135	1,300	1,400
Baltic States	1,420	2,115	2,815
Netherlands	1,765	2,435	3,255

If rationing was designed to provide the population, especially in the cities, with the necessary quantities of food, the quality of that food was an altogether different matter. The quality of bread in particular fell drastically and often the ingredients it included remained a mystery. Apart from wheat flour, rationed bread could contain barley, beets, carrots and potato. The percentage of ground wheat used for the flour was increased from 70–80 per cent (which is standard for white bread) to 95–6 per cent, making the bread darker and harder.[33] Even though today dark bread is considered nutritionally rich, people in the 1940s thought of it as inferior to white bread and the quality of the dark bread was usually poor because the mills were not equipped with the proper machines and as a result contained straw and dirt. Bakers were also sometimes responsible for the poor quality of bread, because they used more water than flour with the result that the bread was tasteless and soggy. The authorities faced with shortages issued ordinances that made the use of substitutes compulsory. In France in 1942 it was decreed that a pack of coffee should contain 60 g of coffee and 180 g of substitutes, like dried chestnuts, soya beans, oak-galls, lupin seeds and date pips. In the same vein, tea was not to contain more than 20 per cent real tea while the rest could be orange peel or leaves of walnut or chestnut trees. Shortages and need drove the authorities, producers and ordinary people to discover the nutritional value of hitherto neglected products and invent substitutes: saccharine instead of sugar, dehydrated vegetables, soya beans and bread made out of beets.[34] Governments encouraged the use of substitutes and a new variety of 'ersatz' products appeared in the market: rayon replaced cotton or wool yarn and the new engines for cars that used wood instead of petrol became so popular that even a 'Salon national des gazogènes' opened in June 1941 in Bordeaux.[35]

When times got harder, people had to resort to eating what they could not have imagined a few years before and new 'recipes' were invented for tulip bulbs in the Netherlands or nettles and locust-beans in Greece. People tried to cope with the scarcity of food and improvised to improve their diet. One of the most usual solutions was to turn the yards of their homes into gardens. City dwellers 'discovered' agriculture and manuals for gardening became very popular. They cultivated leeks, cabbages, tomatoes and potatoes that could enrich their meals, and when it was possible they bred chickens or rabbits. Individual initiatives were often endorsed by the authorities and became official policy. The government in countries like France passed laws that allotted to families or workers' associations uncultivated fields in the cities so that they could grow vegetables. As a result in 1944, according to the French ministry of agriculture, family gardens spread to 75,000 hectares and contributed to the diet of 3,800,000 households throughout the country.[36]

Food shortages created new needs and brought forth new solutions. The most common new phenomenon in occupied countries was the black market. The black market, as Robert Gildea argued in the case of occupied France, was not a single market but rather a network of concentric circles. The wider the market was, the more exploitable it was likely to be. In this system of concentric circles, the widest circle concerned selling to distant and unknown people in Paris or other large towns, which was the most profitable for the farmer and most expensive for the client. The intermediate circle included friends and neighbours and was based on personal, face-to-face contact. In this circle there was a monetary exchange but the prices were reasonable. The third circle was the narrowest and included family members who lived in large cities. In that case money was seldom involved, as farmers would send flour, eggs or meat to their children or cousins as a gift or would get manufactured goods, like shoes, clothes or medicine, in exchange. Quite often, those relatives would sell a part of their deliveries on the black market in the city.[37]

In many occupied countries the occupation authorities tolerated the black market because it was necessary and they could benefit from it. The black market was a necessity to the extent that food shortages occurred and rationed food was insufficient. The prices in the black market were many times higher than the official prices, turning basic foodstuffs into luxury items destined for the consumption of the privileged classes. In Belgium the official price for one kilo of bread was 2.60 francs, while on the black market it was 30 francs in 1941, 45 in 1942 and 49 in 1943. For one kilo of butter the official price was 32 francs, but on the black market it cost 112 francs in 1941, 275 in 1942 and 350 in 1943. One kilo of meat officially cost 34 francs but on the black market one would have to pay 80 francs in 1941, 125 in 1942 and 190 francs in 1943.[38]

The black market dominated everyday life in the cities and had an impact on social relations. The first characteristic concerned spatial mobility. City dwellers left the city in large numbers for short trips to the countryside, where they could purchase foodstuffs that they would subsequently sell on the black market. That situation alarmed the prefecture of Haute-Savoie in France, and in 1941 it prohibited visitors from spending more than four days in the department in an attempt to restrict the quantities of foodstuffs that were siphoned off onto the black market.[39] The second characteristic was that the black market was a cross-class activity. Anyone with access to food or enjoying good relations with the occupation authorities could get involved in the black market. A study on the black market in occupied Denmark showed that of those who were convicted for *sortbørshandel* in Copenhagen 42 per cent were self-employed and 40 per cent were workers.[40] Although the black market was a widespread activity, not everybody made the same profit. One of the most important consequences of the black market was the transfer of wealth to profiteers and go-betweens. The transfer of wealth could be substantial if the black market was controlled by a small number of profiteers. The third characteristic of the black market was that it testified to the failure of centralized control of the occupied economy to supply the official market regularly and to enforce price controls. Usually the black market went hand in hand with incompetent administration, corruption, understaffed agencies and bureaucratic complexities. In occupied Italy the economic police had 1,530 men, although it was initially planned to have 5,000. It was decided that they would not be stationed in one place but move from one city to another in order to avoid corruption and that policemen who broke the law would be deported to camps. German officials attributed corruption to the 'Latin mentality', but it was more a normal consequence of the fact that half of all the goods that reached the market were sold on the black market.[41]

Contrary to popular images of black marketeers, the black market was a widespread activity. To a certain extent it was a 'people's black market', or a parallel market, as thousands of individuals travelled to the countryside to buy foodstuffs that were afterwards sold in the cities. Although after the German invasion and the first weeks of the occupation people left the villages and went to the cities in search of security, this trend was quickly reversed. As soon as the food shortages appeared, city dwellers travelled to the countryside to buy foodstuffs for their families and/or to sell them on the black market. Every morning hundreds of Athenians took the train or the bus for the plains of Beotia, Thessaly and even Macedonia to buy potatoes, vegetables, olive oil and flour, which they sold on their return on the Athen's black markets. The quantities that reached this informal market could be 300 or 350 tons per day.[42] The Security Service in Venice considered the black market a 'necessary evil' and for that reason workers' wives who arrived at the main railway station with sacks of corn flour (for the preparation of *polenta*, a staple food in the region) were not searched by the policemen.[43] The situation was similar in the occupied Soviet territories. A German report in 1942 described it vividly and identified the causes in the following way:

> [T]he urban population, which for the most part has been living in cities or industrial areas for only one or two generations, has relatives in the country by whom it is supplied with food items in exchange for consumer goods. He who flies over or rides through the occupied Soviet area today will notice crowds of people moving along the roads; there are hundreds of thousands of them, and according to the experts their number often may reach a million. These crowds are on the move, either to look for food or, vice versa, to bring food to the cities in order to sell it.[44]

This kind of 'people's black market' saved many people from death but also meant a transfer of wealth from the cities to the countryside. Farmers realized that the food they had was a significant weapon in their hands. The scarcity of food in the cities shifted the power relations between the countryside and the cities. For decades the farmers had sold their products, wheat in particular, at low, fixed prices and received very little in return. Under the occupation the balance between the countryside and the city was reversed in favour of the former.

However, sometimes people who lived in the countryside were also hit by food shortages. This was the case for the villages that were singled out and razed to the ground by the occupation forces, as described below, but also for villages in monocultural areas that did not produce food. The vast majority of the farmers in Languedoc, for instance, were occupied in viniculture and the land was largely covered with vineyards. Because of food shortages during the occupation they had to diversify their cultivation and to add new crops. They extended the cultivated land and grew cereals, sunflowers and cabbages and created small gardens everywhere they could. The other way to make up their deficit in foodstuffs was to revive the barter economy: exchange the wine from Languedoc with meat from the cattle-breeders of the Massif Central.[45] In Greece villagers from mountainous areas would go to the plains to exchange their animal products for wheat; or villagers who produced wheat in one area would exchange it for the olive oil that was produced in another area. That informal market or trade grew independently of the collaborationist government or the occupation authorities. The occupation forces could control the railway lines and some of the main roads but not all the routes that connected the different regions, while the local authorities could only benefit from these exchanges.[46]

From time to time collaborationist governments and the occupation authorities sought to crack down on this 'people's black market'. New stricter laws with heavy penalties were passed against the black market and profiteering, and a wave of arrests and convictions swiftly followed. In these cases the black market of course did not cease to exist but became more organized and was concentrated in fewer hands. As the risk became higher, prices rose, making the foodstuffs only available to the small number of people who could afford to buy them. Another reason for the decline of the 'people's black market' was that travelling within the country, even commuting within the cities, due to the advance of the Allies or guerrilla warfare, became increasingly difficult. The requisition of vehicles by the occupation authorities, the shortage of petrol, sabotage of the lines of communication by resisters, curfews and check-points at the entrances to cities made travelling for ordinary people an expensive and dangerous endeavour. In occupied Greece any person who wished to leave the city had to go to the local *carabinieri* or *Kommandantur* office and fill out the relevant forms in order to obtain a special travel permit. The issue of the permit was quicker if citizens were willing to bribe the officers. Since only one train left Athens each morning for the north of the country, a reservation had to be made several days in advance. Moreover, a trip by train could take a considerable time because of sabotage the railway lines – a trip from Athens to Salonika might last four days. For these reasons many people were ready to pay exorbitant prices to travel by bus, as much as 50,000 drachmas for a bus ticket from Athens to Lamia. Getting a travel permit to the islands was more difficult and whereas the transportation of small quantities of foodstuffs to and from Athens was permitted, no transportation of food was allowed to and from the islands. As far as public transport within the cities was concerned, suffice it to say that in Athens only four street-car lines operated. In general, the communication network that kept the country together broke down; it took six days for a telegram to be delivered from Athens to Patras, while phone calls could be made only within the city limits at a charge of 400 drachmas in public phones.[47] The country was not just divided along occupation zones; it was gradually reduced to a number of isolated regions or self-contained clusters in a fragmented market.[48]

Life in the Cities and the Countryside

Reactions to these new social conditions varied greatly from country to country or within the same country between cities and provinces or between different social classes. Life in the cities for the salaried classes became more difficult, as the cost of living rose faster than wages did. In Belgium before the war a family spent 58 per cent of the monthly income on food; under occupation, between 1941 and 1943, this rose to 70 per cent.[49] A family with two children in occupied France could barely afford the food expenses if the wife did not work.[50] In countries with galloping inflation, like Greece, any rise in wages was actually meaningless because it lagged behind prices. Poverty and destitution hit not only the urban poor, but also social groups that made up the prewar middle class, like professionals and small businessmen. The downward mobility of the upper and middle strata, together with the destitution of the working class in many occupied countries, created an explosive situation. What counted in occupied Greece was not money, education or status, but simply (legal or illegal) access to the two valuable 'currencies': food and gold. With only slight exaggeration one observer reported that a boy selling cigarettes in the street could make more money than a university professor. The same careful observer described the sudden and profound social changes in the following way: 'A great part of the middle class is in danger of being completely ruined. In order to earn their living thousands of families have been obliged to sell their furniture and dispose of other means of savings. In this way a social and economic change is taking place and a considerable portion of the middle class run the risk of being proletarised.'[51]

Food shortages gave birth to a new phenomenon in city life. Long queues began to appear in front of shops. Mostly women but also unemployed and retired men and schoolchildren formed a crowd of hungry, desperate but also determined people. At weekends and on holidays the crowds became larger because working men and women joined the queues. Police acknowledged the potential for disturbances in these long queues as people discussed their daily food problems and as underground organizations agitated against the authorities. Occasionally these queues became the nuclei of 'food riots', such as in the spring and summer of 1942 when marketplaces in Paris became sites of women's demonstrations and street fighting.[52] In Greece the propaganda and protests of the main resistance organization (the left-wing EAM) focused on living conditions, namely the high prices, the low wages, the insufficient rations and the problem of the black market. While for some months in the summer of 1943 the market and the prices were stabilized, after September 1943, as the prospect of the liberation of Greece was postponed, industrialists and merchants increased their prices by 100–200 per cent. The government intervened, suggesting a lowering of the price of certain products of popular demand by 50 per cent. In fact on 19 October a number of shops lowered their prices, while the police patrolled the streets persuading the owners of retail outlets for food and staple products to lower their prices. Some of them did, but most of them preferred to close down. Not for long, however. EAM activists led small groups of people who broke into the shops. Within a few minutes lines were created in front of the pillaged shops and the goods were distributed to those who were there. Some policemen sat and watched, while others joined the crowd. The EAM made no effort to hide its identity; its activists placed notices in the looted shops and declared that they would continue their struggle for the improvement of people's living conditions.[53]

Around the same time as the disturbances in Athens, in October 1943 crowds of workers in Salonika flocked to the offices of the Governor demanding the intervention of the government against black marketeers and profiteers and that the foodstuffs stocked in the warehouses be made available to the public. In fact the occupation authorities closed several large shops and made arrangements for their stocks to be distributed to the public.[54] In provincial towns where the EAM and its military branch the ELAS were strong enough, they tried to enforce price controls by intimidating the merchants. On 27 November 1943 the ELAS in the Evros region in northeast Greece issued a pamphlet warning 'all the flour manufacturers, the big shots of the villages, the important merchants and in general all those who are in business and operate on the black market' in the following words: 'It is necessary, while there is still time, to put an end to the black market and to help the people who are enduring such suffering today. We can do this by conforming to the prices listed below, which the patriot group had decided upon in order that we too shall not be obliged to proceed to executions.'[55] Disturbances became more and more frequent in the cities: crowds broke in and raided shops where food was stocked, trains were plundered, black marketeers were singled out and threatened. One may argue that food shortages gave birth to different forms of illegality. These illegal practices, however, seen from a different angle, corresponded to what E.P. Thompson termed the 'moral economy of the crowd'; they were legitimate because they were 'grounded upon a consistent traditional view of social norms and obligations, of the proper economic functions of several parties within the community'.[56]

In workplaces collective responses to the food problem took a different form. Working classes in occupied countries were particularly hard hit by the combination of high food prices and low wages. The prevailing conditions did not encourage trade union activities but nonetheless, whenever it was possible, workers joined the unions and organized protests. The demands of labour in the different occupied countries were more or less similar: wage rises and increased rations. The effectiveness of these protests depended on the power of the trade unions and the stance of the occupation authorities.[57] While the authorities prosecuted Communists and agitators ruthlessly, they did not want to see the spread of labour unrest. Moreover, since the industrial production in occupied countries was designed to meet German needs, any strike or go-slow in strategic sectors like shipyards, railway and aircraft factories, mines and the metallurgical and automobile industries could be detrimental to the German war effort. Thus employers were caught between the workers and the Germans, and more often than not gave in to the workers' demands. There was an upsurge in labour activity in 1940–1 in Belgium and France against inadequate wages and food rations, which culminated in a wave of strikes in May 1941 in the mines of northern France, the industrial areas of Nantes and Saint-Nazaire and the industrial areas of Liège, Hainaut and Limburg in Belgium.[58] From 1942, however, when Germany began the systematic exploitation of human and economic resources in occupied countries in the framework of total war, labour relations were organized on a different basis. The recruitment of forced labour and the alignment of major industries to the needs of the Reich left little room for trade union activism.

Another collective response to the problem of food shortages was the formation of *ad hoc* local committees. In many Greek towns the inability of the government to collect the harvest and provide sufficient rations drove local people to take the initiative by setting up 'people's committees'. The purpose of such committees was to issue appeals to the government in Athens for food and to control the movement of supplies and prices in the local market. In Athens and other big cities members of professional associations and trade unions formed 'consumers' cooperatives' and demanded from the authorities foodstuffs for their members. These 'consumers' cooperatives' and 'people's committees' were the first nuclei of mobilization in the urban centres: they did not have a political agenda but helped people to overcome the shock of foreign occupation and reconstituted weakened bonds in local societies and workplaces. Civil servants, retired officers, war invalids, lawyers, teachers, workers, students and artisans were among those who set up 'consumers' cooperatives'.[59]

The food situation in the cities became critical before the liberation of the occupied, countries when military operations disrupted or temporarily destroyed the trade networks between the provinces and the cities. In the first months of 1944 the food shortages in Rome became acute. The city was supplied with foodstuffs from the south by train but aerial bombardments had destroyed the railway lines. One hundred trucks were deployed but the quantities they could transport were not sufficient, and bread rations were reduced from 150 grams to 100 grams. The food shortages were so acute that the office of food administration considered the evacuation of part of the population of the city. On the other hand, the attacks of starving people on bakeries forced the German authorities to assign policemen to the lorries that transported flour and bread and to the bakeries.[60]

In many countries during the occupation people were better off living in the countryside than in the cities. True, the occupation troops plundered the countryside, requisitioned animals and vehicles and 'bought' products like butter and meat at nominal prices. However, farmers, in anticipation of the hard times of war and because the harvest was very poor due to the mobilization, hoarded a large part of their crop. As food imports ceased due to the naval blockade and the food shortage in the cities became a certainty, farmers and city dwellers alike realized the importance of the countryside. As we have already seen, new clandestine trade networks between cities and villages emerged, which were very significant. A whole range of economic activities and social relations grew up outside the control of the occupation authorities and the collaborationist governments, together with a transfer of wealth (and sometimes power) from urban centres to the countryside.

At the beginning of the occupation collaborationist governments and the occupation forces tolerated these trade networks and finally legalized the individual transportation of foodstuffs for 'family needs' and the dispatch of 'family parcels' with food. In France more than 13 million 'family parcels', weighing 279,000 tons, were sent in 1942 alone.[61] It was difficult to crack down on these clandestine activities without becoming extremely unpopular, and, on the other hand, these networks were a way, sometimes the only way given the circumstances, to supplement insufficient rations. The crop of 1942 was better than that of the previous year and the inability to collect it meant that food shortages in the cities would continue to occur and exports to the Reich would dwindle. Collaborationist governments and the occupation authorities were determined not to allow this to continue. In 1942 the governments used the carrot and the stick to make the farmers deliver their crop to the government. In Vichy France a special force of *Ravitaillement* officials was established to ensure that delivery quotas were met, partly by centralizing the slaughter of livestock and the manufacture of dairy products, while economic officials tried to enforce price controls in the market and pressed charges against profiteers.[62] In occupied Greece the government introduced a barter scheme to induce farmers to sell their products to the state in exchange for salt, medicine and fertilizers. The whole effort was coupled with a countryside campaign by state officials and gendarmes with a view to determining the agricultural production in the various areas and collecting the quotas.

The campaign was not very successful. In Greece only 50,000 tons of wheat were collected by the state. If we take into account that the delivery corresponded to 20–25 per cent of the total production, then the crop should have been between 200,000 and 250,000 tons. However, statistics show that the production of wheat and other cereals in 1942 was between 580,000 and 650,000 tons (excluding Eastern Macedonia and Thrace, which were under Bulgarian occupation).[63] In other words, most of the crop was hidden and not delivered to the authorities. In France the response of the rural communities was one of non-cooperation. They refused to deliver their quotas and in many cases mayors put themselves at the head of these disobedient farmers. Gildea explains the farmers' attitude by arguing that one of the most important consequences of the occupation was the 'narrowing of horizons', that most people withdrew to their immediate social environment, questioning previous identities or other loyalties.[64] In addition to the 'narrowing of horizons', there were other reasons that may explain the attitude of the farmers. The first was that the crop of 1941 was to a large extent legally or illegally transported to the cities, and little was left for personal consumption; the farmers wanted to make sure that there would be enough food for them and their families in case of another winter of food shortages. Second, the sale of the product to the black market was much more profitable. The government tried to entice farmers to sell their produce to the authorities in exchange for goods that were not in abundance but nevertheless could be found on the black market or from relatives in the cities. Third, if the first year of the occupation had tipped the balance between cities and provinces in favour of the latter, the concerted effort of the authorities was an attempt to restore the previous order, to the dismay of peasants. Finally, the collection drive brought together small and big farmers, local elites and poor peasants and forged new bonds of solidarity against the government and the foreign enemy.[65]

The 'privileged' position of the farmers in comparison with the city dwellers was ultimately threatened by the fortunes of war. The course of the war on the eastern front meant that the Nazis had to rely more and more on the occupied countries to feed their army and civilian population. Quotas were raised and the farmers were obliged to meet increasing demands. In the last phase of the war the annual exports from the General Government were about 550,000 tons of grain and 350,000 to 400,000 thousand tons of potatoes. In 1941–2 2.1 million tons of grain were delivered to the Wehrmacht from the occupied Soviet territories but in 1944 the deliveries increased to 4.8 million tons. In 1940–1 550,000 tons of bread grain were shipped to Germany from France, whereas in 1943–4 there were 792,000 tons.[66] To a large extent thousands of farmers across Europe had been transformed into agrarian labourers for the Reich.

Farmers and Resistance: The Case of Greece

Resistance and guerrilla warfare had serious consequences for the social conditions in the provinces. Greece provides a very good case study of the impact of guerrilla warfare and German counter-insurgency operations in the countryside. In Greece the Communists were able to organize the first nuclei of armed groups in the summer of 1942 by 'defending' the farmers from the tax collectors who supervised the delivery of the crop. Guerrillas showed up suddenly in villages, burnt tax catalogues, removed local authorities and tax collectors, occasionally killed real or imagined collaborators, and distributed the crop that was in the village warehouses to the farmers while keeping a part for the logistical needs of the armed group. The core of the armed resistance was not on the plains but in the mountains, where the state apparatus and the occupation forces were absent, those who clashed with the authorities could take refuge and the guerrilla groups appeared as a force that could restore law and order, in particular eliminating the banditry which had become endemic due to the development of the barter economy. Tensions between the guerrillas and the farmers arose because farmers had to provide food for an increasing number of guerrillas, who would extract it by force if they did not have enough money to buy it. At the heart of the tension, however, were different perspectives: for the guerrillas the crops and the animals were food for consumption, for the farmers they were a means to earn their living.

The development of the resistance presented the collaborationist government and the occupation authorities with a new problem. The military operations against the *andartes* (guerrillas) entailed a great deal of improvization since the occupation troops were inexperienced in combating this new form of war, namely the guerrilla. The mopping-up operations were the most successful tactic for the occupiers, but also the most disastrous for the Greek rural population. From the spring of 1943 the Germans and the Italians began a set of operations to clear the mountains of resisters, a campaign that entailed the systematic burning of villages that provided logistical support to the guerrillas. Together with these mopping-up operations came the reprisals for the killing of German officers and soldiers. The following guidelines were given to the detachments operating in Epirus in August 1943: 'All armed men are basically to be shot on the spot. Villages from where shots have been fired, or where armed men have been encountered, are to be destroyed, and the male population of these villages to be shot. Elsewhere all men capable of bearing arms (16–60 years old) are to be rounded up and sent to Jannina.'[67] In 1943 and 1944 German and to a lesser extent Italian reprisals, which involved razing villages, burning houses, the requisition of foodstuffs and animals and executions of civilians, became frequent in the countryside.[68] Mopping-up operations and reprisals provoked the hostility of the population against the occupiers, but at the same time strained relations with the guerrillas. While they did not want to deliver their crop to the occupation forces, the presence of the guerrillas also constituted a danger.

The countryside suffered not only from the military campaigns but also from economic deprivation. The crop of 1943 was smaller than those of the previous two years of the occupation, due to an unusual drought and unrest in the countryside. German officials estimated that the crop of 1943 was between 280,000 and 300,000 tons, namely less than half those of the prewar years.[69] Moreover, because the distribution of relief aid required the permission of the occupation authorities, the latter made certain that no relief would reach areas where the *andartes* were active. These villages were first decimated by the occupiers and then excluded from the relief scheme. 'Any relief', we read in a report by relief workers in December 1943 about Central Greece, 'in food, medicines, clothing or loans by the Agricultural Bank was strictly forbidden by the German authorities outside a restricted area in the plain which did not include a single burned village, neither did any of these villages need urgent assistance. So the burned villages in the mountains of Oeta, Kallidromon and Orthrys remained without any relief at all.'[70] In the prefecture of Trikala, any relief was denied to 'victims of fire', that is villages razed by the Germans, unless they moved to the town of Trikala. In the same region the inhabitants were forbidden to use road communications or to sow and harvest corn, which had been a staple in the diet of the mountain villagers since the prewar years. The purpose of this policy was to empty these villages so that the guerrillas would be deprived of food, recruits and intelligence.

The German counter-insurgency campaigns and reprisals targeted the mountain-villages that provided the infrastructure for the guerrilla warfare. The misery that the German raids brought to these people is described in the following report: 'They are starved and diseased and their temporary shelters are lamentable. A typical shelter is an improvised place of five or six square metres between two burned and tottering walls, where, with no protection from wind and rain, the people sleep on the ground – healthy and ill, children and animals, all hungry, with no bedding, clothing or shoes.'[71] By June 1944 the Germans, Italians and Bulgarians had raided 1,339 towns, boroughs and villages, of which 879, or two-thirds, were completely wiped out, leaving more than a million people homeless. More than half of these people were victims of counterinsurgency campaigns in Central Greece and Western Macedonia and of the systematic efforts of the Bulgarian occupation forces to drive the Greeks out of Eastern Macedonia and Thrace.[72] 'Malaria is rife everywhere', wrote a relief worker about Epirus, 'together with malnutrition, dysentery and skin diseases. Quinine had disappeared not just from the market but also from the barter exchanges.'[73]

The distribution of relief became an important tool in the hands of the occupiers in their campaign against the resistance. At the same time, the serious flaws of the relief scheme itself were revealed. Greek relief officials received many complaints about the indifference and bureaucratic methods of the commission *vis-à-vis* the plight of the villagers. But that was just the tip of the iceberg. The logic of the relief scheme, which was the regular supply of the cities and the division of the provinces between producing and non-producing, was perhaps tailored to the needs of the Greek population in 1942, but it was very much out of date in 1943–4. It would not be an exaggeration to argue that what happened in 1943–4 was the opposite of what had happened in 1941–2. Whereas in 1941–2 Athens was famine-stricken, in 1943 and 1944 it was the turn of the countryside to face starvation and destruction. The German campaigns against the ELAS guerrillas were catastrophic for the village populations, turning producing areas into burned fields and pillaged villages, and the wealthy provincial towns into refugee settlements. The region of Larissa was the granary of Greece and at the same time had the second highest number of destitute people (130,000) in occupied Greece. Relief, however, did not reach these people. Athens continued to receive one third of the relief until the liberation of the country, while some provinces received less than was originally planned (Thessaly, for instance, received 30 per cent of the planned distribution) or were not even included in the relief plans (like Western Macedonia and Epirus).[74] At the moment when the destruction in the countryside was more than evident, the chief of the commission insisted that 'greater quantities of foodstuffs are required for distribution among people in the *capital*'.[75] The German restrictions on distribution, the ineptitude of the commission (reportedly only one member had experience in relief work and most members were stationed in Athens and avoided field trips to the provinces),[76] and the government policy of prioritizing the urban centres (the capital in particular) at the expense of the provinces resulted in the destitution of the village population. This 'carrot and stick' policy of the occupation forces and the collaborationist government resonated with their political goals, i.e. to wipe out the leftist guerrillas by terrorizing and dislocating the countryside and to appease the urban centres with the relief aid.

The impact of occupation was not the same throughout Europe. It has been argued that the economic, social and political impact of the Nazi occupation in central and eastern Europe was so profound that in many ways it facilitated the establishment of communist regimes in the post-war years.[77] Even though the impact on western Europe was far less dramatic, the changes in everyday life were significant. If the term 'everyday life' is used to describe the ordinary and repetitive in people's lives, then everyday life during wartime was in many aspects very different from everyday life in peacetime. Food shortages, the black market, queues and rationing became part of daily experience under occupation. At the beginning of the occupation especially, when the Germans followed a policy of requisitions and the government machinery was not prepared for the extraordinary conditions that the occupation had created, the scarcity of food became a daily concern. Not everybody was hit in the same way by food shortages. Workers and the urban poor had the greatest difficulties coping with high prices and low wages, although industrial workers received much higher rations than other consumers because of the importance of industry for the German war effort. Food shortages were a problem for people who lived in the cities, not in the countryside. A parallel economic network, however, which involved the black market, barter exchange and 'family gifts', supplied the cities with the necessary foodstuffs and signified a new balance in the social and economic relations between cities and the countryside. In the countries in which the countryside became the site of guerrilla warfare, however, rural populations paid a heavy price. The occupation forces, with their strategy of razing villages, looting, mass executions and taking hostages, turned the rural populations into destitute wartime refugees. Thus, everyday life was in many ways deeply affected during the occupation, and that experience shaped the values, attitudes and expectations of millions of Europeans in the post-war decades.

Notes

1. Alan S. Milward, *War, Economy and Society, 1939–1945* (Berkeley, University of California Press, 1979), p. 132.
2. Stavros Thomadakis, 'Black Markets, Inflation and Force in the Economy of Occupied Greece', in J.O. Iatrides (ed.), *Greece in the 1940s. A Nation in Crisis* (Hanover NH and London, University Press of New England, 1981), pp. 61–80.
3. Gordon Wright, *The Ordeal of Total War, 1939–1945* (New York, Harper Torchbooks, 1968), pp. 111–6.

4. Milward, *War, Economy*, pp. 135–6.
5. Karl Brandt, *Management of Agriculture and Food in the German-Occupied and Other Areas of Fortress Europe. A Study in Military Government* (Stanford, Stanford University Press, 1953), pp. 89–93, 111.
6. Ibid., pp. 131–4.
7. Milward, *War, Economy*, p. 262.
8. Cited in Gordon Wright, *The Ordeal of Total War*, p. 118.
9. Brandt, *Management of Agriculture*, pp. 39–42.
10. Mogens R. Nissen, 'Danish Food Production in the German War Economy', paper presented at the conference 'Food production and food consumption in Europe, c. 1914–1950', Centre for European Conflict and Identity History, Esbjerg, Denmark, 2–4 June 2004.
11. Henry Rousso, 'L'économie: Pénurie et modernization', in Jean-Pierre Azéma and François Bédarida (eds), *La France des années noires* (Paris, Seuil, 1993), vol. 1, pp. 427–51.
12. Rousso, 'L'économie', p. 436.
13. Milward, *War, Economy*, p. 267.
14. Paul Struye and Guillaume Jacquemyns, *La Belgique sous l'occupation allemande (1940–1944)* (Brussels, 1950), pp. 302–3.
15. Gustavo Corni, 'Terzo Reich e sfruttamento dell' Europa occupata. La politica alimentare tedesca nella seconda Guerra mondiale', *Italia Contemporanea*, 209–10 (1997–8), pp. 5–37.
16. Brandt, *Management of Agriculture*, pp. 22–3.
17. League of Nations, *Food, Famine and Relief, 1940–1946* (Geneva, 1946), p. 41.
18. On the Dutch famine see H.A. van der Zee, *The Hunger Winter. Occupied Holland 1944–45* (London, Jill Norman and Hobhouse, 1982). The worst famine during the Second World War, however, occurred not in Europe but in India, where 1.5 million people starved to death in 1943.
19. UNRRA Archives, PAG 4/4.1:9., Memorandum of the Greek Government to the United Nations Relief and Rehabilitation Administration, November 1943.
20. John L. Hondros, *Occupation and Resistance. The Greek Agony 1941–44* (New York, Pella Pub. Co., 1983), pp. 70–1.
21. Mark Mazower, *Inside Hitler's Greece. The Experience of Occupation, 1941–44* (London and New Haven, Yale University Press, 1993), pp. 40–1.
22. FO 371/33175 R610, Berne to FO, 27 January 1942.
23. NARA, Board of Economic Warfare, Greece: Relief Food Distribution by the Joint Relief Commission, 12 June, 1943; Stephen G. Xydis, *The Economy and Finances of Greece under Occupation* (New York, Greek Government Office of Information, n.d.), pp. 23–31.
24. Stavros Thomadakis, 'Black Markets, Inflation', p. 76.
25. Milward, *War, Economy*, p. 248.

26. Bernhard R. Kroener, Rolf-Dieter Müller and Hans Umbreit, *Organization und Mobilisierung des Deutschen Machtbereichs* (Stuttgart, Deutsche Verlags-Anstalt, 1999), vol. 2, p. 226.
27. Brandt, *Management of Agriculture*, p. 418.
28. Robert Gildea, *Marianne in Chains. In Search of the German Occupation of France, 1940–1945* (London, Macmillan, 2002), p. 112.
29. Struye and Jacquemyns, *La Belgique sous l'occupation*, p. 305.
30. Claus Bundgård Christensen, 'Food consumption and the Black Market in Denmark, 1939–53', paper presented at the conference 'Food production and food consumption in Europe, c. 1914–1950', Centre for European Conflict and Identity History, Esbjerg, Denmark, 2–4 June 2004.
31. Kroener, Müller and Umbreit, *Organization und Mobilisierung*, p. 230.
32. League of Nations, *Food, Famine*, p. 23.
33. Paul Maun, *I apostoli mou stin katehomeni Ellada* (Athens, Metron, 2000), pp. 45–52.
34. Struye and Jacquemyns, *La Belgique sous l'occupation*, p. 309; Dominique Veillon, *Vivre et survivre en France 1939–1947* (Paris, Payot, 1995), pp. 188–9.
35. Veillon, *Vivre et survivre*, p. 194.
36. Veillon, *Vivre et survivre*, pp. 171–2.
37. Gildea, *Marianne in Chains*, pp. 115–16.
38. Struye and Jacquemyns, *La Belgique sous l'occupation*, p. 319.
39. Veillon, *Vivre et survivre*, p. 125.
40. Claus Bundgård Christensen, 'Den Sørte Børs. Krisekriminalitet i Danmark fra besættelsen til efterkrigstid 1939–1953', Ph.D. dissertation, Roskilde University, 2002 (I consulted the English summary of the dissertation).
41. Lutz Klinkhammer, *L'occupazione tedesca in Italia, 1943–1945* (Turin, Bollati Boringhieri, 1996), pp. 236–7.
42. Giorgos Margaritis, *Apo tin itta stin exegersi. Ellada: anoixi 1941–fthinoporo 1942* (Athens, O Politis, 1993), pp. 86–97.
43. Klinkhammer, *L'occupazione tedesca*, p. 182.
44. Cited in Brandt, *The Management of Agriculture*, p. 124.
45. Hélène Chaubin, 'L'Hérault', in Dominique Veillon and Jean-Marie Flonneau (ed.), *Le temps des restrictions en France (1939–1949)*, Les Cahiers de l' Institut d' Histoire du Temps Présent, 32–3, May 1996, pp. 171–93.
46. Margaritis, *Apo tin itta*, pp. 107–20, 128–32.
47. NARA 868.00/1250, Istanbul to Secretary of State, 7 July 1943.
48. Stavros Thomadakis, 'Black Markets', p. 65.
49. Struye and Jacquemyns, *La Belgique sous l'occupation*, p. 325.
50. Rousso, 'L' économie', p. 437.
51. NARA 868.48/5324-1/2, Stockholm to Secretary of State, 13 May 1944, enclosure no. 11.

52. Paula Schwartz, 'The Politics of Food and Gender in Occupied Paris', *Modern and Contemporary France*, 7(1), 1999, pp. 35–45.
53. NARA 868.00/1320, Istanbul to Secretary of State, 3 December 1943.
54. NARA 868.00/1324, Istanbul to Secretary of State, 6 December 1943.
55. NARA 868.00/1328, Istanbul to Secretary of State, 18 December 1943.
56. E.P. Thompson, 'The Moral Economy of the English Crowd in the Eighteenth Century', in idem, *Customs in Common* (London, Merlin Press, 1993), p. 188.
57. Gildea, *Marianne in Chains*, p. 120.
58. See the chapter by R. Gildea, D. Luyten and J. Fürst in this volume, p. 47.
59. Mazower, *Inside Hitler's Greece*, pp. 108–9; Margaritis, *Apo tin itta*, pp. 102–5.
60. Klinkhammer, *L'occupazione*, pp. 191–2.
61. Veillon, *Vivre et survivre*, p. 175.
62. Gildea, *Marianne in Chains*, p. 126.
63. NARA, Commission mixte de secours de la Croix-Rouge International, Rapport synoptique sur la production en Grèce, 25 September 1942; NARA 868.48/3655, Geneva to Secretary of State, 3 December 1942; NARA, Foreign Economic Administration, A Survey of Greek Relief, April 1941 to December 1943; NARA, Ministry of Warfare, Greek Agriculture during the War, 11 January 1944; NARA 868.48/5191, Cairo to Secretary of State, 14 February 1944.
64. Gildea, *Marianne in Chains*, pp. 16–7, 128–9.
65. Margaritis, *Apo tin itta*, pp. 156–64
66. Brandt, *The Management of Agriculture*, pp. 34, 133, 564.
67. Cited in Mazower, *Inside Hitler's Greece*, p. 176.
68. Reprisals in the form of mass executions happened, among many other places, in Kalavryta, where 694 civilians were killed in December 1943; Kleisoura, where 215 civilians were killed in May 1944; Komeno, where 317 civilians were shot dead in August 1943, and Distomo, where 300 civilians were executed in May 1944.
69. FO 371/36507 W17916, Stockholm to FO, 29 December 1943.
70. NARA 868.48/5184, Cairo to Secretary of State, 11 February 1944.
71. NARA 868.48/5275, Istanbul to Secretary of State, 29 March 1944.
72. Greek Government Office of Information, *Ruins of Modern Greece 1941–1944. Cities and Villages of Greece Destroyed by Germans, Italians and Bulgars, 1941–1944* (Athens, n.d.), p. 12.
73. FO 371/42356 W6230, Cairo to FO, 21 April 1944, FO 371/43687 R8298, Cairo to FO, 26 May 1944.
74. NARA 868.48/5035, Stockholm to Secretary of State, 25 September 1943.
75. FO 371/36507 W17916, Stockholm to FO, 29 December 1943 (original emphasis).
76. NARA 868.48/5271, Istanbul to Secretary of State, 31 March 1944.
77. Bradley F. Abrams, 'The Second World War and the East European Revolution', *East European Politics and Societies*, 16(3), 2002, pp. 623–44.

–2–

To Work or Not to Work?

Robert Gildea, Dirk Luyten and Juliane Fürst

After the end of the war, to have worked for or with the Germans was generally seen as a form of collaboration – at best economic rather than political collaboration – but in any case a form of betrayal. Directly or indirectly it was seen as working for the German war machine and therefore as contributing to Allied deaths. From the perspective of daily life, however, the question was posed in terms not of political choice but of survival. In response to accusations of collaboration workers, traders and employers might argue that they were forced to enter economic relationships with the Germans, the alternative being that they would have to close their factories, go out of business or lose their jobs. Sometimes claims were even made that putting up some kind of resistance to German demands was evidence of patriotism. Employers agreed to meet German orders, but argued that they had negotiated terms that minimized their contribution to the German war effort or were providing work for individuals who might otherwise be drafted for work in Germany. Workers might claim that they had no alternative but to work for the Germans in the face of unemployment or, forced to work for them, explain that they worked as little as possible, by absenteeism or sickness, go-slows or petty sabotage. This chapter will seek to establish what kind of autonomy of action existed in the world of work even under the most brutal conditions, and how the actions of employers, traders and workers were viewed both at the time and later.

The Impact of the German War Economy

The German occupation had a massive impact on the world of work in Europe. In a first phase, the *Blitzkrieg* of 1939–40 inflicted extensive economic disruption and unemployment in Europe, as a result of physical damage, the break-up of traditional markets, the blockade imposed by the British, and the sudden demobilization of hundreds of thousands of soldiers. Unemployment was rife after the defeats, running to 500,000 in both Belgium and the Netherlands.[1] In a second phase, the German war machine created a new demand for manufactured goods, foodstuffs and labour, so that occupied Europe experienced something of an economic bonanza. Orders came thick and fast from the Wehrmacht, the Luftwaffe, the Kriegsmarine and the Todt

Organisation. There were also orders from the German civil sector, notably, as the war dragged on, for foodstuffs and textiles. Most of this was procured on the open market but shortages and official price fixing meant that the Germans were also big players in the black market. Towards the end of the war, however, the pressure on the German war effort was such that compulsion replaced incentive as the main motor of the war economy, and the screws were tightened on both producers and workers. Nearly 8.5 million workers were drafted from eastern and western Europe to work in German factories in order to replace German workers drafted for military service, although as German armies were driven back, and German industrial areas and cities were bombed, the war economy became increasingly chaotic and ineffective.[2]

The impact on patterns of work varied not only in time but also according to geographical location. Industrialized northwestern Europe was treated more favourably than predominantly agrarian southern and eastern Europe. This was not only because of the value of the economy to the German war effort, but also because of the continued existence of governmental, administrative and corporate structures there, and the resulting possibility of negotiating with the Germans and acting to protect the working conditions of the labour force and keep as much of it as possible at home. In eastern Europe, by contrast, where governmental structures collapsed under the impact of invasion, nothing but local mayors or village elders stood between the working population and German demands. In addition, the mentality of the German forces in the east was very different from that obtaining in the west. While the Danes and Dutch were considered of Germanic stock and invited to collaborate freely, Germans entered the east with an ideology that held local populations to be racially inferior and fit only to be harnessed as slaves to the German war machine. Only the reality of the need to feed and shelter workers if they were to work efficiently tempered the brutal treatment meted out to eastern workers. This chapter will concentrate on the cases of the Netherlands and Belgium, France and Italy, Poland and occupied Russia, predominantly Ukraine, in order to point up these differences.

The German authorities were not monolithic and rivalry between different German agencies shaped conditions in the world of work, even in the east. The Ostministerium under Alfred Rosenberg, which was interested in a permanent, long-term and ideologically inspired conversion of the east into German soil or functioning colonies, found itself constantly at loggerheads with the Wehrmacht, which refused to hand over territory to civilian rule or claimed back stretches close to the front. Similarly, while Albert Speer's armament ministry preferred to employ workers on site, whether in plants and factories taken over by the Germans or in firms with which the Germans had made contracts, Plenipotentiary General for Labour Allocation Fritz Sauckel wanted to conscript foreign workers, first from the east, then from the west, and put them to work in Germany.[3] Tensions between different agencies could give employers and workers scope to play one off against the other to their best advantage.

Negotiating Advantage in Western Europe

Employers generally embraced the opportunity to do business with the Germans, although they had to take steps to ensure they were not accused of collaboration. This could be done by securing the approval of the national government where it still existed, by building solidarity with other employers about their strategy, and also by maintaining good relations with the workforce, lest class revenge be considered at a future point. The attitude of workers to working for the Germans was determined by the level of their wages and rations, and by the degree to which they were left with any labour organization to protect their interests. Despite the constraints they were under in occupied territories, workers sometimes resorted to strike action to put pressure on the German authorities, national governments and employers.

The Dutch economy was integrated into the German war economy with a minimum of fuss. Dutch firms had built up large stocks in the late 1930s in order to be self-sufficient in case of a German attack, and after the capitulation these stocks were immediately turned over to production for Germany. The virtual closure of the German market to the Dutch in the 1930s had been one of the main causes of depression there in the 1930s, but the reopening of that market as a result of the occupation dispelled the shadow of depression and drove up the index of industrial employment in the Netherlands from 100 in 1938 to 117 in 1941. This policy was facilitated by the Dutch administration, through the Ministry for Economy and special agencies or *Rijksbureaus* in which industrialists participated.[4] The Dutch administration was convinced that Germany had won the war, and the idea that the Netherlands would become part of a political and economic sphere dominated by Germany was widespread. The acting Secretary-General for Social Affairs R.A. Verwey saw cooperation as necessary to preserve 'national strength' in this New Europe. The possibility of centralization offered by the German New Social Order seemed more effective to the Dutch top officials than the prewar social order of democracy and pillarization.[5]

Dutch workers were not in general hostile to this new environment. The prewar system of labour relations and collective bargaining (*Rijksbemiddelaars*) continued with some modifications until November 1942, and employers were willing to pay higher wages. In July 1940 the Germans put the socialist union Nederlands Vakverbond (NVV) under the control of H.J. Woudenberg, a member of the collaborationist NSB. Most leaders of the NVV reconciled themselves to the situation and remained in post. In May to June 1942 the Germans set up the Dutch Labour Front, which brought together 100,000 workers, about a third of the prewar NVV membership. Most of these were rural workers, who were not liable for forced labour in Germany at that time and enjoyed a more favourable economic position than industrial workers. Catholic and Protestant unions were dragooned into the Front, and their leaders resigned, supported by the employers' organizations who refused to deal with the Front any longer.[6] That said, clandestine labour organizations were relatively weak and were not able to impose on employers the favourable post-war settlement that Belgian workers were able to achieve.

Conditions for Dutch workers were fairly privileged under the occupation. Unskilled Dutch construction workers could earn up to 25 per cent more working for the Wehrmacht or the Todt Organisation on these sites than on sites outside the war economy.[7] Rations were also good, both because the rationing system was prepared long before the war and proved to be efficient, and because in the Nazi racial hierarchy the Dutch were considered as Germanics. Dutch workers did not go hungry like their Belgian colleagues and had less economic reason to strike.[8] The only strike to obtain higher wages was the strike of the unemployed workers on relief, an atypical section of the working class.[9] The strike of February 1941 in the Netherlands was also political, directed against the persecution of the Jews in Amsterdam. The strikes that broke out in the Amsterdam shipyards a few days earlier were motivated not by material conditions but to protest against forced labour in Germany.[10]

In Belgium economic collaboration was more cautious. It was the only country in western Europe that had experienced a large-scale German occupation in the First World War and had suffered a subsequent economic purge. The economic elite was therefore keen to adopt an economic policy that would keep the factories open and the population fed, while not contributing arms to the German war effort and while protecting the workforce from the threat of conscription into Germany. This policy was called the Galopin doctrine, named after Alexandre Galopin, governor of the main Belgian holding company, the Société Générale, which controlled 40 per cent of Belgian industry. Its instrument was the Galopin Committee, formed in May 1940 of the leaders of the holding companies, banks and industry, which served as a shadow government that decided on economic and social policy and laid down rules about economic relations with Germany. The Committee aimed to involve all industrialists in a given sector in the question of German orders, both to avoid unseemly jockeying for competitive advantage or large profits and to avoid discussion of the patriotic attitude of individual industrialists after the war. Of course the difference between contributing arms to the German war effort and contributing in other ways to the German war machine was not always easy to maintain. Engineering companies controlled by the holdings refused to accept orders which had a clearly military use. If the Germans increased the pressure, the firm would attempt to come to a compromise, accepting part of the order or delaying its delivery.[11] On the other hand, carpenters' yards beyond the control of the Galopin Committee produced barracks for the German army, and many contractors agreed to participate in the construction of German defence works, such as the Atlantic Wall and airports.[12] As a result, the unemployment crisis of May–June 1940 was resolved within a year, when only 100,000 people were looking for a job, a normal level of unemployment.[13]

Unlike in the Netherlands, the system of collective bargaining in each industry – the *commissions paritaires* secured by trade unions after the First World War – was banned by the Germans. Trade unions had to cease their activities. The Germans wanted to replace them by a single trade union for blue and white collar workers, transcending the split between socialist, Catholic, liberal and Flemish-nationalist unions, through a Union des Travailleurs Manuels et Intellectuels (UTMI). Despite the collaboration of the president of the Belgian Socialist Party (POB), Hendrik De Man, and leaders of most labour federations early on, membership of the UTMI in 1940 was only 25 per cent of the strength of prewar unions, and by 1942 it had lost more than half of its members.[14] Similarly, only a few employers ever recognized the UTMI, on the grounds that it was not representative.

Belgian employers seized the opportunity presented by the collapse of the traditional unions and the system of collective bargaining to pursue their own agenda and developed a paternalistic and localized system of labour relations. In a sense this was a continuation of the policy they had developed after the general strike of 1936. In September 1940 a circular of the employers' organization, the Comité Central Industriel (CCI), advised its members to set up factory councils which would provide canteens – of the first importance when food was so short – administer company health insurance and child benefit, provide medical and social services and even give factory land to workers for use as allotments. The members of the factory councils, even if elected by workers, would be vetted by employers. Depending on the balance of power in the factory, they were sometimes former shop stewards, sometimes workers without any previous links to a trade union, and sometimes a mixture of the two.[15] This attempt to construct a 'community of labour' was not unsuccessful. In 1940 many local authorities and labour leaders fled before the Germans, and workers were left to fend for themselves. Their horizons narrowed suddenly. As the sociologist and historian Guillaume Jacquemyns noted, 'in the general collapse the one organization that remained for many workers was the factory, the mine, the workshop or the office, and it was there they headed to find food and safety'.[16] Employers were ready to meet the challenge and played a more central role in the daily life of the workers. They not only provided work, but also filled the gaps left by the labour movement by organizing social help at factory level, supplied workers with extra food to make up the shortfalls of the rationing system, and offered protection against recruitment to work in Germany. As a result workers looked more favourably on employers than on retailers, black marketeers and war profiteers, who often belonged to the same social group as the workers but were seen to have profited unduly and at their expense.[17]

Even this paternalistic system, however, was unable to cushion Belgian workers from the harshness of the occupation. The bread ration, fixed in May 1940 at 450 grams per day was halved to 225 grams in June 1940 for the duration of the occupation, while potatoes were rationed at 500 grams per day, a third of what German soldiers stationed in Belgium were fed. Moreover, people often did not get the rations to which they were entitled. At the same time, wages were frozen by the German authorities, putting access to the black market beyond the reach of most workers. Miners, who received coal as part of their wages, were able to enter the black market on their own account, selling it for five or six times its usual price, but these constituted an elite.[18] Employers themselves became involved in procuring potatoes on the black market to feed their workers, and the German authorities tolerated these goings-on because it was in their interests that workers producing for the German war economy should be decently fed.[19]

None of this, however, was able to break the stranglehold of low wages and inadequate food, and strikes broke out sporadically from the autumn of 1940. These were aimed partly against the employers, protesting against inadequate wages and food supplies, demonstrating the limits of the Galopin system, partly against the Belgian authorities for the 'directed famine' of the rationing system, and partly against the German authorities for holding down wages and – argued the underground press – for causing shortages and hunger by siphoning off all possible resources to Germany. The strikes came to a climax with the so-called 'strike of the 100,000', which began symbolically on 9–10 May 1941, the anniversary of the German invasion, in the Cockerill steel plant, and for ten days mobilized 60–70,000 workers in the industrial areas of Liège, Hainaut and the Limburg coal basin. Communist militants took an active part in the organization of the strike, which was a symptom of the radicalization of the workforce and indicated that the new type of paternalistic labour relations was not effective in keeping social peace. Employers had to find an answer to this new situation by mediating between workers and the Germans. Keen to maintain their autonomy at the factory level, they supported the demands of the workers with the authorities, securing a wage rise of 8 per cent, and refused to give the Germans lists of the instigators of the strike.[20] After this labour leaders remained in secret talks with employers about continuing industrial production under Galopin rules and negotiated the Social Pact of 1944 which laid the foundations of the post-war welfare state in Belgium.

In France defeat and partial occupation in the summer of 1940 provoked recession and unemployment, a situation worsened by the British blockade that cut coal and fuel supplies. German orders that rolled in from the autumn of 1940 came as an immense boost, setting the country to work again. In the Nantes/Saint-Nazaire area of the west of France, for example, the shipyards, which each employed around 3,000 workers, received orders from November 1940 to build destroyers, tugs, torpedo boats, speed boats, U-boats, air-traffic control boats, tankers, transport ships, whalers and trawlers. Associated engineering works received orders for turbines and motors, steelworks for sheet metal.[21] Meanwhile at Nantes the Compagnie Générale de Construction de Locomotives (Batignolles-Châtillon) was devoting 90 per cent of its output to the Reichsbahn early in 1941, and the Société Nationale de Construction Aéronautique du Sud-Ouest (SNCASO) at Nantes-Bouguenais agreed an order in April 1941 to build Heinkel 111 aircraft that was worth 4 million man hours over two years.[22] From May 1942 there was a surge in orders not only from Heinkel of Rostock but also from Junkers of Magdeburg, Focke-Wulf of Bremen and BMW aircraft motors of Munich.[23] To see that these orders were efficiently met, the Germans set up a separate war-economy administration, the Rüstungsinspektion. One of its goals was to increase the number of *Rüstungsbetriebe* or *Rü-Betriebe* producing almost totally for the German military and and *Vorzugsbetribe* or *V-Betriebe* working partly for them.[24]

The biggest orders, however, came not for the shipyards, railway and aircraft factories but for the construction industry, which was required first to build U-boat bases at Brest, Lorient and Saint-Nazaire, and airfields for the Lufwaffe and artillery installations on the Channel coast, and then from 1942 the Atlantic Wall to fend off potential Allied invasion. This enormous programme was promoted by the Todt Organisation, negotiating with one of the industrial cartels set up by Vichy in August 1940, the Comité d'Organisation du Bâtiment et des Travaux Publics (COBTB). This in turn passed huge contracts to construction companies like the Entreprise des Travaux Publics Dodin at Nantes, which themselves often subcontracted to consortia such as the Nantes group of twenty-seven firms set up in July 1943. After the war Henri Dodin, director of the consortium, argued that initially he had refused contracts, but the Germans threatened to requisition his workforce and plant.[25] But accept them they did, amounting to orders of between 50 and 80 million francs working on German defences, out of an estimated 40 billion francs of orders going to the French construction industry as a whole between 1941 and 1944.[26]

To begin with the workforce recruited by Germans for the Todt Organisation was voluntary, but in a rather constricted sense. Local authorities were instructed to close their own public works and hand over building workers, while 30,000 Spanish republicans who were interned in Vichy's refugee camps were transferred to building projects on the coast. From 1942 the need for labour became more intense, and the Germans offered higher wages and bonuses and stepped up the propaganda drive. By August 1942 100,000 workers had been enticed or bullied onto the organization's sites, but this was still not enough. The German authorities pressed Vichy to pass a law on 4 September 1942 allowing it to pressgang workers into jobs required by the national (in fact German) interest. Working for the Reich in France was much more preferable than working for the Reich in Germany, which was required by the Service du Travail Obligatoire (STO) law of 16 February 1943, and nearly 200,000 were working for Todt in France in August 1943. Unfortunately, the transfer of 50,000 workers from the Atlantic to the Ruhr that summer, in order to repair the dams destroyed by the RAF, demonstrated that Todt was less a protection against work in Germany than an antechamber to it, and the workforce began to desert. Things became even worse when the Allies started to bomb the Atlantic coastal towns where the U-boat bases, construction projects and shipyards were sited. Nantes, for example, was bombed on 16 September 1943, killing 812, injuring 1,785 and leaving 20,000 homeless. Panic ensued and 100,000 people or half the population fled into the countryside. Manning levels on sites and in factories working for the Germans fell to 20 per cent. 'Systematic work is as good as impossible', complained the German Labour Office, insisting that the first priority was to ensure that 'workers who have left are brought back to the *Rü-* and *V-Betriebe* as quickly as possible', although many workers had other ideas.[27]

It was generally easier for workers drafted by the Germans to shirk their responsibilities than employers, who later argued that they had had no choice but to collaborate economically with the Germans, for fear of seeing their factory taken over, closed or moved lock, stock and barrel to Germany. This has been termed by historians 'survival collaboration' or 'constrained adaptation'.[28] Keeping quiet about the profits they had made from German orders, such employers also claimed that by staying open they were providing employment for local workers and, if they were in sectors key for the war effort, offered those workers protection against being drafted for forced labour in Germany. After the war they made the case that while accepting German orders formally, they did everything possible not to furnish weapons to the Reich and turned a blind eye to resistance cells within their factories that were sabotaging the production process. The French automobile industry provides an interesting case study. The leading firms such as Renault and Peugeot were put under considerable pressure not only to supply the Germans with trucks but also to persist with the conversion from civilian to military vehicles and parts that had begun in earnest in 1938. Louis Renault seems to have had few qualms about turning his plant over to production for the Wehrmacht, with the result that the factory at Boulogne-Billancourt was bombed by the RAF on 3 March 1942, killing 400 people and putting much of the plant out of action. Renault himself was arrested after the liberation and considered an autocratic *patron* with little support among either his workforce or his competitors. Peugeot, by contrast, was far more astute about navigating a course between collaboration and resistance and was able to survive both the occupation and the liberation relatively unscathed. Peugeot was certainly kept alive by German orders, but it claimed to produce trucks rather than tanks and to have been uncooperative over German demands for a new Focke-Wulf plane. The RAF bombed its factory at Sochaux-Montbéliard on the Swiss border on 16 July 1943, killing 110 people, after which an agreement was made between Pierre Peugeot and a British agent, Harry Rée, that there would be no more bombing of the factory if the firm tolerated sporadic sabotaging of production for Germany by resistance cells within the factory. Sabotage led to the arrest of a number of managers by the Germans and the escape of Pierre Peugeot to Switzerland in October 1944, but also to the fact that he and the firm were not troubled by the French authorities at the liberation.[29]

The Renault and Peugeot cases illustrate very different relations between employers and workers. The advent of Vichy was seen by many in business and the administration as an opportunity to reverse organized labour's gains under the Popular Front for good. Vichy's law of 16 August 1940 set up Comités d'Organisation (COs) to run each industry and effectively assisted the process of cartelization to the advantage of big business, but the task of weaning the working class away from Marxism did not mean that labour organizations were done away with altogether. While the *national* organizations of employers and workers, such as the Confédération Générale du Travail (CGT) and Confédération Générale du Patronat Français (CGPF), were dissolved, *local* trade unions and even their organizations at a municipal (the Bourses du Travail) and departmental level were left intact. Marshal Pétain and the labour minister, former trade unionist René Belin, were explicit that the regeneration of France meant social peace rather than industrial confrontation, and the Charter of Labour finally published on 4 October 1941 was intended to eliminate class war in the medium term by establishing a single trade union for each 'occupational family', merging employers, managers, white-collar workers, foremen and workers, locally, regionally and nationally. In the short term the main provision of the Charter was to bring about the collaboration of all these strata at factory level through the election of factory social committees, which would deal not with running the business but with working conditions and welfare.[30]

The Labour Charter was a powerful challenge to organized labour. A minority of labour leaders saw it as a framework which they could either grasp in order to save the unions, or reject and risk annihilation. Most trade unionists were, however, suspicious of the Charter. They saw it as a trick by which all the gains they had made since 1936 could be rolled back. CGT leaders thought that it threatened the autonomy of trade unions that was consecrated by their own Charter of Amiens of 1906 and left no place for the local and departmental unions of unions based in the Bourses du Travail. The only point at which the Charter really worked was at factory level, with the factory social committees which multiplied in number from 372 in January 1942 to 9,000 in January 1944. They enjoyed a certain popularity because, like the Belgian factory councils, they provided two important services. One was social benefits to cover loss of earnings through illness, or to make payments to deported workers. The other, giving the committees the nickname of 'potato committees', helped to eke out their subsistence through the provision of works canteens, individual allotments or plots of land worked collectively. These services were funded jointly by employers and workers and marked a significant increase in firms' social expenditure, from 15 per cent of the wage bill in 1938 to 34 per cent in 1943, marking the advent of what Le Crom has called the 'providence company'.[31]

Despite cold-shouldering the Charter, the French working class did not demonstrate much militancy in the early phase of the occupation. The strike of the 100,000 in Belgium in May 1941 carried over into the Nord department of France, which was annexed to the same German military administration in Brussels and has attracted the most attention.[32] There was some industrial action in the industrial area of Nantes, at the SNCASO factory of Nantes-Bouguenais in June 1942, and the fact that this occurred in plants harnessed to the German war machine raised the stakes sharply. Vichy and French employers were put under intense pressure by the Germans to settle disputes immediately, which weakened rather than strengthened their hand. And while Vichy was keen to deal ruthlessly with Communists, it did not wish to alienate the mass of the workers, whose hard work and political loyalty it wished to develop.

Strikes were not perhaps the most obvious way to better one's lot under the occupation. More opportunities were offered by the black market, which sprang up in response to the shortage of all sorts of goods, from wine to scrap metal and grain and butter, and the fact that prices on the open market were officially kept down by Vichy. The Germans, who should have closed down the black market, in fact caused it to boom because of their desperate need for materials for the war industry and foodstuffs and luxuries for their own private consumption. The daily tribute they received from the French under the armistice and the artificial overvaluation of the Reichsmark against the franc gave them an immense purchasing power which drove up prices on the black market.[33] This made life extremely hard for consumers on fixed incomes but created openings for those who were able to provide the goods so coveted. Two examples, one entrepreneur and one worker from the Nantes/Saint-Nazaire area, may illustrate the phenomenon. Before the war Roger Flamant had owned a large textile dye-works at Anor in the Nord, which he then sold before going to Morocco to make another fortune. During the war he became a property developer in the resorts of La Baule and Le Pouliguen, buying up large villas and turning them into flats ready to do holiday business after the war. He was well connected with the German authorities, who sold him materials from buildings they had demolished and even lent him lorries to transport them. At the other end of the spectrum was Raymond Couturier, a mechanic and foreman at the SNCASO works at Nantes-Bouguenais factory, who also ran a café called 'L'Envol'. After the Germans arrived he gave up his job at the aircraft factory to concentrate on his café and then made a fortune hiring out horses and carts for the German air base at Château-Bougon and supplying it with black-market goods into the bargain. Not for him the strikes that only ended up with the arrest of militants and the tightening of conditions.[34]

Lost Illusions in Eastern Europe

At the other end of Europe, in occupied Russia, the German authorities and Wehrmacht considered their newly conquered populations as racial inferiors contaminated by Bolshevism and clearly behaved with greater brutality than in western Europe. Over 600,000 Russian workers were conscripted by the Reichsbahn Ost to build road number 4, ensuring effective communications and supply.[35] There was no question of collaboration with Soviet authorities, which evacuated key industries and workers from areas which fell under German occupation in 1941, re-established them in the Russian hinterland and destroyed much of what had to be left behind.[36] However, many local populations in the borderland regions which had been Sovietized and Stalinized by force looked forward to a better deal under German rule. Workers and engineers of the Soviet iron industry centre at Kryvy Rih/Krivoi Rog did everything they could to preserve their plant from destruction by the departing Soviets, while employees in the sugar refineries recovered machinery they had hidden in wells and ponds, or in some cases buried in the ground, and got production going even before the Germans arrived.[37]

The important administrative and entrepreneurial posts were quickly given to Germans or locals claiming German descent, but the occupying power had to rely on the collaboration of the indigenous population in auxiliary positions. Meagre prospects of food, wages and heating at work, as well as anti-Soviet feelings and national sentiments, were enough to ensure a willing workforce. Yet German salaries were by no means high. Most Kiev employees earned less than 500 karbovantsi (the new currency introduced by the occupation regime) per month, enough to buy only a few kilos of potatoes. For example, a woman at a registry office in Kiev was paid 400 karbovantsi and a ration of sugar beet, jam and a small amount of sausage and jellied meat. She ate thin soup and cabbage once a day in the canteen.[38] This was far more than the average Kievan could expect in the hungry winter of 1941/2. Life for industrial workers was equally hard, as the initial German promise of 10 per cent higher wages failed to materialize. The Germans retained the draconian Soviet labour laws, which punished even slight lateness or slowness with harsh prison sentences. However, the fact that few Germans were present or had an adequate grasp of the local language allowed workers to shift easily from chatting and going slow to pilfering for the black market and low-level sabotage. An engineering worker recalled that they tinkered with 'all sorts of junk, mending some things, breaking others. Everybody was working for himself and went away with cigarette lighters, buckets and pans to use in barter.'[39]

In the countryside most of the rural population that had fled before the German armies returned to their home villages. There was widespread hope among the peasantry, who had proven particularly hostile to the implementation of Soviet rule, that the Germans would abandon the kolkhozes and reintroduce private farms. The Germans also courted popularity by supporting the reopening of churches, which had been closed by the 'godless' Communists.[40] Older people in the borderlands remembered the German occupation of the First World War as relatively benevolent.[41] This, together with Ukrainian, Baltic and Ruthenian national sentiments, resulted in an initially warm welcome – newsreels show Soviet peasant women blessing German soldiers with crucifixes and offering them bread with salt – and a subsequent readiness to collaborate with the further war effort.

That said, the conquered territories of the Soviet Union mainly functioned to supply food for the German army on the eastern front and the German population at home. Göring declared in 1941: 'Only those in the occupied regions who work for us shall be assured of adequate food ... even if one wanted to feed all the remaining population one could not do so'.[42] With the food situation deteriorating dramatically in all of the occupied Soviet territories in the course of 1942, an active display of loyalty to the Germans was thus often a matter of life and death. In the absence of Soviet governmental structures, a key role was played by the village elders (*starosty*) and local police units, who were to ensure that the harvest was accounted for properly, pass the required share to the German authorities, supply labour as required and impose law and order in town and countryside, where the German presence was often thin on the ground.[43] Once the confidence of the German authorities had been secured, the *starost'* was literally a 'little tsar'. Ironically, some of these were former Communist Party officials, who now served German rather than Soviet masters.[44] Initiative beyond the call of duty was rewarded with extra land or rights to a private farm, as given, for instance, for the betrayal of thirty members of the Soviet underground in the Oredezhskii raion in the Leningrad region.[45] Many used their newly gained power to settle old scores. The *starost'* of Korolev-Stan near Minsk, who could neither read nor write, denounced three of his neighbours to the German police. Although the main accusation was illegal horse-trading, he made clear that the 'three Soviet activists' had participated in the collectivization drives of the 1930s. When the accused were arrested and executed, he forbade their burial in the village cemetery.[46]

Since Russia was to be Germany's granary, relations with the peasantry were of crucial importance. Yet the nature of this relationship was one of constant debate between the various Berlin ministries and army administrations that had an interest in the situation in the east. Far-reaching agricultural reforms might win over the peasantry but equally endanger the food supply. The German authorities were therefore split on the issue of what kind of procurement methods to employ and in particular whether to maintain or dismantle the kolkhoz system. Depending on the status of the territory in question, the decision of individual commanders and the response of the local population, food procurements took on a wide variety of forms ranging from outright requisitioning by force to enticement to higher productivity through the granting of enlarged private plots, which were not taxed.[47] In the Russian northern territories around Leningrad partial de-collectivization was achieved and yielded high returns.[48] The ethnic German population in Ukraine and some areas in the south benefited from the conversion of kolkhozes into cooperatives, affecting up to 17 per cent of all rural production units.[49] However, at times of severe fighting or military setbacks, even the promise to leave peasants the fruits of their labour on their private plots (which, in 1943, had belatedly been made their property) was broken.

Incessant requisitioning and the decision to leave the kolkhoz structure largely untouched alienated the rural populations and played into the hands of the partisans, who were also known to plunder and pilfer for their own purposes. They exacted retribution against collaborationist *starosty* and police. Often villages were in the hands of the Germans during the day, while at night they were at the mercy of the partisans. The most successful elders and police managed to work with both the Germans and the partisans for the benefit of the local populations. This was an increasingly preferred option in the later stages of the war, when the partisans were interested in obtaining armed manpower and the local police felt it was wise to switch their allegiance.[50]

Western Workers, Voluntary and Forced

Although in the initial phases the German war economy tended to employ workers in their own country, as military demands reduced the availability of Germans for war production so labour was increasingly sucked from occupied areas into the Reich. To begin with this work force went voluntarily and was really a continuation of traditional patterns of labour migration in search of higher wages. With the Russian invasion and the setbacks arising from it, the Germans resorted to forced or conscripted labour, drawing not only on industrial workers but also on the occupied populations as a whole. The number of voluntary and forced labourers in Germany rose from 3.5 million at the end of 1941 to 5.6 million at the end of 1942, 7.3 million at the end of 1943 and 8.2 million at the end of 1944. Over the course of the war the total of 8.4 million foreign workers in the Reich included 80,000 Danes, 375,000 Belgians, 475,000 Dutch, 960,000 Italians, 1,050,000 French, 1,600,000 Poles and 2,775,000 Russians.[51] This did not mean that the Germans obtained all the workers they wanted, for numerous ways were found to avoid labour deportation to the Reich, from finding work in German-controlled factories in one's own country to taking to the hills and forests. Moreover, though workers drafted from occupied Russia were notoriously hard-working, belying myths about their racial inferiority, forced labourers in Germany found all sorts of ways to limit their contribution to the Reich economy, from conscientious laziness and faked illness to absconding and sabotage.

The Danes were in a good bargaining position *vis-à-vis* the Germans, having surrendered without a fight. They provided Germany with 10 per cent of their agricultural production, mainly pigs, butter and fish, as the 'breakfast table' traditionally exported to Britain was now sent to Germany. As a result they were not required to surrender forced labour, but a good supply of voluntary Danish labour nevertheless went to Germany. This was partly because there was a long tradition of Danish construction firms working in Germany, especially in the Hamburg area, partly because there was 35 per cent unemployment in Denmark in the winter of 1939–40 and in Germany Danes were treated and paid like German workers. Following the 'Hamburg agreement' of December 1940 signed in Copenhagen, around a hundred Danish building firms employing 10,000 workers, mostly Danish volunteers, were contracted to work in Germany, 31 firms in Hamburg, 34 in Kiel, 16 in Lübeck, 6 in Rostock and 4 in Berlin. Two cement giants enjoyed special terms. F.L. Smidth, which had established a cement works at Port Kunda in Estonia in 1922 but lost it to the Russians in 1940, recovered the works in 1942 and turned it over to production for the Todt Organisation until 1944. Højgaard & Schultz, the other giant, had a subsidiary called Contractor, which was involved in the building of the Weichselwall outside Warsaw on behalf of the General Government and, following German forces into the Balkans, for the building of the new Prince Eugen Bridge over the Sava at Belgrade, completed in 1942. Meanwhile up to 100,000 workers were employed in building the Danish section of the Atlantic Wall on the west coast of Jutland.[52]

From the Netherlands there was also a tradition of cross-border work dating back to the nineteenth century, interrupted by the First World War and the Depression, but picking up with the German rearmament programme after 1933. The German civil administration in the Netherlands was keen to promote Dutch labour migration to the Reich and the Dutch authorities, especially the Department for Social Affairs, shared the same view. In 1940 and 1941 67,000 Dutch found jobs again as cross-border workers, to whom were added 133,000 'voluntary' workers (men and women). The voluntary nature of their work was qualified by the determination of the Dutch administration from June 1940 to tackle its severe unemployment problem by sending unemployed workers to Germany, refusing them benefits if they did not. Pressure was also put on metalworking firms to send qualified workers to Germany. Many of those summoned to work in the Reich failed to turn up, while about 30 per cent of those employed in Germany did not return after their leave in the Netherlands in September 1940.[53]

The capture of 1.8 million French and British soldiers and 65,000 Belgian soldiers after the defeat of Belgium and France in May–June 1940 relieved some of the pressure on the German economy. POWs were not allowed to be used in war industries under the Geneva convention, but they were soon dispersed from the Stalags in *Arbeitskommandos*, in factories and on building sites, but above all on farms.[54] To these were added voluntary workers whom the Germans sought to attract by offering material advantages and imposing a low wage policy in occupied territory. Belgians had been extremely reluctant to work in Germany during the German occupation of the First World War, even when the British blockade brought both hunger and unemployment, preferring to live at home on the meagre international relief negotiated by the Comité National de Secours et d'Alimentation set up by Belgian bankers and industrialists to head off social unrest. It was not until 1917, when the German military became desperate, that about 120,000 Belgians were finally deported to Germany to work in the war industry.[55] Nevertheless 224,300 volunteered for work in Germany during the Second World War. They expected good wages and living conditions or wanted a job to take care of their families. Among the first to leave were the long-term unemployed. Others, such as Flemish nationalists, also had ideological reasons to go.[56]

Among the French about 10,000 volunteers went to work in Germany per month from the spring of 1941, rising to a peak of 21,000 in July 1942 and a total over the war of about 260,000. They were generally young and working class, often either those seeking to escape a difficult situation in France, such as jailbirds or single mothers, or those who had been brought into close connection with the Germans.

The father of a 22-year-old fitter from Touraine who went to work in Munich in 1942 sold wine to the Germans, while his mother worked for them as a cook.[57] Georges Marchais, who was to become secretary-general of the French Communist Party in 1972, worked at Bièvres outside Paris in 1940–1 for Aktien-Gesellschaft Otto, repairing Focke-Wulf aircraft, before he moved in December 1942 to the Messerschmitt factory at Leipheim near Augsburg. A whole controversy later hung on whether he had volunteered for work in Germany or whether he had been forcibly drafted.[58]

The German occupation of France and the Low Countries closed a traditional destination of Italian migrant workers, who had migrated in gangs to northern Europe to do seasonal work either in the fields or in such industries as the iron mines of Lorraine. In 1931 there were 29,000 foreign workers in the Longwy steel basin, nearly half the population, of whom 18,500 were Italians.[59] At the same time the opportunity to work in the Reich opened up, and under a German–Italian agreement of February 1941 Italy as an Axis partner was to provide 60,000 agricultural workers and 204,000 industrial workers in return for the supply of German goods; Italian statistics suggest that 233,000 Italian workers went to work in Germany in 1941, deployed at key sites such as the Herman-Goering-Werke in Lower Saxony and engineering works in Hamburg/Bremen working for the Kriegsmarine, and sending home very respectable wages.[60]

The German attitude to Italian workers was rather complex. On the one hand, they were the allies of Germany and their workers enjoyed the same wages as their German comrades. They were, however, regarded as racially inferior and, perhaps for that reason, workshy and difficult about their food – rejecting black bread on the grounds, they complained, that they were not pigs. A German–Italian diplomatic incident blew up in September 1941 over issues of work, sex and ultimately race. An Italian syndicalist official in Berlin reported that Italian workers who refused to work were sent to a strict labour education camp and were set upon by guard dogs, provoking Mussolini to exclaim, 'I will not permit the sons of a race which has given to humanity Caesar, Dante and Michaelangelo to be devoured by the Huns'.[61] Moreover, after a German woman in Recklingshausen was shorn and tarred for having sex with an Italian worker, the *Kreisleiter* announced that it would have been better if she had slept with a Norwegian, a Dutchman or even an Englishman.[62]

Polish Workers and *Ostarbeiter*

Poles had long since migrated to work as agricultural labourers on the German East Elbian estates or as miners in the Ruhr. The fears of German nationalists that the German race was being undermined by Slavs brought about the imposition of a *Karenzzeit* or closed season in 1890, which required Polish agricultural workers to return home after the harvest, between 15 November and 1 April each year. After the outbreak of war in August 1914 these workers were required to stay permanently in Germany to support the war economy, a requirement that was extended to the 300,000 Polish industrial workers, most of whom were in the Ruhr.[63] After 1918 the restored Polish government had tried to limit the numbers of Poles going to work in Germany, but the invasion of 1939 reopened the gates to Polish workers who wanted employment in Germany bringing in the harvest. This voluntary labour was, however, inadequate for German needs, and about 100,000 Polish POWs were drafted in by the end of 1939 to complete the work. Since this was still not enough to restock the agricultural labour force in Germany, on 24 April 1940 all young Poles of both sexes aged 16 to 25 in the General Government were declared liable for work in the Reich. Where local mayors cooperated, recruitment was possible, but in some cases whole villages fled into the forests and the Germans resorted to manhunts, hostage-taking and exemplary executions.[64]

Despite (or because of) this brutality young Polish workers did not always conform to the levels of discipline expected by the German authorities. Neither did they socialize only with members of their ethnic group, as required by Nazi regulations. In March 1940 a local official in Leobschütz/Lubczyce (Silesia) informed the local Landrat that:

> in many places it is clear that the Polish workers constantly take time off to get together and that local German workers also take part in these gatherings. Polish workers have already frequently been seen going out for walks and to the cinema with German youths. The obsession of the young Polish girls is all with finery and clothing. Under the pretext that they need to buy clothes without coupons, they obtain advances from the labour office and return after a day's absence without any clothes, having spent the money on things quite useless for work, such as perms and dancing shoes.[65]

Fraternization between Polish workers and Germans was not surprising, given the tradition of communal eating with seasonal Polish labour. An American researcher in Hesse in 1945–6 noted that during the war 'these 'slave labourers' frequently ate at the same dinner table with the peasant and his family, and as long as they worked hard their treatment was no different from that received by German farmhands'.[66] Catholicism was also a strong bond, with Poles attending German churches and priests organizing collections among their parishioners to support Polish workers.

Such intimacy was, however, anathema to the German authorities. German boys going out with Polish girls was one thing, but German girls going out with Polish men was a threat to the honour of German women and the purity of the race. Himmler called for brothels with Polish girls to be set up in towns where Polish men were working in any numbers, and for German women who had disgraced themselves to be shorn or paraded in public with a placard announcing their crime. The *Polnenerlasse* or decrees on Poles issued on 8 March 1940 tried to balance the economic need for Polish labour with the ideology of racial purity. Poles working in the Reich were to be marked out by a special badge, kept away from German 'cultural life' and 'places of amusement', and banned from public transport. Polish workers who had sexual relations with or made indecent advances towards a German woman could be punished by death. For such offences in July 1940 a Polish POW was hanged near Helmstedt, his German partner receiving a prison sentence of two-and-a-half years, and a Polish farmhand was hanged at Hampenhausen in Westphalia, while the following month a Polish worker aged 17 was hanged at Gotha.[67] The contradiction between the informal relations between Poles and Germans, particularly in the countryside, and the sexual apartheid lethally imposed by the draconian *Polnenerlasse* was later the theme of Rolf Hochhuth's play *A German Love Story*.[68]

The campaign against Russia in 1941 transformed the whole character of the war, not least in the world of work. The pressure on the German war economy intensified. Labour was in even shorter supply as successive waves of men and – particularly in the east – women were called up. Despite reservations about using Soviet soldiers infected by Bolshevik ideas, economic need led to Hitler's *Russeneinsatzbefehl* of 31 October 1941 instructing that Russian POWs should be 'extensively exploited for the needs of the war economy'. In fact, the proportion of those who died in transit or were unfit for work was so great that of 3,350,000 Russian POWs taken between June 1941 and March 1942 only 167,000 or 5 per cent of the total were actually put to work.[69] To fill the gaps *Ostarbeiter* or 'eastern workers' were recruited *en masse* after February 1942 from occupied areas of Ukraine and Russia. In the winter of 1941–2 there was a reasonable flow of voluntary workers, with 80 per cent of the first labour quota from Ukraine filled by volunteers.[70] Propaganda was intensive, with a campaign of brightly coloured posters, an itinerant exhibition and a feature film entitled *Come to Lovely Germany*, showing young people laughing and singing all the way to a German farmer's warm welcome. Volunteers were promised a better living, new experiences and the chance to fulfil their patriotic duty by helping to combat Bolshevism. Even the leaders of the two Orthodox churches engaged in the propaganda campaign by calling for participation in the fight against 'Muscovite-Jewish communism'. Brass bands bade farewell to trains bound for Germany. For hungry urban dwellers and disillusioned young people from the countryside these were good reasons to go. One female *Ostarbeiter* recalled that 'we had a certain hope that in Germany we would earn something, and that we would get ourselves some decent clothes. For we saw that all the Germans wore quality clothes, made from good fabrics and well sewn'.[71] Others worked for the Germans in some sort of minor capacity in the occupied territories and simply took the next step of working in Germany, sometimes put in touch by German soldiers with their home farm, shop or small business. Yet another group sought the anonymity of work in Germany to escape from a compromised past, whether their parents had been known Communists or they themselves had been Komsomol members. A 17-year-old girl who had refused to marry a Russian officer her family had rescued from a POW camp in

Simferopol (Ukraine) was denounced by him to the local German commissariat as a communist and daughter of a partisan. She saved herself by going to work in Germany. Another girl remembered that the train to Germany was the only way to evade the unwanted advances of the local German commander.[72]

The merciless and degrading treatment of these first volunteers, which soon became known through postcards from Germany and by word of mouth of returning sick or crippled workers, soon resulted in the flow of volunteers drying up. They were transported in cattle cars, received only meagre food rations and, above all, were forced to wear the *Ostarbeiterzeichen* – a badge marking them out as eastern workers. Meanwhile Soviet counter-propaganda spread stories that young workers were being used in German trenches or sent to North Africa. At the same time the numbers of workers required in the spring of 1942 were vast: 380,000 agricultural workers were rounded up, of whom 290,000 came from Ukraine alone. In addition 247,000 industrial workers were recruited, with 50,000 men and women from Stalino and 30,000 from Kiev. Fritz Sauckel, the Reich's Plenipotentiary for Labour, recruited 1.3 million eastern workers between April and September 1942. Recruitment targets rose steadily, and by late 1943 everyone born in 1926 and 1927 was to go to the Reich.[73] Deportations became the order of the day. Recruitment drives were accompanied by more and more violence, causing more fear and hysteria among the Russian population, who widely believed that being sent to Germany was a death sentence. Great use was made of the local personnel – the *Schuma* (police) and *starosty* (village elders) – in order to deflect popular anger in their direction. They in turn made a flourishing business out of the trade in humans, adding people to lists or deleting them according to financial incentives. In Kharkov it was reported that elders arrested people from their beds and locked them for days in cellars in order to prevent escapes or self-mutilation. Their cruelty often meant that the recruited were in no physical condition to march to the train departure points. If the young men and women failed to show up, severe reprisals were taken, ranging from beatings and shootings to the burning down of their family homes. In Bielosirka (Ukraine) in the autumn of 1942 the German police burned down houses, while the Ukrainian police went through the village collecting young and able-bodied girls and boys. If they did not find the young people at home, they arrested the parents until their sons and daughters gave themselves up.[74] The infamous round-up in the formerly Jewish Kiev district of Podil on 12 July 1942 demonstrated the cruelty, but also the limitations, of the German recruitment terror. Conducted on a Sunday, it missed most city dwellers, who spent the weekend with relatives in the countryside or in the traditional dachas out of town. Moreover the people of Podil had received a tip-off. Of the 1,600 arrested, only about 250 were fit to be deported to Germany.[75] More effective were round-ups which targeted young people in their urban haunts, in cinemas, at fun fairs or simply walking down the street, such as the arrest of 1,400 teenagers in Kiev in May 1942. After the defeat of Stalingrad, the German round-ups became even more brutal and desperate. Orders were given to shoot youths trying to escape and sobbing parents trying to prevent their departure. A Ukrainian girl who escaped a departing train remembers stumbling across a field filled with corpses of less lucky escapees only to fall into the merciless hands of a former school friend of her brothers, who handed her over to the German officers.[76]

Workers' Experiences: The East

By December 1944 nearly 2.8 million eastern workers had been shipped to the Reich, with 2.1 million coming from Ukraine and adjacent areas (army groups South). These included 1,036,810 men and 1,075,334 (50.9 per cent) women.[77] While almost a third of all *Ostarbeiter* were employed in the metallurgical and engineering industries, with another 20 per cent in other industrial areas, about a third were allocated to agriculture and 500,000 girls were sent to German families as domestic servants. What they experienced is a matter for debate. *Ostarbeiter* were often badly housed and fed – sometimes to the point of starvation – and racially discriminated against. They were at the mercy of their German colleagues and superiors. The brutal exploitation of the eastern workers was part of the ideology of the submission of races under the Aryan people and the creation of a political and economic imperium.[78] Initially Göring planned to supply only horse and cat meat to the eastern workers and demanded that a special bread be baked that consisted of 30 per cent sawdust and straw.[79] Early in 1944 eastern workers were given 92 per cent of the bread ration of western workers, but only two-thirds of the meat and fat, a quarter of the sugar and none of the fruit, vegetables, cheese and eggs accorded to western workers.[80] Yet practical concerns about the productivity of labour often went against the requirements of ideology. A manager of the vehicle manufacturing plant of Krupps at Essen, also a member of the SS, argued: 'I myself have no feelings of false sentimentality ... but every creature I require work from has to be fed ... the Russians are good workers provided they get enough to eat'. To make his point he refused to employ workers for whom he had not received proper rations.[81]

The employment of so many workers as farm workers and domestic servants away from the gaze of the authorities also mitigated against ideological rulings that *Ostarbeiter* were to be separated from the German population, strictly housed in camps, allowed to move only in guarded formations and deprived of adequate food and sanitary conditions. Female servants often alluded to a kind of slave trade, 'being bought' by their masters – or more often mistresses. Yet being employed in families with three or more children meant that there was no space for strict segregation.[82] Farmers also frequently ignored the orders of the Party requiring separate tables for their eastern workers. Rules on sexual apartheid between Germans and *Ostarbeiter* were also modulated according to gender. Sexual contact between German men and eastern women was more or less tolerated – only the German Housewives' Association seems to have had 'jealous objections'.[83] The children of female *Ostarbeiter*, who potentially had German blood, were sent to special nurseries for the sake of replenishing the German *Volkskörper*. However, any supposed relationship between a German woman and an eastern man (much more likely since all the men were at the front) was severely punished, with the execution of the man and the shaving and shaming of the woman. Until the middle of 1943 the execution of Polish and Soviet workers for illegal sexual contact with German women rose steadily. In 1944 the responsible department in the security services ordered two to three executions daily. Yet in general executions were less the norm towards the end of the war, when men were more often sent to a concentration camp depending on a racial expert's report on their *Eindeutschungsfähigkeit* (suitability to be Germanicized).[84]

Subjective accounts by *Ostarbeiter* of their German experiences differed considerably. This may well have been a question of perspective. On the one hand, they complained in letters home at the time about their treatment in the Reich. The censorship service reported that 98 per cent of the letters sent home by eastern workers contained negative remarks about Germany, while only 2 per cent had positive things to say.[85] Even the positive comments might be veiled criticism. One postcard to Simferopol read: 'My head spins, 'so good' is our life here ... I now live in a camp just as uncle Iasha' (who had probably been in a Gulag in the 1930s).[86] Other letters were more open and asked their mothers in tears to pray for their survival and return. On the other hand, in a Russian survey of former eastern workers decades later, many described their time in Germany as the best time of their lives. According to their testimony, they enjoyed the relative freedom that work in Germany provided.[87] Many – mostly girls in non-industrial work – also remembered that they were young and carefree and enjoyed being in groups with other young people.[88] After the war former *Ostarbeiters*' tales about German wealth and cleanliness continued to worry Soviet propaganda officials.[89]

Despite the tough work programmes and de-humanizing ideology, there was for the *Ostarbeiter* ample opportunity to subvert German requirements. They were present in enormous numbers, they could speak languages no one in their vicinity could understand, and chaos began to engulf Germany as the war dragged on. On a small-scale, everyday basis they could refuse to wear the sign 'Ost', visit cinemas off limits to them, meet up with *Ostarbeiter* of the opposite sex, trade insults with insults, or resort to various strategies to evade work. So-called *Arbeitsbummelei* – slow and inefficient working – became a mass phenomenon in the later years of the war, despite threats to send *Bummelanten* (shirkers) to labour education camps or concentration camps. The reality was that German industry could not afford to lose manpower, even inefficient manpower.[90] Another possibility for evading work was self-mutilation or the inducement of illnesses. In Nuremberg the sudden rise of a mysterious skin disease among eastern workers almost created a health panic, until it was discovered that the 200 diseased had rubbed their skin with poisonous plants causing boils and infections.[91] More drastic were attempts to escape, a route taken by 45,000 workers each month from 1943. However, over half of the *Ostarbeiter* did not plan to return home – a journey that was unrealistic – but sought to escape the bombing in the Ruhr or to find a better camp with easier living conditions.[92]

Outright resistance was a rarity, despite the German security services' fear of an uprising of eastern workers leading to the collapse of the Reich. In the summer of 1943 Russian workers in Hamburg staged a mutiny, but were brutally put down by Himmler's police.[93] There is evidence of opposition groups in thirty-eight cities with about 2,700 participants.[94] In several factories, young Soviets organized underground Komsomol committees, which held general assemblies and drew up plans for sabotage work. One of the participants, Mariia Grigor'evna Gnipel', described how she would secretly learn how to set the machines in her care and then deliberately induce a malfunction. In the assemblies she and her comrades provided others with advice on how to cause break-downs and rallied public opinion against those who worked conscientiously for the Germans.[95] The largest and best-organized resistance group was the Brotherly Collaboration of POWs (*Bratskoe Sotrudchestvo Voennoplennikh* – BSV), which was organized by an undercover NKVD man in a camp in Munich and run strictly according to the rules of communist underground work. It organized escapes, had contact with communist groups in the German underground and distributed pro-Soviet propaganda. Its well-organized nature, however, allowed the German security services to destroy it most effectively only six months after its foundation.[96]

More effective in the long term were the gangs of *Ostarbeiter* who, hungry and dislodged from their camps by air raids, found refuge in ruins, committed robberies and resisted arrest in the hope of sustaining themselves until the arrival of Allied troops. The centre of so-called *Ostarbeiter* gang activity was Cologne, which had a culture of youthful working-class resistance and was heavily targeted in the bombing of the last few months of the war. Here several gangs of eastern workers were uncovered by the Gestapo – some of whom had connections with more politically motivated German groups such as the last generation of *Edelweisspiraten*. In October 1944 the Ukrainian Mishka Finn and five other eastern workers were publicly hanged for theft, armed robbery and the shooting of guards and well-known Nazi functionaries. Several other smaller groups continued to operate in devastated Cologne, while large-scale groups executed raids on freight trains and engaged in armed clashes with the Gestapo in Essen and Duisburg.[97]

Workers' Experiences: The West

Although the German war economy was massively dependent on eastern workers, recruiting 1.3 million of them between April and September 1942, it could not forgo the contribution of workers from central, western and southern Europe. In the same period Fritz Saukel drafted 339,000 workers from other countries, including 64,000 from Poland, 23,000 from Bohemia-Moravia, 30,000 from France and 55,000 from Italy. However, the supply of labour from Italy, which had traditionally been a key provider, began to dry up. The Italian government needed men for its own armed forces, which rose to 3.4 million in 1942, and for protected war industries. Work conditions in the Reich had received bad publicity, and the fixed rate of exchange steadily eroded the value of wages that workers sent home to their families. In February 1942 the Italian government agreed to provide 320,000 workers, together with 36,000 miners, in exchange for coal supplies, but under the next agreement in February 1943 it managed to negotiate the repatriation of 10,000 workers per month. Sauckel and Speer did their best to slow this down, but in July 1943 there were only 141,000 Italian workers in the Reich. Only the surrender of Italy to the Allies in September 1943 produced a windfall of Italians for the hard-pressed German war machine. About 42,000 Italian soldiers continued to fight alongside the Germans, 20,000 joined the partisans, 24,000 fled to neutral territory, 469,000 found their way home, but 725,000 were captured by the Germans. These were regarded as traitors by the Germans and lost their POW status and were designated Italian Military Internees (IMIs). While 30,000 officers were kept in Oflags, the NCOs and soldiers were put to work in war industries which would otherwise have been closed to them, and those of the worst kind. In February 1944 56 per cent of the IMIs were working in the mining, metallurgy, engineering and chemical industries, also the case for 50 per cent of Soviet POWs but only 17 per cent of French POWs, 58 per cent of whom were working in agriculture. The death rate among Italian POWs was 40 per cent per annum, as against 8 per cent in the case of French POWs and 6 per cent in the case of Belgians.[98] But being worked to death did not make them better workers. As one SD reported: 'The Soviets were gold compared to these Italians'.[99]

Industrial northwest Europe was likewise subject to Sauckel's pressure. In the Netherlands the Secretary-General of the Department of Social Affairs agreed to a decree in March 1942 making all Dutch citizens liable for work in Germany. For the first year only skilled metalworkers were required, and these were recruited by the 'combing-out' of Dutch factories, releasing underemployed workers, sometimes artificially by the closure of factories not geared to war production. Entrepreneurs did what they could to avoid the closure of their firms but welcomed the chance to be rid of bad or militant workers. Workers seldom resorted to strike action; the memory of the repression after the February strike was too painful, while the picking off of individual workers undermined solidarity and collective action. It was each man for himself, seeking rejection for work in Germany on medical grounds or finding jobs in shipyards where the workforce was protected against deportation.[100]

Labour conscription was stepped up another gear in May 1943 with the *Jaarklassen-action*, which divided the population into seventeen age cohorts and required them to register with the employment exchange with a view to being called up. Those who failed to comply were excluded from the food-rationing system. Workers in munitions factories, coal-mining, food production or agriculture were

required to register but were protected by a special *Ausweis*. The requirement of
April 1943 that repatriated Dutch POWs had to return to Germany was a particular
grievance. The Dutch committee of secretaries-general which ran the country was
plunged into crisis. The government in exile and the churches protested, enjoining
civil servants and the police not to cooperate. The April–May strikes of 1943 which
lasted nine days were the first mass popular protest in the Netherlands since February
1941. They involved not only industrial workers but also peasants and the self-
employed, who were also implicated. Forced labour was widely regarded as slavery,
and a strategy with a hidden agenda, mobilizing Dutchmen for German military
preparations against Allied invasion, or to better the German race by obliging
Dutchmen to sleep with German women. The German authorities reacted with
savagery, shooting 130 people, but their nerve was tested. Labour conscripts being
taken away on trains sang the Dutch national anthem, shouted 'Oranje boven!' ('Up
with Orange!') and waved the red flag. Some of those liable for deportation went
into hiding (in August 1943 about 60,000 according to the Germans). Resistance
movements tried to destroy the registers that were used to organize the conscription
and raided offices in order to acquire rationing documents for those in hiding. Dutch
employers working for Germany feared for the loss of their workforce, and even the
economic departments of the German administration were concerned that production
for the German war effort within the country would be compromised. That said, over
500,000 Dutchmen ended up working in Germany, including those rounded up in the
final stages of the war.[101]

For most Dutch workers the issue was not the patriotic one of whether to work
for the Germans or not, since the domestic economy was heavily integrated into
the German one, but the personal risks entailed. The tactic of many Dutch workers
in Germany was to get away from spadework or the factory floor and to find an
easier job driving lorries or in an office. One man, who had worked at home in
a shipyard meeting German orders, found an office job in Germany working for
the Reichsbahn. When it became clear that Germany was collapsing, he returned
home, taking advantage of his job with the German railways.[102] His colleague, who
had worked as a lorry driver and aircraft manufacturer for the Germans at home,
was sent to Germany and built bunkers, then worked in V-2 and synthetic petrol
factories before he managed to get a job as a lorry driver in the transport division of
the petrol factory where he was working, still serving the Wehrmacht but in a more
comfortable way.[103]

Dutch forced labourers complained about the poor food, the low wages, conditions
in the barracks (especially fleas) and Allied bombing – 8,500 Dutch workers died in
Germany. Some deportees had the impression that not the factories but the barracks
were the target because the British and Americans had financial interests in the
firms. Many others did not return to Germany after a period of leave at home. Only
exceptionally was there organized protest in Germany. Workers used other means
to express discontent, such as absconding, small-scale sabotage, cutting corners or

faking illness. Relations between the Dutch and Germans were tolerable; they were aware that not all Germans were Nazis and that especially among older Germans there were Communists, socialists and anarchists, with whom Dutch workers had a good rapport.[104] Sexual intercourse with women from different nationalities, including Germans, was not exceptional, as well as visiting prostitutes in brothels run by the German Labour Front. This could result in workers failing to send home wages to their wives, but there were also many cases of Dutch wives not waiting for their men to return and finding a new partner. Informal rules operated, however; German men saw Dutch men as a threat and relations with married German women were not tolerated.[105]

Forced labour was introduced in Belgium in October 1942. It was a highly sensitive matter, since the memory of forced labour in the First World War was still alive. The secretary-general for Social Affairs resigned and the Church protested openly. Strike action was organized against forced labour, as in one of the leading engineering companies, ACEC, in February 1943. However, many workers put their faith in their paternalistic employers in order to avoid deportation to Germany. The policy of the Galopin Committee was that forced labour was to be limited as much as possible in order to keep the factories working in Belgium, but keeping the factories working also required the goodwill of the occupying authorities, with whom it was decided open confrontation was to be avoided. There was therefore no public protest by the industrialists. An attempt to build a united front of industrialists to withhold lists of their personnel from the German employment agency failed. Instead they preferred to offer prudent and practical support to maintain the link between worker and employer that was the community of labour. Money, food and clothes was given to workers detailed for work in Germany, parcels with tobacco and chocolate were sent to workers once they got there, while contributions to workers' pension schemes and financial support to workers' families to enable them to pay for health insurance were continued.[106] This concern of employers was appreciated; a deportee was 'very pleased' when he received a letter from his Belgian boss.[107]

The imposition of forced labour was a watershed for Belgian workers, of whom 149,542 went to Germany. The underground communist trade union movement – the Comités de Lutte Syndicale and leftist socialist Mouvement Syndical Unifié – which had developed after the strike of the 100,000, challenging the official UTMI and bypassing the remains of the old prewar unions, saw the opportunity to mobilize support on the shopfloor against forced labour and to tackle the widening gap between prices and wages – black-market prices rose eighteenfold between 1940 and November 1943.[108] Although it supported the use of strikes against forced labour, the underground movement preferred to blackmail employers into protecting the workforce, appealing to their patriotism and notions of the community of labour in order to defend workers' interests. While working for Germany was tolerated, war profits were to be 'taxed' for the benefit of the labour force and all notions of stepping up productivity for the Germans were resisted. In December 1943, for example, the metalworkers of the Charleroi Comités de Lutte Syndicale demanded that employers contribute to the *caisses de résistance* for workers in hiding, fund a 50 per cent pay rise for those in work to meet rising food prices, and make adequate food distributions in the factory. They also refused to work overtime or do piecework, demanded proper air-raid protection and continued pay during alerts, and claimed recognition by employers and representation on factory councils.[109] Pressure was also put on employers to accept their responsibilities towards those of their workers who had gone to Germany. One group of workers from Verviers, a textile town on the German border, extracted a bonus from their employer before they went.[110]

The Communists were not the only ones to campaign against forced labour in Belgium. The Katholieke Arbeidersjeugd (KAJ) or Catholic Workers' Youth, which was authorized by the Germans, lobbied the authorities to exempt individuals or groups of young people. In particular they fought, with the Catholic hierarchy, Catholic working women's movements and the secretaries-general, to end the drafting of female labour, emphasizing the moral and psychological risks of 'loneliness, so painful for young women so far from home'.[111] Belgian women were formally exempted from forced labour in March 1943.[112] The KAJ supported those who wanted to go into hiding, either through the parish or the specialist organization 'Hulp aan Voortvluchtigen'. Such help was intended to remove *réfractaires* (draft dodgers) from the influence of Communists, to safeguard the faith, and to eliminate the danger that, excluded from the official circuit of work and rationing, they would resort to crime and banditry. Help was channelled to the KAJ from the government and the Société Générale, while a big industrialist, the Baron De Launoit, supported the parallel initiatives taken by former socialist trade union leaders.[113] Those who did go to Germany to work were supported by KAJ members who went with them, equipped with a letter of recommendation in Latin for the German parish priest and a special prayer book.[114] Helping *réfractaires* became a political issue, since resistance organizations saw it as an opportunity to recruit new members (200,000 went into hiding). The Independence Front, which was closely linked to the Communist Party, did pioneering work in this field. To counterbalance its influence, government support was channelled to a greater degree into the prewar labour organizations.[115]

For the experience of Belgian workers in Germany we have a good source in the diaries procured by the Forced Labour Survey undertaken by the Belgian Centre for Historical Research and Documentation on War and Contemporary Society in the 1970s. Belgians were not at the bottom of the international pile in terms of forced labour and were horrified to see the brutality with which eastern workers were treated – ill-fed, deprived of medical treatment, and refused the use of air-raid shelters. They saw that the Italian IMIs who arrived in the autumn of 1943 suffered even more than Russians and Ukrainians.[116] Belgian workers had problems with the long working hours, made worse by Allied bombing and the lack of periods of leave in Belgium.[117] Flemish workers seem to have had more problems with the long hours than their Walloon colleagues, who were more familiar with industrial work.[118]

Belgian workers in munition factories complained about the strict hierarchy in the factory and the authoritarianism of the foremen, who were always shouting and treated them as if they were children.[119] Such factories were also at particular risk from bombing, which the deportees viewed ambiguously. On the one hand, bombing threatened lives, but on the other it interrupted work, and deportees felt uneasy when forced to repair what the Allies had destroyed.[120] Workers were less likely to strike or attempt sabotage, for which a labour education camp or worse awaited them, than to go slow or absent themselves.[121] Inhabitants of one barrack organized a *charivari* with chairs and lids.[122] One worker joined the football team Flandria because the *Betriebssportführer* made an arrangement to release him from work on the day of the match.[123] Food was in short supply from the spring of 1943, but Jacquemyns observed that 'the country in part feeds its sons working in Germany' by means of food parcels sent by relatives or employers.[124] The tobacco in the parcels was used as high-value currency. 'Tobacco is power, in short supply even among the German population', reflected one worker; Belgians were seen by other nationalities as tobacco traders.[125]

Some workers took a second job outside the factory on a farm. This afforded greater freedom, access to milk and meat in short supply, and the possibility of intimacy with the farmer's wife, whose husband was generally mobilized. Relations between Belgian men and German women were not punished by the Germans as were those with Slavic men, but the sanction of workmates could make up for that: a 20-year-old man was taken to task in a café because he had slept with a married German woman.[126] It is clear that Belgian workers tried to integrate themselves into the towns and neighbourhoods they lived in and that they were not entirely hostile to the German population. One group of workers living in a boardinghouse formed a small band and performed in the *pension*'s café to attract customers.[127] When German power started to collapse, the deportees took their revenge, destroying the barracks where they had been housed, squatting in villas or in country houses, stealing vegetables or chickens from the land, slaughtering pigs, and robbing German refugees who were also on the road.[128]

In France the illusion that work in the Reich was voluntary was maintained for as long as possible. Premier Laval agreed to supply 150,000 skilled workers, so long as 50,000 POWs were released from German camps in exchange, a *Relève* he announced in a broadcast on 22 June 1942. The decline in volunteers, after peaking in July 1942, resulted in the law of 4 September 1942 'mobilizing' men aged 18 to 50 and unmarried women aged 21 to 35. Quotas were effectively imposed on factories, which had to find takers from among their own workforces. As lists of workers who were being drafted for work in Germany were pinned up in factories, so the workforce downed tools. A strike broke out in the SNCF workshop at Oullins, Lyon, on 13 October 1942, and when a hundred strikers were arrested, a rioting crowd accompanied their transfer to Saint-Paul prison. By 17 October 10,000 workers were on strike in the Lyon region and the movement spread to other towns in the unoccupied zone, Saint-Étienne, Clermont-Ferrand and Marseilles.[129] In the occupied zone at Nantes strikes started at the Batignolles-Châtillon locomotive plant on 6 October, at the Société de Mécanique Générale de l'Ouest engineering works (1,100 workers) on 9 October, and at the vast Chantiers de la Loire (1,700 workers) and Chantiers de Bretagne (200 workers) on 12 October. When 1,600 workers at the SNCASO aircraft factory at Nantes-Bouguenais went on strike on 14 October, the *Feldkommandant* ordered a military occupation of the factory, filtered the workforce and arrested those of the designated workers who could be found (many more had got wind of the operation and not turned up). This only inflamed the situation and by 21 October Nantes was in the grip of what one police chief called a 'general strike'.[130] Significantly, the mayor of Nantes sided with the workforce and resigned.

Between 1 June and 31 December 1942 the *Relève* had furnished 240,000 workers for Germany, 135,000 of whom were skilled, mostly from the occupied zone and the industrial areas within them. Fighting for their lives on the eastern front, however, the Germans became increasingly impatient with the shambles of the *Relève*. Now Sauckel decided on a 'second action', which would recruit 250,000 workers, of whom 150,000 would be skilled, in half the time, by 31 March, and the same again by the end of June. Attempts to round up workers in the Peugeot factory of Sochaux in February and March 1943 provoked violent strikes, which exposed the contradictions between different German authorities. For whereas the local military authority or Feldkommandantur supported Sauckel's action, the Rüstungsinspektion followed the line of Armaments and Munitions Minister Albert Speer that French workers working for the Germans were better off in French factories, so that the strike was successful.[131]

Under pressure from Sauckel, but to ensure that French interests and sovereignty were respected, as far as they could be, Minister of Industrial Production Jean Bichelonne, another acolyte of Laval, published the law on the Service du Travail Obligatoire (STO) on 16 February 1943. This established labour service in Germany as an alternative to military service, which had been suspended under the occupation, and applied in the first instance to those born in 1920, 1921 and 1922.[132] While industrial workers were increasingly required to work for the German war economy in France in protected *Rüstung-*, *V-* or, increasingly, *Speer-Betriebe*, the working population as a whole became vulnerable to the labour draft. The regional prefect of Angers, Charles Donati, who visited French workers in Germany early in 1944, was incensed to find that in many cases it was the fit young men who were staying at home and older men, many with families and some former POWs who had converted to the status of 'free workers', who were working in the German factories.[133] Also initially protected were students, who were granted a dispensation until they had finished their examinations in June 1943. These, however, were then caught and suffered the burdens of the occupation for the first time. As the pressure to recruit intensified, even women became liable for STO. A law of 1 February 1944 required the registration for labour service not only of men aged 16 to 60, but of women aged 18 to 45. This violated a fundamental taboo and provoked a violent response from families, communities and the Church in France. 'Family life is still very solid and united in Anjou', reported an official of the Ministry of Information. 'You will never persuade a father to accept that his daughter, even aged 25, will go to work a long way away, beyond his supervision and control'. Given the danger of mixing women of different backgrounds and education, he predicted 'a very lively resistance, not only from ordinary citizens but also from certain mayors, to the registration of women'. The Church's assembly of cardinals and archbishops, which had not come out unambiguously against STO, now strongly condemned this 'serious attack on family life and the future of our country, on the dignity and moral susceptibility of women and their providential vocation'.[134]

In some parts of France, such as Touraine, the response rate to STO was good, but in others, such as the *arrondissement* of Châteaubriant, deep in the Breton interior, the proportion of *réfractaires* in April–June 1943 was 80 per cent. It would be wrong to think that the only alternative to STO was to join the maquis: only 10 per cent of *réfractaires* in fact became *maquisards*. For the vast majority of *réfractaires* the purpose of dodging STO was to increase their chances of survival, which was best achieved by going into hiding. Near Segré in Anjou the son of the stationmaster of La Ferrière-de-Flée hid most of the time in a concealed room above the station, receiving his ration tickets from the daughter of the *secrétaire de mairie* and having lunch regularly with his family.[135] Most did not have so easy a time. *Réfractaires* survived by finding clandestine work, mostly in the countryside, 76 per cent of them with farmers, 10 per cent with rural artisans such as woodcutters and blacksmiths. Since half of French *réfractaires* were workers and only a fifth of peasant background, this meant a large transfer of industrial labour to the countryside. The atttitude of farmers was generally ambivalent. On the one hand, they could plug the labour shortage caused by the absence of POWs and STO workers with a source of grateful workers, who received food and shelter but only 20 per cent of whom were paid. On the other, they were exposed to punishment for hiding young men who were effectively outlaws. As outlaws, without identity or ration cards, *réfractaires* were beyond the loop of the ration system and at risk of arrest. In areas like the Breton interior many mutated at night into masked and armed gangs who took ration-books and identity cards from *mairies*, cigarettes from tobacconists, and money, food, radios and old weapons that had not been handed in from isolated farmhouses. Although there were cases of maquis forming, such as that of Saffré, most *réfractaires* lay low as rural workers and indulged in random acts of what the Vichy authorities called 'banditry' or 'terrorism'.[136]

The experience of French workers in Germany was generally bearable. At the Focke-Wulfe factory at Bremen French workers did the same 60-hour week as their German counterparts, their skills were appreciated by German foremen, and they were impressed by the fact that all employees ate in the canteen together, the managers taking their place in the queue behind workers.[137] A Vichy delegation to factories around Frankfurt and Mainz in February 1944, headed by the regional prefect of Angers, Donati, whose son was on STO, told the French press that French workers were well housed and well fed, with each camp having its own French chef. Among others, STO workers in Lübeck contested this version, saying that they ate only soup, had only four washbasins between 150 men, lived in cold huts and had bomb shelters only five centimetres thick.[138] That said, the French employed plenty of Gallic cunning to skive. The 'Ten commandments of a perfect French worker', a copy of a chain letter found in the possession of a French worker in May 1944, read:

1. Walk slowly in the workshop
2. Walk quickly after knocking off work
3. Go to the toilet frequently
4. Don't work too hard
5. Annoy the foreman
6. Court the beautiful girls
7. Visit the doctor often
8. Don't count on vacation
9. Cherish cleanliness
10. Always have hope[139]

Jacques Hervé, who worked for the municipality of Tours, was sent under STO to Germany in May 1943 and worked near Danzig in a sawmill, a shipyard and a cement factory. 'We didn't do anything,' he said, 'we took things easy', perhaps more out of bravado, to suggest an everday resistance to the German war effort.[140] From time to time STO workers did receive home leave, which was part of the contract, but many refused to return to their German factories subsequently – 28 per cent in the case of large Berlin factories – going to ground as *réfractaires*, so that home leave was cancelled from September 1943.[141] An alternative, in theory punishable as a breach of contract, was simply to revert to the old strategy of the working class, to leave one job where conditions were bad in search of another where they were better.[142] In Germany French workers tended to stick close to friends from their home town or region, but also integrated to some extent with the local population. In Regensburg Germans followed them to the Central Café, seduced by the 'alluring Mediterranean music'.[143] Penalties for relationships with German women were less harsh than those suffered by Poles, and a French officer calculated in 1945 that between 20 per cent and 25 per cent of French workers who had spent more than a year in Germany had fathered a child with a German woman and wanted to bring it home, something that French legislation refused.[144] Other Frenchmen preferred friendships with Russian or Ukrainian women. François Cavanna, who used to join Ukrainian workers meeting to sing and dance on their Sundays on the banks of the Spree, had a particular love for an 18-year-old girl from Kharkov, Maria.

She wore a little navy blue dress, dark blue woollen stockings, a rust-coloured coat with Scottish plaid, lace-up shoes, very 1925, and went bare-headed. She had no other clothes and yet she was not only impeccably turned out, but also a coquette. So were the others, in magnificent shawls, cleaned and mended garments, and polished boots.[145]

Having tried to meet Maria in the infirmary, Cavanna finally caught up with her on the 'death march' westwards before the advancing Soviets. They made love in a farm near Neubrandenburg, before she disappeared.

Sanctioning Work: Collaboration or Survival?

After the liberation of occupied Europe choices about work that had at the time seem morally ambivalent were now redefined in black-and-white terms as patriotic or treacherous. In their defence those accused of economic collaboration with the Germans tried to claim that they had not collaborated as single-mindedly as they might have done or had in some way benefited the local economy. Often they got away with it, either because of the leniency of the judicial process or because of the verdict of the local community.

The charge of economic collaboration was brought first and foremost against employers. The fact that they had accepted German contracts and contributed to the German war effort was impossible to hide. Opprobrium was generally attracted by working too zealously for the German war machine, making large profits, switching activities to meet the German demand, accepting orders which other firms in the sector had rejected, taking part in the process of designating workers to be sent to Germany or asking for German help to quell social unrest. In response employers argued that they had acted under duress, since not to accept those contracts would have entailed the closure or requisitioning of their firm. Staying open was also demonstrated as being of benefit for the local population, offering jobs that might not otherwise have been available. They claimed that they had not given in easily, had quibbled over contracts, produced for civilian rather than military projects, protected their workforce from deportation or allowed go-slows or sabotage to take place.

Belgium was confronted with the issue of economic collaboration for the second time in a generation. After the First World War few employers were brought before the courts, but the penalties had been high. In theory the death penalty was again available for all kinds of work, production for or trade with the enemy, but all sectors of the community saw matters in political or societal rather than in purely legal terms. Even the communist-led Independence Front argued that shopkeepers and businessmen who had traded with the enemy for less than 500,000 Belgian francs should not be brought before the courts. The judge advocate-general, who had a fair degree of autonomy in the matter, took the issue of economic collaboration seriously but came up against the collective discipline imposed on employers by the Galopin doctrine, which made it very difficult to determine individual responsibility. Though Galopin had been murdered by extreme collaborators in February 1944, trade union leaders and employers had agreed to continue the Galopin system and negotiated the Social Pact of 1944, which provided the basis of the Belgian welfare state. The main sectors in which judicial proceedings took place in Belgium were construction, engineering and textiles, which had produced goods for the German army, such as barracks for German troops and uniforms. The socialist Achille Van Acker, who implemented the system of social security in December 1944 and became prime minister in 1945, was much more interested in economic reconstruction and social progress than in an economic purge. Unlike in France, nationalization was never used in Belgium as a punishment for economic collaboration. Social and economic policy was designed to restore liberal capitalism tempered by social reform, as prepared for during the war. Trade unions were also involved in a price and wage policy to cut inflation and this, together with the Allied use of Antwerp as the main entry point for war supplies, produced the so-called Belgian miracle of high economic growth combined with high wages.[146]

In the Netherlands punishment of economic collaboration was in the hands of judicial authorities – the special judiciary (*Bijzondere Rechtspleging*) and a disciplinary juridisction (*Zuiveringsraden*), which included businessmen. The head of the disciplinary jurisdiction, J. Donner, and the minister of justice were of the same opinion that the punishment of economic collaboration was less important than economic reconstruction and the restoration of the 'national community' (*volksgemeenschap*). Unlike in Belgium, where the Galopin Committee had played a political role by deciding itself on the limits of production for Germany, Dutch industrialists had asked the advice of the administrative elite, who allowed them to work for Germany and therefore the government was not inclined to be too critical of the industrialists after the war. Thus very few businessmen were investigated by the special judiciary, most going before the disciplinary jurisdiction, which was more inclined to accept their arguments. Moreover, there had been no great division between employers and workers in the Netherlands during the occupation, unlike in Belgium and France, and public opinion was not much disturbed by the question of economic collaboration, except in the case of the so-called 'bunker builders' (*bunkerbouwers*), contractors working for the German army. At the De Schelde shipyard in Zealand, which had worked for the German navy, a worker complained that his employer had planned to send him to Germany, and the case was taken up by the province's military commander, the supreme political authority at that time, because the shipyard was now involved in the Allied campaign and the cooperation of the workforce was required.[147] This case was exceptional, and the weakness of the illegal trade union movement and Socialist Party relative to Belgium gave the employers virtually a free hand in drafting the Manifesto of the Stichting van de Arbeid (Foundation of Labour). Unlike the Belgian Social Pact, this made no major concessions to the workers, imposed a policy of wage control, and saw off the socialists' project to involve the state more prominently in social and economic life. The low-wage economy contributed to the success of the industrialization programme initiated in the late 1940s.[148]

In France the organized working class, legitimated by the resistance, was outspoken in its demands for the purge of economic collaborators, but came up against the reassertion of state power under de Gaulle and the need to rebuild the economy in both war and peace. High-profile employers such as Louis Renault were arrested, and though he died before being brought to court, his firm was nationalized. More generally, however, business was dealt with after the liberation not by the courts but by Interprofessional Business Purge Committees (CIEEs), set up in each region under a magistrate and including representatives of employers, managers, engineers, technicians and clerical staff. Self-regulation gave a good deal of protection to employers, and engendered corresponding frustration among workers. In Nantes the tramway workers went on strike in December 1944 to demand the dismissal of three Belgian directors they accused of sending workers to Germany and of denouncing a communist militant to the Germans, who had shot him. The CIEE was divided between the labour representatives, who demanded a harsh punishment, and the employers' representatives, advocating leniency, with the prefect in the middle. Eventually the directors were dismissed but received no further sanction. On other occasions employers who should have taken responsibility got off lightly, while managers beneath them received a heavier sanction. Also in Nantes, the deputy-director of the Chantiers de Bretagne was suspended for one year for having threatened workers with deportation to Germany, if they did not work harder, while the director convinced the CIEE that he had protected workers who had engaged in the 'passive resistance' of go-slows.[149]

A second category to feel the anger of the courts and public opinion at the liberation in France were those who had traded with the Germans, on the black market or otherwise. The accusation was that they had taken food out of the mouths of the local population in order to make speculative profits, which had in turn driven up the price of food beyond the means of ordinary people. Committees were set up in each department to confiscate illicit profits under a law of October 1944, but they had very few teeth. In general there was a reluctance on the part of the authorities to look too closely into the ways in which some people had got rich during the occupation, and small fry were more likely to be investigated than big fish. In Touraine two millers, a grain merchant, three wine merchants, a butcher, a builder, a garage owner, a painter and decorator, a shoemaker, a hotelier, a stallholder and a rag-and-bone man went before the Indre-et-Loire illicit profits committee between March and October 1945, but these were relatively small-time crooks. A Vouvray producer had 334,000 francs confiscated, and a foreigner named Szabo had 9 million francs confiscated and a fine of 27 million francs imposed for 'important black-market activities', but his was the only case in that league.[150] Proceedings were more likely where accusations of getting rich were combined with those of cohabiting too closely with Germans.

Madame Morandeau of Coueron, near Nantes, was accused of saying during the war that she preferred one German customer to twenty French ones, and was also said to have indulged in 'veritable orgies' with Germans along with her daughter, while her husband took pictures of them with a camera stolen from work. In her defence she fell back on the usual argument of duress: 'I did like all traders, I served the Germans in my café because I had to, but I never collaborated with them'.[151]

When it came to workers, a distinction was made between those who had stayed at home, who were not troubled even if they had worked in protected factories fulfilling contracts for the Germans, and those who had gone to Germany. Among these, workers who were deemed to have gone voluntarily were at risk of being accused of collaboration. In fact, though 260,000 men and women had worked voluntarily in Germany, only 395 cases came before the Chambres civiques of the Seine, and 71 per cent of individuals accused of voluntary work were acquitted. The liberation authorities took the view that most 'volunteers' had in some way been forced to go by hunger, unemployment or propaganda, and were only interested in the minority whose contribution was politically pro-German.[152] That said, communities sometimes took a harsher view. In Touraine a certain Macret, who had returned to his home town of Loches and was being taken by the police to Tours, was dragged out of the police vehicle and lynched by a crowd of 300, including former political deportees and their families.[153] Some Belgian voluntary workers had expressed their admiration for the New Order while in Germany by wearing buttons with the Flemish lion (symbol of Flemish nationalism), becoming member of the NSDAP or even volunteering for the SS.[154] In the industrial province of Hainaut there were cases of violent confrontations between returning voluntary workers and the core community of miners.[155]

Those who had been conscripted as forced labourers had a better defence, although there was still a widespread notion that they might have escaped going if they had really wanted to, and they were never given the heroic status of resistance fighters who were deported to Germany for political reasons. Since many of those conscripted for STO in France had swelled the ranks of the *réfractaires*, and even joined the maquis, it was argued that others could have done the same. Though a National Association of Prisoners of War and Deportees (MNPGD) was set up in 1945 to link political deportees, POWs and STO workers, those who had been deported for 'acts of resistance' soon broke away to form their own National Federation of Deportees and Internees of the Resistance (FNDIR) and even went to law to prevent STO workers from calling themselves 'labour deportees'.[156] Belgian labour deportees complained about their welcome when they returned home. They were questioned by the police looking for collaborators and voluntary workers, had new goods brought from Germany and German currency confiscated, and were left a meagre 100 Belgian francs.[157] Dutch forced labourers, meanwhile, became the victims of a 'moral panic' stirred up by the state and the churches, and were depicted as demoralized, alienated from Dutch society and a threat to public health.

It was said that they had returned from the barracks carrying venereal disease and argued that unmarried workers returning should be locked up in re-education camps. This was rejected by the social-democratic Minister of Social Affairs W. Drees, who preferred to employ them in the work of reconstruction. However, in order to obtain financial support, Dutch forced labourers had to prove that they had been unable to go into hiding, which was ironic since they had been required to go to Germany by the official employment exchange, which had cooperated with the German recruitment campaigns during the war. Although the forced workers had a specific organization to defend their interests, they did not succeed in obtaining official recognition because of the negative perception of forced labourers, and the fact they were overwhelmingly from the lower social classes.[158]

Liberation was a mixed event for *Ostarbeiter*. On the one hand, there there was a widespread fear in the last few days of the Third Reich that the SS death squads would kill not only concentration camp inmates, but also *Ostarbeiter*. On the other hand, the advancing Red Army took their revenge not only on the Germans but on those who were seen to have been collaborating with them. Komsomol secretary Mikhailov wrote an official complaint about the behaviour shown to liberated female *Ostarbeiter* by members of the Red Army, who regularly attacked barracks and dormitories housing eastern girls. Gang and multiple rapes were frequent occurrences.[159] At the same time, the British and American forces were keen to end the banditry of *Ostarbeiter* gangs by placing them in camps for displaced persons awaiting repatriation to the Soviet Union under the provisions of Yalta. While the vast majority of eastern workers were keen to go back to their families, a sizeable number of them refused to return to the Soviet Union, which re-established the borders of 1941. This was particularly true for former collaborators and inhabitants of the Ukrainian and Belorussian borderlands, who felt that their homeland had passed from one occupation into another. Yet, even among ordinary Russians and Ukrainians, the rumour was widespread that 'all returnees will be severely punished'.[160] In a secret memorandum of May 1946 Politburo member Zhdanov was informed that roughly 300,000 Soviet citizens in western Europe were unwilling to return home. The Soviet desire to reassemble all lost citizens was rooted in the intrinsically suspicious nature of the Bolshevik worldview. While mortally afraid of a fifth column of anti-Soviet Russians and Ukrainians in the west, they also condemned the returnees, who had been contaminated by their stay in Germany and their contact with the west. Consequently, each returning *Ostarbeiter* had to go through several filtration camps, where they were interviewed by NKVD (Ministry of Interior) and SMERSH (counter-espionage) officers in the rough manner typical of Soviet interrogation practice. A secretary in one of the camps recalled: 'They brought these poor girls to the limit. Three or four times they got them in for questioning, always at night... They were not beaten, but morally these girls were killed. There were times when a girl could not stand it any more and fainted. Then they poured water over her.'[161]

Though officially it was concluded that 'only few had been traitors' the legacy of their time in Germany did not leave most former *Ostarbeiter* for the rest of their lives.[162] People at home considered them loose girls – 'as if I had voluntarily eloped with a German officer', in the words of one 16-year-old deported girl.[163] One of the returnees married a lawyer, from whom she hid her past in Germany. When one day she let slip a remark, she found herself divorced within weeks. Her husband's work department had advised him to leave her in order to avoid being tarnished with the brush of treason.[164] Many people were harassed for decades. They were refused the opportunity to study, work or live in certain cities.[165] Girls who openly voiced positive remarks about Germany were arrested and sentenced to long years in camps or exile. One girl spent ten years of her life in the Arctic Circle for confessing that she had eaten at the same table as her German family.[166] For a long time there were widespread rumours that all returning *Ostarbeiter* were going to be deported again – this time to Siberia, Kazakhstan or Central Asia.[167] Returnees from the west were a source of constant worry to a regime that relied on monolithic propaganda to persuade its citizens of its superiority. Individuals' trajectories during the Great Patriotic War became the new class marker, the ticket to a successful or thwarted life in post-war Soviet society.

While most returnees tried to blend back into Soviet society – often attempting to hide the fact they had been to Germany – others were moved to voice their disappointment. Just like demobilized soldiers returning from the western front, former *Ostarbeiter* were in a position to draw uncomfortable comparisons and under-mine the regime's claim to represent the best of all possible worlds. A repatriated *Ostarbeiterin* wrote to a fellow returnee in 1946: 'I cry every day, but crying does not help. I cannot understand how you got used to this kind of life. I went almost out of my mind when I first came back … everything is dirty, there is no soap… Remember what clean girls we were over there, all this is past and only the memory remains.'[168] Another intercepted letter demonstrated that the Soviet fear that contact with Anglo-America corrupted Soviet minds rather than German slavery was not unfounded: 'We could have lived there better, only with Americans as masters and not Germans. I am ready to live there, rather than suffer here.'[169] Others praised the standard of living of German farmers, German cleanliness or their culturedness (in Russian *kul'turnost'* has a more practical, everyday meaning than culture) – all attributes the Soviet Union claimed for itself.[170]

Conclusion

The issues surrounding working for the Germans point up the tension between the need to survive and the danger of taking actions that might, be interpreted then or subsequently, as collaboration with the enemy. The first defence against such accusations was that such actions were forced: non-cooperation would be followed by the business being closed down or moved to Germany, leading to unemployment or starvation. Another practice was to seek legitimation either from the national authorities in place, by acting collectively as employers or by attempting to maintain the sympathy of organized labour or individual workers. It was even possible to claim that some form of resistance had been engaged in while working for the Germans, whether as employers or workers, by gestures of non-cooperation, incompetence, go-slows or sabotage. After the liberation, moreover, the rules of the game changed, and the emphasis was less on economic purging than on stepping up economic production, ensuring a measure of social welfare for populations who had suffered under the occupation, and of course national integration and revival.

Employers undoubtedly made large profits working for the Germans, supplying the wherewithal for the German military machine. Aware of their difficult position, however, they acted where possible to cover their decisions. Dutch employers tried to secure the authorization of the administration before entering into economic arrangements. Belgian employers, stung by the experience of occupation in the First World War and anticipating accusations of collaboration at a future date, formed a collective to work for the Germans only under certain conditions, the so-called Galopin doctrine, and were careful to provide support for those of their workers who were taken to Germany and their families. French employers claimed that the employment they gave to workers in war-related industries saved the same workers from having to go to Germany. Employers often argued that they had fought with the German authorities to obtain the best contract terms or failed to deliver on time. In the case of Peugeot, even low-level sabotage in the factory was permitted in order to buy protection from RAF bombing.

Those who traded with the Germans were in a more vulnerable position, because they had often made vast profits on the black market, draining much-needed resources away from the local community, and could not claim to have given work or protection to anyone else. Even they, however, might argue that they had hidden goods from German requisitioning in order to supply the grey market shared with the local community. For workers, it was necessary to demonstrate after the war that they had not gone to work for the Germans voluntarily, even though in practice they had done so because they were unemployed or because the Germans offered higher wages. Often there was a tradition of cross-border working that simply continued under the occupation. The chance to assume anonymity and start a new life abroad was an attraction for those compromised politically or in a criminal sense. When forced labour was introduced, workers could claim that they had had no choice, although, as with military service, they to some degree had the option of draft dodging or desertion. Working for the Germans on the Atlantic Wall or in Speer's armaments factories at home was a common way to evade the draft and later claim to have resisted work in Germany. Although forced labour in Germany was initially feared as slave labour, and the conditions endured by the *Ostarbeiter* were particularly harsh, conscripted workers found ways of making life more acceptable, and later claim patriotically to have limited their contribution to the German war effort by go-slows, sickness, strike action, sabotage, not returning after home leave, or simply having a good time at the Germans' expense. Poles and Russians might be hanged in the early part of the war for sleeping with German women, but not at the end, while western workers were not disciplined in the same way. At the end of the war, as Germany collapsed into chaos, forced labourers went from factory to camp in search of the best offer, stole and formed gangs for rapine and riot. In many ways the return home was not even seen as a liberation. Forced workers were often suspected of having gone to Germany with some degree of free will and were cold-shouldered by resistance organizations run by those who had been deported for acts of resistance. The shame of the Italian Military Internees was such that their past was best forgotten. Finally, the *Ostarbeiter* retuning to Russia and Ukraine were suspected by the Stalinist authorities and even ordinary people of being German collaborators or corrupt westerners, and might face a much harsher term in a Soviet camp. For them, time spent working for the Germans wars far from being the worst time of their lives.

Notes

1. B.A. Sijes, *De arbeidsinzet. De gedwongen arbeid van Nederlanders in Duitsland, 1940–1945* (The Hague, Martinus Nijhoff, 1966), p. 77; Frans Selleslagh, 'L'emploi', in *1940–1945. La vie quotidienne en Belgique* (Brussels, CGER, 1984), p. 154.
2. Mark Spoerer, *Zwangsarbeit unter dem Hakenkreuz* (Stuttgart-Munich, Deutsche Verlags-Anstalt, 2001), pp. 222–3.
3. Alexander Dallin, *German Rule in Russia, 1941–1945* (London, Macmillan, 1957), pp. 84–103; Alan S. Milward, *The German Economy at War* (London, Athlone Press, 1965), p. 97.
4. Hein A.M. Klemann, *Nederland, 1938–1948. Economie en samenleving in jaren van oorlog en bezetting* (Amsterdam, Boom, 2002), pp. 68–70, 266, 432.
5. Sijes, *De arbeidsinzet*, pp. 91–103, 174. J.C.H. Blom, 'Nederland onder Duitse bezetting 10 mei 1940–5 mei 1945', in *Nieuwe Algemene Geschiedenis der Nederlanden* 15 (Haarlem, Fibula Van Dishoeck, 1982), p. 60.
6. J.P. Windmuller and C. de Galan, *Arbeidsverhoudingen in Nederland* (Utrecht-Antwerpen, Het Spectrum, 1979), 2 vols, I, pp. 83–91.
7. Suzanne Lommers, 'The Influence of War and Occupation on the Distribution of Industry Wages in Denmark and the Netherlands, 1938–1946' (MA thesis, Utrecht, 2003). We are grateful to Ralf Futselaar of NIOD for this reference.

8. Klemann, *Nederland, 1938–1948*, pp. 445–53; Werner Warmbrunn, *The Dutch under German Occupation* (Stanford, Stanford University Press, 1963), pp. 106–11.

9. F. Roest and J. Scheren, *Oorlog in de stad Amsterdam 1939–1941* (Amsterdam, Van Gennep, 1998), p. 196.

10. Roest and Scheren, *Oorlog*, pp. 247, 261–84; B.A. Sijes, *De Februari-Staking* (The Hague, Martinus Nijhoff, 1954).

11. Examples in P. Nefors, *Industriële collaboratie in België. De Galopindoctrine, de emissiebank en de Belgische industrie in de Tweede Wereldoorlog* (Leuven, Van Halewyck, 2000).

12. D. Luyten, *Burgers boven elke verdenking? Vervolging van economische collaboratie in België na de Tweede Wereldoorlog* (Brussels, VUBPRESS, 1996).

13. Fernand Baudhuin, *L'Économie belge sous l'occupation 1940–1944* (Brussels, F. Bruylant, 1945), p. 299.

14. W. Steenhaut, 'Les services sociaux de l'UTMI: un ersatz de son impuissance socio-politique', in *1940–1945. La vie quotidienne*, p. 178.

15. D. Luyten and R. Hemmerijckx, 'Belgian Labour in World War II: Strategies of Survival, Organisations and Labour Relations', *European Review of History-Revue européenne d'Histoire*, VII (2000), pp. 207–27.

16. G. Jacquemyns, 'La Société belge sous l'occupation allemande (1940–1944). Privations et espoirs', in J. Gotovitch (ed.), *La Belgique sous l'occupation allemande (1940–1944)* (Brussels, Complexe, 2002), p. 382.

17. G. Jacquemyns, *La Société belge sous l'occupation allemande, 1940–1944 1. Alimentation et état de santé* (Brussels, Nicholson & Watson, 1950), pp. 379–80.

18. Baudhuin, *L'Économie belge*, pp. 211–13, 243; Jacquemyns, *Alimentation*, p. 220.

19. J. Gérard-Libois and José Gotovitch, *L'An 40. La Belgique occupée* (Brussels, CRISP, 1971), pp. 334, 338.

20. J. Gotovitch, 'La grève des 100.000', in F. Balace (ed.), *Jours de Guerre, Jours de Lutte* (Brussels, Crédit Communal, 1992), pp. 91–100; J. Gotovitch, *Du rouge au tricolore. Résistance et parti communiste. Les communistes belges de 1939 à 1944.Un aspect de l'histoire de la Résistance en Belgique* (Brussels, Labour, 1992), pp. 113–14.

21. Bundesarchiv-Militärarchiv (BAMA), Freiburg, RW24/126, orders from German army, navy and air force, 24 Aug. 1940 to 20 Feb. 1941.

22. BAMA Freiburg RW24/122, war diary of Rüstungsinspektion B, SW France, 24 Feb. to 2 March 1941, 21–27 April 1941.

23. BAMA Freiburg RH36/512, orders on notepaper of Veltrup-Werke K.G., Aachen, May 1942–May 1944.

24. BAMA Freiburg RH36/511, list of 29 Sept. 1941; RH24/174, war diary of Rüstungskommando of Le Mans, 7 Sept. 1942.

25. Archives Départementales (AD) Maine-et-Loire (M-et-L) 74W2, report on Entreprises Dodin by subcommission of Comité interprofessionnel d'épuration dans les entreprises, n.d. but early 1945; AD L-A 132W 161, report of Commissaire de Police des Renseignements Généraux, Nantes, 8 Jan. 1945.

26. Archives Municipales (AM) Nantes 38W27, report of M. Helbert, Nov. 1944; Rémy Desquesnes, *Atlantikwall et Sudwall. La Défense allemande sur le littoral français, 1941–1942* (ANRT, Université de Lille III, 1987), p. 232.

27. Desquesnes, 'Atlantikwall', pp. 161–9 ; BAMA Freiburg RH36/146, report of *Arbeitseinsatzstab*, Nantes, 22 Oct. 1943.

28. A. Beltran, R. Frank and H. Rousso, *La Vie des entreprises sous l'occupation. Une enquête à l'échelle locale* (Paris, Belin, 1994), pp. 22–3, 386. See also Renaud de Rochebrune and Jean-Claude Hazera, *Les Patrons sous l'Occupation. I. Face aux Allemands* (new edn. Paris, Odile Jacob, 1997), pp. 573–6.

29. Anthony Rhodes, *Louis Renault, a Biography* (London, Cassel, 1969), pp. 181–4; François Marcot, 'La direction de Peugeot sous l'Occupation', *Le Mouvement social*, 189 (Oct.–Dec. 1999), pp. 27–46; M.R.D. Foot, *SOE in France. An Account of the Work of the British Special Operations Executive in France, 1940–1944* (London, Frank Cass, 2004), pp. 256–7.

30. The best study of this to date is Jean-Pierre Le Crom, *Syndicats Nous Voilà! Vichy et le corporatisme* (Paris, Les Éditions de l'Atelier/Éditions ouvrières, 1995).

31. Le Crom, *Syndicats Nous Voilà!* pp. 317–18.

32. Étienne Dejonghe, 'Le Nord et le Pas-de-Calais pendant la première année de l'Occupation, juin 1940–juin 1941', *Revue du Nord*, 51 (Oct. 1969), pp. 677–708.

33. Paul Sanders, *Histoire du marché noir, 1940–1946* (Paris, Perrin, 2001), pp. 167–262.

34. AD Loire-Atlantique (L-A) 96W13, officer of civil affairs, La Baule, 15 April 1945; AD Ille-et-Vilaine 217W 218, Chambre civique of Loire-Inférieure, case of R. Couturier.

35. Klaus Tenfelde, 'Forced Labour in the Second World War. German Experiences and European Comparisons', Paper given to the History of Work seminar at St Antony's College, Oxford, 18 Feb. 2005.

36. See 'Znachitel'nye predpriiatiia vyvezheny polnost'iu ... (Dokumenty ob itogakh evakuatsii iz Belorussii) 1941, APRF, Staroe Ploshad', 1995, No. 2, pp. 115–66.

37. Karel C. Berkhoff, *Harvest of Despair. Life and Death in Ukraine under Nazi Rule* (Cambridge, MA, Belknap Press of Harvard University Press, 2004), pp. 152, 155.

38. Berkhoff, *Harvest of Despair*, p. 152.

39. Berkhoff, *Harvest of Despair*, p. 154.

40. Alexander Hill, *The War behind the Eastern Front. The Soviet Partisan Movement in North-West Russia, 1941–1944* (London and New York, Frank Cass, 2005), pp. 58–9.

41. Alexander Hill, 'Popular Reactions to the German Occupation of North-Western Russia 1941–1944', Paper presented at the Annual Conference of the British Association of Slavonic and Eastern European Studies, Cambridge, April 1999, p. 19.
42. Cited in Dallin, *German Rule*, p. 329.
43. Hill, *War*, p. 49.
44. Hill, *War*, pp. 106, 50.
45. Bernhard Chiari, *Alltag hinter der Front. Besatzung, Kollabouration und Widerstand in Weisrussland, 1941–1944* (Düsseldorf, Droste Verlag, 1998), pp. 140–5; see also Hill, *War*, p. 106.
46. Chiari, *Alltag*, p. 143.
47. Dallin, *German Rule*, pp. 320–72.
48. Dallin, *German Rule*, pp. 349–50.
49. Timothy Mulligan, *The Politics of Illusion and Empire. German Occupation Policy in the Soviet Union 1942–1943* (New York and London, Praeger, 1988), pp. 95–7.
50. Hill, *War,* pp. 143–6.
51. Spoerer, *Zwangsarbeit*, pp. 89, 222.
52. Therkel Straede, "Deutschlandarbeiter': Danen in der deutschen Kriegswirtschaft, 1940–1945', in Ulrich Herbert (ed.), *Europa und der 'Reichseinsatz'. Ausländische Zivilarbeiter, Kriegsgefangene und KZ-Häftlinge in Deutschland 1938–1945* (Essen, Klartext, 1991), pp. 143–50; Joachim Lund, 'Den danske østindsats 1941–43. Østrumudvalget i den politiske og økonomiske kollaboration', *Historisk Tidsskrift*, 95/1 (1995), pp. 37–74 (with English summary); Joachim Lund, 'Denmark and the 'European New Order', 1940–1942', *Contemporary European History*, 13/3 (August 2004), pp. 305–21.
53. Sijes, *De arbeidsinzet*, pp. 37, 85–7, 110, 118–19, 134, 365–7, 395, 417–18, 421–43, 625.
54. Yves Durand, *La Vie quotidienne des prisonniers de guerre dans les Stalags, les Oflags et les Kommandos, 1939–1945* (Paris, Hachette, 1987), pp. 61, 78, 83–91.
55. Ulrich Herbert, *Hitler's Foreign Workers. Enforced Foreign Labour in Germany under the Third Reich* (Cambridge, Cambridge University Press, 1997), pp. 105–6; Peter Scholliers, 'The Policy of Survival: Food, the State and Social Relations in Belgium, 1914–1921', in John Burnett and Derek J. Oddy (eds), *The Origins and Development of Food Policies in Europe* (London, Leicester University Press, 1994), pp. 39–53; L. Vandeweyer, 'De verplichte tewerkstelling tijdens de Eerste Wereldoorlog', in *De verplichte tewerkstelling in Duitsland/Le travail obligatoire en Allemagne* (Brussels, Centre de recherches et d'études historiques de la seconde guerre mondiale, 1993), p. 43.
56. Jacquemyns, 'Privations et espoirs', p. 382; Frans Selleslagh, 'L'emploi', p. 157; L. De Vos, *De Tweede Wereldoorlog* (Leuven, Davidsfonds, 2004), p. 375.

57. Patrice Arnaud and Helga Bories-Sawala, 'Les Français et les Françaises volontaires pour le travail en Allemagne', in B. Garnier and J. Quellien (eds), *La Main d'œuvre française exploitée par le IIIe Reich* (Caen, Centre de Recherche d'Histoire Quantitative, 2003), pp. 107–26; AD Indre-et-Loire (I-et-L) 52W 60, report of gendarmerie of La Haye Descartes, 4 Dec. 1944.

58. Nicolas Tandler, *L'Impossible Biographie de Georges Marchais* (Paris, Édition Albatross, 1980), pp. 59–76.

59. Gérard Noiriel, *Longwy, immigrés et prolétaires, 1880–1980* (Paris, PUF, 1984), p. 172.

60. Angela Raspin, *The Italian War Economy, 1940–1943. With Particular Reference to Italian Relations with Germany* (New York and London, Garland, 1986), pp. 284–7; Brunello Mantelli, 'Von der Wanderarbeit zur Deportation. Die italienischen Arbeiter in Deutschland, 1938–1945', in Ulrich Herbert (ed.), *Europa und der 'Reichseinsatz'*, pp. 53–64.

61. Ciano, *Diary, 1939–1943* (London, Heinemann, 1947), pp. 375–6.

62. Raspin, *The Italian War Economy*, pp. 289–92.

63. Ulrich Herbert, *A History of Foreign Labour in Germany, 1880–1980* (Ann Arbor, University of Michigan Press, 1990), pp. 19, 99; Christophe Klessmann, *Polnische Bergarbeiter im Ruhrgebiet, 1870–1945* (Göttingen, Vandenhoeck und Ruprecht, 1978), p. 262.

64. Herbert, *Hitler's Foreign Workers*, pp. 80–3; Alfred Konieczny and Herbert Szurgacz, *Praca Przymusowa Polaków pod Panowaniem Hitlerowskin, 1939–1945. Documenta Occupationis*, X (Pozań, 1976), pp. 355–60, 374.

65. Kreisbauernführer Müller of Leobschütz to Landrat, 21 Mar. 1940, in Konieczny and Szurgacz, *Documenta Occupationis*, X, p. 244.

66. David Rodnick, *Post-war Germans. An Anthropologist's Account* (New Haven, Yale, 1948), pp. 12–13.

67. Reichsführer SS Himmler to Labour Minister, Berlin, and to the Führer's representative in Munich, both 8 March 1940, in Konieczny and Szurgacz, *Documenta Occupationis*, X, pp. 24, 26; Herbert, *Hitler's Foreign Workers*, pp. 65–77.

68. Rolf Hochhuth, *A German Love Story*, trans. John Brownjohn (London, Weidenfeld and Nicolson, 1980).

69. Dietrich Eichholtz, *Geschichte der deutschen Kriegswirtschaft, 1939–1945*, II (Berlin, Akademie-Verlag, 1984), pp. 186–92; Herbert, *Hitler's Foreign Workers*, pp.144–57. Christian Gerlach, *Krieg, Ernährung, Volkermord* (Hamburg, Hamburg Edition, 1998), p. 49, suggests that 85 per cent of Soviet POWs held in the General Government early in 1942 died. Michel Burleigh, *The Third Reich. A New History* (London, Macmillan, 2000), p. 514, argues that 3.3 million out of 5.7 million or 58 per cent of Red Army soldiers captured between 1941 and 1945 died in German hands.

70. Dallin, *German Rule*, p. 430.

71. Berkhoff, *Harvest of Despair*, p. 255.

72. These examples have been collected by Rosa A, researcher at the Archive of the Crimean Republic in Simferopol, who, during the course of her work of collecting information for former *Ostarbeiter* claiming German compensation, kept a diary with some of the startling life stories she encountered in the protocols of the filtration camps. The diary is unpublished and has no archival footnotes. Examples: Starchenko Dimitrii Antonovich; Kasadzhikova Var'vara Mikhailovna, born 1923; Konanenko Nina Ivanovna, born 1921; Greno Mariia Sidorovna, born 1923; Derebianko Nataliia Konstantinovna, born 1924; Tyshchenko Vera Romanovna, born 1927; Rebenko Irina Vasil'evna, born 1924.

73. Berkhoff, *Harvest of Despair*, p. 259.

74. Herbert, *Hitler's Foreign Workers*, p. 170.

75. Berkhoff, *Harvest of Despair*, p. 262; Hans Pfahlmann, *Fremdarbeiter und Kriegsgefangene in der deutschen Kriegswirtschaft, 1939–1945* (Darmstadt, Wehr und Wissen Verlagsgesellschaft, 1968), p. 51; Rolf-Dieter Müller, 'Die Rekrutierung sowjetischer Zwangsarbeiter für die deutsche Kriegswirtschaft', in Herbert (ed.), *Europa und der 'Reichseinsatz'*, p. 240. Herbert suggests that 614 were fit to go to Germany.

76. Berkhoff, *Harvest of Despair*, p. 272.

77. Dallin, *German Rule*, pp. 452–3.

78. Eichholtz, *Kriegswirtschaft*, p. 208.

79. Eichholtz, *Kriegswirtschaft*, p. 214.

80. Eichholtz, *Kriegswirtschaft,* p. 269.

81. Cited in Herbert, *Hitler's Foreign Workers*, p. 211.

82. Susanne Kraatz (ed.), *Verschleppt und Vergessen. Schicksaale jugendlicher Ostarbeiterinnen von der Krim im Zweiten Weltkrieg und danach* (Heidelberg, S. Kraatz, 1995), p. 64; document collection Rosa A; Herbert, *Hitler's Foreign Workers*, pp. 187–92.

83. They objected to the removal of the *Ostarbeiter* badge on the grounds that German men would be less ashamed to be seen in public with them. Harald Bräutigam, *Überblick über die besetzten Ostgebiete wärend des 2. Weltkriegs* (Tübingen, 1954), p. 94.

84. Herbert, *Hitler's Foreign Workers*, pp. 269–73.

85. U. Herbert, *Fremdarbeiter. Politik und Praxis des 'Ausländer-Einsatzes' in der Kriegswirtschaft des Dritten Reiches* (Berlin, JHW Dietz, 1985), p. 287.

86. Kraatz, *Verschleppt*, p. 56.

87. Berkhoff, *Harvest of Despair*, pp. 256–7.

88. Kraatz, *Verschleppt*, p. 84.

89. TsDAHOU (Central State Archives of Civic Organizations of Ukraine, Kiev) f. 1, op. 23, d. 1422, l. 195–196.

90. Herbert, *Hitler's Foreign Workers*, pp. 329–32.

91. Herbert, *Fremdarbeiter*, p. 300.

92. Herbert, *Hitler's Foreign Workers*, pp. 341–5.

93. Edward L. Homze, *Foreign Labour in Nazi Germany* (Princeton, Princeton University Press, 1967), p. 293.
94. Herbert, *Hitler's Foreign Workers*, p. 357.
95. Documents from the former Komsomol archive, now RGASPI, Fond M, 'Sovetskaia Molodezh' v Germanii: Dokumenty antifashistskogo soprotivleniia 1943–1945gg.', *Istoricheskii Arkhiv*, 3. (1995), pp. 63–80.
96. Herbert, *Hitler's Foreign Workers*, pp. 347–50.
97. Herbert, *Hitler's Foreign Workers*, pp. 364–70.
98. Spoerer, *Zwangsarbeit*, p. 228.
99. Herbert, *Hitler's Foreign Workers*, pp. 98–104; Luigi Cajani, 'Die italienischen Militär-Internierten im nationalsozialistischen Deutschland', in Herbert (ed.), *Europa und der 'Reichseinsatz'*, pp. 295–317.
100. Sijes, *De arbeidsinzet*, pp. 213, 219; Klemann, *Nederland, 1938–1948*, pp. 85–6.
101. Sijes, *De arbeidsinzet*, pp. 270, 280–96; Pieter J. Bouman, *De April–mei-stakingen van 1943* (The Hague, Martinus Nijhoff, 1950); Bart van der Boom, *We leven nog. De stemming in bezet Nederland* (Amsterdam, Boom, 2003), p. 77.
102. Ben Kroon, *In het land van de vijand. Mijn jaren van gedwongen arbeid 1943–1945* (Amsterdam, Balans, 2004), p. 48.
103. M. Winters, *Herinneringen aan de Arbeitseinsatz, 1942–1945* (Leeuwarden, Perio, 1990), pp. 15–34.
104. Kroon, *In het land van de vijand*, p. 62; K. Volder, *Werken in Duitsland, 1940–45* (Bedum, Profiel, 1990), pp. 217, 231–6, 263.
105. Sijes, *De arbeidsinzet*, p. 469, 412–59.
106. A. Galopin, Note sur l'attitude du patronat belge à l'égard de l'ordonnance du 30 avril 1942 (Brussels, Archives de la Société Générale); A. Galopin, La politique par l'autorité occupante en Belgique dans le domaine de l'emploi de la main d'oeuvre, 19 octobre 1942 (Brussels, Archives de la Société Générale); M. Van den Wijngaert, *Nood breekt wet economische collaboratie of accommodatie? Het beleid van Alexandre Galopin, gouverneur van de Société Générale tijdens de bezetting (1940–1944)* (Tielt, Lannoo, 1990), p. 70; F. Maerten, *Du murmure au grondement. La Résistance politique et idéologique dans la province de Hainaut pendant la Seconde Guerre Mondiale (mai 1940–septembre 1944)* (Mons, Hannonia, 1999), 3 vols, II, p. 717.
107. Diary M.M., SOMA, Enquête verplichte tewerkstelling.
108. Peter Scholliers, 'Strijd rond de koopkracht, 1939–1945', in *België 1940, een maatschappij in crisis en oorlog, 1940. Belgique, une société en crise, un pays en guerre, 1940* (Brussels, Centre de recherches et d'études historiques de la seconde guerre mondiale, 1993), pp. 245–76; R. Hemmerijckx, *Van Verzet tot Koude Oorlog 1940–1949. Machtsstrijd om het ABVV* (Brussels/Glent, VUBPRESS/AMSAB, 2003), pp. 83–123.

109. Gotovitch, *Du rouge au tricolore*, p. 114; Cahier de revendications des métallurgistes de Charleroi, December 1943, SOMA.

110. Archives of the Royal Palace, Kabinet Leopold III, 255, 'Ordonnance sur le travail', 31 Oct. 1942.

111. Archives of the Royal Palace, Kabinet Leopold III, 168, JOC, 'Le service obligatoire pour les jeunes travailleurs', 15 January 1943.

112. E. Verhoeyen, *België bezet 1940–1944* (Brussels, BRTN, 1993), p. 204.

113. Dirk Luyten, 'De hulp van de werkgevers aan werkweigeraars en gedeporteerden, een bouwsteen van de na-oorlogse sociale verhoudingen?', in *De verplichte tewerkstelling in Duitsland*, pp. 59–80.

114. Louis Vos, m.m.v. P. Wynants and A. Tihon, 'De christelijke arbeidersjeugd', in Emmanuel Gerard (ed.), *De Christelijke Arbeidersbeweging in België 1891–1991* (Leuven, Universitaire Pers, 1991), II, pp. 413–83.

115. Etienne Verhoeyen, 'Londres et l'aide aux réfractaires', in *De verplichte tewerkstelling in Duitsland*, pp. 133–64.

116. See, for example, Diary J.V.A., Diary M.M., Diary G.V.D.P., 'Chronique d'un déporté pour le travail obligatoire en Allemagne ou les tribulations des camarades de 'la Chambre 19' juillet 1943–juin 1945', SOMA, Enquête verplichte tewerkstelling; W.L., Geschiedenis van de tweede wereldoorlog. Gedeporteerden. 'Verplichte arbeidsdienst', SOMA, AB 316.

117. Diary J.V.A., SOMA, Enquête verplichte tewerkstelling.

118. Jacquemyns, *La Société belge sous l'occupation allemande, 3. Les déportés et leur famille* (Brussels, 1950), *passim*.

119. 'Chronique' Diary M.M., SOMA, Enquête verplichte tewerkstelling.

120. 'Chronique' SOMA, Enquête verplichte tewerkstelling.

121. 'Chronique' Diary J.V.A., SOMA, Enquête verplichte tewerkstelling; W.L., Geschiedenis... SOMA, AB 316.

122. W.L., Geschiedenis... SOMA, AB 316.

123. Diary M.M., SOMA, Enquête verplichte tewerkstelling.

124. Jacquemyns, 'Privations et espoirs', p. 335.

125. W.L., Geschiedenis... SOMA, AB 316; K.Volder, *Werken in Duitsland, 1940–45* (Bedum, Profiel, 1990), p. 173.

126. Diary G.V.D.P., SOMA, Enquête verplichte tewerkstelling.

127. 'Chronique'... SOMA, Enquête verplichte tewerkstelling.

128. Diary J.V.A. and G.V.D.P., SOMA, Enquête verplichte tewerkstelling.

129. Jacques Evrard, *La Déportation des travailleurs français dans le IIIe Reich* (Paris, Fayard, 1972), pp. 64–5.

130. AD M-et-L 12W 54, report of *intendant de police*, Angers, 2 Nov. 1942.

131. Jean-Claude Daumas, 'Entre le travail en Allemagne et exploitation sur place: les contradictions de la politique allemande de la main d'oeuvre', in B. Garnier and J. Quellien, *La Main d'oeuvre française*, pp. 234–46.

132. Evrard, *La Déportation des travailleurs*, pp. 74–83.

133. Archives Nationales, Paris, F1a 3870, regional prefect Donati to Laval, 20 March 1944.

134. AD M-et-L 136W 3, departmental delegate of the ministry of information to prefect of M-et-L, 19 Jan. 1944; Michèle Cointet, *L'Eglise sous Vichy, 1940–1945* (Paris, Perrin, 1998), p. 291.

135. Collection Michel Lemesle, letter of Mme Delépine, La Ferrière-de-Flée (M-et-L), 28 Nov. 1973.

136. Michel Boivin, 'Les *réfractaires* au travail obligatoire: essai d'une approche globale et statistique', in B. Garnier and J. Quellien, *La Main d'oeuvre française*, pp. 493–515; Gildea, *Marianne in Chains*, pp. 298–300, 323–6.

137. Helaga Bories-Sawala, 'Aspects de la vie quotidienne des requis en Allemagne', in B. Garnier and J. Quellien, *La Main d'oeuvre française*, pp. 140–2.

138. Archives Nationales (AN), Paris, F1a 3870, regional prefect Donati to Laval, 20 March 1944.

139. Herbert, *Hitler's Foreign Workers*, p. 329.

140. Interview with Jacques Hervé, Joué-lès-Tours, 12 June 1997.

141. Herbert, *Hitler's Foreign Workers*, p. 341.

142. Patrice Arnaud, 'Les logiques d'opposition des travailleurs civils français en Allemagne pendant la Seconde Guerre mondiale: une résistance civile?', in B. Garnier and J. Quellien, *La Main d'oeuvre française*, p. 159

143. AD M-et-L 12W 3, prefect Gaudard of Loire-Inférieure to Intendant du Maintien de l'Ordre, Angers, 3 May 1944.

144. Helga Bories-Sawala, 'Aspects de la vie quotidienne', p. 145, note 42.

145. François Cavanna, *Les Ruskoffs* (Paris, Club Français du Livre, 1979), p. 163.

146. Luyten, *Burgers*; D. Luyten and G. Vanthemsche (eds), *Het Sociaal Pact van 1944. Oorsprong, betekenis, gevolgen* (Brussels, VUBPRESS, 1995); E. Witte, 'Tussen restauratie en vernieuwing. Een introductie op de Belgische politieke evolutie tussen 1944 en 1950', in E. Witte, J.C. Burgelman and P. Stouthuysen (eds), *Tussen restauratie en vernieuwing. Aspecten van de naoorlogse Belgische politiek* (Brussels, VUBPRESS, 1989), pp. 25–9.

147. Dirk Luyten, 'Over strafdossiers en sociale verhoudingen. De Schelde te Vlissingen in de Tweede Wereldoorlog', *Zeeland. Tijdschrift van het Koninklijk Zeeuwsch Genootschap der Wetenschappen.* (2004), XIII, 1, pp. 1–11; Joggli Meihuizen, *Noodzakelijk kwaad. De bestraffing van economische collabouratie in Nederland na de Tweede Wereldoorlog* (Amsterdam, Boom, 2003); Pieter Van Lierop, *Kommunisten in bevrijd Zuid-Nederland. 'Voor één socialistische partij' (september 1944 – juli 1945)* (Amsterdam, Stichting Instituut voor Politiek en Sociaal Onderzoek, 1984), pp. 20–1.

148. Dirk Luyten, 'Op zoek naar sociaal-economische consensus. Sociale pacten bij de bevrijding in België, Frankrijk en Nederland', in M. de Keizer, H. Klemann, D. Luyten and P. Deloge (eds), *Thuisfront*, (Zutphen, Walburg Pers, 2003) pp. 192–205; J.L. Van Zanden, *Een klein land in de 20ᵉ eeuw.*

Economische geschiedenis van Nederland 1914–1995 (Utrecht, Het Spectrum, 1997), pp. 171–82, 192–208.

149. AD L-A 132W 90, dossiers on tramways of Nantes and Chantiers de Bretagne, Dec. 1944–March 1945.

150. AD I-et-L 1305W 54, Comité de Confiscation des Profits Illicites, Indre-et-Loire, March – Oct. 1945.

151. AD Ille-et Vilaine (I-et-V) 217W 217, Chambre civique of L-I, report of gendarmerie of Coueron, 28 Dec. 1944.

152. Anne Simonin, 'Pourquoi certains crimes doivent rester impunis. Les travailleurs volontaires en Allemagne devant les Chambres civiques de la Seine', in B. Garnier and J. Quellien, *La Main d'euvre française*, pp. 563–72.

153. AN 72AJ 160, report of police commissioner, Tours, 20 June 1945.

154. W.L., Geschiedenis... SOMA, AB 316.

155. D. Luyten, 'Prosecution, Society and Politics: the Penalization of Economic Collaboration in Belgium after the Second World War', *Crime, Histoire & Sociétés/Crime, History & Societies*, II (1998), pp. 111–33.

156. Annette Wieviorka, 'La bataille du statut', in B. Garnier and J. Quellien, *La Main d'oeuvre française*, pp. 617–24.

157. Diary J.V.A., SOMA, Enquête verplichte tewerkstelling.

158. Wieviorka, 'La bataille du statut', pp. 617–24.

159. RGASPI f. 17, op. 125. d. 314, l. 40–44; Anthony Beevor, *Berlin. The Downfall* (London, Viking, 2003), pp. 108–10.

160. Documents Rosa A.

161. Cited in Kraatz, *Verschleppt*, p. 72.

162. 'Lish' odinochki okazalis izmennikami', *Istochnik*, 1996/2, p. 56.

163. Kraatz, *Verschleppt*, p. 87.

164. Ibid., p. 92.

165. Documents Rosa A.

166. Kraatz, *Verschleppt*, p. 92.

167. Elena Zubkova, *Polsevoennoe sovetskoe obshchestvo. Politika i povsednevnost' 1945–1953* (Moscow, Rosspen, 2000), p. 39.

168. TsDAHOU f. 1, op. 23, d. 1422, l. 195.

169. Ibid.

170. Zubkova, Polsevoennoe sovetskoe obshchestvo, p. 40.

–3–

Intimate and Sexual Relations
Anette Warring

One evening in May 1945 seven men forced their way into the home of two women. The women were said to have had intimate relations with soldiers of the German occupying forces, and the armed intruders were members of the resistance. The women were taken to a nearby air-raid shelter, and after a brief interrogation their hair was initially cut off with scissors. Subsequently a trimmer was used to shave their heads. Gradually more and more men gathered in the shelter, and they proceeded to pull off the women's clothes and, with black enamel paint, drew swastikas on their exposed backs and breasts. The two women were then forced back on the streets, and, without being allowed to cover themselves up, they had to file past the hundred or more spectators who had gathered there, jeering, shouting and lunging at them.[1]

A European Phenomenon

This scene took place in Copenhagen, but similar cropping incidents took place in France, Belgium, Holland, Italy, Norway, Poland, Czechoslovakia – basically all over Europe. The women had their hair cut off as a punishment for having fraternized intimately with the soldiers of the occupying forces. Everywhere in Europe the cropping incidents peaked during the phase of liberation, but to a varying degree they also took place while the countries were occupied by Germany. In France the first recorded cropping incident occurred in 1943, but in Algeria it was as early as 1941, and in the summer of 1943 the Polish underground sheet *Biuletyn Informacyjny* (Information Bulletin) reported a head-shaving in the streets of occupied Warsaw. In Norway it was as early as May 1940, shortly after the country had been invaded by Germany, and in Denmark, in the late summer of 1940, a large group of young men shaved the heads of a couple of young women whom they accused of 'going out with the Germans'. Eventually, the persecution of fraternizing women was to play a central part in the revolt which brought about the fall of the Danish government in August 1943. While the cutting off of hair was a widespread and common form of punishment, there were nevertheless considerable national and regional differences in the way in which these actions were carried out. In Norway and Denmark, for example, it was a punishment exclusively meted out to women who had fraternized sexually, whereas in France it was used for women accused of all kinds of collaboration.[2] There seems to be no evidence of head-shaving in Soviet territories. Perhaps it did not fit into the official version of events in the post-war Soviet Union, which held that Soviet citizens had not collaborated except for a very few nationalities, which were punished by deportation. Or perhaps this form of popular justice actually did not take place because it was not necessary and potentially dangerous in a state that was keen to preserve its judicial monopoly. While intimate relations between German soldiers and women from the occupied countries occurred everywhere in Europe, they differed in scope and nature and were met with varying responses in the different communities.

Intimate relations between local women and soldiers of the occupying forces, and the question of how such fraternizations should be handled, constituted more than a practical and moral dilemma that had to be tackled on an everyday level. In a profound sense they epitomized and drew attention to the whole conflict of occupation itself, involving wider and politically explosive issues of conquest and race. The female body represented a combat zone between the occupiers and the occupied, between collaborators and resistance fighters. The intimate fraternizations reflected both the national conflict between the German occupying power and the occupied countries, and the internal conflict between collaboration and resistance. However, these conflicts were to a large extent dominated by a shared gender discourse. It was characteristic of the processes of inclusion and exclusion found in the various national and local communities that issues of gender and sexuality played an active part.

War is both a gendered and gendering activity, and consequently we have not only to ask what was the impact of occupation on gender relations, but also in which ways did gender affect the course of occupation? Or, as the American historian Joan Scott puts it: 'Is there a politics of gender in the politics of war? And what does one reveal about the other?'[3] Thus, the widespread fraternizations between soldiers of the German occupying forces and women from the occupied countries represent more than an intriguing appendix to the history of occupied Europe.

Altered Gender Relations

Defeat and occupation changed relations between men and women. Many men were absent from their homes, as prisoners of war, deportees, forced labourers, conscripts or volunteers for the Wehrmacht or the Waffen-SS, as voluntary labourers in Germany, or as members of the resistance working underground. Their absence entailed new responsibilities, but also new opportunities, for the women who were left in charge of the families, economically and otherwise. How radical these changes were varied greatly from country to country. In Denmark approximately 100,000 men accepted work as voluntary labourers in Germany, either for limited or longer periods of time. About 6,000 went to the eastern front as volunteers for the Waffen-SS, and roughly the same number of seamen were unable to return home until the war ended. During the last couple of years of the occupation several thousand men were absent because they were living underground, had fled to Sweden or were in captivity in Germany. In addition about 100,000 men worked voluntarily for the Germans on the construction of the defence system along the west coast of Jutland, which formed part of the Atlantic Wall. During the construction work most of these labourers were accommodated in special barracks and were away from home. Thus, out of a population of approximately four million people, the number of Danish men absent from their homes was fairly high. However, in some of the other occupied countries the destabilization of gender relations was even more far reaching. In France about two million men between twenty and forty years of age were missing, while between four hundred thousand and a million German soldiers of the same age occupied the country. The war caused a huge decrease in the male population in Poland, and the average presence of German soldiers on the territory of the General Government was over half a million. In some areas of the eastern territories the German forces confronted a virtually man-free community.[4]

While many of the men were absent in the occupied countries, the soldiers of the occupying forces were present in large numbers. To the women these soldiers represented both a threat and an opportunity. Depending on the brutality of the warfare and on the particular circumstances in each occupied country, women were to a varying degree and in unknown numbers raped, abused and sexually harassed by German soldiers. In practice the German authorities tolerated rape as part of the warfare in eastern and southeastern Europe but not in the northern and western countries. Initially, German soldiers committed few rapes in villages and towns on Soviet territory, since army brothels, often filled with local women, catered for their needs. It was those who did not have access to this 'commodity' – ethnic German helpers, Hungarian and Romanian soldiers – who became known as the perpetrators of rape among the population. Towards the end of the war, when the situation on the eastern front deteriorated, more and more rape cases, committed by regular German conscripts and officers, were reported.[5] Soviet women were at risk not only from hostile armies; the Red Army and partisan units frequently engaged in mass rapes on Soviet as well as German territory and did not spare Soviet women who themselves had been victims of the war.[6] In Denmark rapes committed by soldiers from the Wehrmacht were rare occurrences, but still, even though the German authorities vowed that such offences would be punished with severity, in actual practice this was far from always the case.[7] Knowing how to handle the advances of a German soldier could be difficult for a woman. On the one hand, she had to think of the reactions of her family and surrounding community. On the other, a rejection could have severe consequences, either if the soldier ignored such a rejection and forced his will on her, or if he reported her for insulting the Wehrmacht. Naturally, the large presence of foreign soldiers also enabled the women to forge intimate relationships voluntarily. The absence of a husband or fiancé offered scope for greater sexual freedom, and the state of occupation also allowed for the possibility of meeting German soldiers without the family and local community knowing or interfering, especially if the women were employed by the occupying power, working in their kitchens, for instance, or as cleaners or secretaries.

Intimate relations between local women and German soldiers challenged the accepted norms and morals surrounding gender, gender relations and sexuality. This fraternization therefore seems to substantiate the widespread idea that the war had an equalizing and democratizing effect on women's situation and on gender relations. At the same time, however, the reactions to the women's fraternizing in general reveal how society's requirements of their national and cultural loyalties had been stiffened because of the state of occupation, which in turn reflected a societal drive for traditionally patterned gender roles. This ambiguity also marked the public debate in Denmark during the occupation. Here the entertainment industry expanded, and eroticism became a popular topic in the literature, films and mass culture of the time. At the same time various specialists and authorities publicly voiced their deep concern for the moral well-being of the Danish youth and of the female population in particular. It was a state of moral panic, which was nourished by the women's overt fraternizations with Germans, and by the dramatic rise in recorded cases of venereal diseases. Fraternization contributed to the destabilization of gender relations and meant both an expansion and a limitation of women's liberty of action.

A Politicized Number

Intimate relations between German soldiers and women from the occupied countries were widespread. The number of children springing from these relations alone suggests that the fraternization was extensive. However, it is impossible to say precisely how extensive it was, as not all fraternizing women had children and not all children fathered by German soldiers were registered as such. But in countries such as Norway and Denmark it is possible to estimate the number of these children with some precision. And, along with police reports, records of cases concerning the transmission of venereal diseases, sources relating, for instance, to the post-war purges and in-depth local studies, these numbers help to define the extent of the fraternization.

During the occupation, the number of women having intimate relations with the German soldiers was a disputed and politicized question. In June 1942 the leading underground newssheet *Frit Danmark* (A Free Denmark) wrote about 'the tarts and the Germans', and stated that only a small percentage of Danish women had committed treason by consorting with German soldiers. However, a few months earlier another underground newssheet, *De frie Danskere* (The Free Danes), had claimed that if you went for an evening stroll in Copenhagen, you could not walk more than five steps without coming across a German soldier with a young girl on his arm. In other words, when the purpose of the propaganda was to express Danish hostility towards the occupying power, the German-friendly girls were seen to be few in number. If, on the other hand, the aim was to rouse people to resistance and incite confrontation with the collaborators, the reported number of German-friendly girls was shamelessly high.

In May 1941 Toralv Øksnevad, the Norwegian voice of the BBC in London, broadcast the following message to his countrymen: 'As we know, the German master race, ruler of nations and world conquerors, is comprised of quite irresistible individuals. However, common Norwegian women can demobilize their conceit-edness without any difficulty, and more than 999 per thousand do so.'[8] The purpose of minimizing the number of women said to be fraternizing with German soldiers was to keep up the fighting spirit among Norwegians, both at home and at the front. By the same token, as well as for reasons of legitimacy, the government in exile attempted at a later stage to censor and classify shocking reports, coming from both Norway and the exile community in Sweden, that between 30,000 and 50,000 women had had relations with the Germans, and that up to 80 per cent of the young girls in certain parts of the Finmark were 'going with the Germans'.[9]

The claim of the 999 per thousand women was completely unfounded, as 400 Norwegian women would then have to have given birth to 9,000 children, which is the officially recorded number of children with a Norwegian–German parentage born during and just after the occupation. Later estimates put the number of Norwegian children fathered by German soldiers at 10,000–12,000, which, according to different methods of calculation, supports a cautious claim that at least 30,000–40,000 Norwegian women found themselves a boyfriend among the German soldiers. Other historians have argued that the number is closer to 50,000.[10] In any case, this is a large percentage out of a population of 3 million.

The officially recorded number of children born of Danish–German parentage during the war is 5,500, but the estimated actual number is a couple of thousand higher.[11] Thus the number of children fathered by German soldiers is lower in Denmark than in Norway, despite the fact that the Danes outnumbered the Norwegians by a million. It should be remembered that the number of German troops in Denmark was considerably lower than in Norway. During most of the occupation approximately 100,000 German soldiers were stationed in Denmark. However, this number increased towards the liberation, where it rose to 250,000 men. By contrast, between 350,000 and 400,000 German soldiers were stationed in Norway for most of the occupation. Calculations show that, most likely, the number of fraternizing women in Denmark was no less than 40,000 to 50,000. This was roughly equal to what the resistance could muster after the last great recruitment for their military stand-by groups during the final months of the occupation.[12]

A thorough survey of the cropping incidents in France suggests that approximately 20,000 French women were subjected to this kind of punishment for having fraternized with German soldiers. But there is no estimate of the total number of women who had performed *collaboration horizontale*, as it was called. However, there is little doubt that the total number of French women having intimate relations with occupying soldiers exceeds the 20,000 shorn women.[13] Already in 1942 Leonardo Conti, Reich Health Leader, reported that more than 50,000 children had French mothers and German fathers, and the following year a major from a German military hospital in France estimated that the number had risen to 85,000.[14] The most reliable calculation is that the total number of French children born as a result of German–French liaisons for the entire territory and for the entire occupation period was as high as 200,000.[15]

In the Netherlands we only have the number of children born during the war of Dutch–German parentage to go by in order to calculate the extent of the fraternization. Here, between 12,000 and 16,000 is cited as the probable number of children.[16] For Belgium, as well as for Greece, Italy and Yugoslavia, there are no definite statistics, and for the occupied countries in eastern Europe we only have estimations from Nazi documents which cannot be taken as reliable. They put the number of German-born children in the Reichskommissariat Ukraine at 10,000. Both German and Soviet sources are likely to underestimate the number of births resulting from German–eastern European alliances. Officially Germans were forbidden to have contact with the Slavic population and were thus unlikely to boast of their paternity. Soviet women knew of the terrible consequences the admission of a relationship of any kind with the occupying forces could have, and would also keep quiet about the fathers of their children. Finally, post-war Soviet identity rested on the image of unified resistance against the invader and was thus unlikely to compile statistics damaging the carefully constructed myth. The fact that relations between Germans and local girls took place in eastern Europe is demonstrated by rather indirect evidence. Post-war records show a high number of Party and Komsomol exclusions of girls who had remained on occupied territory and who had been accused of 'flirtation with Germans'. However, this type of evidence is corrupted, since such smears became standard accusations in political and personal infighting in the years after the war.[17] However, the mere fact that such smears were credible confirms the general existence of the phenomenon, which to date has been vigorously denied by most people living in the former socialist bloc. Indeed, one of the most famous post-war films of life under occupation, *Molodaia Gvardiia*, features a young girl seducing German officers. Of course, she turns out to be in the service of a communist underground organization, yet her ploy could only work if many others had done what she did: befriending the German occupants and engaging in flirtatious and sexual relations.[18] While fraternization therefore occurred in eastern Europe, the lack of quantitative data makes an assessment of its extent impossible.

It is not possible to extrapolate the numbers of fraternizing women in Denmark and Norway to other occupied countries, as the access to birth control and abortion, as well as the incentive to identify a German soldier as the father of one's child, varied from country to country. In addition, studies of post-war era confrontations, such as Fabrice Virgili's *Shorn Women in Liberation France*, are insufficient for estimating the extent of the fraternizing during the occupation, since there are indications that locally the level of confrontation was also determined by factors other than the scale and intensity of the intimate relations between local women and German soldiers.[19] In fact, in areas where the occupying forces were present in large numbers and where the local male inhabitants also socialized with the Germans, there could be a greater tolerance towards fraternizing women, leading to relatively fewer confrontations.

With so few and such uncertain estimates of the extent of the fraternizing in the different countries and regions, the possibility of making comparisons is considerably weakened. Yet regional studies in Norway and Denmark indicate that the concentration of German soldiers was an important factor. In the Finmark German soldiers outnumbered the local population, and in a small municipality such as Sør-Varanger, which had approximately 8,000 inhabitants, there could be up to 60,000 German soldiers stationed from time to time. As in other towns, the Germans were billeted in private homes, so that almost every household had soldiers living with them for long periods of time, which made it difficult if not impossible to avoid forming personal friendships and engaging in intimate relations. In Danish cities such as Ålborg, in northern Jutland, where there was a large concentration of German troops because of the city's strategic military position, the relatively large number of paternity suits suggests that the fraternizing was more intense here than in towns on Lolland and Falster, where the majority of the local inhabitants rarely came into contact with German soldiers.[20]

However, the picture is not unequivocal. Irrespective of the concentration of troops, anonymity could more easily be maintained in the big cities, where a relationship with a German soldier could also more easily be kept a secret. These factors could be conducive to the women's desire to engage in intimate relations with the German soldiers. On the other hand, the soldiers in the cities appeared, to a much larger extent than in the small local communities, as members of an anonymous and brutal occupying power. Opposing forces were also at play in the small communities. Here it was virtually impossible to conceal a relationship with a German soldier, which could prompt a woman to think twice before getting involved with a soldier, but, on the other hand, there was often a readiness here also to look at the man, not just the uniform.

Whether the development of the war fronts and the conflicts between occupier and occupied influenced the extent of fraternization is difficult to say exactly. If, for instance, we look at the statistics concerning the number of Danish children fathered by Germans during the occupation, they do not seem to suggest this. It is true that the number of children with a Danish–German parentage and their relative share of the total birth rate in Denmark continued to increase during the years of occupation.[21] However, to understand these figures properly we also need to keep in mind that the number of German soldiers stationed in Denmark rose proportionately during the occupation.

Did the degree of normality in the occupied countries make fraternization more widespread or not? Again, it is not possible to give a straightforward answer to this question. In some of the occupied countries, such as Denmark, everyday life continued without any major changes, particularly during the first years of the war, which is why it could seem perfectly innocent and not all that deviant to engage in an intimate relationship with a German soldier. Conversely, the collapse of everyday life and extreme living conditions might undermine norms and prompt people to seize opportunities, without thinking about the consequences. Even in the brutal war in eastern Europe, where the German soldiers were mostly perceived as conquerors and murderers, love affairs occurred. Most likely the forces at work varied, and future studies will have to uncover this. The present text will try to give a better understanding of the intimate fraternizations by investigating why and under what circumstances women became intimate with German soldiers.

Fantasies versus Reality

In France they were called *femmes à boche*, in Holland *moffenhoer* or *moffenmeiden*, in Norway and Denmark *tyskerpiger*, *tyskertøser* or *feltmadrasser*. In Ukraine they acquired the name *shliukh-doiche*. Everywhere women who dated German soldiers were given derogatory names branding them as loose. Such relationships could not be explained or considered 'normal' relationships between men and women. Promiscuity and deceitfulness were what sprang to mind. Often these women were also portrayed as unintelligent, ugly and socially disadvantaged, a picture that was evoked in order to explain how the women could bring themselves to form intimate relationships with German soldiers.[22] Even in those rare instances where they were meant to excuse the women's actions, such portrayals were stereotyping and stigmatising for the women. Both in the collective memory and within historical research, the focus has largely been on the reactions triggered by these intimate fraternizations. But what about the women themselves? Who were they, and why did they end up dating German soldiers?

A Danish socio-medical study conducted between 1943 and 1945, entitled *The Girls They Left Behind*, examined various aspects of the German forces' sexual relations with Danish subjects, and, as far as we know, it is the only contemporary survey of its kind.[23] It was conducted by Dr Grethe Hartmann and included 204 women from Copenhagen, randomly selected from the thousand or so individuals who had been reported to the Danish vice squad by the Wehrmacht for infecting German soldiers with venereal diseases. Hartmann's survey showed that the great majority of the *tyskerpiger* were between 17 and 25 years old, and that they had had their sexual initiation at a somewhat earlier age than the average. Very few of them had any political motives for socializing with Germans, and a considerable number of them had worked periodically as prostitutes. Even though – in contrast to the normal group of prostitutes – they did not come from socially disadvantaged families, their own social status was very poor. Their level of education was below average, and they typically had a chequered career with many dead-end jobs. Over a third of them had had dealings with the law, and approximately one-fifth had been charged several times with infecting German soldiers with a venereal disease. Among these women several were characterized as 'retards, spineless and psychopathic'. When Hartmann's book was published in the autumn of 1946, it was perceived as a dismissal of the common stereotype of the *tyskerpiger*, or at least as an attempt to see them in a more balanced light. This was because Hartmann's findings were compared – by Hartmann too – with previous surveys of prostitutes in Copenhagen rather than with the general picture of the entire female population. Moreover, the usual portrayal of these *tyskerpiger* during the occupation had been extremely biased and stigmatizing, supported as it was by underground propaganda. Both in Denmark and abroad Hartmann's book was treated as an 'objective survey', as noted for instance in a Norwegian study, even though one did not have to be an experienced scholar to see that it failed to draw a complete, representative picture.[24] The criterion for selection had been whether the women carried some kind of venereal disease, and they were all women who had been reported by German soldiers as their source of infection. Obviously, among this group there would be an overrepresentation of socially disadvantaged women who relied fully or partly on prostitution, or who had had many sexual partners. In addition it is worth noting that many of the German soldiers would be likely to provide false information, or provide the name of a prostitute, in order to protect their Danish girlfriends from any dealings with the police.[25] Although unique in being the only contemporary survey of its kind, Hartmann's study and its reception at the time reveal more about society's view of women who had intimate relationships with German soldiers than about the women themselves.

Although drawing on a large and varied selection of sources, the few historical surveys that have been conducted on the intimate fraternizations suffer from similar problems of representation, problems that are inevitable when the data being used relate exclusively to women who have been registered in official sources such as police reports, detention papers, documents from court cases and paternity suits, or stem from memoirs and interviews. Consequently, it is impossible to draw a complete sociological and psychological picture of the women in question. What we can conclude with some degree of certainty – on the basis of the research conducted in Norway and especially in France and Denmark – is that we are dealing with a heterogeneous group of women, whose only common trait was that, during a time of occupation, they were dating one or more soldiers from the occupying forces.[26]

Fraternizing women came from all social strata. There were intelligent women as well as 'retards', both ugly and pretty, Nazis, Communists and of no political persuasion. There were prostitutes and women who had relations with only one German soldier. Some spoke openly about their relationships, others kept theirs a secret. There were minors and adolescents as well as older women. They could be unmarried, married, divorced or wives of POWs. There were nationals with a long ancestry, and women with an immigrant background or with German relatives. Some of them worked for the occupying forces or periodically in Germany, while others would never dream of doing that. There were criminals among them, as well as women who had never had any dealings with the law. Some came from Nazi or pro-German families, and some had relatives that were Communists or members of the resistance.[27] The surveys point to the probable scenario that there was an overrepresentation of women in the partner-seeking age, and of women who had left home – in some cases to work for the occupying forces – and who therefore found themselves outside the normal social sphere and control of their families and local community.

A Private or Public Matter?

Why did many of the women in the occupied countries engage in intimate relationships with German soldiers? In occupied countries, facing hard conditions and terror, an intimate relation to a German soldier could be a strategy of survival because of the access to food and the protection from daily threat he could provide. For Jewish women it may have constituted the only hope of survival. Such relationships were founded on fundamental inequality. Some simply fell in love, which is difficult to explain even for a psychologist. From the Danish women's own explanations, however, it is possible to get an idea of the different impulses and situations that could be conducive to starting a relationship with a German soldier. Some of the women initiated intimate relations with soldiers of the Wehrmacht because it tied in with their pro-German or Nazi convictions, while the prostitutes would accept German punters in order to make money. For some women the decisive factor was that the German soldiers were handsome, well-groomed, dressed in uniforms and conducted themselves as true gentlemen, while others did not find the soldiers particularly attractive but saw them as an easy opportunity of gaining experience with men. To others, being in a relationship with a German soldier meant getting access to otherwise inaccessible goods and amusements. Some women used the German soldiers to spice up the dreary everyday life in a provincial town, and went out with them as a revolt against the stifling bonds imposed by parents and a provincial environment. To get a glimpse of the outside world and an opportunity to practise the German learned at school were other reasons for going out with the soldiers. Other women found that the anonymity which the contact with a foreigner could offer enabled them to feel free and to play out their erotic desires. There were also women who, because they worked for the Germans or had German origins themselves, found it natural to socialize with the soldiers, and also to find a boyfriend among them. Last but not least, an intimate relationship with a German soldier often grew out of a chance meeting in a bar, at a dance restaurant, at the baker's, in the park, on the train, at work or in the home where he stayed.

That said, there were many women who, for political or moral reasons, did not dream of or dare to go out with German soldiers because they knew that the those around them would react with scorn. Were the fraternizing women indifferent to this kind of condemnation, or were they simply not aware that they violated the general norms and widespread attitudes in society by socializing with German soldiers? A survey based on interviews with Danish women who dated German soldiers during the occupation reveals that, even though alleged ignorance could serve as an extenuating circumstance, from the outset they fully realized that they overstepped morals of gender and/or national and political norms by engaging in intimate relations with one or more German soldiers.[28] They all knew that they were being frowned upon. Yet there are variations in how conscious they were of the different types of reactions, and here the time factor comes into play. At the liberation all fraternizing women must have known that they risked being held accountable for their actions, even if they did not consider themselves as real *tyskertøser, femmes à boche, shliukh-doiche* or *moffenhoer*. Even if they or their girlfriends had not been harassed or assaulted during the occupation, and even if they had not heard about such incidents or about the condemnations of the underground propaganda, after the August revolt in 1943 they could not have been oblivious to the widespread anger and aggression in parts of the population over intimate fraternizing with soldiers of the enemy. However, it also appeared that what mattered most were the reactions of parents and the local community.

Some women continued their relations with the German soldiers for political reasons, because they were having good fun or simply because they loved their German boyfriends and planned to marry them. Others tried to stop socializing with the German soldiers and restore their reputation, because they were afraid or could not cope with the persecutions and the social isolation, or because the conflicts of war were brought too close to home when a family member or a friend was arrested or deported, or because they had been convinced that it was wrong to consort with members of the occupying force. However, this was very difficult if the woman had already appeared in public with a German soldier, and therefore was known as a *tyskerpige*. Some of the women who moved to another part of the country succeeded in getting rid of their bad reputation, but for the most part their pasts caught up with them. One young woman who came from a small provincial town, where she had been completely ostracized on account of her relations with German soldiers, tried to start all over again by getting a job in another, nearby and bigger town, and by seeking a new circle of Danish friends. But she was dismissed when someone told the people at her new workplace about her past. It was difficult to wash out the stain and escape the past, and in the days following the liberation she was interned.

Both during and after the occupation, the intimate and sexual nature of the fraternizing often prompted the women to excuse their actions and not to perceive their fraternizations as unpatriotic and political actions. They sought legitimacy in an understanding of emotions as a 'war-free zone', and in the popular saying that 'love has no will'. They believed that they could separate the man from the soldier. A French woman who was interned in Jayat at Charente declared 'that it is not a crime to have had relationships based on love with a German when one has had difficulties with one's husband, and in any case, matters of the heart have nothing to do with politics'.[29] A Danish *tyskerpige* expressed it like this: 'I have never believed that I did anything wrong. I have probably always been under the impression that it depends on what you feel.'[30] The notion that one could disclaim responsibility in the name of love and separate the private and the political spheres tallied in many respects with the contemporary view of women. In any case this view was confirmed to the millions of people who after the war could finally watch *Gone with the Wind* and hear the phrase 'War is men's business, not ladies''. However, if a woman appeared in public with a German soldier, she turned herself into a politicized figure regardless of her motives, as socializing with a German soldier signalled acceptance of the presence of the occupying power.

Even if a woman's intimate relationship with a German soldier was not politically motivated, love and war could indeed prove to be a dangerous and political cocktail. In France relatively few of the cropped women were accused of informing, while this was quite a common accusation against the interned *tyskerpiger* in Denmark.[31] To what extent did these accusations hold water? As regards France we do not know, but an examination of all the trials in which Danish women were sentenced for informing during the occupation reveals that approximately three-quarters of the 400 woman found guilty of informing were *tyskerpiger*.[32] Even if those cases where a charge of informing could not be proved, as well as the unknown numbers of informants who were never revealed, are added, it is fair to suggest that only a negligible minority of the tens of thousands of fraternizing women were informers. On the other hand, a large share of female informants were *tyskerpiger*.

A few *tyskerpiger* served as informers for political or financial reasons, or because they were in an intimate relationship with a German policeman or intelligence officer on whom they had become dependent. They typically lived in a deeply criminalized environment.[33] Other *tyskerpiger* informed on underground people or underground activities, either deliberately or due to thoughtlessness. In March 1944 a 27-year-old domestic help told her German financé that a Danish man possessed a gun. The soldier passed this piece of information on to the Gestapo, and the man in question was arrested. She was punished with four years in prison after the war. In October 1944 the conversation between a 21-year-old *tyskerpige* and a German soldier had serious repercussions. She met him by chance in town and jokingly told him that the Germans were so stupid that they did not notice that resistance men received air-dropped weapons right under their very noses. She had learned this from her brother, who belonged to one of the resistance groups who received air-dropped weapons. The Gestapo followed up on this intelligence and called her in for an interview, to which she did not show up at first. But after having been looked up and threatened, according to her own statement, she denounced her brother, who was then arrested. She received a handsome reward. During the post-war purges, she got off with a relatively light sentence of two years' imprisonment, as the consequences of her denouncement were regarded as negligent.[34]

In most of the cases concerning informers, *tyskerpiger* reported people who had attacked them in some way because of their fraternization with German soldiers, either to the Danish or the German police, and more than half of those *tyskerpiger* who were convicted of informing received a relatively light sentence of less than three years' imprisonment. However, the range of motives, the degree of premeditation and the consequences varied greatly. In the autumn of 1944 a 24-year-old domestic help who dated German soldiers reported her neighbour to the German security police of her own accord, because he had called her a *tyskerludder* (German whore). The neighbour was questioned but escaped any reprisals or a sentence. The woman, on the other hand, received a one-year sentence, as the court found that she ought to have realized that contacting the secret police would expose her neighbour to danger. But the outcome of such denunciations could often be far more serious. In December 1944 a 17-year-old girl was called *tyskerludder* and *feltmadras* by a Danish man. When she ran past some German guards, they stopped her and asked her why she was in such a hurry. She told them what had happened and explained that she was afraid of the Danish man, as he was carrying an axe on his bicycle. The guards then escorted the girl to her home. The following day she was asked to point out the Danish man to the Germans, which she did. He was then arrested and deported to Germany, where he was held in several concentration camps and finally became so ill and broken down that the Red Cross took him back to Denmark in April 1945. On account of these serious consequences, the *tyskerpige* was sentenced to six years' imprisonment. The court found that at this late stage of the war, the girl ought to have understood the potentially serious consequences of her actions.[35]

During the post-war purges, it was the actual damage caused to the victim of the denunciation which determined how severely an informing *tyskerpige* was to be punished. However, the motive as well as the degree of premeditation were also taken into consideration. Especially in minor incidents, this could be almost impossible to determine. In some cases more than an average degree of political awareness was necessary in order to keep clear of dangerous situations. It also took a good deal of courage to withstand the pressure of the occupying force, who demanded that the cropped or assaulted women named the perpetrators. To a large extent the denunciations of the *tyskerpiger* were characterized by being unintentional, incidental and something that sprang out of the situation. On the one hand, this led to relatively mild punishments, but on the other hand it also demonstrates how far fraternizing women could be whirled into situations with disastrous political and personal consequences, not only for the people they informed against, but for the women themselves. Few *tyskerpiger* served as informants, yet love and war could turn out to be a far more dangerous cocktail than many women had imagined.[36]

Intimate relations between the occupiers and the occupied could thus have political consequences. In eastern Europe these relationships had not only a political but also a racial meaning. Relationships between 'superior' Aryans and 'inferior' Slavs challenged the propaganda German soldiers were fed in regard to the local population in these countries. Sexual contact with local women was not only a transgression on the part of the women, but also on the part of the soldiers, who deliberately flouted guidelines of non-fraternization and racial purity. In the light of political collaboration with the German occupiers of Ukrainian, Baltic and other anti-Soviet forces, sexual contacts acquired different overtones and could even be interpreted as expressions of mutual commitment. In general, friendship, flirtation and sexual relations had subversive potential for all sides involved – even though or especially because they were regarded as a private matter by those involved.

But did the sexual fraternizing in itself have any effect on the outcome of the war? According to French historian Fabrice Virgili, this was not the case. He claims that the symbolic meaning of the sexual collaboration was inversely proportional to its actual meaning.[37] In any case it is difficult to assess the large-scale effect the sexual relations had on the course of the war. On the one hand they sweetened the life of the occupying soldiers, on the other any emotional attachment to the occupied people could diminish their loyalty and effectiveness as soldiers. Was the fraternizing a political action in itself? The women did not believe so. Yet, to a large extent those surrounding them did. The local population, the German occupying power and the authorities of the occupied countries treated intimate fraternization as a political question. It depended on the eye of the beholder. Was it the motive or the effect which determined whether an intimate act of fraternization can be characterized as a political act? The interpretations do not follow the same pattern, yet are not mutually exclusive. A *tyskerpige*, *femme à boche*, *shliukh-doiche* and *moffenhoer* was both a private individual and a fraternizing woman. A German soldier was both a private individual and an occupying soldier. Intimate fraternizations were both private relationships and a phenomenon that had a political impact upon the relations between the occupying force and the occupied country.

Regulating Intimate Fraternization

In the occupied regions of eastern Europe and the Soviet Union, the Wehrmacht banned all fraternizations by German soldiers. The ban was in accordance with the Nazi race ideology, which viewed the people in these territories as inferior, and which laid the foundation for the Nazi regime's policy of expansion and extermination. The numbers of children fathered by German soldiers in these eastern regions are unknown. Still, it is a large number that gives sufficient evidence that the soldiers ignored the ban. Different kinds of sources indicate indirectly that fraternization did occur in Soviet territories. In May 1943 it was reported in the Komsomol Department of Propaganda and Agitation that Soviet girls, especially pupils and students, were unreliable and flocking in large numbers to German music and dance halls. A popular partisan song of the time ran 'Young girls smile at the Germans/ young girls have already forgotten about their fine boys.../ young girls have forgotten/ that in their homeland, a burning war is waging/ far from Kharkov, far from the Volga/ hot blood is flowing out of their young men... Like a doll for the Germans you build up your hair/ you put make-up on your face, twirling with your head/ but the falcons do not need your white hands/ your young man walks past with contempt.' And after the war protocols of Komsomol mention numbers of young women who were excluded because they had had intimate relations with German soldiers.[38]

The Italian occupying troops in the Balkans were also subjected to a ban on fraternization in principle. But the Italian army in Greece was nicknamed 'Sagapó' which means 'I love you', and the fact that commanders repeatedly ordered soldiers to avoid familiarity with the local population and were anxious about the soldiers' emotional attachments to and intimate relations with local women demonstrates that the ban was consequently not observed in practice. It became a challenge to the conception of the 'superior Italian race'.[39]

In Denmark, Norway, Holland and Belgium as well as the border areas in eastern and northern France, German troops were allowed to fraternize both socially and sexually with the local women. The reason was that the populations in these areas had the privilege of being considered Aryans and part of the Germanic race. However, within the general framework of the Nazi race ideology, such guidelines for interaction were enforced differently, depending on the influence of the SS and on the particular line of policy in each occupied area.

Compared with the other occupied nations, Denmark was granted an exceptional status, as reflected for instance in the Wehrmacht's adopted line on prostitution in the country. To sustain the fiction that the German occupation was a so-called peace occupation that allowed Denmark to maintain its sovereignty, it was crucial to signal that the Danish laws would be respected as far as possible by the occupying power. Therefore the Wehrmacht chose not to ignore a Danish ban on brothels passed in 1906 and refrained from bringing large number of prostitutes into the country to furnish their own brothels, as was common practice in the other occupied countries. The discovery in one Gestapo headquarters of a 'Dienstbuch für Puttenfrauen' must be considered an exception.[40] In Norway, however, there were German brothels and French prostitutes servicing the German troops, and in the Paris region alone thirty-two brothels had been set up for German soldiers in 1941, while the estimated number of unregistered French prostitutes was between 80,000 and 100,000. In Poland a German police proclamation stated: 'Polish women importuning or soliciting Germans are to be taken to houses of prostitution', and brothels under medical control were established by the occupying power. In occupied Ukraine brothels were partially staffed by willing locals and partially by women who had been arrested and forced into providing sexual services.[41] It seems that the Germans more carefully verified the race of prostitutes than the Italians, who also set up brothels where healthy women could serve the soldiers.[42]

The spread of venereal diseases, which threatens to render soldiers unfit for battle, is a nightmare for any army. Setting up brothels for its troops was the German military's attempt to isolate and regulate prostitution, and thereby also to control the spread of venereal diseases. All over occupied Europe, the number of people with venereal diseases skyrocketed. The exact figures for France are unknown, but the Germans were extremely alarmed by so-called 'clandestine prostitution', which took place in hotels, cafés, bars and in private homes. They therefore demanded that the French police interfere to prevent such 'clandestine prostitution'. At the same time, however, they were reluctant to accept the interference of the French authorities in fraternization between German soldiers and local women, as it was perceived as an offence against German military honour.[43]

The same dilemma faced the Wehrmacht over its cooperation with the local authorities in Denmark to stop the spreading of venereal diseases. On the one hand the Wehrmacht wanted the Danish vice squad to actively fight instances of immoral conduct. On the other, they were extremely reluctant for the police and social authorities to clamp down on fraternization out of resentment of Danish–German relationships, or spurred by a political opposition against the occupying power. In a couple of cities collaboration was terminated entirely, because the Werhmacht criticized the police for being too harsh, rounding up under-aged girls with gonorrhoea, or because the Germans felt that the social authorities were persecuting the *tyskerpiger* by handing them over to the public welfare system.[44] Still, by and large Danish–German collaboration worked, motivated by a common interest in controlling rates of infection. During the occupation the number of people with gonorrhoea nearly quadrupled, while the number cases of syphilis was eight times higher than normal. As in the case of the brothels, the Wehrmacht largely respected common Danish practice and jurisdiction with regard to combating venereal diseases. What they seemed to be concerned about above all was tracing and treating the cases, rather than the potential judicial measures. The German military authorities regularly subjected their soldiers to physical examinations, and if they proved to be infected, they had to report the possible sources of infection to avoid facing disciplinary action. The names of the Danish women thus reported by the soldiers were subsequently passed on to the Danish police or health authorities, which then followed the normal procedure of tracing and treating the cases, and sometimes of penalizing the women in accordance with the law, after which they reported back to the Wehrmacht. The Germans also allowed the Danish authorities to vetoe a proposition that women, who sought the company of German soldiers should be equipped with a special *Ausweis*.[45]

In Norway the local authorities also cooperated with the occupying forces when it came to fighting venereal diseases, but here an altogether tougher line was adopted. In contravention of Norwegian laws and judicial practice, and often at the request of the Germans, raids were systematically conducted on bars and cafés, in parks and dock areas, where Norwegian women would normally meet up with German soldiers. The examination and treatment of the detained women was then left to the Norwegian health services. In 1944, to address the spreading problem of venereal diseases, the Norwegian Nazi authorities (NS) passed a bill which, among other things, made it possible to intern anyone who was considered an infection hazard. In addition a register was set up containing information on approximately 3,000 infected women. After the liberation this register was used for the apprehension and internment of *tyskerpiger*.[46]

Due to the spreading hazard of venereal diseases, occupier and occupied had a common interest in clamping down on immoral conduct, but the parties also appealed to a mutual understanding that any nation must be interested in defending its women's decency and honour. In the autumn of 1940 a Danish clergyman noted that the Germans must try to understand the Danes' ill feelings towards women who went out with German soldiers. He wrote: 'During the occupation by French troops of the Rhineland after the World War, many noble Germans feared for the moral integrity of their young people. There was a widespread anxiety that it would lead to frivolity and unbridled passions, the fruits of which would be bitter. Therefore any brave German will also understand that right-minded Danes are anxious that something similar might happen in Denmark. Surely, all Christian Danes and Germans must share a concern that their respective youths are not ruined by flirtation and frivolousness, fornication and impurity.'[47]

In some Danish cities the collaborative efforts to fight immorality led to the formation of local joint patrols that inspected restaurants, streets and other localities with a bad reputation. The Danish police increased its efforts at monitoring the conduct of under-aged girls in particular, and very often the German military command contributed to the collaboration by banning its soldiers from visiting some of these notorious places. German troops also had codes of conduct, especially in the western and northern parts of the occupied territories and in the first years of the war. The guideline was that the soldiers should seek to gain the confidence of the local population – including the women – through good manners and proper behaviour. The Danish authorities tried to refer to this code of conduct whenever the Wehrmacht complained about the censorious attitude among the Danish police and members of the public towards the girlfriends of German soldiers. Thus, in October 1940, when Danish officials from the Ministry of Foreign Affairs and the Ministry of Justice met high-ranking officers from the German legation to discuss this issue, the Danes referred to a passage in the German soldiers' operational order which read: 'Danish women are to be approached with caution'. This was inserted on Hitler's direct orders, and the Danish officials thought that the German soldiers ought to be more aware of it.[48]

The German military authorities themselves were not always satisfied with the level of discipline exhibited by their troops in the occupied territories. On 31 August 1940 General von Brauchitsch issued an instruction that rules of discipline should be impressed on the troops several times a month. He outlined a number of examples to point out that the soldiers did not maintain a sufficiently reserved attitude to the local population, and especially to the women: 'Soldiers of all grades have been meeting common prostitutes on the street and gone in search of places to eat and behave dishonourably … they have taken such women into hotels reserved for Wehrmacht officers and held orgies that do the greatest prejudice to officers living there.'[49] However, it also happened that the Wehrmacht complained over the loose living of the Danish female population, and it did occasionally arrest women who had behaved indecently while in the company of Germans and raided the homes of women suspected of hosting 'orgies' for German soldiers.[50]

Marriage and War Children

The German authorities had an ambivalent attitude towards the relations between local women and German soldiers. Central to their racial policy as well as their policy of occupation in the northern and western countries was that the German soldiers should be able to socialize freely with the local population. At the same time, the soldiers' fraternization with local women was not only a potential security risk, but also threatened to render the individual soldier unfit for combat because of sexually transmitted diseases or because his loyalty and fighting spirit were weakened by his intimate relations with the potential enemy. The Wehrmacht was not blind to this ambivalence, as was also reflected in the German policy on marriage.

In the Czech Protectorate both marriages between Czechs and Sudeten Germans and marriages between Czechs and Reich Germans were considered a problem for the German authorities. Czech–Sudeten German couples made it impossible to distinguish clearly between the two ethnic groups, which in the long term hindered the Nazi goal of Germanization. Marriages of Czech Protectorate citizens, mostly women, and Reich-German Germans, who were part of the military or civil occupying forces and administration, were in particular condemned by both sides. The German partners were accused of undermining official policy and tarnishing German honour. Later, after the German capitulation, the Czech wives of both Sudeten Germans and Reich Germans were considered as traitors and were subjected to public revenge and brutal lynching. However, it seems that demographic and rational arguments prevailed over extreme nationalism, and German mothers with their children were allowed to stay in Czechoslovakia although they had to undergo a thorough examination of their political reliability, apply for Czechoslovak citizenship and were often confronted to humiliating procedures.[51]

In general the German attitude towards marriage between their own soldiers and foreign women was ambiguous and marked by disagreements. The Wehrmacht frowned upon German soldiers who married civilians from the occupied countries, while the SS was concerned with the racial issues involved. For racial reasons a general prohibition of 28 February 1941 preventing German soldiers from marrying foreigners was partly repealed by Hitler, so that it no longer applied in Denmark, Norway and Holland. The repeal was carried out partly because the Norwegian Viskun Quisling had protested against this deeply offensive prohibition, but also because the Norwegian branch of the SS, lead by Terboven, had actively been campaigning for a repeal.[52] However, the Wehrmacht continued to pursue a selective and guarded marital policy based on race, and so it was regarded as a criminal offence for German soldiers to marry without first having obtained a special permit.[53] This permit was issued on the basis of a thorough profiling of the Danish, Norwegian or Dutch women, something which the Danish authorities refused to take part in.[54] They did, however, provide other necessary pieces of information concerning the woman's political background, any previous convictions and her so-called 'morals and reputation'.[55] In Norway it was the *Amtslegen* at the Reichskommissariat in Oslo who issued these certificates of marital eligibility, and in 1942 it was decided that the division of the German Nazi Party in Norway had to be consulted in connection with the political assessment of the woman. The applications were all submitted to Hitler for his final approval.[56]

In the course of 1942 Hitler's decree of 28 February 1941 was tightened, and the different army headquarters issued a stern appeal to German soldiers not to marry women from the occupied countries. It was pointed out that marriage and reproduction only desirable within the German people. Even Nordic women of the so-called Germanic type were not considered part of the German extended family, partly due to their insufficient knowledge of German history and culture. Moreover, the soldiers were reminded that 'a hundred thousand fresh German maidens, together with, sadly, a similar number of young war widows, are waiting in the homeland for the return of our soldiers'. It was made clear that getting married was not a private matter, but played a part in the overall struggle of the entire German people.[57] Furthermore, the Wehrmacht allowed these mixed couples to be married only by German military officials. Local authorities were not permitted to wed couples. In Norway additional provisions were issued, which among other things required that the Norwegian woman should be intellectually equal to her German husband, and that women who were of Saami descent, ill or considered immoral had to be rejected.[58]

There are no certain numbers of how many Danish and Norwegian women married German soldiers during the war, although the Danish authorities tried hard to register these mixed marriages centrally. Indications are nevertheless that there were very few of these marriages. Uneven evidence suggests that in all likelihood there were no more than 400 or 500 Norwegian–German marriages and even fewer Danish–German ones. However, a far greater number of people wanted to get married, particularly if they had had a child together. Thus, approximately 40 per cent of the Norwegian mothers applied for a permit to get married to the German soldier during the first years of the war.[59] However, there were many practical and bureaucratic obstacles that could prolong the process of obtaining approval for several years: countless documents, certificates and declarations had to be procured, and the German soldier had to certify that he could support and provide a home for his wife in Germany after their marriage. It became increasingly difficult to meet this demand, and during the last years of the war it not only seemed less tempting to move to Germany, but many German soldiers were also killed before they could get married. The precondition for getting a marriage permit was that the woman moved to Germany. Not all women followed this rule, but in August 1944 Hitler ordered all German women and children to be sent home to Germany. The order included Norwegian women who had become German subjects by marrying German soldiers. They were sent to Germany on board the ship *Monte Rosa*, under orders to look up the families of their German husbands, with whom they were then supposed to live. Many of them did not reach their destination, however, or found that the address given to them was now a heap of rubble. By the beginning of 1945 conditions in Germany had become so chaotic that the 'repatriation' was in effect called off.[60]

Between the end of the war and 1947, when the last Germans were sent home, thousands of Norwegian women married German soldiers, a sign of the serious nature of the relationships. In Denmark the number of women who married German soldiers was lower, as it was very difficult for them to obtain a marriage permit and to maintain the connection with the German soldier. After the liberation of Denmark relations between German soldiers and Danish women, which had been tolerated during the occupation, were criminalized. During the last months of the war more than 200,000 German civilian refugees poured into the country, where they were segregated from the Danish population in internment camps and kept under strict surveillance. The Danish authorities introduced a ban on fraternization, which due to the overrepresentation of women among the refugees was most often violated by Danish men. However, there were also women who continued to socialize with German soldiers in spite of this ban. It is difficult to assess how consistently the ban on fraternization was enforced, but the sanctions varied from ordering the delinquents to stay away from Germans to imposing fines or suspended prison sentences.[61]

Both in Norway and in Denmark the nationality laws were tightened after the war, in order to target the women who had married their German boyfriends. The laws were clearly discriminatory, as they did not affect men who had married German women. The amendments were applied retroactively so that women who had married German soldiers after 9 April 1940 were stripped of their citizenship, if and when they left their native countries. In this way they became German subjects retroactively when they married German soldiers, and the Norwegian authorities could expel to Germany women who had married German soldiers. Although there were regional differences in practice, the women were for the most part gathered in internment camps along with their children and sent to Germany, even though the

Allies disapproved of this measure and despite reports of the appalling conditions in Germany.[62] In Denmark the practice was much more lenient. Here it was possible for the women to retain their right of citizenship if they applied within a short time limit, and the amendment was repealed by the end of 1948. Very few Danish women who had married German soldiers were interned; the majority of them received a residence and entry permit, unless they had worked for the Germans or carried out Nazi activities.[63] However, during the first years of the war Danish women were only permitted to marry German men if they were able to establish in advance that they would leave the country together with their husbands.[64] In Norway the stringent regulations were only gradually relaxed. In the first two years after the war, approximately one-third of the applications from Norwegian women who were married to Germans and now wished to return to their native country were granted, on the condition that their Norwegian families would cover their travel expenses and support them upon their arrival. According to a new law of 1950, the women could regain their lost citizenship on the condition that they moved back to Norway before the end of 1955, which in effect meant that they would have to break with their families in Germany, as their husbands would not be granted permission to stay in Norway. The situation was worse for those women who ended up in the eastern zone, which was later to become East Germany. Here the conditions were not only harsher, but the women also had to endure having no contact with their Norwegian families until the end of the Cold War. During the late 1980s a critical public debate in Norway paved the way for an amendment, which was passed in 1989 and made it possible for women who had married 'citizens of the enemy state' to regain their lost citizenship.[65]

The children of German soldiers in the occupied countries soon caught the eye of the Nazi leaders. Due to the racial policy some children were more interesting than others. The legal basis and procedures for determining paternity, as well as the issue of the mothers' and their children's entitlement to health care and social care, were part of the Nazi racial and population policies. However, the Wehrmacht also had to take into consideration other aspects of the occupation arrangements.

It was not long before the women in the occupied countries filed the first paternity suits against German soldiers. In Norway it was as early as July 1940, and in Denmark November 1940. As the soldiers had an extraterritorial status, the suits filed against them could not be settled according to the laws of the occupied countries, or in their courts. It was not until 28 July 1942 that Hitler issued 'a decree concerning the care of children fathered by members of the Wehrmacht in occupied countries', which formed the basis of an actual regulation of such cases. Up until then more or less informal agreements were made and different solutions were tried out in an atmosphere of discord between the Wehrmacht, the SS, and the occupying and local authorities in the occupied countries. At first the decree only included Norway and Holland, where there were good possibilities 'of preserving and promoting racially valuable German stock', as noted in §1.[66] According to the decree, expectant mothers were to be offered maintenance in the months prior to giving birth, as well as board and lodging at a maternity home. If the mothers consented, their children could then be placed in orphanages where they would also receive maintenance. In addition, mothers were offered a job if they so wished. Since 1933 similar initiatives had been taken in Germany in order to 'racially secure Germanic blood'. The two organizations responsible for carrying out the Nazi population policy in Germany eventually also supervised the implementation of the policy in the occupied countries. One of them was called Hilfwerk Mutter und Kind and had been founded by the party organization Nationalsozialistische Volkswohlfahrt (NSV). The other organization was Lebensborn Eintragener Verein, which was founded a year later than Hilfwerk Mutter und Kind, under the leadership of Himmler. As was the case in Germany, the two organizations competed in carrying out the work concerning the racial and population policies in the occupied countries.

Besides Germany, Norway was the only country in which the Lebensborn had full control of the cases concerning children fathered by German soldiers. The Lebensborn assumed full financial responsibility for approximately 8,000 out of the estimated 10,000–12,000 children fathered by German soldiers. The organization was able to ensure that the mothers and their children had a place to stay, due to an extensive network of German mother-and-baby homes and orphanages. After Himmler had visited Oslo several times and pronounced himself strongly in favour of the project, Reich Commissioner Terboven handed over the responsibility to a subdivision of the Lebensborn. The Lebensborn project was launched in Norway accompanied by the SS catch phrase: 'after the victory on the battlefield follows the victory in the cradle'. The Norwegian branch of Lebensborn was a large organization, with at least 300 employees in the last years of the war and an annual budget almost as large as that of the Norwegian police. Twelve Lebensborn homes, including maternity homes, mother-and-baby homes and orphanages, were founded, capable of housing several hundred mothers and children. Since these homes could not meet the entire demand, the organization had to buy places in similar Norwegian homes. Even though Norwegian mothers had no legal right to claim financial support, the German authorities granted substantial amounts of money to them and their children. Depending on the mothers' financial situation, they might receive a monthly allowance, as well as subsistence if they lost their ability to work during pregnancy. They might be entitled to have their travelling expenses covered, as well as expenses for delivery, medical examinations, medicine and baby equipment. Lebensborn worked hard at determining paternity. During the war the organization succeeded in doing so in 2,930 cases, and many German soldiers admitted voluntarily that they were the fathers. For the entire war there was disagreement between the German authorities and the Norwegian NS authorities as to whether the children were to be regarded as German or Norwegian. If the children were born out of wedlock, as most of them were, they remained Norwegian citizens. But the Nazis viewed them as 'pro-German outposts within the Norwegian people'.[67]

Much of the Lebensborn's work resembled genuine welfare work, yet their overall objective was to boost the population of Nordic peoples in response to German racial policy. All mothers and fathers were subjected to a racial assessment, and it was also the intended aim to assess their children on a regular basis. Parents had to furnish information about their ancestors, while their own appearance and character were evaluated; and they were photographed, questioned about their political beliefs, and so on. Very few among them were rejected, such as Saami women, but only the 'best' were admitted into one of the Lebensborn homes. During and after the occupation, there were many rumours that the Lebensborn really served as breeding organizations for pure-bred members of the SS. These rumours were rooted in Nazi racial ideology and in Himmler's demented schemes. But overall the Lebensborn in Norway functioned primarily as a German organization that saw to the welfare and care of Norwegian women and their children fathered by German soldiers.[68]

In the Netherlands, which was also included in Hitler's decree of 28 July 1942, Reich Commissioner Seyss-Inquart limited the influence of the SS with the help of the Nazi Party. Here it was the German party organization the NSV which was given responsibility for the care of the German soldiers' children. The current estimate of Dutch–German children born during the war is 12,000–16,000. The organization opened several mother-and-baby homes and was also responsible for determining – according to Nazi racial policy – who were the most eligible to participate in the welfare programme.[69] To discourage racially acceptable unmarried pregnant women from having abortions they were offered places in NSV homes, but the organization did not hesitate to take over children for adoption. Because of the eugenic policy most children ended up in a NSV children's home in the Netherlands or Germany.[70]

If no Nazi organization took responsibility for the social care of the 7,000–8,000 children fathered by German soldiers in Denmark, it was not because the Danes were not important to the Nazis from a racial perspective. Rather it was because Denmark's sovereignty was formally upheld and its democratic institutions allowed to operate under the special status Denmark enjoyed among the occupied countries.[71] The plenipotentiary of the Reich in Denmark, Werner Best, warned the High Command in Berlin against including Denmark in the decree on racial policies of 28 July 1942, as it would reduce the country to an occupied territory like Norway and Holland. After the Danish government resigned in August 1943, the influence of the SS was strengthened, and in January 1944 Himmler announced that a subdivision of the Lebensborn was to be established in Denmark. However, the work progressed slowly, and a Lebensborn maternity home for Danish women was opened in Copenhagen only a few days before the German capitulation in May 1945.[72] In this way the German authorities ended up only dealing with Danish–German paternity suits and disbursing alimony. The paternity suits were at first handled by a conciliation board, but as the suits accumulated, due to a considerable number of the German soldiers not accepting paternity voluntarily, the task was assigned to an actual German court of law. The German authorities imposed their will that the legal basis of the paternity suits should be German, which placed the women and children in a weak position.[73]

'We have no racial policy interest in the French', Hitler stated in the summer of 1941, when for the first time he officially took a position on German soldiers' children in the occupied territories.[74] Neither in France nor in Belgium were any of the Nazi organizations responsible for the welfare work aimed at children fathered by German soldiers and their mothers set up. In the spring of 1941 the Commander of the German armed forces in France suggested that a German civil court be set up in the occupied part of France to settle those paternity suits where French mothers claimed that German soldiers had fathered their children. However, this proposition came to nothing, nor did Reich Health Leader Leonardo Conti's appeal to Himmler, only a few days before the German capitulation in May 1945, to let the Lebensborn take responsibility for the many children of Franco-German relationships, so that they would not be lost to the Reich. In September 1943 the Commander of the German armed forces in Belgium and in northern France suggested that Hitler's decree of 28 July 1942 be extended to include these territories. The proposal was postponed by Himmler, who was opposed to the idea that the racial examinations of the Flemish and Walloon mothers would be carried out by the German armed forces, so that by D-day the conflict of authority had not been resolved.[75]

It was part of the Nazi leaders' plans to Germanize as many as possible of the children 'of pure blood' in the occupied eastern territories. However, the conflict of authority between the SS and Lebensborn, on the one hand, and the Nazi Party and NSV, on the other, delayed the realization of these plans. It was not until October 1943 that a decree was issued by the Führer on 'the care of illegitimate children by Germans in the occupied eastern territories', which dictated how these children were to be registered and how they were to be examined racially. The Reich government was to shoulder the costs of the racially valuable children, and if they were deemed worthy of Germanization, they were to be brought to Germany. That said, the grand scheme and the intricate procedures were never carried out before the advance of the Red Army, which then made a realization impossible.[76]

The Lebensborn and NSV were not the only organizations to which women who were pregnant with a child fathered by a German soldier could apply for support. State and semi-state organizations, private charitable organizations and the Catholic Church also offered help to the woman and her child. But the double shame of bearing an illegitimate child of a German soldier could be a heavy burden to carry. In France the Vichy regime enacted a new law at the end of 1941 which permitted women to give birth anonymously, and after the war the French authorities encouraged returning deportees, refugees and POWs to forgive their adulterous wife and acknowledge paternity of the children of German soldiers. No policy of discrimination or ostracism of children fathered by German soldiers seems to have been carried out by the authorities in post-war France, but it was not unusual for the children to suffer poor treatment in some families and local communities.[77]

After the liberation the authorities in Norway and Denmark had to determine what should be done with the children fathered by German soldiers. In Norway a commission called the 'Krigsbarnsutvalget' debated whether the mothers and children should be sent to Germany. It was decided that the children were Norway's responsibility, yet this decision involved an ambivalent view of the mental state of the mothers and children and was in many respects eugenically inspired. For instance, in the report of the commission the head of one social institution said 'As far as I know, there have been no official examinations of the girls who fraternized with the German soldiers, but based on general experience there certainly seems to be a disproportionate number among them who are backward or anti-social psychopaths – mentally deranged girls even... These are mental defects, which for the most part are hereditary, and there is a certain risk that this hereditary disposition will be reflected in the offspring.'[78] Many of the initiatives proposed by the Norwegian Krigbarnsutvalget – for instance that clergymen had the right to refuse the children certain German names – were founded on a wish to avoid the social stigmatization of the children. To some extent, it was also this consideration which prompted the Norwegian authorities to shelve a large number of the paternity suits that had not been settled during the war.

As in Norway, it was also suggested in Denmark that the children of mixed parentage should be sent to Germany. 'Let Germany keep its "heroic offspring"', was a headline in the leading underground newssheet *De Frie Danskere* (The Free Danes), which further suggested that this 'spawn of dragons' should be sent to Germany, so that 'from its tender years it could get used to life in the snake pit'.[79] This proposal was brought up in the Ministry of Justice, but was never given any serious consideration.[80] Nevertheless, the proposal and the agitation clearly reveal the condemnation with which the German children were met. In the first years after the war, the public was concerned not only with the financial burden constituted by the children, but also with the possibility that the children might later be drawn towards their Nazi German fathers. Other people believed that the children were genetically conditioned for harbouring German, and even Nazi, sentiments. To an unknown degree, children fathered by German soldiers were bullied, humiliated and discriminated against.[81] This was recently officially acknowledged in Norway, when in his millennial New Year's address Prime Minister Bondevik offered an apology to the Norwegian children fathered by German soldiers for the way in which many of them had been treated since the war and in 2005 the Norwegian Parliament agreed a new law to compensate the hardest hit.

In Denmark, too, the authorities broke the law in choosing not to deal adequately with establishing the paternity of children allegedly fathered by German soldiers.[82] Recently, when these children, now adults, have founded organizations in both Norway and Denmark, it has come to light that they believe that the authorities, by not acting in this matter, set aside the interests of the children. Many of them say that they have always felt a great need to know more about their biological fathers, whose identities were often kept secret by their mothers. In this way the mothers' shame and fear of social condemnation have been passed on to the children, who have often experienced a sense of guilt at having been born, leading to considerable identity and welfare problems. Much indicates that the line taken with these children of war was harder in Norway than in Denmark. This difference may perhaps be ascribed to the extensive activities and unique work of the Lebensborn in the country.

Women's Bodies as Combat Zones

The female body and sexuality represented a question of honour and a combat zone between the occupiers and the occupied. The particular sensitivity of the gender issue showed in the fact that many of the conflicts arising between local men and German soldiers grew out of the intimate fraternizations. A French police commissioner reported in 1941 that fights over women between Frenchmen and German soldiers disturbed public order 'because of the mingling of males and females and above all because of the abuse of alcohol'.[83] In Denmark the occupation had only lasted a few days when the Danish police had to intervene in clashes between Danes and German soldiers over a *tyskerpige*. In some cases the clashes were nothing but common street brawls, but in others they were caused by incidents where waiters had refused to serve, or people were shouting and spitting at girls who were accompanied by one or more German soldiers.

The Germans were sensitive to such conflicts, as they saw them as indicators of the general attitude towards the occupying forces. If local people or the local authorities harassed or assaulted women who fraternized with the soldiers, the Germans saw it as an insult against the Wehrmacht. In Denmark the Wehrmacht demanded that individuals who had bothered a *tyskerpige* should be punished more severely than the Danish laws dictated, but at the same time they were very critical of the Danish authorities when they interfered in intimate fraternizations and the conflicts they caused. The role played by the Danish police was a particularly sensitive issue, and very often any dissatisfaction voiced by the Germans over the conduct of the police in such cases led to serious crises in the relationship between local chief constables and German kommandants. Thus, on several occasions the Danish handling of intimate fraternizing between German soldiers and local women was discussed at the highest political level. The first time this happened was as early as 3 May 1940, when the German envoy Renthe-Fink complained over the conduct of the Danish population and police.[84]

It was also a question of honour. 'We are the victors! You have been beaten! The women, even the children, of your country are no longer yours! Our soldiers have the right to have fun, and if you do anything the slight the honour of the German army you will be arrested,' the *Kreiskommandant* of Chinon told a French examining magistrate during a case where the local authorities sought to interfere with what they viewed as an 'incitation of minors to debauchery'.[85] The persecution of German soldiers' girlfriends was not just defamatory against the occupying power. The soldiers also felt that it was an insult against their own personal honour, when their girlfriends were subjected to verbal abuse and various forms of physical harassment. It was considered especially degrading when the harassments took the form of unmistakable symbolic attacks on the girls' moral propriety. After being in a fight with a local man who had insulted his Danish girlfriend by calling her a *tyskerludder*, a German soldier explained that he saw it as an attack on his honour and a challenge to his 'gentlemanly duties'.[86] A closer examination of the various reactions that intimate fraternizations provoked reveals that it was not only the Germans who regarded the women's sexuality as a constituent force in the masculine, local as well as national sense of honour. Female sexuality constituted not merely a combat zone between the occupiers and the occupied; within the occupied cultures it also represented an internal battleground between those who strove for accommodation and collaboration, on the one hand, and those who supported or engaged in resistance, on the other.

After the liberation the general attitude towards women who had been dating German soldiers was markedly negative. But during the occupation responses had been more varied, not least in the first couple of years. Reactions ranged from acceptance to cutting off the women's hair, and within this range of behaviour the women could be met with anything from social isolation and condemnation to illegal propaganda and other types of harassment. In the Soviet territory actions could go further, however, especially if the girl in question was considered to have betrayed partisans or local Communists. It was also by no means always men who led the charge against 'loose' women. Partisan girl Tatiana Logunova recounted in an assembly in Moscow how she cold-bloodedly shot a girl living with a German officer. In the later stages of the war partisan girls were known to have written threatening letters to their former friends, now involved with Germans, warning them to change sides before it was too late.[87] Moreover, in the east women were not only at risk from the society they were seen to have betrayed, but also from those whom they had served. A description of the last days of occupation in Kiev tells that among the last gassed corpses thrown into the ravine at Babi Yar were 100 naked young women from a brothel.[88] The Germans were not to relinquish their conquests – their prostitutes were destroyed like the other valuables they had to leave behind.

In all the occupied countries it seems that women's intimate fraternizing with German soldiers was condemned from the very beginning. Even if they were living in families or local communities where the consensus was to adapt to the presence of the occupying power, it would not take long before they would have to realize that there were other elements of society which took exception to their actions. In the course of the liberation the methods of punishment and the inherent symbolism of the various acts of condemnation were strikingly similar all over Europe, just as cropping incidents peaked everywhere at this stage. Any regional and national differences in the pattern of behaviour can primarily be accounted for in terms of the intensity of the harassments and persecutions that took place during the occupation.

Social isolation – 'the cold-shoulder policy' as the Danes called it, or 'the ice front' for Norwegians – was the least dangerous method of showing contempt for local women's intimate fraternizations with Germans. Even so, it could be very effective and unpleasant. One Danish woman recalled: 'Gradually I became more and more isolated from the people in town, and the atmosphere became more and more tense and unpleasant. In my school the rumour quickly spread that my girlfriend and I were going out with German soldiers. We were frozen out. My girlfriend could not stand it, so she began to stay away from school and was allowed to do so. I managed to stick it out, although I became completely isolated. No one would sit next to me in class, no one would talk to me or have anything to do with me at all. In a sneaky way, the teachers were also in on it.'[89] It is fair to assume that this social strategy was the most widespread one, although we primarily find documentation for it in personal memoirs. Other ways of harassing these *tyskerpiger*, *moffenhoer*, *shliukh-doiche* and *femmes à boche* during the occupation were mentioned in reports monitoring public feeling in the occupied territories. Norwegian reports to the exile authorities in London and Sweden spoke of a widespread indignation at women who consorted with the German troops. However, as mentioned earlier, such reports were far from reliable, as they often served specific purposes of propaganda. Acts of harassment that were reported or intercepted by the German or the local authorities can be traced in the archives. Numbers are difficult to determine but were certainly high. Even in Denmark, where all episodes had to be reported to, and then examined by, a special department of the public prosecutor, which served as a link between the Danish police and the German military, the archive material only shows us the tip of the iceberg. A typical pattern of reaction when local women were seen fraternizing with German soldiers would be to shout profanities or spit at them, push them, refuse to serve them in tearooms or restaurants, send lampoons or threatening letters, instigate rumours and list their names in public. Most incidents took place in public places, when people saw women accompanied by soldiers, or ran into women that they knew were going out with soldiers. Systematic persecutions also occurred in schools and workplaces. Danish sources show that the extent of the persecutions of *tyskerpiger* varied greatly from region to region. Not surprisingly, cities with a large concentration of German soldiers were at the top of the list, but the general level of conflict locally also played a role.[90]

Cutting off the women's hair was the most obvious sign of hostility to sexual fraternization. Both in Norway and Denmark the first *tyskerpiger* were subjected to this kind of punishment at a very early stage of the occupation, even before the underground newssheets began to agitate in favour of such actions.[91] The order of events was apparently different in France. In *Conseils à l'occupé*, published in July 1940, the French socialist Jean Texcier advocated the corporal punishment of women who were dating German soldiers.[92] His plea was soon followed by several underground newssheets which published instructions on how to brand the women and shave their heads. In February 1942 *Défense de la France* reprinted the following text from July 1941: 'You so-called French women who have given your bodies to Germans, will have your heads shaved and you will have a notice put on your backs: "Sold to the enemy"'. You too, you unworthy creatures who flirt with the Germans, will have your head shaved and you will be whipped, and on all your foreheads the swastika will be branded with a red hot iron.'[93] According to the French historian Fabrice Virgili, the first cropping incident was recorded in June 1943, and only after that did the practice become widespread throughout France. Except for Brittany, all incidents occurred in previously non-occupied zones, where there was a hostile attitude towards collaborators as well as the occupying power. The number of cropping incidents rose concurrently with the intensification of the military fighting, and less than one-tenth of these acts of persecution took place while France was still occupied.[94] But as Simon Kitson has shown, French women fraternizing with men of the Axis Powers in Algeria were shorn as early as in 1941. These cropping incidents were initiated not by the resistance but by the Vichy authorities, ostensibly to prevent espionage.[95]

Although the first cropping incidents in Norway occurred in the early stages of the occupation, this did not mean that it became a widespread form of punishment. According to two Norwegian historians, Dag Ellingsen and Kåre Olsen, during the war such actions amounted to sporadic incidents, being on a smaller scale than in Denmark.[96] It was only when the Germans withdrew from the eastern Finmark region in the autumn of 1944 that the phenomenon escalated. However, it was not so much the local population, but rather the Norwegian troops who after their arrival began to shave the heads of *tyskertøse*. In this particular region, where the German occupying forces had far outnumbered the local population, people had largely adapted to the circumstances and shown a considerable tolerance towards fraternization with the German soldiers. These Norwegians also felt that their own troops, once they arrived on the scene, treated them poorly and reacted by composing lampoons when the Norwegian soldiers began to have intimate relations with the women they themselves had shaved in punishment. The comparatively sparse evidence we have of cropping incidents taking place during the occupation is normally explained in terms of the widespread fear of German reprisals. In this connection, it is also worth noting that the harsh condemnations of the *tyskerpiger* issued by the underground press, as well as in the radio broadcasts of the exile government over the BBC, did not call on people to seize these girls and cut off their hair while the German forces were still in the country. Instead, they were a rallying cry preparing for a confrontation once the war was over. Toralv Øksnevad, known as 'the voice from London', noted in a broadcast of May 1941: 'Given the circumstances, severe reprisals from the Norwegian camp are impossible as long as the Germans rule in the country. But those women who do not spurn the Germans will pay a terrible price for the rest of their lives.'[97]

In Norway and France the brutality and scale of the cropping incidents peaked in the period of the liberation. In Denmark, however, such incidents began earlier, notably during the August revolt in 1943, when the government that had cooperated with the Germans was dissolved, and again later in connection with the spontaneous general strikes in the summer of 1944. Ending the official policy of cooperation, the August revolt was really a domestic political confrontation that reflected a turn of the tide in public opinion and heralded the transition from a line of collaboration to one of resistance. Strikes and street fights were aimed not only at the German occupiers but also at collaborators and the general policy of cooperation. Thus the *tyskerpiger* were among the collaborators targeted on the streets and cutting off their hair became an integral part of the revolt in most of the cities. A close analysis of the August revolt reveals that the confrontations targeting fraternizing women fulfilled various purposes in the course of the revolt. In many places the outbreak of strikes and insurrections was the direct result of an intensified and illegal propaganda that *tyskerpiger* be sacked and removed from public places. In some cities the sheer number and brutality of the cropping incidents helped the conflict to gather momentum, while elsewhere, as the revolt began to subside, these actions served as channels for people's pent-up anger, fulfilling their need to find scapegoats. Unlike the scattered incidents that occurred during and after the occupation in general, the cropping actions conducted in the course of the August revolt took place mainly in broad daylight, near the women's homes or workplaces, and with the attendance or participation of large crowds. It was mainly young men who wielded the scissors, but they were acting in a general atmosphere of acceptance, which had been built up by the underground press in the months leading up to the revolt. Initially the leading representatives of the underground movement, including the Communists, were split over the issue of such persecutions, but during the August revolt they refrained from raising any criticism, as they were quick to see the mobilizing and radicalizing effect of the cropping incidents and street riots. Some thought that the anger and rebelliousness could be used more constructively, but at the same time they were not blind to the explosive cocktail of sentiments and motives, national as well as personal, which were partly fuelled by notions of gender and sexual morality and gave rise to the cropping actions.[98] On 26 August the influential underground newssheet *Frit Danmark* (A Free Denmark) gave a severe reprimand to those who had second thoughts about the methods used during the revolt: 'The initial fever of expectation has abated. "Common sense" is returning, and what do we see? "Good" patriotic men, wearing badges to show their allegiance to the King, are beginning to have misgivings about the broken windows and crop-haired "feltmadrasser" graced with swastikas. Free us from this forlorn pity.'

If the proportion of women who had their heads shaved during the occupation was much larger in Denmark than in Norway and France, it is largely due to the two revolts. But apart from that, the cropping of hair still seems to have been a more widespread form of punishment in Denmark than in Norway and France.

Pinpointing the possible causes of this difference in behaviour is not very easy. Illegal propaganda clearly had a major impact on public feeling, and many of the underground newssheets explicitly encouraged the cropping of *tyskerpiger*. Another possible explanation may be that the German reprisals were generally on a much smaller scale than in other occupied countries. The policy of collaboration and efforts to keep the jurisdiction in Danish hands meant that the Danish police and judicial system made an effort to adapt to German interests, resulting mainly in a more severe and randomized practice of prosecution. It was not until after the August revolt in 1943 that it became truly perilous for Danish citizens to harass the girlfriends of German soldiers, as the German security police arrested more and more people on their own accord and court-martialled them. Following the dissolution of the Danish police corps in September 1944, prosecuting incidents of harassment against *tyskerpiger* became an exclusively German concern. In the first years of the occupation even the most brutal cropping incidents would get the assailants no more than a couple of months in prison in accordance with Danish jurisdiction, whereas the sentences passed at a German court-martial could be up to two years of deportation to a German prison.[99]

What codes of conduct were being breached by the women who fraternized intimately with German soldiers, and why were they harassed and shorn? In the eyes of the surrounding community the intimate and sexual nature of the fraternizations seems to have constituted an aggravating rather than a mitigating circumstance. In France, however, it was quite common to exhibit a certain amount of lenience towards prostitution, and, as one newspaper noted, people distinguished between 'prostitution of the soul' and 'prostitution of the body'. Sanctions were primarily aimed at those who were seen to prostitute their soul, as they were considered valid members of the community and were expected to submit to the normal codes of conduct. Jean Texcier made a clear distinction between what was to be expected of prostitutes, on the one hand, and of 'honest women' on the other: 'If you see a girl having a business conversation with one of [the Germans], do not take offence. He will only get what he pays for, and his money is worthless. And remind yourself that three-quarters of French men would not be seen with this woman anyway.'[100] But this picture was not unequivocal. While the professional nature of prostitution was seen by some as proof of the absence of emotional engagement, others felt that the frequent sexual contact with German soldiers legitimized punishing the prostitutes by cutting off their hair.[101]

The extent to which these women's behaviour was seen as a provocation seems to have depended on how public a show they made of their fraternizations. Women who were seen consorting with German soldiers in public were more exposed to harassment and persecution than women who were being more discreet. It was considered a treacherous acceptance of the situation to amuse oneself, for instance by going out dancing or eating at restaurants, with members of the occupying power, which was responsible for everyday hardships such as the scarcity of goods, forced labour, deportations and persecution. It could be perceived as an opting out of the community of people who experienced the occupation as a time ridden by anxiety, oppression, deprivation and suffering. It was also a source of irritation and envy to those around them if such women gained access to sought-after goods, especially if they flaunted these privileges, thereby challenging the normal social order in the community. Earnings made from prostitution were considered more acceptable than the material benefits a woman could gain by consorting with the Germans. In France, accusing the women of being schemers who sought the company of Germans to get access to material goods seems to have been a more widespread phenomenon than in Denmark and Norway, perhaps because the everyday life in France was more deeply affected by the occupation. Women who consorted with Germans because they were socially disadvantaged and lacked the support of a well-to-do family were especially vulnerable to condemnation and persecution, at least during the occupation. After the liberation, however, other social issues could explain the targeting of specific women. Was a woman more likely to be accepted if she were married or engaged to a German soldier? And what if she had a child? The picture is far from conclusive. Some people reacted primarily against what they saw as loose and thoughtless behaviour, while others regarded looseness as a rather innocent offence compared to the commitment of those women who had married representatives of the occupying power. In their own ways both reckless flings and serious relationships could be perceived as potential security risks. Others were primarily outraged by what they saw as a breach of sexual morals, so that while some targeted their anger at those women who had had children with German soldiers, others were more concerned with the question of whether the children had been born outside of marriage. In any case, there is nothing to suggest that the mothers were spared in the acts of retribution.

From a comprehensive sample of police reports it is possible to form an impression of the explanations typically given by Danish men – the assailants were almost exclusively males – as to why they had harassed, assaulted and cut off the hair of *tyskerpiger* during the occupation. Some explained that 'their national pride had been hurt' by the fraternizations of the *tyskerpiger*, but mostly they were provoked by the women's amoral and indecent behaviour. Explanations such as 'she had behaved in a sexually provocative manner' and 'the way the girls were clinging to the soldiers was suggestive', were common. One assailant explained that he had been hurt by a *tyskerpige* because 'her behaviour had been impudent and provocative', and the neighbours of a woman who had taken advantage of her husband's absence and cheated on him with a German soldier were so outraged that they cut off her hair. It was, however, 'not especially because of her association with German soldiers'. Jealousy and anger at being 'rejected in favour of a German soldier' was also one of the reasons given for cutting off the women's hair. A large group of young men explained that they had attacked two young women from their own town, because 'it was sad that several of the young girls went out with the German soldiers as there weren't that many girls in town'.[102] Such statements given by some of the assailants reveal that the cropping incidents were generally motivated by a mixture of jealousy, a wounded national pride and moral outrage at the women's sexual escapades.

Such sentiments were also voiced in the illegal propaganda and can be gleaned from the common nicknames given to fraternizing women in all the occupied countries. In *Défense de la France* they were described as 'unworthy creatures' who had given 'their bodies to the Germans', and a Norwegian illegal paper considered the *tyskertøse* as 'a dirty spot on the name of Norway'. They were immoral and perverse and had 'lost their right to exist'.[103] In Denmark it was common practice in local underground newssheets to publish lists of the *tyskerpiger* living in the area. With headlines such as 'Blacklisted', 'Camp Beds' and 'The Pillory', the papers revealed their names and addresses and suggested isolating them socially or cutting off their hair. The papers were more preoccupied with the sexual behaviour than with the potential security risk of their fraternization. In June 1942 the widely distributed and well-reputed illegal newssheet *Frit Danmark* (A Free Denmark) carried an article that portrayed the *tyskerpiger* as stupid bitches and miserable creatures of low moral standards. They and their 'brood of serpents' were considered a source of both physical and moral infection in society, and were identified with bestial and shameless creatures. The poem 'Hetærer' (Hetaera) was distributed in printed, duplicated and handwritten copies all over the country and sums up the symbolic content of the showdown. It claimed that the intimate fraternizations of the women constituted a shameless open exhibition of sexuality, which offended national pride: 'Women, you who give your favours to a stranger betray your country with no shame. You who shamelessly display your heat, you are a threat to our honour.'

Why cutting off hair became the chosen method of punishment was never explained directly by the assailants or in the illegal propaganda. Apparently it was self-evident that this should be the penalty for engaging in a sexual relationship with a soldier of the enemy. The method was not thought up for the occasion, as more and more countries in Europe were occupied by Nazi Germany, but neither did it stem from a deep-rooted cultural tradition. Over the centuries there were various examples of women who, facing charges of infidelity or of fraternizing with strangers, had had their hair cut off. But other methods of punishment were also deployed in such cases. There is therefore a danger of interpreting the cutting off of hair too rigidly as a symbolic act of punishment which refers to, and can be understood primarily on the basis of, an underlying cultural system. Rather than interpreting it as a cultural sign in the semiotic sense, it should instead be seen as a social strategy or practice deployed to obtain something.[104] By cutting the hair of a *tyskerpige*, *shliukh-doiche*, *moffenhoer* or *femme à boche*, not only her appearance but also her relations to society were altered. The punishment was visible and for a certain duration of time it would bear witness to her treason. It was a punishment of the body that had been given to the enemy, and as such it was a sexualized retribution for a sexual act. That those French women who had collaborated in other ways also had their heads shaven after the liberation only goes to show how profoundly notions of gender and sexuality conditioned the understanding of treason in general. In contrast to the male collaborators, women who had been fraternizing with German soldiers were automatically associated with sexual immorality.[105]

By having their hair cut off, the women were robbed of an important feminine asset, in an attempt to make them look less attractive in a time when cropped hair was certainly not in fashion. This punishment served as a de-sexualization, a symbolic castration of the female, and was simultaneously a demonstration of masculine domination. The level of brutality in the cropping incidents during and after the occupation varied greatly. In some cases only a few tufts of hair were cut off, while in others the women had their heads completely shaven, were stripped, painted and branded like cattle. Physical violence also occured, although rapes were seldom committed in connection with these incidents. This was arguably the assailants' way of underlining their contempt for the women and of expressing their own sense of moral high ground. Still, there were many examples of returnees or Allied soldiers forming relationships with women who had previously been intimate with German soldiers, just as there are witness accounts indicating that it was not uncommon to see an assailant who had cut off a woman's hair trying to look her up again, presuming that she would be sexually available.[106] The sexual nature of the punishments was an additional source of humiliation and shame to the victims, whereas the assailants generally sought to play down its seriousness and its implications. A French police report noted for instance: 'No brutality was carried out on S. She was simply stripped and her backside slapped.'[107] Similarly, in Denmark it was not uncommon to reduce an assailant's sentence on the grounds that the victim's hair 'would grow out again'.

Women who had fraternized sexually with representatives of the occupiers were automatically considered and portrayed as promiscuous. They were punished not only for behaving against the national interest, but also for offending the public norms of sexual morality. The female body and sexuality constituted a combat zone because women were central markers by which a society could take bearings of its own characteristics and unifying force. On a mental plane the fate of the nation was equated with the fidelity of its women. During occupation – and other national crises where the sense of nationality was closely associated with biological concepts of inheritance and origin – the line between acceptable and unacceptable sexual behaviour was sharply drawn. If the women did not fulfil the expectations of respectability and virtue, and live up to the ideal, which tradition and convention set up in respect of practices of sexuality, reproduction and marriage, they became a threat to the survival of the nation and the very order they were supposed to maintain. By their intimate fraternizations, the women challenged the national and masculine ownership of women's sexuality in the occupied countries. Punishing them was an attempt to re-establish male dominance and reinstate traditional gender roles.

During the occupation, retributive acts of harassing, condemning or cutting the hair off women who consorted with German soldiers also functioned generally as public warnings against collaboration, and as reminders of a future showdown after the liberation. These persecutions could also have a radicalizing effect on the conflicts with the occupying power, as well as on the conflicts between collaboration and resistance. However, after the liberation, when the cropping incidents increased considerably in number and brutality, the persecutions ceased to have such propagandistic purposes. As the war was most brutal in the occupied part of the Soviet Union, the women who had fraternized and even had a child with a German soldier could face the most tragic fate. After the Germans had left, the women became social pariahs, were deported or shot by the Red Army or disappeared in the Siberian Gulag.[108] In none of the newly liberated western countries did 'rendering the enemy sexual favours' become a criminal act according to the new laws implemented during the purges. Nevertheless, everywhere tens of thousands of women who had fraternized sexually with Germans were arrested and interned for shorter or longer periods of time. Some of them were under suspicion of, and charged with, other forms of collaboration as well, while others were interned simply because they had dated German soldiers, or because they were carriers of venereal diseases. In some cases the women were interned in order to protect them from mob justice, but this turned out to be a case of setting the fox to keep the geese, as the women often faced similar acts of retribution during either their arrest or their imprisonment. In many cases, the arrests had an inflammatory rather than a calming effect on public feeling.

Some voices, though not many, were critical of the way in which fraternizing women were treated. The argument aired was that, to re-establish a society based on the rule of law, it was necessary to stop people taking the law into their own hands. The majority of people, however, felt that the women should pay the penalty for their actions and thought it unfair to punish those who had great sacrifices during the occupation, and, in the heated atmosphere of the summer of liberation, had overstepped the boundaries of acceptable behaviour, especially if the women who had made life easier for the occupying power were let off scot-free. Very few people therefore protested against the treatment of these women. One of those who did, however, was the Norwegian psychologist and anti-Nazi campaigner Johan Scharffenberg, who felt that the women should not be held accountable, because they had been the victims of their own passions. He noted: 'The sex drive is a primitive instinct that is far more powerful than national sentiments, which are a more recent product of civilization.' To the renowned Danish theologian and commentator Hal Koch, it was not the women's own sex drive or emotions that had weakened their judgement, but rather their social conditions. He accused those who condemned the *tyskerpiger* of not taking their share of the responsibility for the social problems which had driven the women into the arms of the German soldiers: 'Where were we when they grew up surrounded by poverty, sin and squalor? Should we now be sitting comfortably, pointing our fingers at them? I say to you again: Have you taken leave of your senses, or what are you thinking?'[109] While showing compassion and understanding, such defences primarily saw the women as victims and ignored the possibility that dating Germans during the occupation could in some cases have been a deliberate choice. By portraying the fraternizing women exclusively as victims, such critiques of the treatment they received found very little support in the early years after the occupation.

Notes

1. Københavns opdagelsespoliti, protokol over anmeldte krigsforbrydelser og tabte sager 1945, j.nr. 2280–30. Københavns Byret, afdeling 10 A, sag nr. 170/45 afsagt 4.9.1945. Østre Landsret, I. afd. sag nr. 304/45 afsagt 20.12.45.

2. Fabrice Virgili, *Shorn Women. Gender and Punishment in Liberation France* (Oxford: Berg, 2002), p. 61; Simon Kitson, *Vichy et la chasse aux espions nazis 1940–1942. Complexités de la politique de collaboration* (Paris: Autrement, 2004), pp. 114–17; Kaare Olsen, *Krigens barn. De norske krigsbarna og deres mødre* (Oslo: Forum Aschehoug, 1998), p. 247; Anette Warring, *Tyskerpiger under besættelse og retsopgør* (Copenhagen: Gyldendal, 1994), pp. 75–6; Biuletyn Informacyjny, konspiracyjne czasopismo SZP-ZWZ-AK, 3.VI.1943.

3. Joan Scott, 'Rewriting History', in M.R. Higonnet, Jane Jenson, Sonya Michel and M.C. Weitz (eds), *Behind the Lines. Gender and the Two World Wars* (New Haven and London: Yale University Press, 1987), p.26.

4. Hans Kirchhoff, J.T. Lauridsen and A. Trommer (eds), *Gads leksikon om dansk besættelsestid* (Copenhagen: Gads Forlag, 2002); Fabrice Virgili, 'Enfants de Boches – the War Children of France', in Kjersti Ericsson and Eva Simonsen (eds), *Children of World War II* (Oxford: Berg, 2005); Madajczyk Czestław, *Polityka III Rzeszy w okupowanej Polsce, T. I and II* (Warsaw: Panstwowe Wydawnictwo Naukowe, 1970), pp. 239, 242, 263; Rolf-Dieter Müller, 'Liebe im Vernichtungskrieg. Geschlechtergeschichtliche Aspekte des Einsatzes deutscher Soldaten im Russlandkrieg 1941–1944', in Frank Becker, T. Grossbötting, A. Ozwar and R. Schlögl (eds), *Politische Gewalt in der Moderne* (Münster: Aschendorf, 2003), pp. 239–67.

5. Karel Berkhoff, *Harvest of Despair: Life and Death in Ukraine under Nazi Rule* (Cambridge: Harvard University Press, 2004), pp. 114–15, 217, 302.

6. Karel Berkhoff, *Harvest of Despair,* p. 222; RGASPI f. 17, op. 125, d. 314, l. 40–44; Anthony Beevor, *Berlin: The Downfall* (London, Penguin, 2001), pp. 108–10.

7. Udenrigsministeriet, 84.C.2.B./40–45; Statsadvokaten for særlige Anliggender, AS 38–215.
8. Quoted in Dag Ellingsen, 'De norske "tyskertøsene"': Der myter rår', in: Dag Ellingsen, Inga Dora Björnsdottir and Anette Warring, *Kvinner krig og kjælighet* (Oslo: Cappelen, 1995), p. 16.
9. Kaare Olsen, *Krigens barn*, pp. 235–45.
10. Kaare Olsen, *Krigens barn*, p. 13; Dag Ellingsen, 'De norske "tyskertøsene"', pp. 19–25. Knut Einar Eriksen and Terje Halvorsen, *Norge i krig. Frigjøring* (Oslo: Aschehoug, 1987), p. 251.
11. Georg Lilienthal, *Der 'Lebensborn E.V.' – Ein Instrument nationalsozialistischer Rassenpolitik* (Frankfurt am Main, Akademie der Wissenschaften und der Literatur, 2003), p. 257; Arne Øland, 'The countability of Danish Children of War', in Kjersti Ericsson and Eva Simonsen (eds), *Children*, pp. 60–2
12. Kaare Olsen, *Krigens barn*, p. 69; Anette Warring, *Tyskerpiger*, pp. 25–6.
13. Fabrice Virgili, *Shorn Women*, p. 1.
14. Georg Lilienthal, *Der 'Lebensborn E.V.*, pp. 200–1; Phillippe Burrin, *Living with Defeat. France under the German Occupation, 1940–1944* (London, Arnold, 1996), p. 207.
15. Fabrice Virgili, 'Enfants de Boches', p. 144.
16. Georg Lilienthal, *Der 'Lebensborn E.V.'*, p. 257; Monica Diedrichs, 'Stigma and Silence: Netherlands Women, German Soldiers and Their Children', in Kjersti Ericsson and Eva Simonsen (eds), *Children*.
17. Local party archives hold the protocols of exclusion hearings (files inspected in Simferopol, Volgograd and Riazan) . While no exact quantification of cases based on accusations relating to sexual collaboration has been carried out, the predominance of the theme is apparent in 1945–6. For political jostling see TsDAHOU f. 7, op. 5, d. 618, l. 131–3
18. *Molodaia Gvardiia*, which entered the post-war literary scene as a novel by the esteemed Soviet writer Aleksandr Fadeev and was subsequently made into a film, recounted the tale of a heroic Komsomol underground organization. One of the heroines was Liubov Shevtsova, whose duty it was to befriend and spy on the German soldiers stationed in the nearby town.
19. Fabrice Virgili, *Shorn Women*, p. 2; Anette Warring, pp. 156–87.
20. Kaare Olsen, *Krigens barn*, p. 247; Anette Warring, *Tyskerpiger*, pp. 78–127.
21. Statistisk Årbog. Justitsministeriet, 1. kontor, div. Journalsager 1940, 1941 and 161,1–981/1942;161,1–986/1943; 161,1–1–1282/1944, 161,1–1972/1945–1951.
22. Monica Diedrichs, 'Stigma and silence', pp. 151–2; Dag Ellingsen, 'De norske "tyskertøsene"', pp. 40–5. Anette Warring, *Tyskerpiger*, pp. 26–31.
23. Grethe Hartmann, *The Girls They Left Behind* (Copenhagen: Ejnar Munksgaard, 1946).

24. Sigurd Senje, *Dømte kvinner* (Oslo: Pax Forlag A/S, 1986), p. 52.
25. Grethe Hartmann, *The Girls They Left Behind*; Anette Warring, *Tyskerpiger,* pp. 31–42; Anette Warring, 'Danske *tyskerpiger* – hverken ofre eller forrædere', in Dag Ellingsen, Inga Dora Björnsdottir and Anette Warring, *Kvinner krig*, pp. 105–7.
26. Fabrice Virgili, *Shorn Women*, pp. 177–9; Anette Warring, *Tyskerpiger*, pp. 26–66; Kari Helgesen, '...f.t. siktet som tyskertøs', *Historisk Tidsskrift*, no.3 (1990), pp. 285–310; Luc Capdevila, 'La collaboration sentimentale: Lorient, mai 1945', in François Rouquet and Danièle Voldman (eds), *Identités feminines et violences politiques (1936–1946)* (Les Cahiers de l'IHTP, no. 31, 1995), pp. 67–82.
27. Anette Warring, *Tyskerpiger*, pp. 37–8.
28. Anette Warring, *Tyskerpiger*, pp. 37–66.
29. Quoted in Fabrice Virgili, *Shorn Women*, p. 26.
30. Quoted in Anette Warring, *Tyskerpiger*, p. 65.
31. Fabrice Virgili, *Shorn Women*, pp. 12, 16, 127; *Tyskerpiger*, Anette Warring, p. 67.
32. Retsopgøret med landssvigerne. Beretning til Justitsministeriet afgivet af det Statistiske Departement (Copenhagen, Statens Trykningskontor, 1958). Ankenævnet i henhold til § 8 I lov nr. 260 af 1.6.1945.
33. Ankenævnet i henhold til lov nr. 260 af 1.6. 1945, nr. 241.
34. Ankenævnet i henhold til lov nr. 260 af 1.6. 1945, nr. 38, nr. 369.
35. Ankenævnet i henhold til lov nr. 260 af 1.6. 1945, nr. 1, nr. 7.
36. Anette Warring, *Tyskerpiger*, pp. 73–4; Anette Warring, 'Danske *tyskerpiger* – hverken ofre eller forrædere', in Dag Ellingsen, Inga Dora Björnsdottir and Anette Warring, *Kvinner krig*, p. 139.
37. Fabrice Virgili, *Shorn Women*, p. 9.
38. Juliane Fürst, 'Heroes, Lovers, Victims – Partisan Girls during the Great Fatherland War', *Minerva*, Vol. XVIII, Numbers 3–4, Fall/Winter (2000), pp. 38–75. Quotation from p. 61.
39. Davide Rodogno, 'Italian Soldiers in the Balkans: the Experience of the Occupation (1941–1943)', *Journal of Southern Europe and the Balkans*, vol. 6, no. 2 (2004).
40. Grethe Hartmann, *The Girls They Left Behind*, p. 22; Anette Warring, *Tyskerpiger*, p. 12.
41. Karel Berkhoff, *Harvest of Despair*, pp. 114–15, 148.
42. Sigurd Senje, *Dømte kvinner* (Oslo: Pax Forlag A/S, 1986), p. 29; Dag Ellingsen, 'De norske "tyskertøsene"', p. 24; Phillipe Burrin, *Living with Defeat*, p. 205; Fabrice Virgili, *Shorn Women*, p. 24; Landau Ludwik, *Kronika lat wojny I okupacji, Vol. I* (Warsaw: Panstwowe Wydawnictwo Naukowe 1970), p. 60; Davide Rodogno, 'Italian Soldiers in the Balkans'.

43. Robert Gildea, *Marianne in Chains* (Oxford, Macmillan, 2002), pp. 76–9
44. Statsadvokaten for særlige Anliggender, månedlige indberetninger, Esbjerg, Feb. 1941; Ribe, April 1942; Udenrigsministeriet, 84.C.2.b, Socialministeriet, 3. kontor, 262/1944, 313/1941, 49/1943, 262/1944, 429/1944, 436/1944, 510/1944 and 511/1944.
45. Udenrigsministeriet, 84.C.2.b.
46. Kaare Olsen, *Krigens barn*, pp. 291–5; Guri Hjeltnes, *Norge i krig. Hverdagslivet i krig* (Oslo: Aschehoug, 1987), p. 174–5.
47. *Kolding Kirkeblad*, Dec. 1940; Statsadvokaten for særlige Anliggender, AS 34–23. Own translation.
48. Udenrigsministeriet, 84.C.2.b.; Statsadvokaten for særlige Anliggender, AS 0–2154.
49. Bundesarchiv – Militärarchiv, M 747/46781.
50. Statsadvokaten for særlige Anliggender, AS 34–76, AS 38–348, AS 48–383 and Månedlige indberetninger.
51. Michal Simunek, 'German Mother and Czech Father – Czech Mother and German Father', in: Kjersti Ericsson and Eva Simonsen (eds), *Children*.
52. Kaare Olsen, *Krigens barn*, pp. 164–5.
53. Udenrigsministeriet, 13 Tys.1/8a/1940–45.
54. Justitsministeriet, 1. kontor, Q 2779/1941; Q 2483/1941.
55. See e.g. Statsadvokaten for særlige Anliggender, AS 0–7885, AS 0–7888, AS 0–7892, AS 0–8059.
56. Kaare Olsen, *Krigens barn*, p. 168.
57. Bundesarchiv – Militärarchiv, M 747/46781.
58. Kaare Olsen, *Krigens barn*, p. 168.
59. Anette Warring, *Tyskerpiger*, p. 141–5; Kaare Olsen, *Krigens barn*, pp. 171, 175.
60. Kaare Olsen, *Krigens barn*, pp. 212–23.
61. Ditlew Tamm, *Retsopgøret efter besættelsen* (Copenhagen: Jurist- og økonomforbundets Forlag 1985), p. 587; Henrik Havrehed, *De tyske flygtninge i Danmark 1945–1949* (Odense: Odense Universitetsforlag, 1987), pp. 226–7; Anette Warring, 'Bag pigtråd. Tyske flygtninge i Danmark 1945–1949', in Karen Hjorth, Grethe Ilsøe and Minna Kragelund (eds), *Kan, kan ikke. Vil, vil ikke. Kvindeliv i perspektiv* (Copenhagen: ARKI Varia, 1996), pp. 31–58.
62. Kaare Olsen, *Krigens barn*, pp. 304–9, 316–17, 325–31.
63. Justitsministeriet, 3. kontor, 114 A/1945; Anette Warring, *Tyskerpiger*, pp. 144–5.
64. Udenrigsministeriet, 21 D.8; Justitsministeriet, 3. kontor, 114 A/1945; Justitsministeriet, 1. kontor, 3514/1945.
65. Anette Warring, *Tyskerpiger*, p. 146; Kaare Olsen, *Krigens barn*, p. 386; *Kontrast*, no. 2/3, 1986.
66. Reichsgesetzblatt, Teil I, nr. 83; Justitsministeriet, div. journalsager, 1941; Kaare Olsen, *Krigens barn*, p. 20.

67. Kaare Olsen, *Krigens barn*, quotation pp. 35 and 24.

68. Kaare Olsen, *Krigens barn*, p. 67.

69. Georg Lilienthal, *Der 'Lebensborn e.V.'*, p. 257; Monica Diedrichs, 'Stigma and Silence', pp. 152–3.

70. Monica Diedrichs, 'Stigma and Silence', pp. 154–5.

71. Arne Øland, 'The Countability of Danish Children of War', in Kjersti Ericsson and Eva Simonsen (eds), *Children*; Justitsministeriet, 1. kontor, div. Journalsager, 1940, 1941 and 161,1–981/1942, 161/1–986/1943, 161,1–1282/194, 161,1–1972/1945–1951.

72. Georg Lilienthal, *Der 'Lebensborn e.V.'*, pp. 193–4.

73. Udenrigsministeriet, 84.C2/1940–45; Reichsgesetzblatt, Teil I, nr. 79, Berlin, 25.8.1943.

74. Notits, Reichskanzelei, 27.6.1941, 'Der Führer hat entschieden', quoted in Georg Lilienthal, *Der 'Lebensborn e.V.'*, p. 169.

75. Georg Lilienthal, 'War Children in Nazi Race Policy', paper at the conference 'German–Norwegian War Children – An International Perspective', Oslo, 15–17 November 2002; Fabrice Virgili, 'Enfants de Boches.

76. Georg Lilienthal, 'War Children in Nazi Race Policy'; Roman Hrabar, Sofia Tokarz and Jacek E. Wilczur, *The Fate of Polish Children during the Last War* (Warsaw: Panstwowe Wydawnictwo Naukowe, 1970), p. 147, suggest that over 200,000 children were deported from Poland, but the number and how many of these children were of German–Polish couples are unknown.

77. Fabrice Virgili, 'Enfants de Boches'.

78. Krigsbarnsutvalget, 9.7.1945–3.11.1945, Indstilling til Sosialdepartementet, p. 48, quoted in Dag Ellingsen, 'De norske "tyskertøsene"', p. 13.

79. *De Frie Danske*, April 1945; see also *Frit Danmark*, June 1942.

80. Justitsministeriet, 1. kontor, 160, 6/1945.

81. Memories of war children published in Arne Øland, *Horeunger og helligdage* (Copenhagen: Det Schønbergske Forlag, 2001).

82. Arne Øland, *Horeunger og helligdage*.

83. Quoted in Robert Gildea, *Marianne in Chains*, p. 76

84. Udenrigsministeriet, 84.C.2.b; Statsadvokaten for særlige Anliggender, månedlige indbretninger fra politimestrene.

85. Quoted in Robert Gildea, *Marianne in Chains*, p. 30.

86. Statsadvokaten for særlige Anliggender, AS 34–435.

87. Juliane Fürst, 'Heroes, Lovers, Victims', pp. 38–75.

88. Karel Berkhoff, *Harvest of Despair*, p. 303.

89. Quoted in Anette Warring, *Tyskerpiger*, p. 77.

90. Anette Warring, *Tyskerpiger*, pp. 78–88.

91. Kaare Olsen, *Krigens barn*, p. 247; Anette Warring, *Tyskerpiger*, p. 76.

92. Jean Texcier, *Conseils à l'occupé* (Paris, 1940); Fabrice Virgili, *Shorn Women*, p. 66.

93. Quoted in Fabrice Virgili, *Shorn Women*, p. 67.

94. Fabrice Virgili, *Shorn Women*, pp. 61–74.
95. Simone Kitson, *Vichy et la chasse aux espions nazis 1940–1942*, pp. 114–17
96. Kaare Olsen, *Krigens barn*, p. 247; Dag Ellingsen, 'De norske "tyskertøsene"', pp. 22–23.
97. Quoted in Dag Ellingsen, 'De norske "tyskertøsene"', p. 246.
98. Anette Warring, *Tyskerpiger*, pp. 104–128.
99. Statsadvokaten for særlige Anliggender, AS 14–196, AS 17–181, AS 24–140, AS 26–84, AS 27–398, AS 27–423, AS 27–439, AS 32–99, AS 34–671, AS 34–683, AS 36–474, AS 56–81, AS 56–80, AS 65–182, AS 66–215, UK 2117.
100. Jean Texcier, *Conseils à l'occupé* (Paris, 1940).
101. Fabrice Virgili, *Shorn Women*, p. 24.
102. Statsadvokaten for særlige Anliggender, AS 7–34, AS 12–106, AS 13–17, AS 48–159, AS 48–833, AS 48–483, AS 48–431, AS 36–376, AS 36–112, AS 27–79, AS 46–151, AS 48–1756, AS 7–34. UK 441, UK 1709, UK 120, UK 455.
103. Quoted in Fabrice Virgili, *Shorn Women*, p. 67; Kaare Olsen, *Krigens barn*, p. 246.
104. Ulrik Langen, 'Ritualer, symbol, tekst og praksis', in Ulrik Langen (ed.), *Ritualernes magt* (Copenhagen: Roskilde Universitetsforlag, 2002), pp. 13–18.
105. Fabrice Virgili, *Shorn Women*, pp. 12, 192; Anette Warring, 'Køn, seksualitet og national identitet', in *Historisk Tidsskrift*, no. 2 (1994), p. 299.
106. Ebba Drolshagen, *Det skal de ikke slippe godt fra* (Copenhagen: Det Schønbergske Forlag, 1999), p. 140; Fabrice Virgili, *Shorn Women*, p. 211; Kaare Olsen, *Krigens barn*, pp. 247–9; Anette Warring, *Tyskerpiger*, pp. 44–7.
107. Fabrice Virgili, *Shorn Women*, p. 193.
108. Mentioned in an interview with the sculptor Gavrilovyi about his time in Rokossovskii's Army, winter 1941, published in *Mokva, Voennaia*, Moscow 1995, p. 591; Rolf-Dieter Müller, 'Liebe im Vernichtungskrieg', pp. 239–67.
109. Johan Scharffenberg, 'Gjerningen og gjerningsmannen', *Morgenbladet*, 29.1.1948; Hal Koch, 1947, quoted in Erik Knudsen and Ole Wivel (eds), *Kulturdebat 1944–48* (Copenhagen: Gyldendal, 1958).

–4–

Schooling as a Cultural Interface
Pavla Vošahlíková, Bénédicte Rochet and Fabrice Weiss

Schooling has always served a number of functions at the interface of political, social and religious organization and daily life. It shapes national and local loyalties, religious and secular values, occupational structure and social mobility. It holds in tension the interests of a number of partners: the state and local community, churches and religious organizations, and not least families. The process of state-building tended to prioritize the national over the local, the secular over the religious, social stratification over social mobility. In occupied Europe these tensions became much more explicit, as the German Reich sought to use schooling as an instrument to consolidate political dominance, racial superiority and economic supremacy. Even the Nazis, however, were unable completely to eliminate the influence of traditional partners in the education process, and it is the aim of this chapter to explore the struggle between the German state under Nazi rule, on the one hand, and local and national communities, churches and families on the other. Three main areas will be concentrated on here in order to explore the balance between the German project and the strategies of traditional partners: Alsace-Moselle and Belgium in western Europe, and occupied Czechoslovakia and Poland in central and eastern Europe.

Patterns of German Control

Not all countries and regions which fell under German occupation saw massive changes. In France, for example, there was no programme of Germanization or Nazification. Education remained under the control of the Vichy state's ministry of education. The German presence gave an opportunity for the Vichy state to purge undesirable personnel, such as Jews, freemasons and those with foreign parents, from teaching positions in the universities and schools. The influence of the Catholic Church in education, virtually eliminated under the Third Republic, was now increased, but not so as to threaten the supremacy of the secular state in education.[1] The main concern of the occupying authorities was military security, and for this reason paramilitary organizations such as boy scouts were banned in the occupied zone. Another German obsession was the productivity of French agriculture, which was considered backward and unable to produce enough resources for the Reich. Every June schools in the west of France were ordered to close so that children could be sent into the fields to find and destroy the Colorado beetles that infested the potato crop.[2] Otherwise French schools and schoolteachers were left to get on with their jobs as usual, unless they became politically suspect.

Belgium was similar to occupied France in that it was under German military administration but retained, if not a government, then its state bureaucracy, including the national education department. The Germans had plans to make the Free University of Brussels, which was French-speaking and run by a board of directors of liberal or socialist tendencies, into a 'Germanic bastion' in western Europe. They allowed the university to reopen after the capitulation on the condition that it accept a German curator who would have control of the professors, students and internal reform of the university. They also considered annexing the small German-speaking area of the country around Arlon, as they had Luxemburg, and demanded more extensive teaching of German in the schools of this area. To see off the latter threat the Belgian authorities found a compromise solution under a decree of 10 August 1942, increasing the number of hours of German teaching but insisting too on the primacy of French in order to retain ties with French-speaking Belgium.[3] Elsewhere Belgium remained a bilingual country, with French and Flemish as the official languages, and the Catholic Church as a major player in the education system.[4]

In the core of the Greater German Reich, things were different. Alsace-Moselle, which had been lost to France in 1918 and was then recovered, together with the Grand Duchy of Luxemburg were incorporated into the German system of administration by *Gauleiter*. The intention was not only to integrate this region politically, but also to make the people fully part of the German nation. In the eastern part of the Moselle the population spoke a German dialect, while to the west of Sarrebourg and Thionville it spoke French, which in 1918–40 was also the official language and that of the dominant class. To combat this the German authorities reorganized the school system to conform to the German model and attempted to eliminate Catholic education. Privileged under the terms of the reincorporation of Alsace-Moselle into France in 1918, and protected in theory under the German-Catholic Concordat of 1933, ordinances of 12 September 1940 and 30 June 1941 in the Moselle and Luxemburg nevertheless announced the suppression of the denominational organization of state education. State schools were now interdenominational *Gemeinschaftsschulen*, and from December 1940 private religious schools were closed.[5]

The German authorities began a programme of sending teachers from these annexed regions for retraining in the Old Reich, while teachers from the Old Reich were seconded to teach in the new territories. From 5 August to 30 September 1940, 750 teachers of the Moselle took part in a fortnight of training classes in the Saarland and the Palatinate, followed from October by teachers from Luxemburg. These training classes were organized with the collaboration of the NSDAP and the NSLB (Nationalsozialistischer Lehrerbund, the Nazi teachers' union) and were to familiarize the teachers both with the German school system and with the principles of National Socialism.[6]

The elision between Germanization and Nazification became explicit in the case of the establishment of the Hitler Youth in the annexed territories. From October 1940 training for the youth of the Moselle was organized, with several hundred young people going to Saarbrücken to take part in mass meetings and gatherings. Early in 1942, through their school, children were subject to a census with the aim of enrolling them in the Hitler Youth, which became compulsory under the ordinance of 4 August 1942. This was backed up by four summer camps in 1942, set up by the German authorities to intensify the propaganda for the Hitler Youth. Each brought together 100 young people from the Moselle and 100 from Germany, to raise awareness of the unity of German youth, to undergo physical and military preparation and to be indoctrinated in National-Socialist ideals. This culminated in a ceremony on 10 September 1943, the day of the Party, when 2,200 young people were brought to Metz and 1,200 of them marched in front of the civil and political authorities.[7] Meanwhile an elite of the youth was trained in Adolf Hitler schools. One was set up in the Moselle at Fénétrange, in the buildings of the Catholic boarding school of Notre-Dame-de-la-Providence, while in Luxemburg an Adolf Hitler school for boys was established at Clervaux and a Napola for girls at Kolmar-berg in 1942.[8] Separated from the influence of their family and their traditional environment, the pupils were subjected, more than in the traditional educational cycle, to National Socialist indoctrination, whose precepts were found in every subject studied.[9]

In central Europe there had long been rivalry between ethnic Germans and Slav populations. The interests and identities of the Slav peoples were defended after 1918 by their own states, notably Czechoslovakia and Poland. Victory, occupation and the control of administration by the annexation of areas with a significant German population and the establishment of regimes such as the Protectorate of Bohemia-Moravia and the General Government of Poland, however, gave the Germans the opportunity to dismantle the national systems of education in these states and push through a programme of Germanization. This entailed the closure of native-language schools as soon as German schooling could be established; the liquidation of the ruling class of the new Slavic states by the destruction of their universities and the downgrading of the secondary education system; limiting the education of girls above elementary level; and the elimination of Jews altogether from the education process.

In his post-war trial K.H. Frank, the foremost representative of the Sudetenland Movement and a long-standing member of the Czechoslovak Parliament, admitted that before the occupation, and even before the annexation of the Czech border areas, there was 'a general plan to get rid of excessively developed Czech institutions', which was adopted after March 1939 by the Department of Education and Schools in the Reich Protector's Office.[10] In the Sudentenland, occupied after Munich, Czech schooling had disappeared even before the rest of Czechoslovakia was occupied and well before the beginning of the Second World War. Parents and pupils who wished to maintain Czech as a medium of instruction were subject to personal abuse and official persecution. Czech teachers in the border areas were amongst the most socially threatened professional groups. Alongside representatives of the Czechoslovak state (policemen, postmen) they were the first ones to be persecuted and driven out. Then, according to an official report of the Protectorate Ministry of the Interior of 14 October 1939:

immediately after 16th March of this year numerous buildings and classrooms of Czech state schools were confiscated and occupied and Czech pupils and teachers were prevented from being taught and teaching. These measures were either carried out by German citizens themselves, while the Czech population was not given any protection, or a direct order was issued by the German authorities. Children from the schools thus closed were sent randomly to other villages, in which they were often unable to attend school because of various obstacles.[11]

More than thirty Czech primary and secondary schools for over 2,500 pupils were closed in the brief period from mid-March to mid-September 1939. Simultaneously all equipment in the abolished schools was destroyed or stolen. Czech children fared worst in Jihlava and Brno, where many secondary and grammar schools, business colleges, teacher-training colleges and a music school were also closed.[12]

The Nazis decided to close Czech institutions of higher education soon after the war started, but they started preparations much earlier. They were well aware that institutions of higher education, primarily Prague's Charles University, were seen by the public as part of a national cultural heritage and that its closure would not only shatter its students and professors but would also affect the whole of society. As early as 2 May 1939 demands to abolish the Czech University were voiced at the Prague German University. On 28 October 1939, the anniversary of the founding of the Czechoslovak Republic, mass anti-Nazi demonstrations and strikes were held in major Czech towns, counting on a rapid defeat of Nazi Germany by the Allies. A medical student, Jan Opletal, was mortally wounded, and his funeral on 15 November became the occasion of another anti-Nazi rally. The Germans exploited the opportunity of their military success in Poland to clamp down on Czech students and higher education. On 17 November they raided student halls of residence, singling out nine students for execution and deporting 1,200 to concentration camps. Charles University and other institutions of higher education were closed for three years in the first instance. Only German institutions of higher education, closed to Czechs, remained open as the Reich sought to prevent the revival of a national intelligentsia.[13]

At the secondary level the composition of the student body in Czech schools changed dramatically. Jewish pupils and students were first excluded from classes where they were taught together with Germans. Private schools were established for them in Germany and occupied countries, even in ghettos. However, from 1941 Jewish schools were in general not allowed to operate, and Jewish children were banned from being taught privately. The definitive ban on all Jewish schools in the Third Reich and occupied countries was issued on 30 June 1942.[14] Female students were also discriminated against. Under ministerial regulations, for example, the number of girls sitting the Maturita exam in individual grammar schools in the Protectorate was not allowed to exceed 10 per cent of the total number of school leavers.[15]

In occupied Poland the educational fate of Polish children depended on what zone they lived in. In Pomerania and West Prussia, where there was a large German population, the object, as in the Czech border areas, was to assimilate a section of Slavic youth. Elsewhere, as in the Warthegau (Poznań) region, where Germans made up only 7 per cent of the population, the task was to downgrade the schooling of Poles to a bare elementary minimum, up to the age of 12, with teaching in German to be progressively established.[16] Heinrich Himmler stated that 'the goals of a Polish four-grade elementary school are simple arithmetic up to 500; writing one's name and the acceptance of a principle that it is the Divine instruction to show obedience towards Germans, humility, diligence and deference. I do not consider reading useful.'[17] Slightly more generous, E. Wetzel and G. Hecht stated in their plans for Polish schools that merely the most fundamental skills in arithmetic, reading and writing were allowed to be taught. The teaching of subjects important from a national perspective – geography, history, the history of literature and PE – was banned. School was required to prepare pupils for work in agriculture, forestry, as well as simple activities in industry and crafts.[18] A. Greiser, who was directly involved in the Nazi administration of Poland, expressed similar sentiments when he said that Polish children were to master the German language 'to such a degree that a pupil will comprehend simple verbal instructions without problems in his future job, in addition to reading short printed and hand-written instructions dealing with work procedures, operating machinery, etcetera; he will master the four fundamental arithmetical skills; he will understand volumes, measurements, weights and how to write them down. Other subjects, including PE, are not to be offered in the intended school curriculum.'[19] Not all Polish children received even this schooling. In the General Government Polish schools were closed after the German occupation and Polish children were not allowed to attend schools designated for German children. The reason given, in this dumping-ground of the Reich, was that Polish children needed no education, not even an elementary one.[20]

For all the force and decisiveness of the German educational project, the question must be posed: how far were the German authorities able to assert their domination by the remodelling of education systems and how far were rival partners able to negotiate a defence of their own interests, subvert the intentions of the occupying forces, exploit the contradictions of their policies, or even resist? In western Europe educational institutions had a greater ability to offer opposition than in eastern Europe, where the limited indigenous schooling that was allowed to subsist was put to grander uses or paralleled by clandestine networks of schooling. Teachers as a body dragged their feet over plans to relocate, retrain or reorganize them for the benefit of the Nazi educational project. Churches, which were heavily implicated in schooling at all levels, sought to protect the interests of religious education. Local and national communities took measures to preserve their own language and culture. Resistance was not open and dramatic as much as small-scale, inventive and organizational activity by schoolteachers and professors, churches and families making the most of the resources to hand and the tactics that were possible. It was an everyday resistance, using the 'weapons of the weak', but no less effective for that.

University Clashes

Although German policy was that the German Reich should tolerate only German universities, in parts of occupied Europe university staff and academics found different ways of perpetuating higher education. In central and eastern Europe, where repression was harshest, university life was where possible reinvented in secret, while in western Europe universities were either moved into unoccupied territory, as in France, or stayed put and battled for survival, as in Belgium.

In the Protectorate of Bohemia-Moravia, Charles University in Prague and other Czech higher learning institutions were closed in 1939, formally for three years. University dignitaries maintained their positions, in anticipation of a reopening, but university teaching staff were often persecuted as representatives of the Czech intelligentsia. Some university workplaces were preserved, such as teaching hospitals and research institutes, where secret progress was made in areas as diverse as the development of penicillin and motor cycle design. The Protectorate Government of Emil Hácha repeatedly attempted to free students who had been arrested in exchange for displays of loyalty towards the Nazi regime, but without success. Many undergraduates went to work in industry while continuing their university education at home, under the informal guidance of professors and lecturers. The three year closure of higher education expired in the autumn of 1942, which was, ironically, the time following the assassination of Acting Reich Protector Reinhard Heydrich. Terror in the Protectorate culminated in that period and any concessions to Czech interests were unthinkable.[21]

Higher education in Poland was able to reinvent itself more imaginatively. Academics and students from the University of Poznań, which was closed by the Germans and reopened as a German university in 1941, fled to Warsaw, where they founded a clandestine University of the Western Territories in the city and its suburbs in November, with faculties of humanities, theology, law and medicine. The students, sworn to secrecy, numbered 1,200 in 1943. Even larger was the clandestine University of Warsaw itself, which had 3,500 students and 300 university teachers in 1944, before the Warsaw uprising, a secret community attending lectures in vocational schools and private homes.[22]

At the outbreak of war in September 1939 the University of Strasbourg was moved to the French interior and reopened at Clermont-Ferrand, which remained in the non-occupied zone in 1940. Since the armistice was only provisional and France had not officially surrendered Alsace-Moselle, it was still called the University of Strasbourg. This infuriated the Germans, who reopened the German University of Strasbourg, which had existed under the Second Reich, in 1941. They forced the return of the Strasbourg university library in December 1940 by threatening to confiscate the Sorbonne library, which they controlled in the occupied zone, but they were less effective at ordering the return of students and staff from Clermont to Strasbourg. It was not until they invaded the non-occupied zone in 1942 that the Germans were able to close down this 'fictitious' university and round up its students for return to the Reich.[23]

In Belgium the German authorities gradually asserted control of the Free University of Brussels, but were ultimately frustrated by the actions of academic staff and students. Known in the prewar period as a bastion of freemasonry with many Jews on the staff, and as having taken a stand on anti-fascist issues, it became a target for reform by the German authorities. Staff who had fled to France in May 1940 were investigated to check their political reliability and connections. The German authorities assumed a right of veto over appointments to vacant chairs (17 September 1940) in order to keep out 'undesirable' professors. Under the German ordinance of 28 October 1940 universities were immediately to dismiss all professors, lecturers assistants and students of Jewish race.[24] The German curator of the Free University brought in 'Gastprofessoren', or German professors, who were supposed to be the 'antidote to the old atmosphere in the Belgian universities'. He also sought to replace the board of directors by a small office under his direct authority and to appoint to vacant posts himself in order to build up a teaching staff more responsive to Nazi ideals. These measures were rejected by the Free University, and the university's board of directors decided in November 1941 to close the university unilaterally. The Germans made several attempts to reopen the university, but without success. Those responsible for the decision to close and the leaders of students' associations were imprisoned until March 1942. University staff were prohibited from teaching or holding any other public office. After the closure, 583 students from the Free University were accommodated by the Catholic University of Louvain, in spite of their radically different philosophical views, as patriotism triumphed over traditional sectional interests. The students benefited from the suspension of a requirement that students of Louvain were to practise the Catholic religion. Other students organized themselves with the teaching staff to set up clandestine courses. The Free University did not reopen its doors before the liberation.[25]

The Catholic University of Louvain had a rather different experience. Under the canonical supervision of the Vatican and enjoying the support of the Belgian episcopate, which formed its board of directors, it was able openly to defy German directives and retain its autonomous status as a Catholic university during the occupation. Indeed the Germans were wary of a conflict with the religious authorities, a *Kulturkampf*, which would compromise the maintenance of law and order. The Third Reich was not prepared to go down a path of persecuting the Catholic Church in Belgium.[26]

Shortages, Subversion, Secrecy

The limits of Germanization were set not only by the influence of rival partners, but also by the contradictions in German policy that those rivals could exploit. The policy of Germanization was at odds with the logic of war, which required the greatest possible numbers of Germans to be mobilized for military activity, rather than teaching non-Germans in the Greater Reich. And while Germanization required the emasculation or destruction of the dominant educated class in non-German areas, the war economy also required trained experts to serve as technicians and managers in industry, agriculture and other essential services, who could not simply be brought in from Germany.

Initially the progress of the German takeover was measured, and families were able to take action to ensure a national education for their children. Immediately after the annexation of the border areas, during the so-called Second Republic (September 1938–March 1939) and also in the first years of the Nazi occupation of the entire Czech territory, many Czech parents in these areas resolved the issue of their children's education by sending them to school in the interior, where Czech-based instruction still continued. However, this route was closed stage by stage and after 1942 it was impossible, except for some rare instances, to continue this practice.[27]

The pressure to Germanize and the need to conscript all able-bodied Germans for war were in tension, and the lack of German teachers to undertake the Germanization of non-German youth became increasingly acute as the war stepped up. In the summer of 1940 the Reich Protector's Office reported that 110 new German teachers were needed for the territory under its control. Without this increase, it said, it would be impossible to provide teaching in the Protectorate's German primary and secondary schools.[28] Yet suggestions that German teachers be exempted from military service fell on deaf ears. In the Bohemian lands the German authorities were thus required to keep on Czech teachers, or even give them back their jobs in schools. Their presence in schools, which was supposed to be only temporary, contradicted the original policy of the country's new rulers. A secret report of the *Gauleiter* of Liberec in north Moravia of 5 November 1941 stated that 'positions held by German teachers beginning their military service, including those of head teachers, have had to be filled in many cases by Czech staff, which is not particularly desirable in politically unstable villages in racially mixed areas. Our recent efforts may thus go completely to waste, or in any case are threatened.'[29]

In Poland likewise it was difficult to recruit specialist teachers for German schools, not to mention for schools for Polish children which had German as the medium of instruction. Because German distrust of local teaching staff was greater than in western Europe or even in the Bohemian lands, it was impossible to remedy the situation by even the temporary recall of Polish teachers. This resulted in a desperate state of school teaching, which was often provided by people who did not have any teaching experience, whose own education rarely went beyond the elementary level, and whose mastery of German was generally limited. German sources, especially school inspector reports, and post-war research conducted by Polish school authorities show that the original occupations of these teachers were, for example, 'a blacksmith, baker, farmer, gamekeeper, female shop assistant, milliner, waitress and maid' scarcely the shock troops of the German racial project.[30]

While it was German policy to close down non-German universities and other institutions of higher education, at least in the core of the Reich, technical and vocational training was allowed to flourish. Industrial production located in the Bohemian lands, for example, was very important for the Third Reich. Any stoppages of operation due to the shortage of skilled labour would have represented a huge loss for German industry. The Germans felt that workers with secondary education would more than meet the demands of Czech industry, with German nationals occupying managerial posts. Similarly, medical training could not be totally ignored, and the only Czech institution of higher education that functioned in the Protectorate during the occupation was the College of Veterinary Medicine in Brno. In the last years of the war an attempt was made to combat the shortage of local doctors through Reinhard Heydrich bursaries, which allowed access to university education in Germany to racially and politically reliable students, but for obvious reasons the demand on the Czech side was minimal.[31]

Even in the General Government of Poland, where the occupation regime was exceptionally ruthless, local vocational, technical and agricultural education was tolerated, at least until 1943. A new state technical university was even set up in Warsaw in the spring of 1942. There was a huge interest in this form of education amongst the Polish public. Vocational training provided, at least temporarily, some protection against forced labour in the Third Reich. In addition, the vocational school often served as a cover for grammar schools and even higher education to operate clandestinely. It has been estimated that 65,000 Polish students completed their secondary studies in this way during the occupation years, while thousands more even graduated from universities.[32]

Subversion took place not only within the official system but also outside it, in secret. The Poles had long experience under partition in the nineteenth century of clandestine schooling, which offset the official schools of Prussians, Russians and Austrians. This reflex returned with a vengeance under Nazi–Soviet occupation. *Komplety* or parallel schools were set up at all levels to sustain Polish national education and perpetuate the training of elites. At secondary level, as we have seen, the *komplety* functioned within vocational schools. Of 90,000 secondary school students before the war, about 60,000 took *komplety* in 1943–4, and 18,000 even took the underground baccalaureate. Primary schools were still authorized to teach the rudiments; at this level schools taught the whole curriculum in the villages, beyond the purview of the authorities, while in the cities 37,000 schoolchildren were attending underground *komplety* in 1943–4, about one student in every three or four.[33]

One way of compensating for the inadequacy of German education and ensuring the survival of national schooling was to develop extra-curricular activities. Heydrich, the Acting Protector of Bohemia-Moravia, thought that 'it will undoubtedly be necessary to bring the younger Czech generation together in a way that will promote education outside the school, and will help – especially because it is not possible to arrest all Czech teachers – to remove it from their environment. Knowing the Czech attitude to these matters, it will undoubtedly be best done through sport.'[34] These views were shared by Emanuel Moravec, a prominent Czech collaborator who became minister of youth education. He established the Curatorium for Educating Children and Youth, a leisure organization which was for all young people aged 15 to 18. It employed German instructors, who selected and trained further Czech staff. In fact, despite the exceptional support provided for this organization by the Nazi administration, especially in the final years of the occupation, it did not fulfil the hopes placed in it. Political events and training courses failed to arouse the enthusiasm of the Czech youth and effectively suffered a boycott as the end of the war approached. Rather than complementing official schooling, the Curatorium ended up working against it, as for example in October 1943, when all schools were instructed to release young people for up to four half-days a week to undertake the recycling of textiles, paper, scrap metal and other raw materials, under the supervision of the Curatorium.[35] The Curatorium was most successful in the area of sport, but even then unwittingly provided a cover for banned sports associations, such as the Sokol (Falcon), or sheltered the resistance activities of young people.[36]

Teachers as a Corporation

In September 1941 Reinhard Heydrich, the new Acting Protector of Bohemia-Moravia, called all Czech teachers without exception 'a gang fostering opposition to the Czech government'.[37] On various occasions he suggested their physical liquidation as the best solution, and some teachers did not survive the wave of arrests and executions known as the first Heydrichaide. Even Heydrich, however, conceded that Czech teachers were necessary, but would have to be retrained. They were therefore sent on retraining courses organized by the Reich's Central Institute for Education and Teaching (Zentralinstitut für Erziehung und Unterricht) at Rankenheim near Berlin, with history, geography and biology on the agenda.[38] The decision to run these courses for selected Czech teachers was taken before Heydrich's arrival in Prague, namely in June 1941, and the first group of teachers left on 28 September 1941. They continued at Rankenheim until 1944, when the bombing grew so severe that the courses were relocated to Prague. Though they did not overtly protest, there is little evidence that Czech teachers retrained with any enthusiasm.

The practice of transferring teachers to the Old Reich for retraining was also inaugurated in Moselle and Luxemburg. It served three purposes: to improve their knowledge of the German language, to instil National-Socialist principles, and to deal with the critical lack of teachers – as a result of their conscription - within the Reich itself. In February 1941 the teaching profession in the Moselle was divided into two groups. The first was composed of teachers who had a good command of the German language and were young and dynamic (under 40). A second group was composed of those whose professional competence was below average or whose political loyalty was questionable. The period of employment in the *Altreich* was set at one or two years for both groups, with the prospect of returning earlier to the Moselle if they performed well.[39]

This system was implemented in both the Moselle and Luxemburg in April 1941. In the Moselle it provoked a veritable teachers' uprising. The large majority of the teachers concerned demanded a meeting with the school administration in Metz with a 'great irritation but a strong stubbornness', stating that they had never agreed to these transfers to the Old Reich. The protest was less resistance in a political sense than the defence of their interests as a profession or corporation, but was none the less effective. On 25 April *Gauleiter* Joseph Bürckel relaxed the position for married women but insisted that male teachers who refused would have their property confiscated and be refused re-entry at the border.[40] The impact on the teaching profession was in many ways counter-productive. A report on the city of Metz in September 1941 said that while their professional abilities were good, their general attitude was considered 'a too French spirit'.[41]

In Luxemburg a similar opposition got under way. At a meeting of 350 teachers in October 1941 tempers ran high against an official statement of the *Gauleiter* by a school inspector. A fine equivalent to a quarter of their salary was to be levied against all teachers unless they guaranteed in writing that they would dissociate themselves from the leaders of the opposition. Only a few did so. The rest declared their solidarity with their colleagues and placed the defence of the educational community above their personal interest. Particularly galling for the authorities was the fact that two teachers who were affiliated to the VdB (Volksdeutsche Bewegung) not only joined the opposition but also remained close to the leadership insofar as they did not use their right to opt out. Apparently the feeling of belonging to a corporation had taken priority over political activity.[42]

In Norway an attempt by the collaborationist Quisling government in February 1942 to regiment all children aged between 10 and 18 into a Nazi youth organization, the NSUF, and all schoolteachers into a new organization, Norges Lærersamband

(Norwegian Teachers' Corporation), which would also oblige them to educate children in Nazi ideology, was effectively opposed by a joint front of teachers and families. About 200,000 parents petitioned against their children's forced membership of NSUF, a clandestine committee of teachers organized a collective resignation from the new teachers' organization, and the Norwegian bishops also issued a protest. A majority of the 14,000 Norwegian teachers followed the boycott either by conviction or because of pressure from colleagues, although the number quoted varies from 7,000 to 12,000. Although the authorities did not accept the resignations and 600 arrested teachers decided to accept their membership, the protest was perceived as a great success and became an international news story, and the youth organization never became successful. The actions of parents and teachers frustrated the government's effort to Nazify the schools and were of great importance for the Norwegian civil resistance.[43]

Culture Wars

Schools were not only at the interface between Germanization policies and professional interest, they were also at the interface between Germanization and patriotic identities. The remodelling of school textbooks, the imposition of Nazi symbols and ritual and, in the core part of the Reich, the prohibition of speaking any other language than German were obvious vehicles of Germanization and Nazification. And yet means were found either to oppose this alien culture or to subvert it in ways that made it less powerful and effective. Commissions required to revise textbooks in a pro-German direction dragged their feet, Nazi rituals and ceremonies were gently mocked, indigenous languages were used in private by pupils and teachers, prayers and religious education were perpetuated not only outside the school but within it, and the regimentation of the youth was contested by teachers, priests, parents and ultimately young people themselves.

In Belgium there was no question of imposing the German language, but the question of what textbooks were to be studied became a stand-off between the Belgian and German authorities. Belgian textbooks of the interwar period aimed to stimulate a patriotic spirit after the first German occupation and often described the Germans as enemies of the fatherland and their military as wild armies which plundered, burned and killed. A German ordinance of 13 August 1940 required the deletion of all references considered 'abusive for the German honour'. *L'Histoire générale* of Frans Van Kalken and V. Clobert's *L'Histoire de Belgique* were banned. In October 1940, under pressure from the German authorities, the secretary-general of education set up a commission to scrutinize, revise and standardize textbooks at all levels of teaching. It was made up of inspectors or teachers from the state sector, but did not include representatives from Catholic education. From the outset *Militärverwaltungschef* (MVC) Reeder announced his requirements: subjective comments, such as passages hurtful to the German people, had to be deleted. Another ordinance required that all books prohibited in Germany, in particular by Jewish authors, should be banned equally in Belgium. The commission published ten lists with comments on textbooks, but made use of every opportunity not to be decisive or speedy. Members of the commission were poorly motivated, disagreed with each other, cited a lack of resources in wartime and encountered the opposition of classroom teachers to change. Most serious, the Catholic establishment was not part of the commission and did not recognize its decisions. The German authorities lost patience and began to take their own decisions. They prohibited some textbooks and made changes to the lists of the commission. Often the books in question, in spite of many controls, were hidden and not destroyed.[44]

In Bohemia-Moravia civic education was abolished in schools of all types in order to prevent it from being used as a vehicle for patriotic education. History, geography and biology did not disappear from the school curriculum but their contents had to be adapted to suit the interests of the Third Reich, notably its racial theories.[45] Clearly existing textbooks did not, in general, comply with these new requirements and therefore they had to be revised or withdrawn under the supervision of the Department of Culture and Politics attached to the Office of the Reich Protector. At first, in 1939–40, it was deemed adequate to cover or black out offending passages in standard texts. However, these spatchcocked and disjointed texts lent themselves to popular ridicule and became a rich source of jokes. The security apparatus of the occupation authorities considered popular jokes to be potentially subversive towards the Reich, and to hinder the re-education of the younger generation. Gradually, the revised textbooks had to be withdrawn for recycling and were replaced by provisional, Czech–German texts.

School life in the Greater Reich was a highly politicized environment. From their first day at school, the pupils were confronted with a regime that was very different from what they had known until then. The opening of school establishments was accompanied by a renaming of the school, often after a hero of the National Socialist Party, and a modification of the interior decoration. It was not rare then to find symbols of the NSDAP or the army on the walls, or pictorial reproductions of the emblematic figures of legendary Germanic heroes.[46] Portraits of Hitler and Nazi dignitaries were supposed to hang in the corridors as well as in the classrooms. At the beginning of each school year and term a colours parade was imposed on each school establishment. After the school register had been taken, the head, teaching staff and pupils were to assemble around the flagpole for the raising of the swastika, followed by the *Deutschlandlied* (German anthem). In the Moselle, as of 4 October 1940, an ordinance introduced the Nazi salute into school establishments, to be observed at the beginning and end of the school day.[47] From the start of the year 1941 prayers at school were definitively prohibited while the Nazi salute became obligatory at the beginning and the end of each class. It was not easy to put into practice this symbol of affiliation to the Third Reich and loyalty to Hitler. One school inspector reported that the teachers, far from imposing the Nazi salute, failed to set an example. 'The pupils', he wrote, 'do not respect the requirement of the Nazi salute because the teachers themselves did not observe it.'[48] On the other hand, open resistance was also dangerous. A group of students of the Lycée of Metz who called themselves 'Espoir Français', and replaced the Nazi flag by a board duster for the trooping of the colours, covered over pennants on war memorials reading 'für das Reich' by ones reading 'für Frankreich', sang the *Marseillaise* and shouted 'vive de Gaulle' in the school corridors, were decimated by a wave of arrests in June–July 1941.[49]

In territories annexed by the Reich, the use of languages other than German in public spaces was prohibited. Although a German dialect was spoken in the eastern part of the Moselle, the fact that French was banned gave its use a new subversive currency. In Moselle schools French was used outside school and even inside school during the break.[50] Rather than shirk their studies, children organized French composition contests, which were read secretly one after the other during the breaks. In fact language may have been less significant than the group solidarity of Lorrainers confronted by an influx of pupils and teachers from the Old Reich into their schools. One Moselle girl, Marie-Josèphe Lhote-Crée, who attended a secondary school in Metz, recalled that 'the breaks sometimes had a perfume of conspiracy which heartened them. Small clans of Lorrainers were formed which, looking carefully around and taking care not to be overheard by Germans from the Reich, commented on political events in as much as they knew about them.' The class was split in two by the arrival of a German girl in Tyrolean costume called Ursel, some, like Marie- Josèphe, becoming her admirers, others rejecting her. The fact that her father turned out to have been in the SA was of less significance for Marie-Josèphe than the recognition that, after the triumph of her theatrical production, Ursule won from the whole class so that Marie-Josèphe was no longer special.[51]

The Power of Religion

The presence of religion, especially the Catholic religion, has often been seen as an obstacle in the way of the totalitarian ambitions of the Third Reich. Catholicism was a dominant force in many of the new territories annexed by the Reich, giving it many of the problems that it had encountered by the absorption of Catholic southern and western Germany in 1871. In some areas, such as occupied Poland, where Catholicism was seen to be a source of Polish nationalism, the Germans were as hostile to the Church as they had been during the *Kulturkampf* of the 1870s. Elsewhere, as in Moselle/Luxemburg and in particular Belgium, the influence of the Catholic Church in education set important limits to what could be achieved in the Germanizing and Nazifying project.

In the Polish territories incorporated into Germany (Pomerania, Silesia and the Warthegau) the Church was allowed very little autonomy and any religious teaching that subsisted was not allowed to be in Polish. In the Warthegau the Catholic Church was almost non-existent, only 6 per cent of churches remaining open.[52] In Pomerania the use of Polish for religious ceremonies was restricted: the mass was in Latin, while the sermon and some hymns were in Polish. In the General Government, unlike in the annexed territories, the Polish hierachy remained. Private Catholic schools there and the Catholic University in Lublin were closed but religious instruction continued in clandestine schools. These loopholes were enough for the Catholic religion to subsist and sustain the preservation of a Polish identity.[53]

From the start of the annexation of Moselle and Luxemburg, symbolized by the expulsion of the bishop of Metz, Mgr Heintz, on 16 August 1940, the German authorities made clear their desire to undermine religious affiliation and above all to eliminate religion from the school system. Unfortunately Catholicism was part of the familial, local and regional identity, preserved in the case of the Moselle from the anticlerical onslaught of the Third Republic because it was part of the German Empire in 1870–1918.[54] While it was possible to shunt together state and religious schools in non-denominational schools, it was not possible to eliminate religious education from them. The first step of the authorities was to try to ensure that religious instruction was given by the teachers themselves, not as traditionally by priests coming into the schools, and yet the Catholicism of many teachers, themselves responsive to the demands of families, was unquestionable. During the visit of an inspector in 1941 to a Metz school, an open conflict occurred between the inspector and the schoolmaster. The inspector pointed out that the prayers at the beginning of lessons were now prohibited and launched into a diatribe against religion. 'In a great irritation the teacher declared that he would not admit any critical remarks about the Catholic Church and would not be wounded in his religious convictions by him.'[55] School authorities had to reprimand the teachers several times on that matter, while the continuing presence of priests in schools was frequently observed.[56] Even the Nazi regime had to recognize that there were limits to what they could achieve as the school, family, Church and teaching profession all combined to frustrate their efforts. In February 1941 Martin Bormann admitted to *Gauleiter* Joseph Bürckel that it was too early to prohibit religious education in the schools of the Moselle, while insisting that in time it would have to disappear. He hoped that religious instruction would be given not by the clergy but by the teaching staff, because even if they had religious tendencies they were judged less dangerous than the clerical personnel. Permission to teach religion would be given only to those clerics who were loyal towards the National Socialist state. If a chaplain died or was moved, great care would have to be taken that no other priest was appointed to this position.[57] In this way Hitler's deputy confessed that there was virtually nothing that could be done to eliminate the influence of the Church in such newly annexed areas of the Reich.

The Battle for Youth

One of the ambitions of Nazism was to exploit tensions between generations and genders in order to win over young people, both male and female, to dedicate their energies to the German nation and race. The intention was to monopolize the organization and indoctrination of youth, separating it from the rival influences of family, school and Church. By the same token, however, family, school and Church attempted to exert a restraining influence, in order to keep young people within the norms and structures which had been built up over the years. By and large, the Nazi project worked well when it focused on offering young people excitement and new challenges, but it had much more difficulty when the pressures of the war effort made it imperative to use young people both as forced labour and for military purposes.

The Hitler Youth was the most important vehicle for mobilizing youth, and its appeal should in no sense be underestimated. In the Moselle, young people were attracted by the dynamism and breadth of activities proposed by the movement, in which they sensed liberty and independence as well as discipline and leadership, a sort of counter-power against the restrictions usually imposed by parents, the Church and the school. A French report about the city of Metz and the valley of the Fentsch, written in January 1945, admitted:

> Many young Lorrainers still have the memory of exciting moments experienced in German organizations. If most young Mosellans, still influenced by their parents or other educators, endured the Nazi mystique rather than embraced it, some intelligent young people took up the attractive challenges offered by the Hitler Youth as a game... All this leads to indiscipline. You only have to ask certain parents about this: they no longer recognize their own children since these have been wholly under the authority of German youth leaders. It is quite normal to want to escape home at 14, especially these days. But now some children are challenging their parents, criticizing their decisions and their ideas. This lack of respect towards parents goes along with a general rudeness shown by children in public offices and at school.[58]

Gender roles as well as generational hierarchies were called into question by the experience of Mosellan youth under the occupation. The language spoken to girls, that they belonged to the German people and that the nation counted on them, was new and unusual. The 'Faith and Beauty' movement, which was popular in Metz, made it possible for a majority of girls to practise sports and other activities, which before the war would have been restricted to higher social classes. Music, singing and dancing, sports like tennis, swimming, canoeing and riding, lessons in domestic science and first aid, as well as competitive professional examinations, were widely available and made possible a certain form of emancipation. This was combined with dedication to the community during both the harvest period and the winter actions, when they undertook many tasks which until then were traditionally forbidden to them. Some, like Marie-Josèphe Lhote-Crée, Ursel and their friends, were recruited into the school first-aid unit and enjoyed the privilege of not having to rush for the cellars like the other pupils when the air-raid warning sounded. 'They were seen patrolling the school during the alerts, helmeted rather like Minerva, sporting their armbands, their first-aid kit around their waist, gas mask slung across their shoulder, swaggering at each step.'[59]

Some of the activities of the Hitler Youth were designed to develop their links to the local community. During the summer of 1943, for example, a toy-making competition was held by the Hitler Youth, the profits from which would go to the Winter Help programme. The city of Metz and the surrounding area made over 10,000 toys, which raised more than 30,000 reichsmarks. Such charitable activity and generosity was designed to win over the population to the cause of the National Socialist Party.[60] However, the stick was used as much as the carrot to ensure the success of the Hitler Youth. Parents who did not enrol their children in the Hitler Youth were refused help with the costs of schooling (*Kinderbeihilfe*).[61] By the same token, membership of the Hitler Youth became compulsory for any young person who wanted to continue study at secondary school.[62]

Overall, the development of the Hitler Youth challenged the authority of the family, Church and school, and these partners in education were often prepared to fight back. Some parents used the traditional methods employed to avoid military conscription, citing their children's vaccination programmes, diseases, physical or mental disorders.[63] Schoolteachers took exception to the vandalism and disrespectful behaviour that seemed to be legitimated by the Hitler Youth and tried to discourage it.[64] A local youth leader at Thionville involved young people in football matches or card games in the café on a Sunday, speaking to them in French, isolating them from German organizations.[65] Priests kept children busy with choir practice and services in order to keep them away from the Hitler Youth. One curé let his choirboys out through the vestry door while the Hitler Youth leader was waiting at the main church door for them to emerge from mass.[66] The Metz report of January 1945 concluded on the more favourable note that 'we owe it to our young priests and some schoolteachers who remained in the Moselle for having in part safeguarded our youth. If national-socialism did not flourish in the Moselle it is both because of its opposition to Christianity and because of the humanism incarnated by France.'[67]

In spite of the obligation to join the movement, rates of membership of the Hitler Youth never reached 100 per cent.[68] The military setbacks of the German army, such as Stalingrad, led to many objections and growing opposition. The Germans became aware that the ranks of the Hitler Youth were becoming thinner. The French language began to be heard again and comments such as 'in a fortnight the Americans will arrive' were expressed. In 1943 ten leaders of the Hitler Youth were attacked in the streets of Metz at night. In reply the German authorities strengthened their patrols and, according to them, succeeded in reducing by 80 per cent infringements of the 1940 ordinances which imposed a range of curfews on young people.[69]

Increasingly the logic of education clashed with the logic of war and the war economy. German attempts to win over the youth were increasingly undermined by their need to dragoon them into forced labour and then military service. On 6 June 1943 *Gauleiter* Joseph Bürckel introduced compulsory labour work service for young people in the Moselle. The authorities were adamant that this was also a means of forging the German people, and imposed fines and other sanctions on parents whose children did not enrol. But parents were also ready with excuses as to why their children should not work, such as illness or the danger of air raids. Air raids were not an excuse for the authorities. On the contrary, from 1943 pupils of the higher classes of the secondary schools had to serve in the FLAK (Flieger Abwehr Kanone), or anti-aircraft artillery. Still wearing the badges of the Hitler Youth but now under military discipline, 500 young people of the Moselle, including fifteen pupils aged 16 and 17 from the Sarreguemines secondary school for boys, were assigned to the city defence as *Luftwaffenhelfer* (air force auxiliaries). A few young people managed to avoid this service by hiding or fleeing over the French border, but most served for fear of provoking reprisals against their families.[70] Finally, towards the end of the war, after the establishment of the *Volkssturm* on the orders of the Führer on 25 September 1944, all able-bodied men aged 16 to 60 were officially called up and assigned to specific units. Of the 2,148 men drafted on 8–9 November 1944 in the Metz city district, there were 80 youths aged 16 to 18, including 35 who were only 16.[71]

In Belgium, where the ability of civil society to oppose such measures was greater, the imposition of forced labour destroyed what influence the Germans had with young people, driving them into the arms of the schools, universities and Church, which protected them and set limits to the effectiveness of German power. On 5 February 1943 a German ordinance obliged first-year students to interrupt their studies on 1 May and work for six months in Belgian industry. The universities joined forces and sent a letter of protest to the occupying authorities. They refused to collaborate and to transmit the directive to the students, which was eventually done by the collaborationist press. In March 1943 lectures were raided by the Gestapo and Belgian *gendarmerie*. Panic ensued, and courses were deserted by the students. The German authorities demanded lists of students under the threat of a permanent closure of the universities. While the Dutch-speaking University of Ghent acceded, the French-speaking university of Liège and the Catholic University of Louvain refused to submit lists. Despite threats that Louvain University would be closed down and the students sent to Germany, on 23 May 1943 the rectoral council backed the decision of the rector, Mgr Van Waeyenbergh, to stand fast. As a result the rector was arrested and imprisoned for eighteen months, but the university stayed open.[72]

In June 1943 the forced labour obligation was extended from university students to school sixth-formers. Head teachers were required to hand over lists of sixth formers to the *Werbestelle*, but they referred the matter at once to the state education department. On 24 July 1943 the education department instructed head teachers not to submit lists of pupils and tried to negotiate with the military authorities to have this order lifted. However, in some schools there were serious incidents when head teachers were arrested and the school searched. The heads of the church schools of the diocese of Tournai met at Kain during the summer of 1943 and declared that they were not prepared to collaborate in this way with the enemy. They were arrested, but the education department secured their release. It was often the same heads who at the beginning of the new school year in September 1943 took the risk of admitting sixth-formers who in theory were liable for forced labour, thus preserving them from the draft.

Conclusion

Schooling under the German occupation was thus not simply a vehicle for Germanization and Nazification but an interface at which partners which had traditionally competed for control of education – the state, the churches, teaching bodies, families – continued to compete. Naturally the balance of power between these partners now favoured the Third Reich or states subject to its control, but other partners found different ways of preserving their authority. Some wider factors gave them additional advantages. First, the German and Nazi regime did not have a monolithic approach to education in occupied Europe: while the core area was subjected to fairly ruthless Germanization and Nazification, outlying areas were not and were able thus to preserve their own education systems virtually intact. Second, plans for Germanization often came into conflict with other German plans for waging the war and mobilizing economies for the war effort. Thus when German teachers were required to fight, indigenous teachers who might otherwise have been removed had to be redeployed, while technical and vocational education was maintained to supply skilled workers, technicians and managers for the war effort and acted as a front for more conventional education programmes. In western Europe, where indigenous governments or administrations were still active, bureaucracies were able to cushion the demands of the German authorities in such matters as the revision or otherwise of textbooks. Elsewhere, in central and eastern Europe, where there was no state-level opposition and Germanization was applied most seriously, a whole subculture of clandestine education developed in order to maintain national culture and national elites, reviving practices that had been evolved in the period of subjection to the German and Russian empires before 1917–18. These clandestine systems demonstrated most effectively the resilience of the other partners traditionally involved in providing education: the churches, the teachers and families. In some areas, such as occupied Belgium, the Catholic Church, which was in any case dominant in education, was able to block German plans not only in regard to university administration but also in the conscription of forced labour from amongst students. In other areas, such as Norway, the teaching body put paid to the attempts of the Germans and the Quisling regime to dragoon them into becoming agents of the Nazi project. Everywhere families, with the best interests of their children at heart, did what they could to preserve traditional modes of education and oppose movements such as the Hitler Youth that set children against their families. This crucial activity is unfortunately one that we know very little about and merits serious future research.

Notes

1. Nicholas Atkin, *Church and Schools in Vichy France, 1940–1944* (New York and London, Garland Publishing Inc., 1991).
2. Robert Gildea, *Marianne in Chains. In Search of the German Occupation, 1940–1945* (London: Macmillan, 2002), p. 81.
3. Archives CEGES, AA 43/22, Investigation of Secretary-general of Education, M. Nijns, on his activities during the war, Brussels, March 1946.
4. Baudouin Groessens, 'L'enseignement: du fondamental au secondaire', in Jean Pirotte (ed.), *Pour une histoire du monde catholique au XXème siècle, guide du chercheur* (Louvain-La-Neuve, 2003), p. 405.
5. Robert Krantz, *Luxemburgs Kinder unter dem Nazi-Regime 1940–1944. Ein dokumentarbericht* (Luxemburg, Editions Saint-Paul, 1997), I, p. 32; Archives Départementales, Moselle (ADM) 1W 6, *Amtsblatt für das Schulwesen in Lothringen n°1*.
6. H. Hiegel, 'L'enseignement en Moselle sous l'occupation allemande de 1940 à 1944', *Cahiers lorrains* (1983), pp. 227–48.
7. ADM J7110, German report on the Hitler Youth in Moselle, 1940–4.
8. Hiegel, 'L'enseignement en Moselle', pp. 227–48; Robert Krantz, *Luxemburgs Kinder*, I, pp. 437–557.
9. Herma Bouvier and Claude Geraud, *NAPOLA. Les écoles d'élites du Troisième Reich* (Paris, L'Harmattan, 2000), p. 23.
10. *Perzekuce českého studentstva. Dokumenty* [Persecution of Czech Students. Documents], (Prague, 1945), p. 132.
11. František Bosák, *Česká škola v době nacistického útlaku* [The Czech School during the Period of Nazi Oppression], (České Budějovice, 1969), part II, p. 467.
12. Bosák, *Česká škola*, p. 468.
13. *Perzekuce českého studentstva*, pp. 61ff.
14. Józef Wulf, *Lodz. Das letzte Ghetto auf polnischen Boden* (Bonn, 1962), pp. 45ff.; Rolf Eilers, *Die nationalsozialistische Schulpolitik. Eine Studie zur*

Funktion der Erziehung im totalitären Staat (Cologne and Opladen, 1963), pp. 98–103.

15. Rolf Eilers, *Die nationalsozialistische Schulpolitik*, p. 19. On the discrimination against girls regarding their access to education, see the Nazi pedagogue Rudolf Benze, *Erziehung im grossdeutschen Reich. Eine Überschau über ihre Ziele, Wege und Einrichtungen* (Frankfurt-am-Main, Diesterweg, 1943), pp. 13ff.

16. On education in occupied Poland, see Czesław Madajczyk, *Okkupationspolitik Nazideutschlands in Polen 1939–1945* (Berlin, Akademie-Verlag, 1987), pp. 343ff.

17. Marian Walczak, *Nauczyciele wielkopolscy w latach wojny i okupacj 1939–1945* (Poznań, Instytut Zachodni, 1974), p. 25.

18. Walczak, *Nauczyciele wielkopolscy*, p. 21ff.

19. Walczak, *Nauczyciele wielkopolscy*, p. 18ff.

20. Madajczyk, *Okkupationspolitik Nazideutschlands*, p. 344.

21. Jiří Doležal, *Česká kultura za protektorátu. Školství, písemnictví, kinematografie* (Czech Culture under the Protectorate) (Prague Národni filmový archiv, 1996), pp. 50ff.

22. Józef Krasuski, *Tajne szkolnictwo polskie w okresie okupacji hitlerowskiej 1939–1945* (Warsaw, Państwowe Wydawnictwo Naukowe, 1977), pp. 303–5. We are grateful to Jacek Tebinka for help with this section.

23. Léon Strauss, 'L'Université de Strasbourg repliée. Vichy et les Allemands', in André Gueslin, *Les Facs sous Vichy* (Clermont-Ferrand, Institut d'Études du Massif Central, Université Blaise-Pascal, 1994), pp. 87–112.

24. Barbara Dickschen, 'L'AJB et l'enseignement', in Jean-Philippe Schreiber and Rudy Van Doorslaer (eds), *Les Curateurs du Ghetto. L'association des Juifs en Belgique sous l'occupation nazie* (Brussels, 2004), pp. 233–60.

25. Bénédicte Rochet, *Les Universités belges pendant la Seconde Guerre mondiale. Le cas particulier de l'Université catholique de Louvain et de l'Université d'État de Gand* (Louvain-la-Neuve, Université Catholique de Louvain, 1998), pp. 10–20; André Uyttebrouck and A. Despy-Meyer, *Les 150 ans de l'ULB (1834–1984)*, (Brussels, 1984), p. 39.

26. Rochet, *Les Universités belges pendant la Seconde Guerre mondiale*, pp. 10–20; *Le Diocèse de Tournai sous l'occupation allemande* (Tournai, 1946), p. 110.

27. Jiří Doležal, *Česká kultura za protektorátu*. pp. 64–6.

28. Central State Archives Prague, Archives of the Reich Protector's Office, Box 1802, secret report of 27 August 1940.

29. Josef Orlík, *Opavsko a severní Morava za okupace. Z tajných zpráv okupačních úřadů z let 1940–1943* (The Opava Region and North Moravia during the Occupation. From Secret Reports of Occupational Authorities between 1940–1943) (Ostrava, 1961), pp. 92–3.

30. Walczak, *Nauczyciele wielkopolscy*, pp. 14ff., 27. See also Józef Krasuski, *Tajne szkolnictwo*, pp. 19ff.

31. Jiří Doležal, *Česká Kultura*, p. 50f.
32. Czesław Madajczyk, *Okkupationspolitik Nazideutschlands*, pp. 348–53.
33. Jacques Sémelin, *Unarmed against Hitler. Civilian Resistance in Europe, 1939–1943* (Westport, CT, Praeger, 1993), p. 79.
34. *Chtěli nás vyhubit* (They Wanted to Exterminate Us) (Prague, Naše vojsko, 1961), p. 153; Vojtěch Dolejší, *Noviny a novináři* (Newspapers and Journalists) (Prague, 1963), p. 417.
35. *Věstník (protektorátního) ministerstva školství* (The Gazette of the [Protectorate] Ministry of Education, issue 17, no. 165, p. 332, 25 Nov. 1943.
36. Josef Kliment, *U obětovaného presidenta. Rukopis paměti část II* (With the Sacrificed President. Handwritten Memoirs, Part II), p. 108; Archives of the National Museum, Prague, Josef Kliment papers, box 23.
37. *Chtěli nás vyhubit* (They Wanted to Exterminate Us), p. 153.
38. Rudolf Benze, *Erziehung im grossdeutschen Reich*, pp. 79ff.
39. Archives Municipales, Metz (AMM) 1Z6, Chief of civil administration of Lorraine Moselle, school affairs section, to school representatives in Lorraine Moselle districts, 18 Feb. 1942.
40. AMM 1Z6, Chief of civil administration of Lorraine Moselle, school affairs section, to school inspectors of Metz, 25 April 1941.
41. ADM (Archives Départementales Moselle) 1W211, *Arbeitsstelle für Volksforschung im Deutschen Ausland-Institut Stuttgart*, 19 Sept. 1941.
42. National Archives of the Grand Duchy of Luxemburg (ANGDL), A 2–2 271 , Chief of civil administration of Luxemburg, Section II b, to school inspectors, 22 Oct. 1941; Circle chief, Political commissar, to permanent representative of Chief of civil administration Dr Siekmeier, 25 and 28 Nov. 1941; Permanent representative to Circle chief Dr Schroeder, 6 Dec. 1941; Circle chief, Political commissar, Dr Schroeder, to permanent representative of Chief of civil administration, Dr Siekmeier, 16 Dec. 1941.
43. Berit Nøkleby, 'Holdningskamp', in Magne Skodvin (ed.), *Norge i krig* (Oslo: Aschehoug, 1984–7), IV, p. 78; Hans Fredrik Dahl et al. (ed.), *Norsk Krigsleksikon 1940–45* (Oslo: J.W. Cappelens Forlag, 1995), pp. 258–60, 305–6, 309; Hans Fredrik Dahl, *Quisling. A Study in Tyranny* (Cambridge, Cambridge University Press, 1999), pp. 255–62. We are grateful to Anette Warring for this paragraph.
44. Mark Van den Wijngaert, *Schoollopen in oorlogstijd, het dagelijkse leven van middelbare scholieren tijdens de duiste besetting* (Brussels, 1988), p. 23; Archives CEGES, AA 43/22, Investigation of Secretary-General Nijns.
45. Kurt-Ingo Flessau, 'Schulen der Partei(lichkeit)? Notizen zum allgemeinbildenden Schulwesen des Dritten Reichs', in K.-I. Flessau, Elke Nyssen and Günter Pätzold (eds), *Erziehung im Nationalsozialismus* (Cologne, Böhlen, 1987), pp. 65ff.

46. E. Heiser, *La Tragédie lorraine* (Sarreguemines, Pierron, 3 volumes, 1978, 1979, 1983), vol. 3, pp. 53–4.

47. ADM 1W6, *Amtsblatt für das Schulwesen in Lothringen no. 1.*

48. ADM 331W , Chief of civil administration of Lorraine Moselle to all teachers of Lorraine Moselle, 21 Feb. 1941.

49. Bernard and Gérard Le Marec, *Les Années Noires. La Moselle annexée par Hitler, Documents et Témoignages* (Metz, Editions Serpenoise, 1990), p. 197.

50. AMM 1Z32, Chief of civil administration of Lorraine Moselle to all teachers of Lorraine Moselle, 21 Feb. 1941.

51. Marie-Josèphe Lhote-Crée, *Claire à l'école allemande* (Sarreguemines, Pierron, 2003), pp. 23–4, 36–7, 50, 58–9.

52. Ian Kershaw, 'War and "Ethnic Cleansing": the Case of the 'Warthegau', in K.G. Robertson (ed.), *War, Resistance and Intelligence. Essays in Honour of M.R.D. Foot* (Barnsley, Leo Cooper, 1999), p. 91.

53. We are grateful to Jacek Tebinka for help with this section.

54. L. Sidot, *L'Identité française dans la Lorraine annexée et nazifiée. Une Logique de l'être.* (Mâcon, Gourdon, 1995), pp. 34–5.

55. AMM 1Z6 , Chief of civil Administration of Moselle, explanation, 11 March 1941.

56. ANGDL A 2–2 123 , City Office of Education, Luxemburg, 29 June 1941; AMM 1Z32, City Office of Education, Metz, to all school heads, 28 Feb. 1941; ADM 1W754, State Governor of Westmark and Chief of civil adminisration of Lorraine Moselle, Section V, to all school heads, 4 Sept. 1941.

57. ADM 1W6, Representative of Führer to *Gauleiter* of Westmark, 10 Feb. 1941.

58. ADM J7110, Ministry of National Education, Direction of Popular Culture and Youth Movements, report of mission on 'Alsatian and Lorrainer Youth', 29 Jan. 1945.

59. Marie-Josèphe Lhote-Crée, *Claire à l'école allemande*, p. 61. On the enthusiasm of German children for the Hitler Youth see Nicholas Stargardt, *Witnesses of War. Children's Lives under the Nazis* (London, Jonathan Cape, 2005), pp. 31–5.

60. ADM J7110, German report on situation of Hitler Youth in 1940–4.

61. ADM 1W211, Report of a discussion with the *Ortsgruppenleiter* of Algrange, 1941. *Kinderbeihilfe* was a kind of school benefit.

62. AMM 1Z48a, circular of 11 Sept. 1941.

63. AMM 1Z48a, circular of 11 June 1942.

64. AMM 1Z48a, circular of 11 June 1942; letters between school heads and direction of Hitler Youth for Metz City and Metz district, 16 Jan., 19 Feb., 3, 4 and 11 June, 22 and 23 Dec. 1942, 9 Feb., 8 and 16 March, 6 and 8 May 1943; AMM 1Z48b, 10 Oct. 1943, 15 Feb. 1944.

65. ADM 1W211 Report of *Kreisleiter* of *arrondissement* de Thionville, end 1942.

66. H. Hiegel, 'Les mesures anti-religieuses du national-socialisme en Moselle, 1940–1945', *Mémoires de l'Académie Nationale de Metz* (1982), pp. 70–108.

67. ADM J7110, Ministry of National Education, Direction of Popular Culture and Youth Movements, report of mission on 'Alsatian and Lorrainer Youth', 29 Jan. 1945.

68. ADM 1W756, School inspection report for 1942–3.

69. ADM, J7110, German report on situation of Hitler Youth in 1940–44; the decrees on the protection of youth were 9 March and 7 Nov. 1940.

70. ADM J7110, Report on the activities of the Hitler Youth in Lorraine, in particular Metz, n.d.; Bernard and Gérard Le Marec, *Les Années Noires* (Metz, Editions Serpenoise, 1990), p. 197.

71. AMM 27Z9, Figures from lists dated 8–9 Nov. 1944, *Volkssturm Westmark, Arbeitsbataillon, Kreiskommandostab* Metz.

72. Dirk Martin, *De Rijksuniversiteit Gent tijdens de bezetting, 1940–1944, levend met de vijand* (Ghent, 1985), p.19; Frans Van Kalken, *Histoire des Universités belges* (Brussels, Brussels Office de Publicité, 1954), pp. 117–18.

–5–

Resisters

From Everyday Life to Counter-state

Olivier Wieviorka and Jacek Tebinka

In the whole of occupied Europe, the 'resistance' – defined as an organized movement – was a minority phenomenon. If resistance had been able to defeat the Germans or Italians alone and take power, it would not have been 'resistance' but a strong revolutionary or insurrectional movement. It was obviously not so, even if the figures differed from one country to another. Between 1 per cent and 3 per cent of the French, 2.4 per cent of the Belgians and 1–2.5 per cent of Danes were involved in the resistance during World War II, a proportion far from the 10 or 15 per cent of Poles who were committed to the struggle against the German occupier.[1] However, alongside these underground but structured movements there were other forms of resistance during the Second World War. Involving mainly civilian populations, they were generally based on civil rather than military opposition, protesting, for example, against rationing. These protests were usually peaceful, rejecting the use of violence. They were able to mobilize masses rather than just the elite working, for example, for the Special Operations Executive (SOE). They were also spontaneous, whereas resistance was supposed to be an organized movement. It may therefore be possible to make a distinction between resistance in general and civil resistance,[2] a distinction which to some extent coincides with Martin Broszat's distinction between *Resistenz* (unorganized protest) and *Widerstand* (organized and structured resistance).

Over and above such differences we can, however, point out the main features uniting these two kinds of resistance. Resistance, first of all, implies an intention to fight the occupier or its allies. A man who helps Jews to escape for money cannot therefore be considered as a resister. Resistance is a commitment – a desire to participate in a concrete and collective action against the occupier or its ally. Even when the action is individual, it is linked to a collective action which aims to oppose the new order in a collective way. Resistance also involves transgression. The resister obviously disobeys when his or her action breaks the law. It implies risk and danger – even when the resister seeks to minimize these.[3]

On the whole the issue is not to offer a definition of resistance but to explore whether and how everyday life was able to assist resistance, whatever its shape, by providing a fertile ground. This contention goes against the grain of much received wisdom. Resistance is often presented as an ideological enterprise in which people are fighting for noble values such as freedom or democracy, or for their country's sake. Resistance is equally presented as a fight aimed to help the Allies militarily. It should therefore be closely connected to the war rather than to the parameters of everyday life. To suggest that everyday life contributed to this struggle might therefore appear self-contradictory, since it lacked two important dimensions: ideology and military aims. Likewise, in western as in eastern Europe, resistance is often presented in a heroic way. The resister is described as a hero, pulling off incredible exploits, such as derailing trains or organizing bold ambushes. This picture, enhanced by many books and films, does not easily mesh with the image of a resistance deeply rooted in everyday life. Can a resister also be a man or woman peacefully demonstrating against food rationing?

The part played by everyday life in the resistance movement is therefore quite difficult to gauge. We can of course consider that the great deprivation endured by occupied peoples provided a fertile ground for underground activity. It gave good reason to denounce German or Italian plundering and to debunk the myth of the so-called 'new order'. Cold and hunger might equally pave the way for struggle. They could help to mobilize masses to protest against the occupiers' rule by demonstrations, strikes and so on. They could also help to organize people by giving them concrete and understandable objectives. It may have been easier to organize a demonstration against forced labour than to send plans of the Atlantic Wall to London. Daily life opposition might be a way of challenging the position of those employers and authorities who decided to work hand in glove with the occupiers. Further, everyday life might be a way to build a 'counter-state' able both to challenge the established power, exposing its inability to run the country, and to enforce its own rule, so that the resisters' law was now obeyed by the local population. On the other hand, we could also consider that everyday life was of no interest either for the resistance or for the Allies. Receiving intelligence and the organization of ambushes or train derailments were certainly helpful, but scarcely belonged to the sphere of everyday life.

This general pattern leads us to consider the links woven between resisters and the local population. The ability to use everyday life as a reason for struggle suggests that the resisters were both 'in' and 'out' of the community. To understand the problems of the population meant that resisters had to share these problems, living the occupation as ordinary people. But organizing the fight also meant, on the other hand, that resisters were strong enough to overcome the monotony of everyday life and to mobilize people. It meant that resistance organizations had to give a political meaning to petty dissent or opposition, that is to transform *Resistenz* into *Widerstand*. In this sense, protesting against the curfew was not only a way of obtaining extra hours of leisure but also a way of defying German or Italian orders. These ambivalent realities therefore gave the resisters a status as brothers as well as protectors.

Everyday Life: A Fertile Ground

The Food Problem

Generally speaking, resisters considered everyday life a fertile ground for combat. The kind of occupation imposed by the Germans or the Italians of course varied from one country to another, and no one could seriously compare France and Denmark to Poland or Russia. But one common factor linked all occupied countries despite their differences: they were all subject to the occupiers' law and had to provide goods and labour to the victors. To feed their own people and to win the war, Germany and Italy were willing to plunder subjugated countries and to that extent were extracting their national wealth. At the end of the First World War Germany, under Allied blockade, was on the verge of starvation, despite her pillaging of conquered territories, particularly in eastern Europe. The situation was different in the Second World War. The occupied territories were much better organized economically. Moreover in 1939–44 there was much more territory in German hands. Besides important industrial centres in the defeated countries, they now possessed the agricultural regions, both in eastern and western Europe: Yugoslavia, Poland, Bohemia and Moravia, Russia and Ukraine, together with Denmark, France and the Netherlands.[4] In France between 34 per cent of industrial production (in the first half of 1942) and 45–50 per cent (in the spring of 1944) was sent to Germany.[5] In addition the Germans took 240,000 tons of the 1,150,000 tons of meat produced in France.[6] In the Netherlands during the first years of occupation the Third Reich took one-seventh of food production and one-third of industrial output. Belgium was forced to send 72 per cent of its exports to Germany in 1941 and played an important role in German armaments. Moreover, some elements of the business establishment in western European countries, of which a good example was Denmark, accepted the fact that economic cooperation with Germany would benefit them and their societies.[7] This general trend became more obvious after the defeat of Wehrmacht in the battle of Moscow in December 1941. The Germans increased their economic exploitation of the conquered territories, especially in eastern Europe, in Poland and in the Soviet Union. In the Polish territories annexed to the Reich and in the General Government all large and medium-sized industrial properties were confiscated and put to work for the German war machine.[8] Plundering by the occupiers was of course not the only cause of shortages, which were also explained by the war in general and the disruption of national and international markets. The economic pressure exerted by the Germans, however, undoubtedly worsened the situation.

Daily life was thus substantially transformed between 1940 and 1944. To begin with people suffered from critical shortages. On 23 September 1940, for example, all French people received a food ration card which guaranteed them 1,327 daily calories, compared with 3,000 before the war. Apart from food, many other things were in short supply, such as coal, shoes, oil and clothes. In Belgium rations were similarly low and in addition the rationing system was inefficient so that people did not receive the rations to which they were entitled. Some people, especially in the industrial areas, went hungry.[9] The food situation was even grimmer in eastern Europe. In occupied Poland the lowest food rations provided between 623 and 834 calories daily. Polish Jews had to make do with rations of a mere 300 calories, which without provisions from outside the ghetto meant starvation.[10] Generally in eastern European countries even these starvation rations were impossible to obtain. This could lead to disaster, as in the Great Hunger in Athens during the winter of 1941–42.[11]

This bleak situation, however, was not always the rule in occupied Europe, and there are some counter-examples. For most Danes, for example, daily life was not altered significantly until the last year of the war. The average consumption of calories was only reduced from 3,300 to 3,150, even if the reduction was not equally distributed. In Denmark, ironically, the average consumption of meat, sugar and butter during the war was higher than in Germany.[12]

Shortages of food, fuel and clothes nevertheless provided a strong basis for resistance organizations, especially when the situation during the war contrasted sharply with that prevailing in the interwar period. In 1939 a Belgian miner had 700 grams of bread, butter or margarine, eggs or cheese, meat and fruit for his lunch. In 1941 this was reduced to three slices of bread and a little jam.[13] This deterioration was obviously difficult to tolerate and opened the way to resistance propaganda.

Clandestine newspapers naturally exploited the mood. Shortages were often presented as proof that the Germans were ransacking the occupied countries. 'The Germans receive 1500 grams of sugar per month, the French only 500', explained *Défense de la France*. 'Malnutrition is the most powerful weapon Hitler has to destroy France.'[14] 'Our "guests" will have 46 per cent more than a state of 40 million inhabitants for their consumption. This plunder has no precedent in history', asserted *Libération*, a clandestine newspaper published in the northern zone.[15] To highlight rationing was a way to point out the authorities' inefficiency and hence to contest their legitimacy. It was also a means to debunk the myth of collaboration by showing that the new order was simply to serve the Italian and German interests. To that extent propaganda tried to stir up people's anger and to transform bitter feelings into a patriotic and resistant attitude.

Subsistence was a fertile ground for resistance activity because it deeply concerned every citizen in every country. Many people resorted to the black market and hence broke the law. Others spontaneously hid their harvest or their cattle. In France, for example, peasants took around 250,000 tons of meat (21 per cent of overall production) for private consumption or for sale on the black or the grey markets. Disobedience thus became a means of survival. Moreover, people grumbled more or less openly against shortages while queuing up for hours. Such petty dissent might be risky. In Paris, for example, a woman was arrested in January 1941 because she criticized the Vichy state and accused the Germans of plundering the country. Another person was arrested because he recited two poems celebrating Charles de Gaulle.[16] These actions, however, cannot be considered as resistance, even though they broke the law. In the case of the black market they were motivated by private interest, whereas resistance tried to convey a general one. Besides, the risks were generally negligible, even when people criticized the authorities. However, by disobeying the law and opposing the Germans' will, ordinary people could live their everyday life as a way of resisting the occupier, even if the occupier did not consider this kind of action a real threat. The resistance thus had a seductive but difficult task: to convert these widespread feelings of frustration into collective action capable of challenging the rules of the new order.

Various ways were used, first to obtain material concessions and second to undermine collaborationist rule. The clandestine press tried to present the peasant's private consumption (or even black market sales) as a patriotic duty, a way to resist the law of the occupier. Demonstrations also took place. They were often organized in western Europe by communist movements for which such modes of dissent were tried and tested.[17] They generally mobilized housewives, giving social elements who were traditionally not used to committing themselves politically, such as women, a way to become involved. In the rue Daguerre in Paris, the demonstrations were led by Lise London, Arthur London's wife.[18] The police were reluctant to repress such demonstrations where women and sometimes children were on the front line. However, such protests were not organized throughout Europe because of the danger. In occupied Poland any open political demonstration would be suicidal in the face of the harsh German policy of ruthlessly punishing Poles and the Jews with the death penalty or concentration camps for minor offences.

It was, however, possible to launch other movements arising out of daily life, such as strikes for food or wages, in order to protest against occupation.[19] In Belgium in May 1941 a great strike broke out – the so-called strike of the 100,000. It mobilized 70,000 workers for seven days and was successful in that wages were increased by 8 per cent. The Communist Party played an important part in the process, which was the starting point of the development of an underground trade union movement, the Comités de Lutte Syndicale.[20] In northern France a similar strike broke out in May 1941, as 100,000 coal miners stopped working. The lack of soap, of food and of coal offered a favourable ground for this spontaneous movement, even if the Communist Party helped to organize it. The strikers risked harsh repression. In fact 450 people were arrested and 244 subsequently deported. The clamp down dissuaded miners from attempting such a movement again, but the 'great strike', as it has been called, was on the whole a success. It showed that it was possible to transform corporate claims into a political movement and to link class conflict to a patriotic fight.[21]

The same pattern can be observed in Greece. On 12 April 1942 a postman collapsed in Athens from starvation. Some of his workmates demanded a ration increase, a demand that was rejected by the head of the office. On 13 April a strike broke out and the government was obliged to yield. Rations were increased and the strike leaders set free. As in the French case, the movement had been mainly spontaneous. But the EAM helped it by persuading the strikers to hold out.[22]

It was definitely more difficult to strike when an intermediary between the strikers and the Germans, such as collaborating authorities or local owners, did not exist and the occupying forces used terror and collective reprisals from the very beginning. On 13 December 1940 four hundred workers in the Warsaw tram garage went on strike. The Gestapo immediately arrested the leaders of the strike and threatened their immediate execution if the workers did not return to work within ten minutes. The argument was convincing. During the following years, as the occupiers' terror escalated, strike actions in the General Government were rare. Successes, such as the small pay rise secured in spring 1943 by workers at Warsaw's radio engineering factory, were exceptional.[23]

Forced Labour

Forced labour also offered a fertile ground for the resistance movements. In the face of total war the Reich was keen to replace German workers who had gone to the front by foreign workers. In France forced labour (the *Service du Travail Obligatoire*) was established in February 1943 and thousands of people (probably more than 600,000) were conscripted to work in German factories. This pressure often led people to hide to avoid forced labour. Such actions cannot be considered as resistance because draft dodgers did not always intend to fight or resist the Germans. They generally just wanted to protect themselves, even if such an action was frustrating for the Reich, which was trying to exploit the European workers for total war. Some movements, however, did become a real threat for the occupiers. In the Netherlands a two-day strike in February 1941 against the persecution of Jews was part of a broader movement. Metal workers went on strike to oppose forced labour in Germany, while unemployment relief workers were mobilized because of material grievances. In Greece the fear of forced labour created a kind of pre-insurrectional atmosphere in February 1943. Strikes paralysed Athens, a great demonstration organized by the EAM took place on 5 March 1943, involving more than 7,000 people. This mobilization obliged the collaborationist authorities to surrender and give up the forced labour project. As a result, Greeks provided only 16,000 workers, a mere 0.3 per cent of the labour force in the Third Reich.[24] In the Netherlands the decision to send the Dutch POWs freed in 1940 back to Germany as part of a plan to oblige Dutch workers to go to Germany provoked a massive strike in 1943, the so-called *april–mei stakingen* (April–May strikes). The Germans reacted violently.[25] In France some young men chose to join the maquis instead of working in Germany, but they in fact remained a minority. In the Isère department 30 per cent of draft dodgers joined the maquis, while in the Aude it was only 6 per cent. That said, these minorities amounted to thousands of people. It was thus a difficult challenge for French resistance organizations suddenly to integrate thousands of draft dodgers and to convert them into fighters. This example, however, clearly reveals ways in which organized resistance could convert *Resistenz* into *Widerstand*.

Despite opposition to the deportations in the occupied countries during the period of the war, the number of civilian labourers and POWs on German territory amounted to 12 million, of whom 8,435,000 million were civilian workers, forced and voluntary. Every conquered state was affected by deportations to Germany, although to differing extents: forced and voluntary workers included 2,775,000 Soviet citizens (32.6 per cent of all civilian workers), 1,600,000 Poles (18.9 per cent of the total), 1,050,000 French (12.5 per cent), 960,000 Italians (11.4 per cent), 355,000 Czechs (4.2 per cent), 475,000 Dutch (5.6 per cent), 375,000 Belgians (4.4 per cent) and 80,000 Danes (0.95 per cent).[26]

Indoctrination

Finally, some countries were directly threatened in their daily life by the indoctrination attempts of Nazism or fascism: Italianization in some parts of Greece, Nazification and (re-) Germanization of parts of France, Belgium, Poland, Slovenia and Czechoslovakia annexed to Germany.[27] Furthermore, driven by the vision of *Lebensraum* in the east and the extermination of the Jews, anti-Slavic racism, and the hope that *Blitzkrieg* would bring the defeat of the Soviet Union in 1941, the Germans prepared fertile ground for the development of the resistance movement on the occupied Soviet territories. Berlin did not even decide to create small satellite states, such as Croatia, or the Baltic states of Estonia, Latvia and Lithuania, where the Wehrmacht was welcomed in summer 1941 as the liberator from Soviet rule. There was a similar situation in Ukraine, where the Germans needed collaborators and fuelled the hatred of the Ukrainians against Jews and Poles, but did not intend to form a puppet Ukrainian government as they had done during the First World War.[28]

Generally, attempts to win sympathy for Nazi ideology did not gain much support in the occupied countries. Attempts to use communism as a spectre after the Stalingrad defeat did not work even in the eastern Europe that had been occupied by the Soviet Union earlier, in 1939–41. On the contrary, the Red Army victories contributed massively to the popularity of the communist resistance in the west. One might add that everyday life under the German occupation and the high level of reprisals reduced the numbers of those eager to serve the conquerors. In spring 1943 in Katyń, near Smolensk, the graves of 4,300 Polish officers murdered by the Soviets three years earlier were discovered. The Germans tried to use this as an argument to recruit Poles to serve them, but without success. In German newsreels shown in the cinemas of the General Government, SS divisions formed in other occupied countries were paraded on screen, with the question 'Where are the Poles?' The audience usually came back, 'In Auschwitz'.[29]

The resistance movement tried to oppose Nazification or Italianization in the context of daily life. In Poland it took over clandestine teaching at all levels to preserve Polish culture and identity. In Alsace some families tried to maintain French customs and traditions although this was forbidden by the German authorities. In Norway a huge protest led by the teachers' trade union prevailed against the Nazification of the schools in 1942.[30] The struggle against Nazification was thus often carried out in the sphere of daily life, not in order to help to defeat the German armies but mainly to preserve a national or a collective identity that was endangered by the occupation.

Germanophobia was sometimes a fertile ground which linked daily life to mass movements. In Denmark in 1940–3 there was not a favourable social and political climate for more active forms of resistance, let alone guerrilla warfare. Compared with eastern Europe the occupiers were scarcely visible in everyday life. In the summer of 1943, after the successes of the Allies and the fall of Mussolini in Italy, the public mood in a traditionally anti-German society changed. The wave of strikes in Denmark in August 1943 led the Germans to order the Danish government to impose martial law, including the death penalty. Until then strikes, unlike in other occupied countries, had been treated as an internal Danish affair. They were a product of the collaboration policy they were seeking to overthrow. The government, which had tried to protect the country from the harsher forms of occupation as the price of economic cooperation with Berlin, was forced by the strikes to refuse the German demands and resigned. The revolt in August 1943 represented the important transition from collaboration to resistance, but the emergence of a dual power between the legal and the illegal political forces was only in embryo until the next wave of strikes in the summer of 1944, which constituted almost a national revolt. It started in Copenhagen at the end of June. The workers struck partly to protest against a German curfew and, with the whole capital at a standstill, the Germans cut off the water, gas and electricity and all means of communication. This revolt was important and led to the death in combat of about a hundred people, quite a heavy toll although not comparable with the quarter of a million inhabitants who died during the Warsaw uprising in August and September of 1944. The strike in Copenhagen ended with compromise. The Germans withdrew the Schalburg Corps – the Danish Nazi force – from the capital and lifted the curfew, and the strike came to an end.[31] These strikes had the effect of involving ordinary Danes in the struggle by giving them a part to play, whereas military resistance, mainly led by the SOE, was supposed to be restricted to a small elite of professionals.

Everyday life, from the rationing, forced labour and indoctrination angles, obviously provided fertile ground for the resistance forces in occupied Europe, helping the clandestine movements to popularize their fight by propaganda and to organize their struggle by various means such as strikes, demonstrations, sabotage or – occasionally – guerrilla warfare. There was in fact a strong basis for doing so, as everyday life was able to generate spontaneous and hidden protest – by hiding the harvest or cattle, becoming a draft dodger or listening to the radio. In the spring of 1944, 70 per cent of radio owners in western Europe were listening to the BBC – a very impressive figure.[32] In many ways the resistance was able to transform such individual and spontaneous forms of *Resistenz* into *Widerstand*, a general and organized protest against occupation. Occupation, however, did not always breed favourable conditions for the development of the resistance. In the Netherlands, Bohemia and Moravia quite a favourable economic situation and the relatively light burden of the German rule in 1939–42 prevented the development of an underground movement. The attempt on the life of Reinhard Heydrich, Reichsprotector of Bohemia and Moravia, undertaken in Prague on 27 May 1942 by the British SOE with the permission of the Czech government in exile, did not change the situation. Himmler's deputy died a couple of days later in hospital. In retaliation the Germans shot 192 men from the village of Lidice and 32 from Lezaky. After the assassins were found, betrayed by one of their parachutist colleagues, and killed in combat, the occupying authorities unleashed savage repression. Subsequently, however, they revised their tactics and tried to avoid antagonizing the population and driving them to resistance.[33]

Investigating the Resistance Strategy

Divided or United Societies?

Daily life issues offered a good basis for resistance because they were common and frequently led people to despair. These motives, however, seem insufficient to explain mass mobilization. The social changes provoked by the occupation have also to be taken into account. To some extent rationing and forced labour were divisive forces. They generally increased the geographical gap between the countryside, which was often able to live in autarchy, and the towns, which were deprived of almost everything. In France townspeople were starving, especially in the north, but the countryside was often prosperous. A similar situation could be found in other occupied countries. In the General Government the everyday life of the rural population in 1939–44 was easier than that of the urban population. Villages located close to the bigger towns were better off thanks to the food they could smuggle onto the black market. On the other hand, the partisan movement based in the countryside provoked repression. In Poland, Yugoslavia and the Soviet Union this often took the form of pacification of whole villages, with the murder of men, women, children, and the elderly.[34]

New social divisions appeared too. Wage earners suffered, caught between inflation and frozen wages. The group particularly afflicted in the General Government comprised the intelligentsia, civil servants and teachers who had lost their jobs and had to sell their belongings. Peasants, in contrast, were advantaged because they could at least eat what they were producing. While Germans or Italians controlled economic resources, those near to them, such as police or customs officers, were favoured. Alongside the occupation authorities arose a group of informers betraying Jews, gypsies and members of underground movements. The black market made up an inseparable part of everyday life in occupied Europe. It presented enormous possibilities for quick profits at the expense of the rest of the society. In effect a new group was forming – the black marketeers.[35] Forced labour also had unequal effects. In France peasants, students and some workers such as coal miners avoided it, but others, generally factory workers, were Fritz Sauckel's main target. Everyday life was clearly not the same for everybody.

On the other hand, rationing and forced labour could serve as unifying factors. Apart from the happy few, everybody in occupied countries suffered cold and hunger. Everybody was fearful of being rounded up and sent to Germany. To that extent, occupation conditions can also be considered as a factor of social unification. The occupation to a large extent eliminated many of the social and political conflicts that prevailed before the war. Social and political hatred vanished or appeared secondary. Hatred of the occupiers mingled with patriotic feelings as a unifying factor. Of course, this should not be overestimated. The occupation also generated new conflicts, for example between winners and losers. Some elements of the ruling classes, such as industrialists, were doing 'business as usual' with the occupiers. Old conflicts did not vanish but took on a new shape during the occupation. For example, many anti-communists, in Greece and elsewhere, became collaborators. Overall, however, the new situation involved by the occupation offered ways to unite people and overcome old conflicts.

Uniting People

In order to unite people, resistance organizations often used symbols such as patriotic emblems or rituals of commemoration. This process was obviously strengthened by the BBC in occupied Europe. Thanks to its wide diffusion, it helped to shape public opinion – even in occupied territories – and was therefore able to create some kind of consensus. It was sometimes able to deliver clear instructions to the population. In France monuments celebrating the Great War were often decked with flowers, sometimes spontaneously, sometimes on the orders of Free France. The 11th of November was also celebrated by many people in Belgium. In the Netherlands people wore a carnation, which was the royal symbol, while in Denmark wearing a badge in honour of the King was a widespread phenomenon. On the territory of the General Government in Poland people laid flowers on the graves of national heroes on 3 May, the prewar Constitution day. Candles were also lit on the graves of Polish heroes and national memorials on All Souls Day and Independence Day (11 November), while anchors painted on the walls of buildings symbolized the Polish underground movement. Even such symbolic acts could lead to repression. On 15 February 1944 the Germans executed forty men in the centre of Warsaw. On the site of the executions groups of people in prayer lit candles. The German police reacted by shooting them and those who survived were immediately arrested.[36]

Were these acts signs of resistance? They cannot always be considered so. The risk was not always high: by acting in such a way, civilians were just expressing a feeling of patriotic protest without really endangering the occupiers, and these petty demonstrations of protest were not always linked to a collective action of resistance. But by encouraging this kind of action, resistance organizations were able to establish the fight on a national and depoliticized ground, which was a means to overcome social divisions and to bring together very different people.

The problem, indeed, was to gather different social classes in the same movement. Old organizations such as political parties or trade unions were somewhat hampered because they were not necessarily used to rallying people in such a way; nor were they easily able to develop the new types of struggle required by the war. Political parties recruited on ideological and social grounds, which by definition perpetuated conflict. In a democracy Marxists were necessary against nationalists, conservatives against social democrats. Old political habits died hard. In Mediterranean countries such as Greece political parties were essentially based on clientelism.

The occupation, however, dismantled these connections. Scarcity prevented bosses from handing out favours because there was nothing to distribute: neither *panem* nor *circenses*. Trade unions, meanwhile, recruited on a narrow basis, which was occupational or professional (skilled workers, unskilled workers, white-collar workers, peasants). These old kinds of organization were, on the whole, not suited for the new context created by the war because they were not able to recruit on a national basis.

This general pattern, of course, must be refined. In Belgium the trade unions were obliged to make way for a single union, the Union des travailleurs manuels et intellectuels (UTMI), which soon came under German control. Some leaders of the prewar trade unions were involved in this new union, often motivated by political and ideological concerns. Other leaders started to fight the new union, primarily using the clandestine press. Before the war Belgian trade unions were closely linked to political parties – there was a Catholic and a socialist union – and to the state, with the unions, for example, paying out unemployment benefits. From 1941 clandestine unions emerged which were novel in two ways. They were based on factories and aimed to organize all workers, regardless of their political opinion, even if in reality they were either communist (the CLS) or radical-socialist (Mouvement Syndical Unifié).[37] In Denmark old parties, organizations and associations were the most important channels of recruitment to the resistance movement. These examples serve to play down the novelty of resistance organizations. However, if they were not new, they sometimes appeared to be so, such as the Front National in France or the EAM in Greece. These seemed to transcend old conflicts that had often paralysed prewar political life. The EAM, for example, rejected the old Greek debate between Venizelists and royalists, and the Front National in France avoided dealing with the problem of the Church – for so long a poisonous conflict. By partly focusing their attention on everyday life, they appeared political and were hence able to gather people coming from various sides, above all if they used strong national symbols.

New Leaders?

These formations were often led by new leaders, unknown before the war. Georges Guingouin in the Limousin (France) was a great resistance leader but before the war was an unknown schoolteacher. The KKE (the Greek Communist Party) put a woman, Chryssa Chatzivassileiou, in the first line, an astonishing exception in a country where politics was run only by men. This traditional picture underwent changes during the war, and in September 1944, at the very end of the German occupation, a third of Greek women were involved in the resistance, which made the country one of the most feminist in Europe.[38]

Maybe this is not so surprising. Because resisters depended on the resources and functions of daily life, the home was sometimes very important to the recruitment and the participation of women in the resistance. It was one of the consequences of the politicization of daily life and the undermining of the boundary between the public and the private sphere. By transforming daily life problems into political issues (arguing, for example, that rationing was not just a problem of bread but the result of the occupiers' plundering), the resistance gave it an ambivalent status. The home was both a sanctuary where it was possible to forget the cruelty of war and a space opened up by the strains and stresses of the war and occupation.

The emergence of new leaders also increased the feeling of novelty. Repression increased the possibility of promotion in the underground movement, as the most active members of the resistance were mostly in their twenties and thirties. People in their forties were often in the top positions in the underground movement. This was very different from the age structure of prewar organizations.

The new leaders were not disconnected from everyday life. On the contrary, they often shared ordinary people's lives, a phenomenon which was new in many countries where a gap frequently separated leaders from the rank-and-file. A simple fact explains this. Apart from some special cases, resisters seldom lived totally in the underground movement and thus faced the problems of everyday life like other people. Even a great resister such as Pierre Brossolette in France was obliged to teach at the Lycée Sévigné until 1942 and kept a bookshop for two years. Clandestine formations were generally unable to pay their members, so that to survive resisters had to keep their jobs. Having a job was both a necessity in order to survive and prudent, since sudden disappearance might attract police attention. Last but not least, some resisters kept their jobs in order to help their organizations professionally. Postmen, railway employees, printers and even mayors were often more useful in post than if they quitted to join guerrilla movements.

To a certain extent, this view seems to contradict the resistance experience. Resisters have often been described as mavericks, heroes or outlaws, living in underground circles cut off from the reality experienced by ordinary people. In France memoirs written after the war by former resisters and the films seeking to describe their actions, such as *L'Armée des ombres* and *Lucie Aubrac*, have popularized this vision. This representation is to a large extent a myth. Resisters often shared the common everyday life, a fact that has been seen as a handicap, since they were not able to resist full time. It was also an advantage, however, as being involved in everyday life helped them to understand people's feelings and establish networks in a wider community.

Protecting People

For these reasons, resistance movements were sometimes able to organize people on an everyday life basis. The Belgian underground trade union movement could survive only in the factory. In Greece the EAM set up local and regional committees to mobilize the masses on a territorial or occupational basis by involving people according to their social roles. The EAM followed the Communist Party pattern by organizing people at a grassroots level and on a local basis: in the village, town or city neighbourhood. It also had a trade union organization (the Greek Workers' Liberation Front), a youth organization (United Panhellenic Youth organization) and a welfare organization (the National Solidarity). In France this trend was less widespread. But movements and networks did nevertheless recruit in specific spheres and some organizations were especially devoted to specific targets. Thus the ORA (Organisation de Résistance de l'Armée) tried to attract officers, while the Front Uni de la Jeunesse Patriotique aimed to recruit young people. This pattern was useful in mobilizing the masses against the occupier by keeping contact with ordinary men and women.

By protesting against rationing and scarcity, resistance movements were able to mobilize the masses to involve them in social struggles. As we have seen, they were able to focus propaganda on the problems of everyday life and to organize demonstrations and strikes. A further step was sometimes reached when the resistance was able to build a counter-state, that is, to replace a disqualified power and enforce a new legitimacy. This new role was sometimes imaginary when the resister was seen as a modern Robin Hood, reactivating popular legends. In Provence (southern France) the resister was often compared to the 'provençal bandit', mythologized after the eighteenth century. Such representations were more often based upon reality when the population regarded the resisters as their protectors. To achieve this, resisters used various means. Some actions in daylight obliged the occupiers to give up unpopular measures such as forced labour in Greece. They also protected civilians in clandestine ways. Some movements provided false papers to people facing persecution, such as Jews, Communists and families of resisters. They could often rely on a favourable ground. In some townships, civil servants spontaneously issued false identities to those being sought by the police, falsifying registers and giving certificates to people who needed them. This strategy was sometimes a risky one, because many false papers derived from the same source, attracting police attention. The resistance could play a part in this scheme, by centralizing this source and providing those on the run with papers coming from different regions. *Défense de la France*, for example, printed thousands of false identity cards and made false rubber stamps. It used models coming from many places, such as northern France or Burgundy, and was able to dispatch complete kits to the whole of France. Resisters living in Britanny were often given papers from Franche-Comté, which complicated police enquiries. In the Netherlands a national organization, Landelijke Knokploegen (LKP), took charge of this process. It launched 233 raids on government offices (May 1943–September 1944) to steal identity and ration cards.[39]

Jews could also be helped. Neighbours sometimes sheltered children when parents were deported. This was the case for 4,000 children in the Netherlands. Some priests issued false baptism certificates and hid children in religious boarding schools or monasteries, as depicted in Louis Malle's film *Au Revoir les Enfants*. Overall, 75 per cent of the French Jewish community was saved by ordinary people acting in this spontaneous way. Attempts were also made to organize this rescue in a much more structured way. Thus the Notre-Dame de Sion congregation, devoted to the conversion of the Jews, and the Organization pour le Sauvetage des Enfants (OSE), a Jewish structure devoted to rescuing children, tried to establish regular channels to hide Jews. In the General Government the secret Council for Aid to Jews (Rada Pomocy Żydom 'Żegota') supplied Jews hidden outside the ghetto with money, shelter, medical help and false documents. The financial means for this were sent by the Polish government in exile and Jewish organizations from Allied and neutral countries.[40]

Movements could also try to save people by sending them to a safe place – abroad in general but also to the so-called Free Zone in France until 1942. Here they could sometimes also rely on very old traditions. Smugglers were used to crossing frontiers, especially out of France over the Jura or Pyrenees or in Norway or Denmark, where crossing the border had never been a problem. Smugglers or people used to travelling abroad converted their know-how during the war, helping people to freedom sometimes for money, sometimes for nothing. From France about 40,000 people succeeded in getting to Spain, of whom 23,000 intended to fight in North Africa.[41] Some 20,000 Jews were rescued by crossing the Spanish or Swiss border.[42] In Denmark 7,000 Jews were saved, sent to Sweden in 600 or

700 shuttles in October 1943, a rescue which had huge patriotic resonance. These rescues started with private initiatives and were channelled by social and political networks – churches, political or professional associations and even the police. Once again the resistance was able to structure what began as a spontaneous initiative. The same process can be observed in France, where Protestant organizations such as the CIMADE and other Christian or Jewish structures (Scouts or the OSE) sometimes worked together to rescue Jews.

In the same way, networks and movements such as the Comète or Pat O'Leary networks in Belgium organized channels to help resisters or Allied soldiers to escape. From this point of view the resistance was the only structure able to combine local initiatives, frequently spontaneously born, but unable to work on a stable basis. Geographical context, however, played a great part in this kind of action. France, Norway and Denmark were obviously at an advantage compared to Belgium or Netherlands. While 80,000 Norwegians were able to reach Sweden during the war, only 200 Dutch people succeeded in getting to Great Britain.

Resistance movements sometimes also destroyed files which were used by the occupier for round-up or forced labour. In the night of 10–11 February 1942 the Dutch resistance movement set fire to the building of the Arbeitsamt (the German labour office) in Amsterdam, but the files survived. In February 1944 a band led by Léo Hamon burnt the STO census in Paris. In France and Belgium the maquis helped the *réfractaires* (forced labour draft dodgers) to hide in forests or mountains.[43] In the General Government the Polish Home Army (Armia Krajowa) killed some of the German Arbeitsamt officers and burned the files of tax offices in order to make the collection of taxes and compulsory food deliveries difficult. In some countries the resistance was strong enough to organize rationing instead of the authorities subjected to the occupiers. In Greece, for example, the EAM was able to fix prices and make requisitions. At Argalsti (Pelion) wood prices and wages were decided by the new local administration.[44] In a parallel way the resistance was able to protect civilians, but civilians were also able to protect resisters. Concierges kept silent, even when they witnessed strange comings and goings. Shopkeepers acted as mail boxes, where resisters left and received messages. *Défense de la France*, for example, used a bookshop called *Le Vœu de Louis XIII* for that purpose.

Liberated Zones

Resistance movements were sometimes even able to rule liberated zones. Some 'free zones' were liberated before the arrival of the Allies. Such cases occurred in states where a strong partisan movement existed, able to remove the occupiers from part of the territory, for example in the Soviet Union, Poland, Yugoslavia, France, Greece, Slovakia and Albania. When the resistance took power, it had to deal with everyday problems such as rationing, taxation and schooling. Power was sometimes exerted in a conventional way, when the resisters were merely restoring the old order. But sometimes it took the form of a utopia, when they tried to enforce new rules articulating a kind of revolution.

In France the plateau of Vercors in the Alps was liberated for two months (9 June–21 July 1944) by the resistance, starting just after the Allied landings. On 3 July the Republic was officially organized but the new administration had been working since 9 June. A civil administration (the Comité de Libération Nationale du Vercors) was in charge of civil affairs, even if it was in practice subject to the military. This republican authority took two main courses of action. First it tried to preserve the Vercors from a military and civilian point of view. It organized the rationing and watched over the mail (which was censored) and the comings and goings of the inhabitants. But also took the political initiative by abolishing the Vichy regime, decking houses with flags and above all by punishing traitors and collaborators. A hundred individuals, mainly French notables, were jailed and a court martial set up which handed down five death sentences in 43 days.[45] A similar experiment took place in Burgundy, in the Aignay-le-Duc area, in August 1944. As in the Vercors – but on a smaller scale – this area, free of Germans for a month, acted as a counter-state. The *maquisards* controlled rationing and taxes. A court martial was set up but the purge was so benevolent that the clandestine prefect, Jean Bouhey, stated that the maquis was too tolerant of Vichy supporters.[46] These examples show that resistance did not always aim to set up a revolutionary power. To that extent the French free zones cannot be compared to the Commune experiment of 1871. They did not invent utopian measures and they rejected violence, for there were few death penalties. Above all they wanted to get back to normality, to restore the republican regime in a symbolic way (decking houses with flags) and legally (abolishing Vichy law).

'Free zones' were not able to survive without help from the Allies. That meant that it was very difficult for resistance organizations to convert daily life protest into armed struggle. The only ways were guerrilla actions and uprisings. The former were impeded by the lack of weapons, as experienced by the French maquis, while the latter were hampered by the military superiority of the occupiers. Uprisings in Paris and Prague ended in success thanks to the rapid movement of the Allied forces, which could help the insurgents. This was not always the case. In Poland in July and August of 1944 the territory around the town of Skalbmierz, about 1,000 square kilometres, was liberated by the partisan forces and called the Pińczów Republic. It was a result of cooperation between the non-communist forces – the Home Army (Armia Krajowa – AK) and Peasant Battalions (Bataliony Chłopskie – BCh) – and the Communist People's Army (Armia Ludowa – AL). For a couple of days the partisans were able to retain power, but in the end they were too weak to effectively oppose the German forces and to hold the territory. Attempts to seize the area close to the Sandomierz bridgehead established by the Red Army failed, and the Germans reoccupied the lost territory, destroying the Republic.[47]

The case of the Warsaw uprising was different. Stalin was opposed to the victory of the Home Army, and indeed the elimination by the Germans of the largest Polish centre of the independence movement was in his interest. The uprising, which was supposed to last a couple of days, turned into a sixty-three-day combat. The Home Army captured a large part of the capital of Poland. Authority was taken over by an administration loyal to the Polish government in exile. The Poles tried to build the structures of the state and organize the judiciary and social services under the constant bombardment of the German forces.[48]

In other countries, however, the free zones administration took another turn, because the resisters, mainly the Communists, wanted to organize a revolutionary power. This was possible for a while, when the occupier in fact agreed to surrender control of certain areas. In Greece, for example, the EAM tried to enforce a *laocratie* which was based upon self-administration, involvement of new categories (mainly women and youths) and popular courts. In Yugoslavia and Albania the liberation of certain territories by the communist resistance movement in 1944 was the first phase of the establishment of communist power. This strategy was sometimes successful when the occupiers gave up territories, concentrating on the control of major cities and the main axes of communications. It was sometimes a failure. In Greece, for example, the British military presence there in the autumn of 1944 explained the failure of the Communists, who lost the civil war that ended in 1949.[49]

Such resisters' administrations were sometimes positively viewed by civilians. So long as the resisters delivered food and goods to the villages and prevented plundering by the occupying forces, their authority was generally accepted. But this pattern was not always the rule. Liberation was sometimes synonymous with reprisals. The enthusiasm of the inhabitants of Warsaw after the outbreak of the uprising in 1944 wore thin, as the struggles continued and life under constant fire and bombardment became more and more difficult. According to British historian Joanna Hanson, 'whilst some people treated the insurgents as faultless heroes, others regarded them as the instigators of their suffering and the murderers of their families and children'.[50] In France, too, people were sometimes hostile towards the resistance – mainly the maquis – because it attracted the attention of the Germans, which often led to reprisals. Nazi propaganda exploited this feeling by criminalizing resisters. In the newsreels projected in the cinemas and on many posters, resisters were often presented physically and morally as crooks and murderers. Such propaganda sought to arouse strong feelings of fear, and this fear was sometimes shared by ordinary people.

In fact, the Germans often took for granted the fact that resisters and local inhabitants were accomplices and practised a harsh policy of collective reprisals in retaliation for resistance attacks. In Russia, Belarus, Yugoslavia and Poland whole villages were burnt and the inhabitants shot. The reprisals policy was also especially severe in Greece, where 70,600 were executed, as against 50,000 killed in combat.[51] In France, Belgium and Denmark repression was less severe, with the exception of tragic examples such as Oradour-sur-Glane. For these reasons, civilians often feared the presence of resisters. Moreover some resisters enforced their rule by violence. In Greece self-administration was sometimes used by the EAM/ELAS to eliminate their opponents by setting up a kind of revolutionary order. A similar situation obtained in Yugoslavia, where, apart from the war with the Germans and Italians, there was an internal conflict between the communist partisans of Tito and the Chetniks, who were loyal to the government in exile. Resisters might even be criminals who plundered the population, stealing goods and raping women. In France the maquis Le Coz (a good example of black maquis) was a group of bandits which terrified the population of the Loches area in Touraine.[52] The frontier between criminality and resistance was in this case totally erased.

The historian can of course try to make a distinction between mere crime and resistance. When an action was taken in the general interest to help resisters and the Allies, it cannot be considered as a real offence. To steal food for the maquis or to shoot a collaborator who threatens to denounce resisters cannot be regarded as a mere criminal act. But to commit such an act simply to become richer or to get rid of a rival cannot be described as resistance. To that extent the motive and not only the nature of the act helps historians to distinguish between resistance and crime. In 1944, however, such a distinction was sometimes difficult for the victims to accept. The shopkeeper who had been robbed saw himself as a victim and was not necessarily inclined to make a subtle distinction between criminal and patriotic robberies.

Conclusion

Historians are on the whole inclined to consider everyday life as one matrix of resistance. Daily life was so difficult that rationing, forced labour and indoctrination stirred up civilians, sometimes leading them into dissent or revolt.

In the beginning, some people undertook spontaneous *Resistenz* by breaking the law, hiding, demonstrating, and so on. Such actions were not meaningless, even when they were undertaken in a private interest, because of the politicization of everyday life. This politicization was due to two factors. The occupying authorities helped the process by criminalizing social relations – ruling, for example, that the black market was an attack on the new order. The resistance, on the other hand, supported the process by giving a political or nationalist meaning to the actions of everyday life. Selling meat to the black market in France was not merely a commercial transaction; it was also the way to deprive the Germans. French peasants were thus able to reconcile their private interest with patriotism. In different ways occupiers on the one side and resisters on the other increased the politicization of everyday life and gave a collective sense to the gestures of everyday life. In this way the actions of everyday life were never simply that. Meaning was given to them both by the enemy and by the resistance. The coalminers' strike in northern France started as a merely corporate movement. By their harsh repression, however, the Germans transformed it into a patriotic protest, a meaning that was in turn enhanced by the resistance forces in their propaganda.

Clandestine organizations were often able to base their action on this fertile ground. They exploited daily problems in their propaganda to capitalize on civilian indignation and upgrade it to *Widerstand*. They used these problems to mobilize the masses by launching strikes or demonstrations. In some liberated zones resistance was even able to seize power and to enforce its rule against the collaborationist one. The occupiers of course tried to react. In their propaganda the Germans often presented resistance as a criminal enterprise. Moreover, collective reprisals aimed to deter people from joining or supporting the resistance, by showing in a bloody way that collective protest was a very risky means of action.

Everyday life was thus a fertile ground for resistance, but it was not the only one. There were other kinds of mobilization. When the resistance adopted military tactics (spying, mounting ambushes, or conducting guerrilla warfare), its activity was not focused on everyday life but plainly devoted to war. The link between the two spheres is not obvious, even if the maquis and uprisings show that it was possible to convert a daily life protest into an armed struggle. However, the military part of the resistance should not be overestimated. In Belgium the resistance contributed to the speedy capture of Antwerp, which was crucial for the supply of the Allied armies. But in Greece in 90 per cent of cases military action was not dangerous for the Germans. In addition a very heavy price was paid. Between March 1943 and the liberation of Greece in October 1944, 2,369 Germans were killed and 4,204 were wounded. At the same time, 21,255 Greeks were killed and 20,000 arrested in German counter-insurgency campaigns, while 1,700 villages were destroyed.[53] In a similar way, the French resistance never really endangered German troops, even if it played a significant part in 1944 by giving the Allies intelligence and helping the troops to free some areas, such as Brittany. It is therefore not possible to contrast a useless daily life resistance with a useful military one. The first certainly played a part by forcing the occupier to mobilize troops to maintain order and by creating a dangerous atmosphere for the Germans or the Italians. The military struggle, on the other hand, did not always play a decisive part, except perhaps in Yugoslavia and the USSR.

The part played by everyday life in shaping resistance depended on many factors. One important parameter was of course the rule of the occupying authorities. High pressure could drive people to despair and thus to resistance, while a smooth occupation would lead to accommodation rather than to revolt. From this point of view, Norway, Denmark, Belgium and even France could be opposed to eastern (Poland, Russia) or southern countries (Greece, Yugoslavia). But even these distinctions do not always work. Strong reprisals, for example, could also crush strikes and hinder resistance action by depriving it of social support, as in northern

France in 1941. On the other hand, a smooth occupation, as in Denmark, could lead to open revolt. Other factors therefore also played a significant part, for example the military situation and ideology, such as Germanophobia. Optimism might lead people to commit themselves, as in France or in Warsaw in 1944, but the contrary is also true. The arrival of the Allies might lead to wait-and-see attitudes. The ability to take into account the people's will was also fundamental. Sometimes everyday life was considered by the resistance movements as the main issue. They hence focused their attention on this, which helped them to shape their organizations and even to build a counter-state, as in Greece, Poland or the Limousin. Subordinated to the government in exile in London, the Polish underground state during the Second World War was even able to organize into three main parts: 1) the Representation of the Government in Exile (Delegatura Rządu RP na Kraj) responsible for the underground administration, judiciary and education, 2) the Home Army – military forces in Poland) and 3) Rada Jednoœci Narodowej (nucleus of the underground parliament – gathered together all the main non-communist political parties).[54]

These trends were of course favoured by the prewar situation. When war and occupation led to the collapse of a weak state and the dismantling of old types of political formations (parties or trade unions), resistance easily superseded the old structures and was able to impose its rule, as in Greece. On the other hand, everyday life might be ignored or underestimated when the resistance preferred to make war rather than to mobilize civilians, or when the old structures were able to persist. In France, for example, the state apparatus remained strong until 1944 and the old organizations were to a certain extent able to keep a hold on the population, even if they had been discredited by the defeat and occupation. To that extent, everyday life played a great part in shaping resistance organizations, but this part varied, partly because of the occupiers' rules, partly because of the national contexts.

The part played by everyday life must not be overestimated, even if it has sometimes been considered as a very important factor. We should not be led astray by politics of memory after the war. After the war, it was important for societies to build a new consensus and daily life experiences were integrated in the national resistance memory. This trend led to an overestimation of the importance of signs of protest, such as flowers on national monuments, which are now considered as bold acts of resistance. By building such a myth, the political authorities sought to define resistance as a mass movement and show that collaboration and occupation had always been unpopular. It was a way to avoid civil war (France), or to unite divided societies (Belgium), or to legitimate the new power (Poland). This was of course an optimistic view, but it was generally impossible to tell the historical truth in 1945. The experiences of daily life during the occupation therefore gained significance but were also distorted by being put into the context of national history. Conversely, the heroic tales of the resistance movement's actions were given authority and importance when the collective narrative could demonstrate a link to the daily life and will of the people. To that extent, the link between daily life and resistance is certainly a historical issue, but it is also a memory problem, deeply rooted in the national memories built after 1945.

Notes

1. For Denmark, 1 per cent represents the standing force at the liberation, 2 per cent the global number of resisters during the whole period, 2.5 per cent the proportion of the population over 15 years involved. See Hans Kirchhoff, *Samarbejde og modstand under besættelsen* (Odense, Odense Universitetforlag, 2001), p. 186, and Aage Trommer, 'Rekruttering til modstandkampen', in Hans Kirchhoff, John T. Lauridsen and Aage Trommer (eds), *Gads leksikon om dansk besættelsestid 1940–1945* (Copenhagen, Gads Forlag, 2002), pp. 389–92.
2. This point is made by Jacques Sémelin in *Unarmed against Hitler. Civilian Resistance in Europe, 1939–1943* (Westport, CT, Praeger, 1993).
3. Pierre Laborie, 'L'idée de Résistance, entre définition et sens. Retour sur un questionnement' in *Les Français des années troubles* (Paris, Points-Seuil, 2003), pp. 65ff. Olivier Wieviorka, 'A la recherche de l'engagement', *Vingtième siècle, revue d'histoire*, 60 (Oct–Dec. 1998), pp. 58–70.
4. Peter Liberman, *Does Conquest Pay? The Exploitation of Occupied Industrial Societies* (Princeton, Princeton University Press, 1996), pp. 36–40.
5. Arne Radtke-Delacor, 'La place des commandes à l'industrie française dans les stratégies de guerre nazies de 1940 à 1944,' in Olivier Dard, Jean-Claude Daumas and François Marcot (eds), *L'Occupation, l'État français et les entreprises* (Paris, ADHE, 2000), p. 22.
6. Alfred Sauvy, *La Vie économique des Français de 1939 à 1945* (Paris, Flammarion, 1978), p. 131.
7. Peter Liberman, *Does Conquest Pay?*, pp. 41–3; Czesław Madajczyk, *Faszyzm i okupacje 1938–1945. Wykonywanie okupacji przez państwa Osi w Europie, vol. I: Ukształtowanie sie zarzadów okupacyjnych* (Poznań, Wydawnictwo Poznańskie, 1983), pp. 295, 324 ; Phil Giltner, 'The Success of Collaboration: Denmark's Self-Assessment of its Economic Position after Five Years of Nazi Occupation', *Journal of Contemporary History*, vol. 36, no. 3 (2001) pp. 485–92.
8. Jan Tomasz Gross, *Polish Society under German Occupation. The General-gouvernement 1939–1944* (Princeton, Princeton University Press, 1979), pp. 92–7.
9. Guillaume Jacquemyns, 'La société belge sous l'occupation allemande (1940–1944). Privations et espoirs', in José Gotovitch (ed.), *La Belgique sous l'occupation allemande (1940–1944)* (Brussels, Complexe, 2002), pp. 295–434. See also

J. Gérard-Libois and J. Gotovitch, *L'An 40. La Belgique occupée* (Brussels, CRISP, 1971), pp. 330ff.

10. *Okupacja i ruch oporu w dzienniku Hansa Franka 1939–1945*, vol. 1: 1939–42 (Warsaw, Książka i Wiedza, 1972), p. 335.

11. See Polymeris Voglis, 'Surviving Hunger', in this volume, pp. 22–4.

12. John T. Lauridsen, 'Forsyningssituationen', in Hans Kirchhoff, *Samarbejde og modstand*, pp. 161–4.

13. Guillaume Jacquemyns, 'La société belge'.

14. 'Kollaboration', *Défense de la France* 2, 10 September 1941.

15. 'Dépenses budgétaires', *Libération (nord)*, 24 November 1941, quoted by Alya Aglan, *La Résistance sacrifiée. Le Mouvement 'Libération-Nord'* (Paris, Flammarion, 1999), p. 79.

16. These examples are given by Dominique Veillon, *Vivre et survivre en France 1939–1947* (Paris, Payot, 1995), p. 129.

17. Rudi Van Doorslaer, *De kommunistische partij van België en het sovjet-duits niet-aanvalspakt* (Brussels, Masereelfonds, 1975), p. 157; Fabrice Maerten, *Du murmure au grondement. La Résistance politique et idéologique dans la province du Hainaut pendant la seconde guerre mondiale (mai 1940–septembre 1944)* (Mons, Hannonia, 1999), 3 vol; vol. 2, pp. 690–3.

18. Paula Schwartz, 'The Politics of Food and Gender in Occupied Paris', *Modern and Contemporary France*, vol. 7, no. 1, (1999), pp. 35–45.

19. F. Roest and J. Scheren, *Oorlog in de stad Amsterdam 1939–1941* (Amsterdam, Van Gennep, 1998).

20. José Gotovitch, *Du rouge au tricolore. Les communistes belges de 1939 à 1944. Un Aspect de la Résistance en Belgique* (Brussels, Labor, 1992), pp. 110–15.

21. Etienne Dejonghe and Yves Le Maner, *Le Nord dans la main allemande* (Lille, La Voix du Nord, 1999), pp. 192–5. See also the chapter 'To Work or Not to Work?' by Robert Gildea, Dirk Luyten and Juliane Fürst in this volume, pp. 47, 50.

22. Mark Mazower, *Inside Hitler's Greece. The Experience of Occupation, 1941–1944* (New Haven and London, Yale University Press, 1993), pp. 123–4; Peter D. Chimbos, 'Greek Resistance 1941–45: Organizations, Achievements and Contributions to Allied War Efforts against the Axis Powers', *International Journal of Comparative Sociology*, vol. 40, no. 2 (1999), pp. 258–9.

23. Tomasz Szarota, *Okupowanej Warszawy dzień powszedni* (Warsaw, Czytelnik, 1988) (see in German: *Warschau unter dem Hakenkreuz: Leben und Alltag in besetzten Warschau 1.10.1939 bis 31.7.1944* (Paderborn, 1985, pp. 151–4.

24. Mark Mazower, *Inside Hitler's Greece*, pp. 75–6, 118–22.

25. P.J. Bouman, *De April–mei stakingen van 1943* (The Hague, Martinus Nijhoff, 1950). See above, p. 64.

26. Czesław Madajczyk, *Faszyzm i okupacje 1938–1945. Wykonywanie okupacji przez państwa Osi w Europie, vol. II: Mechanizmy realizowania okupacji* (Poznań, Wydawnictwo Poznańskie, 1984), pp. 593–4; M. Spoerer, 'Recent

Findings on Forced Labor under the Nazi Regime and an Agenda for Future Research', *Annali dell'Istituto Storico Italo-Germanico in Trento*, XXVIII (2002), pp. 385–6; Mark Spoerer, *Zwangsarbeit under dem Hakenkreuz* (Stuttgart-Munich, Deutsche Verlags-Anstalt, 2001), p. 222; Peter Liberman, *Does Conquest Pay?* pp. 44–6.

27. Alan E. Steinweis, 'Ideology and Infrastructure: German Area Science and Planning for the Germanization of Eastern Europe 1939–1944', *East European Quarterly*, vol. 28, no. 3, (1994), pp. 335–47.

28. Michel Heller, Aleksander Nekrich, *Utopia in Power. A History of the USSR from 1917 to the Present* (London, Hutchinson, 1986), pp. 393–9; Truman Anderson, 'Germans, Ukrainians and Jews: Ethnic Politics in Heeresgebiet Sud, June–December 1941', *War in History* vol. 7, no. 3, (2000), pp. 325–51.

29. Norman Davies, *Rising'44. The Battle for Warsaw* (London, Macmillan, 2003), pp. 115–16; Michael Burleigh, *The Third Reich. A New History* (London, Macmillan, 2000), pp. 455–7; Czesław Madajczyk, *Dramat katynski* (Warsaw, Książka i Wiedza, 1989), pp. 36–56.

30. See above, pp. 139–40.

31. Bjorn Schreiber Pedersen and Adam Holm, 'Restraining Excesses: Resistance and Counter-Resistance in Nazi-Occupied Denmark 1940–1945', *Terrorism and Political Violence*, vol. 10, no. 1, (1998), pp. 60–89; Hans Kirchhoff, 'Denmark. Background Determinants: The Socio-economic and Political Factors', in Bob Moore (ed.), *Resistance in Western Europe* (Oxford, Berg Publishers, 2000), pp. 105–6.

32. Jean-Louis Crémieux-Brihac, 'La France libre et la radio', *Mélanges de l'Ecole française de Rome*, 108/1 (1996), p. 73.

33. Czesław Madajczyk, *Faszyzm i okupacje 1938–1945*, vol. I, pp. 84–8; William Mackenzie, *The Secret History of SOE: Special Operations Executive 1940–1945* (London, St Ermin's, 2002), pp. 317–20.

34. Truman Anderson, 'Incident at Baranivka: German Reprisals and the Soviet Partisan Movement in Ukraine, October-December 1941', *Journal of Modern History*, vol. 71, no. 3 (1999) pp. 585–623; Jonathan E. Gumz, 'Wehrmacht Perceptions of Mass Violence in Croatia, 1941–1942', *The Historical Journal*, vol. 44, no. 4 (2001) pp. 1015–23, 1030–32.

35. Jan Tomasz Gross, *Polish Society*, pp. 109–13. See also above, pp. 27–30.

36. Władysław Bartoszewski, *Warsaw Death Ring 1939–1944* (Warsaw, Interpress, 1968), pp. 288–91; Władysław Bartoszewski, *1859 dni Warszawy*, (Cracow, Znak, 1984), p. 546.

37. Rik Hemmerijckx, *Van Verzet tot Koude Oorlog. 1940–1949. Machstsstrijd om het ABVV* (Brussels-Ghent, VUBPRESS/AMSAB, 2003). See above, p. 46.

38. Peter D. Chimbos, 'Greel Resistance 1941–45', pp. 257–8; Margaret Polous Anagnostopoulou, 'From Heroines to Hyenas: Women Partisans during the Greek Civil War', Contemporary European History vol. 10. no. 3 (2001), pp. 481–501.

39. Dick van Galen Last, 'The Netherlands', in Bob Moore (ed.), Resistance in Western Europe (Oxford-New York, Berg), 2000, p. 201.
40. Richard C. Lukas, *Forgotten Holocaust. The Poles under German Occupation 1939–1944* (New York, Hippocrene Books, 1990), pp. 147–51.
41. Robert Belot, *Aux Frontières de la liberté. Vichy, Madrid, Alger, Londres. S'évader de France sous l'occupation* (Paris, Fayard, 1998), p. 681
42. André Kaspi, *Les Juifs pendant l'occupation* (Paris, Le Seuil, 1991), p. 363.
43. *De verplichte tewerkstelling in Duitsland/Le Travail obligatoire en Allemagne. 1942–1945* (Brussels, Centre de recherches et d'études historiques de la deuxième guerre mondiale,1993).
44. Tomasz Szarota, *Życie codzienne w stolicach okupowanej Europy* (Warsaw, Państwowy Instytut Wydawniczy, 1995), pp. 249–50; Mark Mazower, *Inside Hitler's Greece*, p. 293.
45. Gilles Vergnon, *Le Vercors. Histoire et mémoire d'un maquis* (Paris, Éditions de l'Atelier, 2002), pp. 94ff.
46. Maurice Lombard, 'Les maquis et la libération de la Bourgogne', *Revue d'Histoire de la Seconde Guerre Mondiale*, 55 (July 1964), pp. 29–54.
47. *Polski czyn zbrojny w II wojnie światowej. Polski ruch oporu 1939–1945* (Warsaw, Wydawnictwo Ministerstwa Obrony Narodowej, 1988), pp. 709–11.
48. John Erickson, *The Road to Berlin. Stalin's War with Germany*, vol. II (London, Phoenix Giants, 1996), pp. 269–307, 634–40; Norman Davies, *Rising '44*, pp. 245–79; Richard C. Lukas, *Forgotten Holocaust*, pp. 182–219.
49. M.R.D. Foot, *SOE. The Special Operations Executive 1940–1946* (London, Mandarin, 1993), pp. 334–46; Thanasis D. Sfikas, *The British Labour Government and the Greek Civil War. The Imperialism of 'Non-Intervention'* (Keele, Ryburn Pub., 1994).
50. Joanna K.M. Hanson, *The Civilian Population and the Warsaw Uprising of 1944* (Cambridge, Cambridge University Press, 2004), p. 257.
51. Tom Dyson, 'British Policies toward Axis Reprisals in Occupied Greece: Whitehall vs. SOE', *Contemporary British History*, vol. 16, no. 1 (2002), pp. 11–12.
52. Robert Gildea, *Marianne in Chains. In Search of the German Occupation 1940–45* (London, Macmillan, 2002), pp. 337–8; Bernard Briais, *Un Dossier noir de la Résistance. Le Maquis Le Coz* (Saint-Cyr-sur-Loire, Alan Sutton, 2002).
53. John L. Hondros, *Occupation and Resistance. The Greek Agony 1941–1944* (New York, Pella Pub. Corp., 1983) , p. 162.
54. Richard C. Lukas, *Forgotten Holocaust*, pp. 40–60; Józef Garliński, 'The Polish Underground State', *Journal of Contemporary History*, vol. 10, no. 2 (1975) pp. 219–59; Marek Ney-Krwawicz, *The Polish Resistance Home Army 1939–1945* (London, Studium Polski Podziemnej, 2001).

–6–

Resistance, Reprisals, Reactions
Geraldien von Frijtag Drabbe Künzel

In March 1942, two and a half years after the German invasion of Poland and only a few months after the Japanese attack on Pearl Harbour, the American novelist John Steinbeck wrote *The Moon is Down*.[1] In this novella, Steinbeck tells the story of the occupation of a mining and fishing town by a foreign army. The villagers display no inclination to cooperate. Initially resistance is passive, but the more compulsion the occupiers use, the more openly the villagers seek confrontation. When winter arrives, the relations between occupier and population have frozen. The escalating violence of which both the populace and the occupiers are guilty blocks the way to peaceful coexistence. In the end the old mayor (symbolizing the 'old' – democratic – order) is taken hostage and is eventually shot in retribution for anti-German acts. For the occupiers this all means defeat: the moon is down.

This dramatic sequence of events, Steinbeck shows us, was in a sense inevitable, because the occupation lacks legitimacy and the violence carried out by the occupiers was therefore illegitimate and condemnable. The violence used by the resistance, on the other hand, is accepted and approved – even if the villagers themselves suffer the reprisals and their mayor is executed. Forty years later the Dutch author Harry Mulisch wrote on the same topic. The story of his bestseller *De Aanslag* (The Assault)[2] plays against the background of the German occupation of the Netherlands (1940–5). The novel opens with an assault in the street where the protagonist Anton Steenwijk lives. The victim is a collaborating Dutch policeman, the culprits are two Dutch resistance fighters. The assault is followed by German reprisals: because the body is found in front of their house, Anton and his family are arrested; his parents are shot with twenty-nine other hostages; his parents' house is burned to the ground.

At first glance the relationships and lines of division appear once again to be straightforward: a 'bad' policeman is killed by 'good' Dutch people – rightly – and the 'bad' German occupier kills innocent civilians – wrongly. However, in the course of the story (and in the course of Anton's life) it becomes clear that the situation is more complicated. The motive of the two resistance fighters was not only political but emotional, given that these two (the female and male resistance fighter) had an adulterous relationship and the assault served the purpose of being together. Their victim was not so much a confirmed and powerful Nazi as a diligent fusspot official, who considered it his duty as a civil servant to carry out orders from above. Although a monument is erected and the Dutch resistance is honoured for its heroism after the war, Anton starts to wonder whether this particular assault was brave and laudable or rather pointless: was it really worth the casualties?

Steinbeck and Mulisch wrote fiction, but were assaults on occupiers fictive (Germans and Italians alike, as well as their collaborators)? Was the shooting of innocent people fictive, or the razing of villages in retribution for anti-German or anti-Italian acts? And what about the reactions of the resisters, survivors of the targeted community and others? Did they always react the same way? Was their reaction always unanimous?

This chapter is about collective punishments, but not only that: it is also about reactions, at that very moment and in the long term. Acts of resistance which elicited acts of retribution and those retributions themselves inevitably had an impact on the lives of ordinary citizens. Perhaps they could have continued their daily lives more or less as normal in the lull of war violence. Resistance and reprisals brought an abrupt and jolting end to any possibility of remaining aloof. How did they now, as ordinary citizens, judge the sequence of violent acts, starting with the act of resistance which had provoked the reprisal and mostly ending in a bloodbath in which their neighbours, acquaintances or relatives had died? How did they judge the resistance after they had directly or indirectly become the target of German reprisals? Did these reactions and judgements change over time? This last question introduces the question of memory. To elaborate this issue in detail would lead too far from the subject of this chapter. However, it should be made clear that there is a difference between (immediate) reactions to events and the way these events and reactions are memorized.

These questions are linked to the relation between the occupying forces and the local population, but also – and one might say especially – to the relation of the resistance to the rest of the population. It thus touches on the basis of the post-war myth which is widespread in previously occupied Europe: the (collective) myth of the (collective) resistance, according to which the resistance was as brave as it was unimpeachable and enjoyed broad support from the population. In his masterful work on post-war Holland, France and Belgium, Pieter Lagrou found differences in the organization of national memory (and remembrance) but not in the image of the resistance as such: in each of these countries the resistance as a heroic and broadly supported movement was up to 1965 the dominant discourse.[3] In other parts of Europe, as well as in the former Soviet Union, the myth of a massively supported resistance is no less stubborn.[4] This simplified view of a unified people under terroristic control and totalitarian rule started to erode during the decades that followed. In part, this was a consequence of altered national and international circumstances. The end of the Cold War, for instance, encouraged new approaches to the subject. Doubts were thrown upon the undifferentiated divide between occupied and occupier, oppressed and oppressor.

In the spirit of the 'old' myth, however, and along the lines of Steinbeck's fiction, one might expect the inhabitants of a targeted community to regret the losses suffered, but also to bear them with pride: their dead were after all sacrifices brought by the community to the fight against the occupation – the fight they were fighting together, alongside the resistance. In fact this was not always the case. The reactions of the targeted local population varied. The sceptical protagonist of Mulisch's story has many equivalents in the world of non-fiction.

General Patterns

Collective punishments were a tradition in many western European armies during the nineteenth century, as well as in the Ottoman Empire. Already in the Franco-German war of 1870, the Prussian army arrested French notables with the aim of using them as human shields.[5] 'There can only be a question of forbearance towards people and goods if the nature and aim of a war permit it', the German army staff stipulated in 1902.[6] The Hague peace conference and treaties of 1907 forbade collective punishment explicitly. The German government had signed the treaties but its army did not keep to them in practice. In military circles collective punishments were not considered to be at odds with the *ius in bello*. During the First World War the German army regularly made use of hostage-taking and executing innocent people, a weapon aimed at intimidation and retribution. In occupied Belgium this resulted in more than 6,000 dead. In the years preceding the invasion of Poland it emerged that the German army chiefs thought no differently about the matter.[7] In the preparations for *Fall Gelb* (the attack on Belgium, the Netherlands, France and Luxemborg) general Wilhelm von Brauchitsch named hostage-taking explicitly as a possible 'security measure'.[8]

So it was not entirely unexpected that holding groups of citizens, even whole communities, accountable for acts with which they had nothing to do became a commonplace in the parts of Europe occupied by Germany – with the possible exception of Denmark.[9] Collective punishments became an essential component of German occupation politics. The imposition of money fines and compensatory work (*Sühneleistungen*) was a relatively mild variant; taking innocent civilians hostage and killing them, as well as destroying their possessions, belonged to the more brutal forms. Three major groups of citizens were the target of the German hostage policy: Jews, notables and Communists.

In the parts of the Balkans and Greece occupied by the Italian forces, the situation was not much different. The responsible army commanders had gained ample experience of repression in the African colonies of Libya, Somalia, Ethiopia and Eritrea. Hostage-takings took place relatively rarely, however, though Mussolini had determined in 1941 that for each dead Italian soldier twenty Croat civilians should be killed. It was more common to avenge acts of resistance by destroying possessions (whole villages) and incarcerating inhabitants elsewhere.[10]

The local populations were not confronted with collective punishments in the same way or on the same scale in every location in occupied Europe: the context in several respects differed substantially from one occupied territory to another and from one period to another. Ideological, territorial, military-strategic, economic and racial aims and interests of the occupiers varied; the composition of the local population did as well, and all these variations had an influence on occupation policy.

Poland, for instance, had partly belonged to the German Imperial Reich before 1919. After the German attack of September 1939 these formerly German provinces were annexed. Other parts were destined to become a German colony. Racially, Poles were seen as *Untermenschen*; economically, as cheap slave labourers. Towards Denmark and Norway, invaded in April 1940, the German regime had no colonial claim. The inhabitants of these countries were seen as 'racially highly qualified'. Norway was governed by a civilian regime, the Reichskommissariat. The attack on the Netherlands was part of a larger German attack on the neighbouring western countries in May 1940. Luxemburg and some eastern regions of France and Belgium awaited annexation. Because of its strategic importance, Belgium was placed under German military rule, as was the occupied northern zone of France. Like Norway, the Netherlands were governed by a Reichskommissariat. The military conquest of the Balkans from April 1941 onwards had different rationales for the different occupying forces. For the Nazi regime, the invasions of Yugoslavia had mainly a military purpose, as a means to safeguard the southern border. More recent studies suggest that Italy, Germany's southern ally, was to a large extent motivated by considerations of race. The German invasion of the Soviet Union in June 1941 was propagated as an outright *Weltanschauungskrieg*, as both a racial and an ideological battle of the 'Aryans' against the 'Jewish Bolsheviks' or 'Bolshevik Jews'. The tenor of new research suggests that other – economic and territorial – aims were closely interwoven.[11]

These differences resulted in different attitudes towards the native population. Of course the context of the occupation, the way the relations between occupier and occupant evolved, also influenced the occupier's attitudes towards occupied populations. But in some parts of Europe, where inhabitants lived who were not seen as 'worthy', the occupied displayed much more violence at a much earlier stage than elsewhere. In these parts the local population was faced with collective punishments earlier and more regularly than in others. In Poland, for instance, the climate was right for excesses from the start. 'We cannot kill fourteen million Poles, but we can take care of breaking their spines forever', were the eloquent words of Hans Frank, appointed in September 1939 as general-governor of what remained of western Poland.[12] Only a few months after the German conquest of Polish territory 106 innocent civilians were shot in a reprisal action in Warsaw. The occasion was the murder – a non-political one – of two German soldiers in the city. In the spring of 1940 Frank's deputy Arthur Seyss-Inquart gave orders to shoot 169 civilians in retaliation for the murder and robbery of a German family.[13] In the Czech protectorate, too, a hard line was taken from the beginning. A few months after the German invasion the police rounded up about 1,900 students after there had been an open demonstration against German measures. A small minority was brought to trial and sentenced to death; the others (of whom a large number were innocent) were interned at Oranienburg.[14]

Compared to this, the actions taken by the occupying forces in the northern and western parts of Europe were at first quite mild. Terror was confined to incidents like the crushing of the Amsterdam strike and the reprisal for a British attack on the Lofoten islands, both in the spring of 1941. Leaving aside the hunt for Communists and the persecution of Jews, it was generally the case that the German Reichskommissariat in the occupied Netherlands and Norway acted rather cautiously. It was the policy there to induce the native population to join the Greater German Reich voluntarily. In both countries there were civilian casualties during the first two years of German occupation, but in most cases these were death sentences imposed for acts of resistance. Until the summer of 1941 acts of sabotage were rare. Collective punishments often took the form of fines. Arresting and killing innocent hostages were barely tried methods.[15]

In Belgium and France, too, the occupation authorities held back during the first year of occupation. The German leadership in Paris and Brussels, respectively headed by Militärbefehlhaber Otto von Stülpnagel and Alexander von Falkenhausen, valued a good understanding with the local population. In Belgium, during the first year of occupation, there had been a few impressive strikes, but only one German had been assassinated by the resistance.[16] As in Norway and the Netherlands, occasionally rails were bent, cables were cut or Wehrmacht targets were attacked. In Belgium the number of such assaults had risen to 419 by March 1941.[17] Nevertheless, during the first year of occupation, resistance in north and west Europe was not so much a military threat as an annoyance and a threat to prestige.

In all occupied territories and in areas where Wehrmacht troops were still operational, one can see a clear sharpening of German repression from the late summer of 1941. This development was in part a reaction to the general increase in resistance to the German presence. To reign in and avenge this resistance, two measures of collective punishment in particular became popular: internment and the execution of innocent civilians (in other words, hostages). The Oberkommando der Wehrmacht (OKW) gave instructions in this vein, spreading many (and sometimes contradictory) decrees among the commanders in the field in the last quarter of 1941. One of them indicated that German occupation authorities should at all times punish 'a number of hostages with different political backgrounds': 'It is important that there should be among them well-known leading personalities or their relatives, whose names may be made public. According to the political background of the culprits, hostages from a corresponding group will be shot.'[18] The Italians followed a similar strategy concerning hostages: around the same time the Italian military governor of Montenegro decided to keep a number of civilian hostages as guarantors of Montenegrin behaviour.[19] Another significant German decree which circulated in mid-September 1941, and had the aim of combating communist resistance, made the recommendation that for every German soldier's death fifty to a hundred hostages should be killed in reprisal.[20]

In many places it did in fact become German policy to avenge the death of a German or pro-German individual with the deaths of several hostages. From June 1941 hostage-taking and the execution of hostages occurred with increasing frequency. With regard to the implementation of the decrees, it mattered whether a country was administered directly by Wehrmacht authorities or not. In Norway and the Netherlands the Wehrmacht was not in charge, and here there were the strongest deviations from the decrees. Moreover, the resistance developed quite slowly in the Netherlands. The first assault by the resistance on a person, for instance, was not carried out until January 1943. This helps to explain why it was only in the summer of 1942 that a hostage-taking policy was begun. In France and Belgium, both Militärbefehlshaber saw the recommended severity as exaggerated, but took the OKW decrees, albeit reluctantly, as guidelines for their policies.[21] In particular, in the former French departments Nord and Pas-de-Calais assaults on Germans and their collaborators grew in number. In Lille, for instance, four German soldiers were killed in August 1941. The same month Von Falkenhausen announced that assaults on German persons from that time onwards would be avenged by the shooting of hostages: for one German killed, five hostages would be executed. This ratio was much less out of proportion than the one proposed a month previously by the OKW (1:50).[22]

Von Falkenhausen's own announcement, however, became the directive for Belgium. All prisoners were from then on hostages (*Haftgeiseln*). In addition the police also imprisoned hundreds of innocent notables (*Wahlgeiseln*). In practice it was mostly *Haftgeiseln* who died in reprisal actions. The first time this happened was in September 1941, when in the vicinity of Lille two more assaults were carried out on German trains taking soldiers on leave. Von Falkenhausen responded with the execution of five communist prisoners.[23]

Von Stülpnagel carried out a similar policy in the part of France under his authority. He also saw little good in the massive hostage executions proposed by the OKW. He wrote an infamous letter in which he pronounced himself against 'Polish methods' on French territory. Shortly after this, in the spring of 1942, the old general resigned. Nevertheless, in the autumn of 1941 he had twice given orders to execute large groups of hostages. After his departure, too, massive executions were carried out. By October 1942 more than four hundred French civilians had become casualties of such actions.[24]

These numbers pale in comparison with the number of hostages killed in the east and in the Balkans in this period. In Serbia, as an extreme example, up to the autumn of 1942 a guideline was followed to avenge each dead German with the deaths of a hundred civilians, every wounded man with the deaths of fifty civilians. What this led to became evident in October 1941, when an assault in Krajusevac in which 36 Wehrmacht soldiers were wounded (of whom ten fatally) was answered with the execution of more than two thousand men from the village's surroundings.[25]

In some parts of the Balkans, rivalry between the two Axis partners had an impact on the effectiveness of the reprisals. On some occasions, especially during 1943, Italian generals refused to join the Germans and Croats in anti-partisan operations; at other times the Germans organized this kind of military operation within Italian areas of occupation to the bitter resentment of Italian military commanders. In general, however, fascist Italy's repression in the Balkans did not deviate significantly from German policy. In an infamous memorandum circulated in March 1942 the Italian general Mario Roatta prescribed for the battle against partisans not 'an eye for an eye, a tooth for a tooth' but 'a head for a tooth'.[26] The results of this became clear in the parts of Yugoslavia occupied by the Italian army. In the province of Ljubljana alone more than 3,500 partisans were 'liquidated' in the summer of 1942. At first Italian actions in Greece were more tempered, but in the course of 1942 terror was introduced there as well. In August of that year, dozens of local shepherd shelters had already been destroyed in the vicinity of Lamia. In revenge for resistance actions, it became the general policy to raze villages, execute a number of male inhabitants and deport the rest, and take relatives of resistance fighters hostage. The Italian military followed this policy in practice more than once.[27]

In the German protectorate of Bohemia-Moravia, German terror increased in the autumn of 1941 after Reichsprotektor Constantin von Neurath was replaced by the head of the Reichssicherheitshauptamt, Reinhard Heydrich. He made it his task to bring order to these formerly Czech provinces. In this process he did not shy away from violence, so that within several months hundreds of Czechs had already been sentenced to death or shot as reprisal hostages. German terror reached its dramatic high point only after his death. On 27 May 1942 Heydrich was killed in an ambush by partisans near Lidice. The same day an order came from the highest authorities to take 10,000 prominent civilians hostage. A number of them were to be shot the same evening. At the last moment Berlin pulled back from carrying out these measures. Instead, martial law was proclaimed, and it was announced that large numbers of hostages would be killed if the culprits had not been tracked down before the end of the following month. Berlin did not wait for this, however. In June 1942 Hitler gave the order to raze Lidice, execute the male inhabitants, send the women to concentration camps and send the children, to the extent they were judged 'suitable for Germanization', to German families. This was done. Of the village and its few hundred inhabitants, little remained. More than eighty children not eligible for placement in German families were gassed in Chelmno.[28]

For the Czechs these draconian measures were a novelty, but further east, in Ukraine, German troops had by then long abandoned any principle of proportionality. The German response to a series of explosions in Kiev in September 1941 became infamous; in retribution more than 30,000 innocent people, all Jews, were massacred at Babi Yar, a deep ravine on the outskirts of Kiev.[29]

Reprisal actions on this scale did not occur elsewhere in occupied Europe. But the reality of war for civilians did begin to resemble more closely that in the east. After the German invasion of the Soviet Union, the climate in all of occupied Europe hardened considerably, and from then on the relations deteriorated by leaps and bounds. The more territory the Axis powers lost, the greater the readiness of the population in these areas to put up (armed) resistance. More and more often the occupation army resorted to collective punishment measures like hostage executions.

At the beginning of 1943 the Italian army lorded it over central Greece, and the village of Domenikon was razed to the ground by the occupying forces. A summary table compiled by the Command of the Italian 3rd Army Corps on operations conducted against bandits in February 1943 in the sectors of Kastoria, Trikala, Lamia and Thebes-Aliartos reported that around 120 bandits and 32 *favoreggiatori* had been killed and 107 persons shot in reprisals, and that aerial bombardments had caused an unspecified number of deaths and injuries. The document does not state whether these were civilians, whether they had been interned in previous actions, or whether they had been captured during the operations. When the Italian Supreme Command demanded that Carlo Geloso explain the shooting of hostages, he replied that the intensification of the rebel insurgency, the extreme mobility of the bands, and the impending invasion of Greek territory justified such a vigorous reaction. Geloso wrote that his methods were not excessive, for the bands did not have territorial objectives to defend; it was consequently necessary to punish the local people for acts of collusion by destroying their dwellings and interning them. Unleashed by Geloso, General Cesare Benelli, commander of the Pinerolo Division, announced that, in the event of acts of sabotage against the Larissa–Volos railway line, fifty Greek citizens detained in the concentration camp would be shot. In the same period, on the Greek peninsula, the Italians resorted to heavy aerial bombardments which struck military targets and civilians indiscriminately, whilst during rounding-up operations a number of villages were razed to the ground.[30]

In the west and north of Europe one can see from the spring of 1943 a growing tendency towards violent acts – both of resistance and by the occupation forces. In the autumn of 1943 the number of violent reprisal actions in the Netherlands increased explosively when the German security police began the so-called 'spruce-action'. At that moment it was decided to respond to assaults on Dutch collaborators with *Gegenterror* (counter-terror). More than fifty Dutch people were killed by snipers as they went about their business unsuspecting.[31] In Norway native Nazis were involved in comparable reprisal actions.[32] In Belgium, where 1942 had had a very bloody end, armed resistance reached a climax in 1943. In the first half of 1944, 167 persons were killed in 163 assaults. The response of the occupation authorities was not long delayed. In total 305 political prisoners were shot as hostages between November 1942 and August 1944. Besides this, snipers were also used in Belgium. They carried the responsibility for dozens of other deaths.[33]

After the Allied landings on the Normandy coast, mass killings also took place in parts of Europe outside the Balkans and the east. The devastation and massacre of Oradour-sur-Glane in June 1944 was an excess until that point only seen in the Balkans, Poland and occupied parts of the Soviet Union. In the last months of 1944 and the beginning of 1945, while large areas of occupied Europe were already liberated, the northern part of the Netherlands was confronted by months of German terror. Without having their guilt established, persons under suspicion were shot on the spot or locked up as *Todeskandidat* – hostages who could be executed at any opportune moment. Often the German authorities waited until a resistance action had taken place which in their eyes required a harsh response. The number of members of the resistance arrested in these reprisals and subsequently executed ran into the hundreds.[34]

Almost everywhere in occupied Europe, at a certain moment in time, civilians became aware of this particular weapon being used by the occupier: collective punishments. In many places people were confronted with hostage-taking and shooting. Sometimes they themselves, their friends or relatives were the target. Maybe they asked themselves what had been the logic of arresting and killing innocent people. The answers could have been many. Collective punishments were part of war logic, but they were also intended as a means of repression or as an act of retaliation. Many purposes could be served; sometimes many logics were in fact working together simultaneously.

Resistance and the Local Community: Support or Resentment?

As has been indicated, resistance and reprisals were transnational phenomena. Countless villages and cities in Europe experienced resistance actions and collective reprisals. Although every case of resistance and reprisal was unique, there are also patterns in the reactions of the local populations. How the local population reacted depended among other things on the way the reprisal was executed, the number of casualties and the size of material losses. The reaction also depended on the act of resistance itself and factors such as whether the resisters were locals or outsiders, and whether the victims were locals or randomly picked, notables or Communists.

Almost everywhere, in every targeted community, one could find anger and grief. But this anger was not always (exclusively) directed against the occupier who was responsible for the reprisal. In some cases the local population primarily resented the resistance that had provoked the reprisal. Sometimes the reprisal led to heated debates on the usefulness of sabotage. This was not restricted in time; later, when events had become memories, acts of resistance still often elicited mixed feelings – not least among the relatives of persons killed in the reprisals which ensued. In their version of the past, the resistance is portrayed much less positively than in the national memory of the occupation.

These observations are based on a number of western European cases that have been studied more closely. One of these cases is the French city of Nantes.[35] In this medium-sized city at the mouth of the Loire, a young Communist from Paris opened fire on the Feldkommandant of Nantes, Lieutenant Colonel Karl Hotz, on 20 October 1941. The victim died. This assault was the first resulting in a death outside Paris. The capital had been rocked in recent months by violent acts of resistance, but outside Paris things had remained relatively quiet up to this point. The assault alarmed the German authorities, who assumed, correctly, that the armed resistance had shifted its operating ground. The victim was not just anybody either, but the highest local commander. Probably, these facts contributed to the decision to take severe measures. Days after the assault the Militärbefehlshaber in France announced the counter-measures:

> Cowardly criminals in the pay of London and Moscow shot the Feldkommandant of Nantes (Loire-Inférieure) on the morning of 20 October 1941. To date the murderers have not been arrested. To expiate this crime I have ordered that fifty hostages will be shot in the first instance. In view of the gravity of the crime, fifty more hostages will be shot if the guilty parties are not arrested before 23 October at midnight. I am offering a reward totalling 15 million francs to inhabitants who contribute to the arrest of the culprits.[36]

Executions indeed took place on 22 October: six victims were residents of Nantes who were held in the fort of Romainville in Paris; eighteen were taken from prisons in Nantes; twenty-seven others were communist prisoners from the Choisel camp near Châteaubriant.

That the Germans would line these people up in front of a firing squad was not clear either to the local population or to the French city government when they gave their first reaction on 20 and 21 October. Here it is quite important to underline that the Nantes hostages shot were mainly local notables, while those at Châteaubriant were interned Communists from all over the country. French local authorities hastened to express their disapprobation for the assassination. The mayor and the city council condemned the act in a published appeal to the population as a cowardly murder and asked the residents of Nantes to help in tracking down the culprit(s). For many French officials the assault was an example of senseless violence, which put unnecessary pressure on the good relations between the German and French authorities. From the letters sent to the *préfecture* and *mairie*, it became evident that residents of the city for the most part thought no differently. Various social organizations in the city and department made it known that they condemned the assault.

Their protests could not have prevented the first wave of executions. The second series of shootings which was threatened if the culprits were not found before midnight on 23 October was stayed, however. In the hours preceding the time set for an ultimatum many submitted petitions to the German authorities to prevent the executions. Some of these writings were remarkable. Marshal Philippe Pétain, for example, wrote a letter in which he offered his life in exchange for that of the new batch of hostages. The families of hostages who had already been shot pleaded for the lives of others. It cannot be said with certainty that these appeals made the Germans decide not to shoot more hostages. Other reasons may have contributed, such as the growing disagreement between different German authorities about the usefulness of mass collective punishment. No more hostages were executed in reprisal for the assault on Hotz. For many residents and their government, the tragedy proved the counter-productivity of resistance. The resistance had unnecessarily disturbed the relatively good atmosphere and peace in the town and put the lives of innocents at risk.

In the occupied Netherlands acts of resistance were also not always welcomed positively by the civilians who were the targets or likely to become targets of German reprisals. This was the case for instance in August 1942, when the first execution of hostages in the Netherlands took place.[37] In this episode, as in Nantes, the conscious choice of the German authorities to exploit the hostage-taking and the execution for propaganda purposes had a decisive influence on the Dutch population's reaction. Before the shooting, during the summer of 1942, hundreds of Dutch people had been taken hostage.[38] Other measures had already been taken against Communists in the latter half of 1941. The Sicherheitspolizei had taken many prisoners and put these 'hostages' on convoys to German concentration camps across the border.[39] A massive taking of notables as hostages did not take place in the Netherlands until the summer of 1942. These hostages, more than 1,400 in total, were interned in a Catholic seminary ('Beekvliet') and were if not national then local celebrities; a small number of them had held office.[40]

At the time the Dutch population reacted nervously to the arrest of so many local notables and nationally prominent figures. This feeling was strengthened by the announcement of Wehrmachtbefehlshaber Friedrich Christiansen in mid-July that the lives of these hostages would henceforth be the guarantee of peace and order in the country. A climax was reached a month after that when the execution of hostages hung in the balance.[41] The occasion for this was an incident in Rotterdam on 7 August in which a local communist resistance group had planted explosives on a stretch of railway in the city centre. The intention was to blow up a train with German soldiers on leave, but a delay upset the plan. Instead of the packed train, a Dutch railway official making his rounds on a bicycle hit the explosives. He was seriously injured. Although no casualties had occurred on the German side, Christiansen demanded, probably with support from the OKW, that several of the Beekvliet hostages be shot.[42] The next day an official statement appeared in the Dutch newspapers:

> On August 7 irresponsible elements carried out an assault on a railway train of the German Wehrmacht in Rotterdam. A Dutch railway official became the victim of this

assault in the course of carrying out his duties. If those guilty of this assault do not report to the police before Friday August 14 or are not identified with the help of citizens, the punishment will be carried out on a number of hostages who stand as the guarantors against such acts of sabotage by order of the Wehrmachtbefehlshaber in the Netherlands. The arrest of the guilty parties is thus in the interest of the whole population, in order to avoid this retaliation against the hostages. A reward of 100,000 florins has been set on prompt reports to an office of the German Wehrmacht or the police leading to the seizure of the perpetrators. All reports will be treated confidentially.[43]

On the German side this experiment was awaited with high expectations; never before had threats been made against the lives of innocent citizens. 'It will be interesting, how it will work out, and to see if it will be necessary to have hostages' heads roll', the Gesandter of the Auswärtiges Amt, Otto Bene, had reported in a letter to his superiors in Berlin.[44]

The announcement caused the required disturbance among the people of Rotterdam, which increased further after the arrest of more well-known Rotterdam residents. There was a widespread assumption that the German authorities would avenge the assault on hostages from Rotterdam. One day before the ultimatum, the *Nieuwe Rotterdamsche Courant* newspaper published two declarations on its front page. The first declaration was signed by thirty-two Rotterdam notables who by no means were known as pro-Nazi. Among them were doctors, harbour barons and other members of the liberal professions, but also judges and officers of justice. The text of their declaration said that 'they thought it desirable that the Rotterdam citizenry state clearly that they consider the bomb attack on the railway bridge of Friday 7 August in Rotterdam an irresponsible act which exposes entirely innocent fellow citizens to mortal danger'.[45] The second declaration came from the (politically neutral) Church Councils of the combined Protestant communities in Rotterdam. Their representatives declared in the message that they severely condemned this 'act of sabotage'.[46] In other ways too the population of Rotterdam criticized the assault. In several neighbourhoods in the city signatures were collected to express condemnation of the resistance action.[47]

Not only in Rotterdam, but also in the Catholic seminary of Beekvliet, the atmosphere was tense. Because it was not made known who was to be shot until just before the ultimatum expired, no hostage knew if he would live or die. This shared uncertainty strengthened the feeling of a shared fate. A ban on correspondence with the seminary imposed from 8 August and a halt to all contact with the outside world added to this feeling. On 14 August, just after midnight, the German guards took five hostages aside. They were taken the next morning to a remote estate in Goirle and shot by firing squad.[48]

That day the German authorities reported their deaths in all the daily newspapers.[49] The reaction to this report was great and possibly different from the one German authorities had hoped for. Whereas before the shootings the population of Rotterdam had condemned the assault in passionate terms, now this disapproval was directed at the German authorities. 'What is yet to be said ... about this shameful act?', the editors of the popular clandestine national paper *Vrij Nederland* asked on 19 August 1942: 'We think of the victims, of their families, of the hostages from whose midst they were shot away. Of the revenge to come? Of the account to be settled? That too! And may God then have mercy on the deluded German people!'[50]

The national paper *Het Parool*, also clandestine, judged similarly: 'a senseless cruelty' was the view six days after the shooting[51] and in a subsequent issue the editors spoke out strongly once again:

> To the endless series of their shameless acts ... the Germans have added one, the shooting of five Dutch hostages, which will live on in history as a model of German baseness ... We can only keep silence. But one thing should be asserted: the murder will have an entirely counter-productive effect! For in the hearts of our tormented people, hatred of the intruder who condemns it to death while waving the German code of 'honor' and 'conscience' becomes more and more deeply ingrained.[52]

That the criticism of the illegal press was devastating is hardly surprising, but, given this kind of presentation, the many German observers in the country also openly doubted the success of the act of retribution. They did not fail to notice that the effect of the shooting on Dutch society was tremendous.[53] Intelligence services spoke of a population that was 'deeply shocked'.[54] Höherer SS- und Polizeiführer Hanns Albin Rauter, chief of police and SS forces in the Netherlands, considered the 'shock' desirable. He wrote on the matter to his superior in Berlin:

> Strong pressure must be exerted if the will of the occupation power is to be imposed. The 1,200 hostages have 50,000 friends and acquaintances, and all of Holland trembles at the thought that somewhere sabotage might be carried out. The aim and purpose of the hostage-takings has now gradually become clear to the Dutch.[55]

Not everyone on the German side saw the turmoil caused by the executions in such a positive light. In a meeting at Christiansen's military headquarters at the Netherlands, in the beginning of October 1942, this event was evaluated. The military intelligence service thought the execution had been partly responsible for the fact that relations between the occupying power and the population had become completely frozen:

> With this, the last possibilities for a good understanding between the occupying force and the Dutch people have been lost forever. An unprecedented rejection, an unknown hatred against Germany is gaining ground in the Netherlands. The possibility must be kept in view that in an Alarm-Fall [the name given to an Allied attack] the present forced passivity of the Dutch will swing round to the most brutal opposite.[56]

From that moment the hostage community was left alone,[57] and threats to execute innocents were only made in highly exceptional circumstances.

It is notable that after the war, in the local resistance history of Rotterdam, the execution of hostages occupied a remarkably modest place. This can be explained in part by the fact that other events which took place around the same time had more far-reaching consequences for the harbour city: the German bombing of May 1940, which destroyed large parts of the city, and the hunger of the winter of 1944–5, which caused hundreds of deaths among the civilian population. What may have played a role is that those who carried out the assault were from Rotterdam and ultimately paid for their struggle against the occupiers with their own deaths.

More than in the history of Rotterdam, the executions acquired a place in the history of the Beekvliet hostages. In the tightly knit hostage community, the episode was (and is) a significant shared experience. In their history the executions constitute a dramatic low point: in their remembrance of the hostages, the executions are central. That is shown by the date chosen by the Committee of Former Hostages (founded in 1946) for the annual act of reunion and remembrance: August 15. The utility of the act of resistance which provoked the execution did not give rise to debate after the war.

In other places and at other times, however, reprisals did give occasion to reconsider the usefulness of armed assaults. Sometimes they gave rise to vehement debates inside the resistance. This was the case, for instance, in Belgium. Because assaults on Belgian collaborators were for a long time punished more lightly than those on German persons and goods, the illegal Belgian Communist Party gave its members instructions to take the former category as its target.[58] In Poland, too, the violent action of a prominent resistance leader was cause for divisions within the resistance.[59] Major Henryk Dobrzański Hubal, called by the Germans 'the crazy major', was a keen horseman and a member of the Polish Olympic team for the 1936 Games in Berlin. During the Polish–German war of 1939 he was second-in-command of the 110th Cavalry Regiment. After the defeat he refused to take off his uniform and, despite orders to disarm, he continued with a group of soldiers a guerrilla fight in the Kielecczyzna region, waiting for the western powers' offensive. At the beginning his unit numbered no more than thirty, but by the beginning of 1940, despite the severe winter, it had increased to 200. On 13 March 1940 the representative of the command of ZWZ (Związek Walki Zbrojnej, Union for Armed Struggle) told Hubal to demobilize his detachment. The order was fulfilled only in part, because some soldiers still stayed, with the major leading the fight.[60]

However, the very presence of Hubal's detachment brought German repression down on local communities. The Nazis burned several villages to the ground and killed 700 people. There were still new volunteers joining his detachment, but the feelings among the local population were slowly becoming hostile as the number of victims rose. The Germans were using provocateurs in the area of Hubal's activity who were pretending to be his agents trying to enlist new soldiers. Potential volunteers quickly fell into a carefully prepared trap. The underground army's command was seriously concerned because it caused problems with the recruitment of new members.[61] The Commander-in-chief of ZWZ, Stefan Rowecki, wrote to Paris in a report of 15 April 1940: 'In Konskie the insane manifestation of Hubal, who twice refused to obey an order to dissolve his guerrilla group and initiated military action, has been paid for by the life of many peasants... I am chasing Hubal, I want to send him abroad, in the future I will bring him before the courts.'[62]

In occupied Holland resisters debated the whole issue of the use of violence a few months before the liberation. The incident which provoked this took place on the night of 6–7 March 1945.[63] That night four members of a local resistance group dressed as Waffen-SS forced a car to stop. They had devised a plan immediately before to rob a meat convoy bound for Germany, but to do this they needed a truck and they did not have one. Such a truck would have to be acquired. To acquire one the four resistance members set out for the Woeste Hoeve, a well-known establishment in the woody surroundings of Hoenderloo. When they heard a heavy engine, they decided to act, supposing the approaching vehicle was a truck. Instead it turned out to be a BMW cabriolet. One of the resistance members had already stopped the car and, without knowing it, was standing face to face with Hans Albin Rauter, Höherer SS- und Polizeiführer, who had just signed an order forbidding the stopping of cars at night outside residential zones. The resister asked the SS man to identify himself; Rauter answered with several shots. This was the signal for the other resistance members hiding in the bushes to empty their sten guns into the car. Though they assumed they had killed everyone in the car, Rauter was still alive and was found only the next morning. Because he was too weak to make a decision on the reprisal himself, his commandant did so for him, probably after discussions with other authorities. It was decided to execute a large number of *Todeskandidaten*, the figure rising in the end to 263. They came from several German prisons in the Netherlands and were shot in different locations in the Netherlands: in Amsterdam, The Hague, Utrecht and Amersfoort, among other places. The largest group (more than a hundred prisoners) was taken to the Woeste Hoeve and shot there.

Unlike the reprisal in Nantes and Rotterdam, this bloodbath was given very little publicity by the German occupiers. The name of the more important victim of the assault was not mentioned – not surprising, perhaps, since the German authorities did not like to boast about the vulnerability of their highest police officials. Still, the news of the executions reached the population quickly. The large number of people shot was an embarrassment to the resistance and caused them to think through once again the question of the purpose and usefulness of violence. Had it really been necessary, and, if so, had there not been an alternative to the excessive use of violence? The highest organ of the Dutch resistance met to discuss this question but did not arrive at a unanimous answer. All those present agreed that the assault had been very unfortunate, but differed on the question of whether violence should subsequently be avoided. For the rest, they exonerated the resistance members involved of all blame; they could not have acted otherwise. Their vain attempt to prevent the execution near the Woeste Hoeve also spoke in their favour; they went there armed but saw upon arrival that the execution had already taken place. It is evident from the reports in the illegal press how much these circles struggled with the evaluation of the assault. Some newspapers doubted the political background of those involved in the assault. The suggestion was made that the assault had not been the work of the resistance but of rival German authorities.[64]

After the war the commemoration of these events was initiated not by relatives of the victims, but by a high resistance organization. It paid for the monument (a wooden cross on a pedestal) which was unveiled on the spot barely two months after the liberation. The inscription on the pedestal, 'Here on 8–3–45 the German invaders brutally murdered 117 sons of the Fatherland', pointed to the victims, but their bereaved families did not play any part in the commemoration. Nor did the local municipality. This can be explained in part by the fact that the executions were carried out at different locations. The backgrounds of those executed also played a role. Only a few of them came from the neighbourhood of the assault and the reprisal. The people shot were a group of men gathered together almost randomly, sharing only the fact that they were in German prisons at the time of the assault. The majority of them were members of the resistance, but they also included black marketeers and criminals. That the victims were not a coherent group probably explains the fact that neither the bereaved nor the local municipality of Hoenderloo cultivated the memory. Only in 1991 did a number of relatives of the victims decide to set up the Monument Woeste Hoeve Foundation. The foundation's main aim was to finance a plaque with the names of the victims. A year later a glass plate with 117 names was placed behind the cross.[65]

In the post-war period the question of whether the March 1945 assault had served a useful purpose surfaced with a vengeance from time to time. Did this act of resistance justify the more than 250 dead? Already in 1946 the leader of the resistance group responsible sought public attention. He took responsibility for the assault, declared the act to have been meaningful and judged the German reprisal to have been out of proportion.[66] In the public debate, the illegitimacy of the reprisal was beyond doubt, but the question as to whether the men who carried out the assault had done their job properly, whether they had gone for their guns too soon, was a cause for dispute. Lou de Jong, the most authoritative Dutch historian of the war, made a judgement in 1980. In his book he wrote with extraordinary severity about the assault, considering irresponsible 'an act of resistance, undertaken with the intention of getting a German truck, which led to the shooting of 263 Dutch people'.[67] The dubious grounds for the assault made it difficult to see the 'Woeste Hoeve' merely as a symbol of German terror. In post-war memory, the 'Woeste Hoeve' is also a synonym for the amateurism of the Dutch resistance.

Another case that could be mentioned here is that of Ascq, a small town in the former occupied territory governed by Von Falkenhausen (Belgium and the two northern French departments), studied by Robert Gildea.[68] In this town resisters placed an explosive charge on the railway near the station. This charge exploded on the evening of 1 April 1944, when a German military train carrying SS troops passed. None of the passengers was wounded and the train was not even badly damaged, but the broken line endangered the transport of troops from Brussels to Lille (and further to the Channel coast). Immediate counter-actions were taken in accordance with the latest instructions: 86 inhabitants were shot, 62 of them on the railway line where the train had stopped.

As in Hoenderloo (but unlike in Nantes and Rotterdam some years before) publicity was given to the events only after the reprisal had taken place. In a communiqué, issued by the Oberfeldkommandant of Lille, it was said that the troops had acted in self-defence: 'The population must know that any attack on German units or individual soldiers will be responded to by all means required by the situation. The example of Ascq must be a lesson. In the nature of things it is inevitable that innocent people will suffer when such things happen. Responsibility lies with the criminals who make such attacks.'[69] Two months later, six locals, all railway workers, were found guilty by a German military court. They were condemned to death and executed.

As in Rotterdam, the reprisal seriously harmed the good relations between the local authorities and the occupying forces. Prominent citizens, like the prefect and the archbishop of Lille, protested. On BBC radio Ascq and Lidice were compared by a French commentator. In the first years after the war the general opinion hardly changed. Anger towards those responsible for the reprisal was predominant. Some, like the mayor, held the German people as a whole responsible. In his opinion, this people 'should be excluded from humanity'.[70] Others, like the new vicar, distinguished between Nazis and the German people. In August 1949 the perpetrators of the massacre were brought to trial. The verdict: eight (of the nine in court) were condemned to death.

Following the immediate post-war years, some in and outside the community of Ascq sought reconciliation. Those involved were mostly religiously inspired. A leading role was performed by the Archbishop of Lille, Cardinal Liénart, and the Pax Christi movement. Liénart urged president René Coty to commute the death penalties, lest they be carried out in 'a spirit of vengeance'.[71] Pressure for a pardon was also brought to bear on Coty from some of the widows of those massacred. They were duly released, and in March 1957 a service of reconciliation, at which Cardinal Liénart officiated, was attended by Monsignor Schoeffer, head of the German section of Pax Christi and bishop of Eichstatt in Bavaria. Twenty years after the massacre a group of survivors and families of those massacred went on a pilgrimage to Rome. There they were blessed by the Pope: 'Happy are you who have turned hate into love, vengeance into friendship and war into peace'.[72]

For a long time, the commemoration of the resisters who had been shot by the Germans for the attack (the *fusillés*) was closely interwoven with the commemoration of those massacred (the *massacrés*). This was illustrated in 1947, when General de Gaulle unveiled a plaque dedicated to the memory of both the *massacrés* and the *fusillés*. There was a good reason for this: men from both groups were local men. In due time, however, tensions started to grow. As Gildea suggests in his article, there were tensions under the surface as early as the 1960s. More recently, in the FR3 film *Ombres portées* (1994), which dealt with the fiftieth anniversary of the massacre, this became even more evident. During an interview a widow of a *fusillé*, for instance, mentioned that inhabitants of Ascq held her husband responsible for the tragedy: 'I told myself that my husband had not done anything wrong, because there were no victims on the German convoy, and then he was obeying orders.'[73]

A similar phenomenon can be observed on the occasion of the commemoration of the bloodbath in the French village of Maillé (Touraine). On the night of 25 August 1944, coinciding with the liberation of Paris, a German convoy ran into a *maquisard* ambush in that municipality. The damage on the German side was not serious – only three wounded – but that didn't prevent a revenge operation being mounted. The next morning a small German unit took revenge in a horrific manner on the population of Maillé. Within a short time, 126 civilians, a little under a quarter of the population, had been slaughtered. Houses were set on fire and dynamited. Not long after the liberation, a plaque was unveiled in memory of the victims of 'Nazi barbarism'. In 1948 the village received the *Croix de Guerre* for 'the sacrifice, spirit of resistance and heroism of the village'. That distinction did not, however, bring an end to the ambivalent sentiments of the survivors. Because of the synchronicity of their tragedy and the national festivities around the liberation of Paris on 25 August, this commemoration has always been extremely difficult. The heroism of the resistance in general was recognized, but this particular operation hit them hard and implicitly they wondered if it had been worth it. What they feared most in the years after the war (until today) was that the recognition of their loss would be overshadowed by reverence for the resistance.[74]

The inhabitants of Civitella also developed a difficult relationship with the resistance. In this small village of 800 people in the Tuscan hills, partisans shot three German soldiers dead on 18 April 1944. Different stories circulate about the incident to this day. Whether the partisans had the intention of killing the soldiers or only wanted to get hold of their weapons, for example, is a question which remains unanswered. Whether they acted in self-defence or opened fire themselves is also unclear. What is certain is that, after the shooting, the partisans left the scene and left the bodies lying in the village.[75]

A little more than a week later SS troops took revenge. On 29 June 1944 they stormed into the local church, where a mass was being held. All present were rounded up on the village square. Others who had not attended mass were taken from their homes, which were then set on fire. On the square a selection process then took place. More than 100 men were set against the wall of a school building a short distance away and shot dead. The remaining villagers, mostly women and children, were chased from the village. In the nearby villages of La Cornia and San Pancrazio the SS also took revenge. There were 97 casualties, women and children among them.[76]

Francesca Cappelletto, who wrote about this bloodbath in 1998, indicates a remarkable discrepancy between the official national memory and the local memory of the massacre, that of survivors and fellow villagers or inhabitants of the immediate area.[77] The official reading of the events is one of a courageous act of resistance against fascism/National Socialism, but according to Cappelletto the events were evaluated very differently by the survivors. From many interviews it became clear to her in the first place that most survivors saw the events as an apocalypse, a 'watershed', 'the stereotype of paradise lost'.[78] Beforehand everything was peace and tranquillity, at least in the eyes of those interviewed; afterward, the troubles began. In the second place, Cappelletto notes that many survivors did not approve of the partisan action, but on the contrary saw it as senseless and irresponsible, and are still indignant at the absence of an apology from the former resistance. One survivor whom Cappelletto interviewed for her research stated: 'They [the partisans – GvF] should come to me and say ... then I would forgive them, otherwise, I will keep this sorrow forever... If the president of ANPI [National Association of Italian Partisans] would say to me "it's true, we made great mistakes in Civitella", then all of us would be more...'[79]

That the local memory stands in complete opposition to the national one became evident during one of the recent post-war memorial ceremonies, when the local population made it clear in no uncertain terms that it considered the official days of remembrance a violation of its memory and sentiment.[80] Alessandro Portelli, who also wrote about the episode, took the view that the story did not end with a contrast between national and local memory. According to this writer, one should speak of a multiplicity of memories, all one way or the other ideologically and culturally mediated.[81]

There is certainly a multiplicity of memories in the case of the bloodbath in the Dutch town of Putten.[82] In October 1944 one of the worst German reprisals in the occupied Netherlands was carried out. The occasion was an assault on a Wehrmacht vehicle, in which several German officers were fatally shot, inside the boundaries of the rural municipality of Putten. In revenge for the assault the German police evicted the entire village, set fire to the centre of town and deported the male population to the German concentration camp of Neuengamme. In the *Aussenlager* of Neuengamme near Ladelund in Germany, 552 of the 600 deported men from Putten perished.

The way many in Putten dealt with the past shows a remarkable similarity to the way the massacre in Ascq was managed. In the first years after the war the trial of the Germans who were responsible for this injustice was at the centre of attention. The punishments, far too lenient in the view of many, caused disappointed and sometimes enraged reactions in Putten and elsewhere. What remained was the great sorrow for the many dead. Putten was swathed in mourning, and in the broad surrounding area the Dutch population felt deep sympathy for the stricken town.

In those years of shared mourning no need was felt to reconstruct the sequence of events or to examine the question of the purpose of the assault and the responsibility for it. There was quiet agreement not to dig too deeply into this already so painful past, out of reverence for the dead and compassion with the bereaved. Even the scholarly Netherlands Institute for War Documentation (NIOD) kept to this informal oath of silence by stopping its inquiry into 'Putten' in 1947 and putting the collected materials under an embargo for fifty years. In 1949 a monument was unveiled in remembrance, figuring a woman in traditional dress with a handkerchief in her hand and her gaze directed towards the old church where the men had been herded together. On the pedestal a biblical text is inscribed: 'and God shall wipe away all tears from their eyes' (Rev. 21:4) The choice of the monument is eloquent of the local memory of the event and what dominated in it: not the victims, nor the resistance fighters or the barbaric occupation, but the grief of the bereaved, the widows.[83]

After this period of shared mourning a remarkable distancing took place between the national and the local view of 'Putten'. While in the national memory 'Putten' became a fossilized symbol of German terror, on the same scale as Oradour in France and Lidice in Czechoslovakia, the profoundly religious population of Putten sought (like many in Ascq) reconciliation – not so much with those responsible for the repression but with the population of Ladelund, where most of the deported men were buried. This Putten *Sonderweg* of reconciliation led in 1964 to the laying of wreaths by the pastor of Ladelund at the monument in Putten and in 1974 to the foundation of the Committee Putten–Ladelund.[84]

The 'revolution' of the 1960s, which led in the Netherlands to a more critical view of the loyal and law-abiding attitude of the Dutch and the amateurism of the resistance, in large part passed Christian Putten by. But it did not pass by several national papers, which at the beginning of the 1970s raked up the past which had been declared taboo and asked questions about the organization, the purpose and the success of the assault. The amateurish planning, the divisions in the resistance group, the 'cowardly' leadership – all of this was raised and set against the background of the reprisal. This did not implicitly shift the question of guilt, but it did expand it to those responsible for the assault. Those who were still alive did not wait long to make their voices heard, in an attempt to justify their action, but the many critical reports cast doubt on the legitimacy of that action.[85]

It is noticeable that the community of Putten hardly took part in this discussion. This changed towards the end of the 1970s, when it became the subject of the discussion. In a television documentary in 1977 an eminent Dutch psychiatrist related the high mortality rate among the men deported from Putten to their religiosity. Their religiously inspired resignation to fate and their work ethic had supposedly made them tame sheep who could be led without a struggle to slaughter. Although the people of Putten could not be held accountable for the German retaliation, the men deported from Putten (and in fact the whole community of Putten) were held responsible by the doctor for their fate in the concentration camp. The implicit message was that the religious, 'backward' climate in the town was in part the cause of the 'tragedy of Putten'. It need hardly be said that the Putten community was not much taken with this view. In the public discussion which followed, it defended its religiosity and fought the notion that religion had led to a fatal fatalism. It was – according to this view – precisely the power of faith that had saved the deported men from a worse fate and led to the survival and return of at least a few of them.[86]

Nowadays, rumours are silenced and debates are closed. It is notable that both memories, the national and local, have grown closer once again. On the local level the suffering of the bereaved is still the central concern, but there is also more interest in the fate of the deported. The German municipality of Ladelund is always invited to participate in commemorations. National interest in the tragedy was evident from the publicity around the sixtieth anniversary. A television documentary broadcast on that occasion drew a large number of viewers. It should be said that this documentary was about how the surviving Germans responsible for the bloodbath looked back on it. The discussion on the senselessness of the assault and the debate about the alleged passivity of the Putteners were not given any attention.[87]

Conclusions and Suggestions for Further Research

Much has been written on the repressive politics of the occupation forces and on the reprisals in occupied Europe. Some generalizations can be made. To begin with, collective punishments, in which groups of innocent civilians were punished for others' actions, took place all across occupied Europe. It is no exaggeration to state that they were part of the reality of occupation.

Collective punishments were varied: some were mild, others extremely severe. We have limited ourselves in this investigation to the more severe kind: western European cases in which innocent people paid for an act of resistance which had taken place in their vicinity by being deprived of freedom, of life and also of possessions. Such collective punishment hit civilians in different parts of Europe, but it is important to note that this punishment was not imposed everywhere on the same scale and with the same regularity. Differences can be partly explained by the ideological, tactical and strategic considerations of the occupying forces. Some population groups were seen as racially inferior; some areas as militarily or economically of lesser importance. The most brutal action was often taken against that population and in those areas. Small deviations, caused by the personal views of the local authorities, also occurred. The attitude of the local population to the occupation also influenced repressive occupation policy. In countries where a large resistance movement was active, it was stricter than elsewhere. In those countries, collective punishments were more frequent.

Until late in 1941 the occupied western and northern parts of Europe were largely spared massive reprisal operations. The populations in the east and in the Balkans, on the other hand, were confronted with terror on a huge scale from the beginning. Collective punishments were structural there. In countries such as Norway, the Netherlands, Belgium, France, Italy and Greece they took place more often from the autumn of 1941 onwards, but they retained a more incidental character. Only in the closing months of the Second World War was the situation in the various parts of occupied Europe virtually equivalent. Horrible bloodbaths took place everywhere in that final phase.

Violent reprisals naturally hit the local population, but it is more difficult to make generalizing comments on the responses to them. In this chapter we have explored several different reprisals; only in a few cases have we been able to elaborate on the manner in which the stricken community and the bereaved survivors responded to events. On the local reactions to bloodbaths in eastern Europe and the Balkans this article has little to tell the reader. Perhaps the question of language plays a role here; some sources have remained unused because they simply could not be read. But it is an open question whether there are such sources. One gets the impression that less research has been done on this subject in some countries. Everyday life, seen from the perspective of the 'ordinary' civilian, is not equally popular in every national war historiography. In some countries, such as Italy, the Netherlands and France, there are comparatively high levels of interest in 'history from below' and regional studies appear regularly. The experiences of ordinary citizens under the occupation have been traced more frequently in these countries – and so also has the response to reprisals in local communities. In some countries, like Italy, France, the Netherlands and Belgium, the post-war myth of the national resistance is more open to discussion than in others. This has led to more (and more critical) writing on cultures of remembrance. In general, more publications in which the unanimity of the resistance and the rest of the population has been questioned have appeared in those countries. In these and similar publications attention is also given to the evaluation of the acts of resistance which provoked reprisals.

Research into the reactions of the stricken population to collective punishments has necessarily resulted in an impressionistic picture. One can, however, discern a few patterns. In each case studied, the reprisal left deep scars on the local community and in most communities the reprisal disturbed relations with the occupation forces. A notable outcome of this research is that relations with the resistance often suffered as well after a reprisal. In many of the cases studied the act of resistance which provoked the reprisal was seen critically. Frequently, both at the time and after the war, the resistance was reproached for having exposed the local population, innocent civilians, to revenge actions. Often there was no single shared memory, but a fragmented whole: a rich and varied collection of individual, collective, national and local memories. However that may be, relatives of victims usually had a different version of the past from that held in the national culture of remembrance, in which adoration of the resistance was for a long time central.

Each community naturally has its own unique history and context which could explain the local reaction, but it is an open question whether more general factors or circumstances can be identified. In all likelihood they can. The nature of the reprisal itself played a part. The number of victims and the scale of physical destruction in the community undoubtedly had an effect on the local population's response. One can expect the shock to have been greatest in places where a reprisal was carried out for the first time. The blow of the reprisal was also more easily absorbed when there were no immediate deaths, but threats came first. In this situation, in which a public campaign was linked to the reprisal, the population and those who carried out the assault were purposely involved in the revenge action. Whether the community was spared or not depended on the resistance turning themselves in. The population also had plenty of time to translate its fear into anger at the resistance.

In the case of Nantes and Rotterdam, we see that these last factors coloured the immediate reaction of the local population. A publicity campaign was part of the policy and this meant that the populace followed events closely. In both cities the population and its authorities, threatened with the execution of prisoners from their midst, condemned the assault. In Rotterdam this sentiment was completely overshadowed by the rage caused when the Germans indeed shot five hostages. This remained the case in Rotterdam after the war. The residents of Nantes have a different recollection. They were threatened by a second wave of executions after the first executions had taken place. Attempts to prevent this disaster were undertaken by various parties: groups of French citizens and authorities hastened to condemn the assault again in writing. In the end, the German authorities decided to cancel the second wave of executions planned and though it is not at all clear that this was a result of their writing, many saw in this the proof that an attitude of loyalty (and condemnation of acts of resistance) could prevent deaths. After the war, the population of Nantes persisted in this view, which is doubtless why de Gaulle paid it only the most perfunctory of visits in January 1945. Probably it is this which explains the difference with the memory of the 'Rotterdam' execution, in which the preceding resistance action is no longer a subject for debate.

In these early cases, an appeal to the culprits to turn themselves in preceded the hostage executions, but with later reprisals this was rarely the case. The act of retribution in Putten and Ascq, for example, was exploited less for publicity than the execution of the hostages in Nantes and Beekvliet had been some years before. The fate of the deported men of Putten was not connected to the hunt for those who carried out the assault, for instance. The execution of a few residents and the clearing and burning down of the town were not aimed at that. In the press the measures taken were not given a great deal of space. Elsewhere as well, reprisals followed mostly within twenty-four hours of an assault, without much publicity being given to them. In such cases, the population outside the targeted village had hardly any idea of the horrors which had taken place. In some places, the scale of the reprisals became clear only after months had passed. The inhabitants could not know one of the consequences of the Germans' retribution – the high death rate among the deportees. That more than 90 per cent of them would not come back alive was only apparent after the war. Only after the war was the utility of the act of resistance drawn into question.

How severely the act of resistance was condemned was related to the victims' background. People from Hoenderloo, in which municipality more than a hundred *Todeskandidaten* were shot in March 1945, hardly responded to the executions. After the war, too, they did not play a prominent role in the remembrance of the executions by firing squad. No critical tone was struck among them about the resistance leading to this revenge operation. Why not? Could it be because that only a single person among the victims came from the region where the assault had been carried out? In many cases, however, the victims were chosen from a community in the area where the assault had been carried out by the resistance. In small communities, above all, the dead and deported were known. The grief was more personal and identification with the victims was not difficult. Grief and anger at the deaths of known people made condemnation of the resistance more obvious and also more straightforward.

Finally, one can point at the relation to the resistance fighters. Cappelletto, in her research into Civitella, observed: 'a local Partisan was "almost forgiven" by the inhabitants because "he is one of us". Partisans from outside, however, were not forgiven.'[88] In the evaluation of the act of resistance in other places, the background of the perpetrators also played a role. In his description of the events in Nantes, Robert Gildea suggests that the reaction of the population would have been very different if no resident of the town had been shot but only communist prisoners from elsewhere.[89] Would these observations not also hold for other reprisals? Is it not logical that people respond more vehemently when 'strangers', 'outsiders', expose them to dangers than when known people do?

Research into collective punishments and the responses to them of the targeted local population has shown, besides general patterns, variations and differences. Variations in the nature of the reprisals had to do with the policy followed locally. In turn that had to do with the ideological and tactical considerations of the occupation authorities and the entire national climate in particular countries. One can point to places spread across the map of Europe which were hit by reprisals; most of those places are in the Balkans and eastern Europe. In reprisal operations there was always immaterial and material loss to be mourned, but in these areas they were greater than elsewhere.

The cases demonstrate that reactions to dramatic events varied, at the time and long afterwards. Different factors have been pointed to for a possible explanation: the time, the form and the scale of the reprisal; the relations between those who carried out the resistance action, those shot and those affected by their deaths. An important similarity which holds across national boundaries has, however, also been brought to the surface: despite the differences, these kinds of reprisal almost always led to discussions on the usefulness of violent resistance actions. Almost always the judgement was more negative at the local level, among members of the targeted community, than it was at the national level. After the war, this occasionally led to striking divergences in the memory of the events and the views of the resistance. The post-war myth of the resistance was rarely swallowed in these communities.

These conclusions are, as has been said, based on a fairly limited investigation and thus to be taken as provisional. Reactions at the local level to assaults in eastern Europe and the Balkans have remained outside our consideration. The question is, however, whether there is reason to assume that the results of this investigation should not also hold true of other cases. Complementary research should move in that direction.

Notes

1. J. Steinbeck, *The Moon is Down* (London, Heinemann, 1942).
2. H. Mulisch, *De Aanslag* (Amsterdam, Bezige Bij, 1982).
3. P. Lagrou, *The Legacy of Nazi Occupation. Patriotic Memory and National Recovery in Western Europe, 1945–1965* (Cambridge, Cambridge University Press, 2000); idem, 'The Politics of Memory. Resistance as a Collective Myth in Post-War France, Belgium and the Netherlands, 1945–1965', *European Review*, Vol. 11, No. 4 (2003), pp. 527–49.
4. R. Bosworth, *The Italian Dictatorship. Problems and Perspectives of the Interpretation of Mussolini and Fascism* (London, Arnold, 1998), pp. 186–92; T. Judt, 'The Past is Another Country. Myth and Memory in Post-war Europe', in I. Deák, J.T. Gross and T. Judt (eds), *The Politics of Retribution in Europe. World War II and Its Aftermath* (Princeton, 2000), pp. 293–323; A. Weiner, *Making Sense of War. The Second World War and the Fate of the Bolshevik Revolution* (Princeton, Princeton University Press, 2001), p. 160.
5. E. Verhoeyen, *België bezet 1940–1945* (Brussels, BRTN educatieve uitgaven, 1993), p. 416.
6. M. Messerschmidt, 'Völkerrecht und "Kriegsnotwendigkeit" in der deutschen militärischen Tradition', in: M. Messerschmidt, *Was damals Recht war... NS-Militär- und Strafjustiz im Vernichtungskrieg* (Essen, Klartext, 1996), p. 193.
7. Messerschmidt, 'Völkerrecht und "Kriegsnotwendigkeit",' pp. 191–229.
8. *Sonderbestimmung für die Verwaltung und Befriedung der besetzten Gebiete Holland, Belgiens und Luxemburgs* (29 October 1939). International Military Tribunal (IMT). *Trial of the Major War Criminals* (Nuremberg 1947–9), Vol. XXX, 210–13, PS–2329.
9. N. Hong, *Sparks of Resistance. The Illegal Press in German-Occupied Denmark, April 1940–August 1943* (Odense, Odense University Press, 1996), p. 200ff.;

H. Umbreit, 'Auf dem Weg zur Kontinentalherrschaft', in B.R. Kroener, R.-D. Müller and H. Umbreit, *Das Deutsche Reich und der Zweite Weltkrieg*, Vol. 5/1 (Stuttgart, DVA, 1988), p. 191.

10. E. Collotti, 'Zur italienischen Repressionspolitik auf dem Balkan', in L. Droulia and H. Fleischer (eds), *Von Lidice bis Kalavryta. Widerstand und Besatzungsterror* (Berlin, Metropol, 1999), pp. 105–24; G. Rochat, *Guerre italiane in Libia e in Etiopia* (Paese, Pagus, 1991), pp. 95–6 and 84–5; C. Madajczyk, 'Terror und Repression des Dritten Reiches im besetzten Europa', in Droulia and Fleischer (ed.), *Von Lidice bis Kalavryta*, pp. 27–9.

11. Umbreit, 'Auf dem Weg zur Kontinentalherrschaft', pp. 28–95.

12. Ibid., p. 187.

13. Madajczyk, 'Terror und Repression des Dritten Reiches im besetzten Europa', p. 19.

14. Umbreit, 'Auf dem Weg zur Kontinentalherrschaft', p. 188. See above, p.

15. Ibid., p. 189.

16. W. Weber, *Die innere Sicherheit im besetzten Belgien und Nordfrankreich 1940–1944* (Düsseldorf, Droste, 1978), pp. 55–9.

17. Verhoeyen, *België bezet*, p. 306.

18. IMT, Vol. 6, pp. 120–9 and Vol. 27, p. 374, PS–1590.

19. The Military Government of Montenegro – Ufficio Affari Civili, 6 November 1941, *Internment and Police Measures*. Ufficio Storico Stato Maggiore dell'Esercito Italiano (USSME) N1–11 – Diari Storici, file 463.

20. Weber, *Die innere Sicherheit*, p. 69ff.

21. Madjaczyk, 'Terror und Repression', p. 21; IMT, Vol. 27, p. 364, PS–1588.

22. Weber, *Die innere Sicherheit*, pp. 73–7; Verhoeyen, *België bezet*, pp. 416–17.

23. Weber, *Die innere Sicherheit*, pp. 73–7.

24. On the German hostage policies in occupied France see S. Klarsfeld, *Livre des otages. La politique des otages menée par les autorités allemandes d'occupation en France de 1941 à 1943* (Paris, Les Éditeurs français réunis, 1979).

25. Messerschmidt, 'Partisanenkrieg auf dem Balkan. Ziele, Methoden, "Rechtfertigung"', in Droulia and Fleischer (ed.), *Von Lidice bis Kalavryta*, pp. 69–70.

26. M. Legnani, 'Il giner del general Roatta, le direttive della II Armata sulla repressione antipartigiana in Slovenia e Croazia', *Italia Contemporanea*, 209–10 (Dec. 1997–March 1998), pp. 156–74.

27. Robotti, 5 November 1941, USSME, M3b84; 'Pinerolo' Division command, 24 August 1942, USSME, N1–11 – Diari Storici, file 984; 26th Army Corps command, 27 September 1942, N1–11 – Diari Storici, file 972; General Carlo Geloso commander-in-chief of 11th Army to all dependent Army Corps, 8 October 1942, USSME N1–11 – Diari Storici, file 1054; Notizario 3D, 16 October 1942, USSME N1–11 – Diari Storici, file 1192; 'Pinerolo' Division to Grevena's garrison command, USSME N1–11 – Diari Storici, file 1232; USSME N1–11

– Diari Storici, file 1089. We are grateful to Davide Rodogno for these passages on the Balkans.

28. On Lidice see M. Kárný, '"Heydrichiaden". Widerstand und Terror im "Protektorat Böhmen und Mähren"', in Droulia and Fleischer (ed.), *Von Lidice bis Kalavryta*, pp. 51–63.

29. On Babi Yar see A. Anatolij, *Babi Yar. A Document in the Form of a Novel* (London, Cape, 1970). Also K.C. Berkhoff, *Harvest of Despair. Life and Death in Ukraine under Nazi Rule* (Cambridge MA, Belknap Press of Harvard University Press, 2004), pp. 65–9.

30. 11th Army to the German General Staff southeast, 26 February 1943, Monthly relation on the political and military situation, USSME, N1–11 – Diari Storici, file 1266A. Thanks to Davide Rodogno, who wrote this passage.

31. E.A. Cohen, 'Schuldig slachtoffer. De derde Befehlshaber der Sicherheitspolizei und des SD in Nederland', in A.H. Paape (ed.), *Studies over Nederland in oorlogstijd*, 1 (The Hague, SDU, 1972), pp. 192–210.

32. R. Bohn, '"Ein solcher Spiel kennt keine Regeln". Gestapo und Bevölkerung in Norwegen und Dänemark', in G. Paul and K.M. Mallmann (eds), *Die Gestapo. Mythos und Realität* (Darmstadt, Wissenschaftliche Buchgesellschaft, 1995), p. 473.

33. Verhoeyen, *België bezet*, pp. 416–20; Weber, *Die innere Sicherheit*, p. 186.

34. G. von Frijtag Drabbe Künzel, *Het recht van de sterkste. Duitse strafrechtpleging in bezet Nederland* (Amsterdam, Bert Bakker, 1999), pp. 213ff.

35. The reconstruction of the history of Nantes is largely based on R. Gildea, *Marianne in Chains. In Search of the German Occupation of France 1940–1944* (London, Macmillan, 2002), pp. 243–59.

36. Cited in Gildea, *Marianne in Chains*, p. 248.

37. G. von Frijtag Drabbe Künzel, 'Het Duitse gijzelingsbeleid', in S. Jansens *et al* (ed.), *Een ruwe hand in het water. De gijzelingskampen Sint-Michielsgestel en Haaren* (Amsterdam, Het Spinhuis, 1993), pp. 137–227.

38. The taking of the hostages was sourced in the guidelines mentioned earlier which the OKW sent to the local commanders towards the end of 1941 (among them the *Wehrmachtbefehlshaber* in the occupied Netherlands, Friedrich Christiansen); message Seyss-Inquart (17.3.1943), Netherlands Institute for War Documentation Amsterdam (NIOD), archive 61–76, file 3D; telex Harster (17.7.1942), NIOD, archive 77–85, file 129B; *Het Proces Christiansen* (The Hague, SDU, 1952), *passim*.

39. L. de Jong, *Het Koninkrijk der Nederlanden in de Tweede Wereldoorlog* (The Hague, 1969–91), Vol. 8, p. 163.

40. Frijtag, 'Het Duitse gijzelingsbeleid', pp. 153ff.

41. Politische Lagebericht D. Hatenboer (13.8.1942), NIOD, archive 77–85, file 27A; Frijtag, 'Het Duitse gijzelingsbeleid', pp. 174–5.

42. De Jong, *Het Koninkrijk*, Vol. 6, pp. 66–7; *Het Proces Christiansen*, p. 24.

43. *De Telegraaf* (8.8.1942).

44. Message O. Bene (10.8.1942), NIOD, archive 207, file 731–265542.

45. *Nieuwe Rotterdamsche Courant* (13.8.1942).

46. Ibid.

47. De Jong, *Het Koninkrijk*, Vol. 6, pp. 71–4.

48. Proces-verbaal H. van Dam (31.8.1949), National Archive The Hague, Centraal Archief voor de Bijzondere Rechtspleging (NA-CABR), file H. Probsting; proces-verbaal M. van Heerenbeek (9.6.1945), NA-CABR, file H.F.W. Küthe.

49. *De Telegraaf* (15.8.1942).

50. *Vrij Nederland* (19.8.1942).

51. *Het Parool* (21.8.1942).

52. Ibid. (25.9.1942).

53. Lage und Stimmungsbericht Feldkommandantur Utrecht, 26 (29.8.1942), NIOD, archive 1–12, file 26C.

54. Meldungen aus den Niederlanden, 108 (25.8.1942), NIOD, archive 77–85, file 36B; Politische Lagebericht D. Hatenboer (20.8.1942), NIOD, archive 77–85, file 27A; monthly report of Feldkommandantur Breda (August 1942), NIOD, archive 1–12, file 26C.

55. Letter of Rauter to Himmler (10.9.1942), in N.K.C.A. in 't Veld, *De SS en Nederland. Documenten uit SS-archieven, 1933–1945* (Den Haag, SDU, 1976), 812, No. 216.

56. Protokoll der Besprechung der Bef. und Kommandeure am 2.10.1942 beim Wehrmachtbefehlshaber, NIOD, archive 215, file 1000810–1000812.

57. Notwithstanding the execution of two more hostages in October 1942.

58. Verhoeyen, *België bezet*, pp. 418–19.

59. We are grateful to Jacek Tebinka for the passage on Poland.

60. B. Kobuszewskiego, P. Matusaka and T. Rawskiego (eds), *Polski ruch oporu 1939–1945* (Warsaw, Wydawnictwo Ministerstwa Obrony Narodowej, 1988), pp. 82–4.

61. *Armia Krajowa w dokumentach 1939–1945*, vol. 1: IX 1939–VI 1941 (Wroclaw, Ossolineum, 1990), pp. 341–2.

62. Ibid.

63. On the assault and the reprisal, see H. Berends, *Woeste Hoeve 8 maart 1945* (Kampen, Kok Voorhoeve, 1995); De Jong, *Het Koninkrijk*, Vol. 10b, pp. 438–47.

64. *Het Parool* (17.3.1945 and 27.3.1945).

65. www.oorlogsmonumenten.nl.

66. J.H. Middelbeek, *Ik draag U op… Systeem en werk der Nederlandsche Binnenlandsche Strijdkrachten, getoetst aan de lotgevallen van lokale eenheden (Apeldoorn en omgeving)* (Apeldoorn, s.n., 1946).

67. De Jong, *Het Koninkrijk*, Vol. 10b, p. 446.

68. R. Gildea, 'Resistance, Reprisals and Community in Occupied France', *Royal Historical Society*, 13 (2003), pp. 163–85.
69. Cited in Gildea, 'Resistance, Reprisals and Community', p. 169.
70. Cited in Gildea, 'Resistance, Reprisals and Community', p. 179.
71. Cited in Gildea, 'Resistance, Reprisals and Community', p. 179.
72. Cited in Gildea, 'Resistance, Reprisals and Community', p. 181.
73. Cited in Gildea, 'Resistance, Reprisals and Community', p. 182.
74. Gildea, *Marianne in Chains*, pp. 327–8 and 396–7.
75. A. Portelli, 'The Massacre at Civitella Val di Chiana (Tuscany, June 29, 1944). Myth and Politics, Mourning and Common Sense', in *The Battle of Valle Giulia. Oral History and the Art of Dialogue* (Madison, University of Wisconsin Press, 1997), pp. 141, 142.
76. Francesca Cappelletto, 'Memories of Nazi-Fascist Massacres in Two Central Italian Villages', *Sociologia Ruralis*, Vol. 38, No. 1 (1998), pp. 69–85.
77. Portelli, 'The Massacre at Civitella', pp. 140–60.
78. Cappelletto, 'Memories of Nazi-Fascist Massacres', pp. 70, 82, 83.
79. Ibid., p. 79.
80. Portelli, 'The Massacre at Civitella', p. 142.
81. Ibid.
82. On Putten see M de Keizer, *Putten. De razzia en de herinnering* (Amsterdam, Bert Bakker, 1998).
83. www.oorlogsmonumenten.nl; www.oktober44.nl.
84. De Keizer, *Putten*, pp. 307ff.
85. Ibid.
86. Ibid.
87. This documentary, 'Op de drempel van het grote vergeten', was broadcast in two parts, on September 27 and October 4, 2004. For reactions see the channel's website: www.info.omroep.nl/ncrv.
88. Cappelletto, 'Memories of Nazi-Fascist Massacres', p. 81.
89. Gildea, *Marianne in Chains*, p. 247.

Conclusion
Olivier Wieviorka and the Team

Everyday life was deeply disrupted in Europe between 1939 and 1945. In a sense it may even be irrelevant to speak of 'daily life', since the lives of ordinary people were governed by extraordinary, bewildering and unpredictable events. People faced new and terrible problems. First of all they were exposed to hunger, a scourge that had all but disappeared in Europe in the twentieth century. They now spent a great deal of time looking for food and the wherewithal to meet their most basic needs – clothing, heating, transport. They were subjected to rationing, obliged to queue, tempted to supplement their meagre rations by buying on the black market. Some famines occurred – as in Greece in the winter of 1941–2 or the Netherlands in the winter of 1944–5 – not to speak of the terrible situations in the Jewish ghettos and generally speaking in eastern Europe. Ordinary people were forced to work for the enemy, either in factories at home or, after being deported, in factories in the Reich. This recalled the slavery of the Ancient world or serfdom, which had vanished in Europe apart from, perhaps, in the Gulag system of the Soviet Union. Ordinary communities faced collective reprisals, as the German and Italian armies used collective punishment to ensure a peaceful occupation for their troops, by both threatening civilians and making resisters unpopular. They could be deprived of entertainment (when cinemas were closed or the curfew imposed), fined collectively as towns or villages, taken hostage and shot, or be burned alive in their communities, in a hundred places from Lidice to Oradour-sur-Glane.

Daily Life, a Relevant Notion?

These phenomena might be considered extraordinary and thus excluded from so-called everyday life. And yet daily life is not to be confused with normalcy. It may be conditioned by extraordinary and abnormal events. These, between 1939 and 1945, concerned not a minority of the population but millions of people. During the 'Great Patriotic War' 20 million Soviet civilians died, including 2.8 million Jews. Nearly 8.5 million workers were drafted from eastern and western Europe to work in German factories. Rationing was in force in all European countries, even if it was less harsh in the Netherlands or in Denmark than in Poland or Ukraine. Moreover, these phenomena were not sporadic, but lasted for five or six years. Sometimes conditions were easier than at other times. The end of the war was the harshest time in western Europe, but countries like Poland suffered occupation intensely for the full duration of the war. Affecting millions of people and lasting for years, these extraordinary events shaped everyday life in the whole of occupied Europe.

To this extent, everyday life was quite different during the war from what went before it. And yet some of these phenomena were not entirely new. Hunger had struck Ireland in the nineteenth century and the Soviet Union in the 1930s. Forced labour was widespread in eastern Europe in the nineteenth century, even if it was serfdom rather than slavery. Even collective reprisals were not new. They had been tried by the Germans during the First World War, even though they were forbidden by The Hague conventions. In the Soviet Union whole families were deported in the Dekulakization campaign, while during the purges of the 1930s close relatives of suspected enemies of the people were arrested and detained. Daily life during the Second Word War was hence linked to a past which, occasionally, was not far removed from the present. It brought back memories, sometimes coloured by nostalgia, as in the case of motorized societies rediscovering horses and oxen, sometimes by fear, as forced labour recalled Russian serfdom or the deportation of labour that had taken place from Belgium and northern France in 1914–18.

The novelty of the situation, in other words, lay not in the conditions themselves, since famine, serfdom and collective reprisals were not unknown in the recent European past, but in the fact that they were brought together at one historical moment and affected most of the European population. European societies had to cope with hunger, forced labour and collective punishment *at the same time*, which was quite new, except perhaps in Stalin's Russia. Though Ireland was struck by the Great Hunger in the 1840s, it did not have to cope with forced labour or collective reprisals. During the Second World War, however, the impact was cumulative, which explains why societies were affected in such a deep way. This accumulation is not surprising because the situation encountered by the occupied societies was not explained by a single cause. The so-called 'Nazi domination' in fact embraced three different processes: war, occupation and a new political order.

War, Occupation and New Order

War, of course, disrupted everyday life. It exposed civilians to violence, a modern violence which led to the mass killing of civilians, whether in land fighting or by aerial bombing. As the war became a total war, German and Italian forces mobilized resources in occupied territories to support their war economies. Daily life was disrupted because civilians were plundered, starved, drafted and dragooned into helping the Axis to win the war. In so far as resistance developed in opposition to these demands, the repression of resistance belonged to the logic of war.

The logic of occupation was to some extent different. In this case enemy forces disrupted everyday life not because they were engaged in fighting, but because they were omnipresent. Soldiers were billeted on homes, occupied schools and hotels, invaded theatres, cinemas and public transport. The occupying authorities sometimes imposed their own languages, always imposed a curfew and their new symbolic universe of flags, public notices and road signs. Their presence provoked a variety of reactions. Some preferred to keep silent to show their disapproval, as illustrated by the 1942 novella of the French writer Vercors, *The Silence of the Sea*. Others preferred to resist, sometimes with violence. The occupation, however, also offered new challenges and opportunities. Some industrialists were happy to work with a rich and greedy client who allowed them to run their own businesses and offered good profits. Militants whose ideology was close to that of the Nazis or fascists found new ways of registering their commitment, in collaborationist parties or in organizations such as the Wehrmacht, Hitler Youth or SS. Some people were satisfied by plundering their Jewish neighbours – taking their flats or goods or eliminating economic or professional rivals. Men and especially women found new opportunities for sexual encounters, as thousands of men were away from home, in Stalags or German factories. Some nations, as in Ukraine or the Baltic states, even saw the Germans as their liberators from Soviet rule and were willing to collaborate with them. In these ways occupation was more ambivalent than war.

Finally, some events that disrupted daily life were due neither to war nor to occupation. They were imposed by the new political order brought in by the Nazi and fascist victory. In many places Nazis and fascists tried to reshape states and societies by imposing their own ideology and culture. This led them to destroy Jewish communities and attack their racial enemies. In the core of Europe they looked to destroy some national identities in order to pave the way for further German or Italian colonization. To achieve this, the occupying authorities used various means. They obliged ordinary citizens and especially school pupils to speak German or Italian, purged or forcibly retrained local teachers, banned church schools, had portraits of the Führer or Duce hung in schools and other public buildings, and required the fascist salute at ceremonies. In some Slavic countries, such as Poland, the occupying authorities tried to eliminate the local elites, by smashing the existing school system, especially secondary schools and universities, and even by the mass murder of the educated class.

These three main factors – war, occupation, political *Gleichschaltung* – were closely associated but combined in different ways according to place. In Poland the horrors of combat were experienced mainly at the beginning and the end of the war, but Poles were subjected to an extremely harsh occupation, both for racial and economic reasons. Denmark, on the other hand, suffered much less because it was not militarily strategic, because the Danes were highly regarded from a racial point of view and because they were supposed to be the 'larder of Germany', feeding it with their agricultural products. In the occupied territories of the Soviet Union people faced a tough occupation, a violent war and the imposition of Nazi rule. This multiform reality explains how despite a common pattern based on three common pillars – total war, occupation and political reshaping – outcomes were very different across occupied Europe. The experience of occupation by European populations depended on the economic interest of the country and its military importance for the occupiers, together with the political outlook of the winners – Italians or Germans.

Conditions varied not only according to place but also according to time. The policy of the occupying forces was directly influenced by the course of the war. From this point of view, the war against Russia (June 1941) and the state of total war (1943) were two important steps. They brought about a process of radicalization and increased the pressure exerted on populations, especially in terms of rationing, forced labour (introduced in France in 1943) and reprisals. On the other hand, the growing pressure of total war on Germany, intensified by the many fronts and Allied bombing, also made her less able to ensure supplies of foodstuffs, control the forced labour force, or contain resistance. Paradoxically, greater repression went hand in hand with decreasing effectiveness.

Daily life may be considered as a by-product of the policy of the occupiers, but not every problem was their responsibility. Some difficulties were the result of war in general, which disrupted old economic relations. The famine in Greece in 1941–2 is explained partly by German and Italian policy, but also by the blockade imposed by the British. The Dutch famine of 1944–5 was caused by the division of the Netherlands into two main areas, one controlled by the Germans and the other by the Allies. Supplies could not circulate from one area to another, not least because the Allies were reluctant to feed the enemy zone. In France shortages were mainly due to German plundering; but they were also caused by the snapping of the commercial ties linking metropolitan France to the outside world, especially her empire. In Belgium shortages can be partially explained by the inefficiency of the rationing system. To give one final example, the bombing suffered by the populations of occupied Europe's towns and cities was, after 1943, less the work of the Luftwaffe than that of the British and American air forces. Reality and perceptions of reality, however, did not always mesh, and for most of the occupied populations the occupiers were held responsible for their fate, a factor which explains people's disillusionment when the occupying forces withdrew and their problems remained.

Narrowing or Widening Horizons?

The collapse or weakening of nation-states under foreign occupation meant that societies fell back from defence of their country onto the defence of smaller circles – of the individual, family, local community, corporation or religious grouping. Horizons narrowed as people thought less about the survival of their country, more about needs and loyalties closer to home. The search for food haunted every mind. If a mother was alone because the husband was a prisoner of war or working in Germany, finding milk became a real nightmare which took much time and cost a good deal of money if it had to be bought on the black market. Queuing for food might take three or four hours a day to get almost nothing in the end. Economic disorganization and the fragmentation of markets forced people back onto a barter economy and local exchanges. In the labour sphere, collective bargaining was abandoned and replaced, as in Belgium, by local or factory agreements – or the liberality of an employer. The private sphere, finally, became a kind of sanctuary where it was possible to forget war, occupation or political pressures.

On the other hand, the collapse or weakening of the nation-state might also widen people's horizons. Sent to work in Germany, many Soviet workers discovered that the situation in the capitalist hell was far better than in the workers' paradise – a conclusion also reached by Russian soldiers, the *frontoviki*. When the war was over, some even thought that they had had 'the best times of their lives' in Germany. French POWs who had worked on German farms often returned home with the same impressions. Women whose husbands were away found themselves at the head of the family farm or business or confronted by the possibility of new romantic experiences. As the traditional family was put under pressure, so opportunities arose for a kind of female emancipation. Many young people complained that they had lost their youth, but those, for example, who joined the Hitler Youth, or were recruited to anti-aircraft or civil defence units, were removed from their local communities to face dangerous and exciting challenges. The war, finally, was a world war. Just following its progress on the map certainly widened people's horizons. Their fate depended on events taking place far away. This consideration obliged people to be interested in foreign matters which they might have neglected before 1939, and to link their destiny with that of others – to live in communion with the whole world and to be concerned, if not passionate, about it.

Material Needs and Moral Choices

People under occupation were confronted by serious material problems, but they also faced difficult moral choices. Daily life in fact was highly moralized and politicized: individual choices could not avoid being judged on moral or political grounds. Sexual relations, for example, were no longer only a private matter ruled by the heart. Women had affairs with Germans for sentimental as well as material or ideological reasons, but, whatever their motivation, their behaviour was judged by their fellow citizens, who did not consider the matter to be private. 'German girls' were seen as traitors whose behaviour threatened the honour and integrity of the family, local community and indeed nation. If they were insulted by their fellow citizens, their German protectors could take the view that the honour of the Wehrmacht was being impugned, and if the women denounced the insulter, who was then arrested and deported, national security was seen to be at stake. So love became a question of international relations and women's bodies a 'combat zone' between competing communities. To that extent, the frontier between the private and public spheres collapsed. Working for the enemy was also a moral and political issue. To go to work in Germany was not usually a genuine choice, even for those who were in a formal sense volunteers. They were driven to accept work in Germany because of unemployment, which was a real problem in countries such as France and Belgium in 1940, and because higher wages in the Reich seemed very attractive. This choice, however, was also a moral and political one, because their labour sustained the German war machine. Even forced labour posed moral dilemmas, because there was the alternative of trying to escape it by going into hiding or joining the resistance. On the other hand, failure to go could result in the punishment of one's family or sanctions against the local community, so that patriotism came into conflict with narrower loyalties.

These moral and political choices, moreover, were far from simple, because people were deprived of familiar ethical guidelines. In some countries, such as the Soviet Union, Poland, Yugoslavia and the occupied parts of the Soviet Union, the state collapsed, while in others, such as France, Greece and the Bohemian Protectorate, the state was induced to collaborate, and rival resistance movements, some communist, some non-communist, laid claim to an alternative legitimacy. In Yugoslavia the alternative legitimacy proposed by the resistance was split because of the struggle between Mihailović's Chetniks and Tito's partisans. For the French it was hard to disobey the Vichy regime, which appeared to be a legitimate power, and those who did disobey faced rival calls from de Gaulle and the communist resistance. For some Soviet citizens, who had suffered under Stalin's regime during the 1930s, the choice between defending the Soviet Union and the possibility of survival by working for the Germans was certainly not obvious. Churches might provide ethical guidance, and in places such as Poland the Catholic Church assumed a new importance trying to defend national identity and culture, while in Belgium it protected people against forced labour or persecution. In other cases, however, churches did not always deliver a clear message – for example, whether it was a duty to do forced labour if recruited – and sometimes shared some of the values and aims of the occupying forces, above all anti-communism and anti-Semitism. For these reasons individuals had to fall back either on a personal moral assessment of the challenges they faced, or looked to guidance from their families or those in authority in the local community, such as clergy, mayors or employers. These choices were certainly difficult to make and the burdens heavy to carry for ordinary people; but this situation also offered them a kind of freedom. As the traditional authorities collapsed or were contested, people came to rely on their own judgements and feelings, a situation which allowed them to use, in a very concrete way, a liberty of choice.

The Revenge of Society

Daily life was characterized by hardship and suffering, and yet the pressures under which ordinary people were put provoked social responses. Occupied societies were not a soft wax which the Germans or the Italians could model at will. Societies reacted, sometimes violently, sometimes in more measured and imaginative ways.

The problems encountered by populations in their daily lives offered a fertile ground to resistance networks. Rationing was exploited by resisters to discredit German or Italian policy and to popularize their fight. To obtain wage increases workers tried to bargain – as in the Netherlands until 1942 – but they also went on strike, like the Warsaw transport workers in December 1940 or the coalminers and metalworkers of northern France and Belgium in May 1941, risking a brutal response because of the threat they posed to the Axis war machine. Forced labour was highly unpopular and thus offered a perfect target for resistance movements. These concentrated their propaganda on it, tried to organize the draft dodgers by helping them go underground, giving them false identity papers and money, or even recruited them into paramilitary structures like the *maquis*. Attempts at Germanization or Nazification generated opposition that was expressed symbolically, by wearing national colours or commemorating national heroes and anniversaries, but could also, when the international balance of power shifted, trigger national uprisings, such as the Danish revolt of June–July 1944 (initially triggered by a mere question of curfew) or the famous Warsaw uprising of August 1944.

Armed struggle, however, was not always popular among populations because it could – and in fact often did – provoke reprisals against local communities. The taking up of arms by civilians was forbidden under international law governing the terms of occupation. The Axis powers therefore treated armed civilians as terrorists and also took the view that communities thought to be harbouring terrorists should be punished, not least to drive a wedge between resisters and local populations. While resistance organizations often posed as protectors of local communities, they were not above exploiting them on their own account and were frequently distrusted, even feared, as pernicious forces that only served to attract the wrath of the occupying forces.

Rather than resort to arms, local populations were more likely to improvise 'weapons of the weak' which were less risky and more imaginative. After all, the main task for most people was to survive occupation rather than to bring it to a violent end. Survival strategies often meant generating new social networks or new social practices. These in themselves demonstrated the vigour of associational life and the depth of civil society. They showed that whatever the totalitarian ambitions of the Axis powers, there were limits set to what they could achieve by the societies they occupied.

To cope with rationing, for example, people resorted to parallel economies where food was more freely available if at higher prices. These economies were varied, from the exchange of goods by post on a family basis, between town dwellers and country cousins, to locally based barter economies, trips made by townsfolk to the countryside, where they had or hoped to find contacts with producers, to a much more professional long-distance black market which often involved the occupying forces themselves. Faced by the threat of forced labour, and given the dangers of striking, workers resorted to a range of options, from blackmailing employers into offering them protection from going, or providing them or their families with material support if they had to go, as in Belgium, to finding work in German factories on their home soil, whose workforce was protected under German regulations from the labour draft. Workers who did end up going to Germany did not suffer slave labour, and those from the west initially enjoyed periods of leave. Some foreign workers perfected all sorts of tricks to make life easier. These included various forms of time wasting – called *Arbeitsbummelei* by the Germans – moving to different factories or easier jobs on lorries or farms, voicing insults and low-grade revolt among workers of the same nationality, and finally descent into a gang existence as the Third Reich fell apart.

The Germans and Italians did not try to impose their culture and ideology uniformly, but even where they did, they found themselves opposed by rival institutions with rival values. Though the nation-state was weakened or destroyed by occupation, other bodies such as local communities, schools, churches and families stepped in to protect local, national and religious cultures. The Catholic Church maintained the autonomy of its University of Louvain, which in turn protected its students from the forced labour draft, and more widely in Europe maintained its grip on young people through catechism, choir practice and youth associations even when its confessional schools were closed down. The German attempt to use the official school system to impose German culture in central Europe was undermined by its need to fall back on local teachers when German teachers had to be drafted into the army, and by whole networks of clandestine schools and recognized schools delivering syllabuses at a much higher level than they were supposed to. Teachers rediscovered a corporate identity in their opposition to being retrained for the Nazi project, and officials dragged their bureaucratic feet over projects to revise school textbooks. Meanwhile, families, teachers and churches found common cause in quietly frustrating attempts to recruit young people into the Hitler Youth.

Occupation offered challenges to daily life and stimulated a variety of survival strategies. These in turn provoked major social changes which outlasted the war. From a demographic point of view, family life was severely disrupted by occupation. There were, for example, thousands of children fathered by Germans in occupied territories, most of them illegitimate – 7,500 in Denmark, 10–12,000 in Norway, 8–16,000 in the Netherlands and 50–70,000 in France. War and the aftermath or war also saw a surge in the divorce rate. In France, for example, the number of divorces rose from 37,618 in 1945 to 64,064 in 1946, before declining to 31,268 in 1956. Marriages followed a similar pattern, rising in France from 393,000 in 1945 to 517,000 in 1946 and falling back to 312,300 in 1955. There was a similar marriage boom in the Netherlands, with the rate rising from 15.6 per thousand in 1945 to 22.8 in 1946, falling to 16.6 in 1955, while in Belgium the marriage rate climbed from 7.7 per thousand in 1935–9 to 9.3 per thousand in 1946–50. Marriage and divorce rates followed the same pattern in Denmark. In 1940 there were 35,262 marriages and 3,472 divorces; these rose to 37,524 and 5,365 in 1944 and 40,257 and 7,500 in 1946, declining to 39,910 and 6,943 in 1947. In the Soviet Union, however, the marriage rate fell mainly because there were simply not enough men of marriageable age, partially because new legal and social forces made men reluctant to commit to marriage. The government freed men from the obligation to pay alimony for illegitimate children, so that the birth rate climbed from a low of 11.2 per thousand in 1943 to a post-war high of 27.0 per thousand in 1951. Polish data show that the birth rate rose from 11.2 per thousand in 1936–8 to 18.5 per thousand in 1948–50. In France the birth rate, which was 13.7 per thousand in 1940, rose to 21 per thousand in 1946. The stresses of daily life thus both threatened traditional family structures, by exposing them to great shocks which led to divorce, and strengthened them by encouraging new couples to marry or at least to have children – the origin of the post-war baby boom. The family unit, subject to immense pressures by war and occupation, demonstrated how effective it was at surviving those pressures and recreating itself for new challenges.

Daily life also contributed to a reconfiguration of social structures. The problems posed by war and occupation divided societies in new ways between winners and losers. The traditional basis of social prestige was severely shaken, and social status was no longer defined by culture, education or qualifications. What mattered was the ability to secure food or make money, a change that on the whole favoured peasants, shopkeepers, industrialists and those collaborating with the occupiers. People without such advantages, such as workers, town dwellers and public service employees, faced a tougher situation. Issues of daily life thus divided societies in new ways. Even rationing had its own rules, giving different amounts to workers and non-workers, young and old. In some countries, such as Greece or Yugoslavia, the shock of occupation was so great that divisions were never overcome. The need to confront common threats and common dangers, however, also brought people together in a common consensus against the occupiers. Sometimes, as in France or the Netherlands, the myth of national unity was more powerful than the reality. The memory of hardships endured, the sense that sacrifices had not been equally shared and a frustration that the purge of profiteers was incomplete led to a great deal of social unrest, including violent strikes in 1947. In some countries, such as Denmark, youth was both praised because it was involved in the clandestine struggle and feared because it had developed an anti-authoritarian culture which might endanger the social order. Daily life thus left difficult legacies that had to be managed when the war was over.

The Legacy of Daily Life

The legacy of daily life was ambivalent. Traumatized by the war, occupation and the imposition of fascist rule, people simply aimed to return to a normal state of existence in respect of food, clothing, accommodation, family life, work – and traditional values. These aspirations could not be fully realized immediately after the war because of the destruction and hardship the war had inflicted, but they can explain the subsequent success of the affluent society. Deprived of their basic needs during the war, people were in fact ready to support a society based upon the consumption of material goods. Significantly, the opposition to consumer culture during the 1960s in France, Italy and Germany never had the support of the older generations, who had lived through the war and experienced hunger and deprivation, but was orchestrated by their children, who criticized their selfish materialism. At the same time, however, people dreamed of another world, of reaching new horizons and securing a kind of New Deal. This was clearly not the case in some countries, such as Denmark, where a welfare state had been built during the interwar period. But in other countries, life seemed so hard during both the war and the interwar period that people, whether in France or Greece, Poland or the Soviet Union, now set their sights on a new social contract. 'Back to normalcy', which seemed adequate after 1918, was now no longer so. This aim was sometimes shared and managed by the elites. In France, for example, politicians were well aware that after the war it was impossible to restore the old republican system and that a new economy and new society had to be founded. In Belgium employers and workers had already negotiated a social pact in 1944 that became the basis of the post-war welfare state. While the late Stalinist regime failed to implement far-reaching changes in its governance, it too underwent a certain process of re-identification. The post-war years saw concessions regarding the existence of a growing consumer culture, the continued rise and establishment of a professional Soviet middle class and the abandonment of iconoclastic, revolutionary policies.

All these elements suggest that everyday life is not a marginal subject. The ordeals suffered by ordinary people as a result of war and occupation were at the core of everyday life. Hunger, forced labour, family break-up, lost opportunities were, in fact, the 'people's war' in occupied Europe. There were clearly differences between western and eastern Europe – no one can seriously compare the Danish case to the fate of Poland – but despite this all over Europe people faced the same problems (hunger, forced labour), were subjected to the same temptations (collaboration) and devised manifold strategies of survival (sometimes involving resistance).

This everyday life, moreover, was not closed in on itself. It had a real effect on the course of the war. It is not that the war was won or lost because of daily life. What mattered above all were military operations. The Axis war machine, however, depended on mobilizing resources and labour from the countries they occupied, and in that sense total war impinged on daily life. That said, daily life did not simply amount to what was left after the Axis had had its fill. On many occasions the occupiers had to take into account the reactions of the population. They understood that they could not 'Polonize' France, nor should they unleash a new *Kulturkampf* against the Catholic Church in Europe. Moreover, for ordinary people survival meant not only feeding themselves and finding work but defending the families, workplaces, trade unions, churches and local communities which structured their daily lives and which were, in turn, structured by their daily lives.

Issues of daily life also shaped the post-war period. Popular aspirations not only to recover a decent standard of living but also to reach a New Jerusalem forced the political elites either to define another social and political contract, as in western Europe, or to resort to a policy of repression, to dampen people's hopes, as in eastern Europe. The success – or failure – of the new authorities depended on their ability to establish a new political and social consensus. This consensus was partly based on the possibility of giving a political meaning to the wartime experiences of ordinary people. Resistance and collaboration were, on the whole, minority phenomena, so that a patriotic or national sense had to be given to daily life. Some powers succeeded in such an enterprise. In France, for example, all French people, even POWs, were considered resisters by the Gaullists and Communists, as a way to reintegrate them in the national community. When the authorities were too weak or divided to provide this common meaning, the national community remained shaken and divided. This situation could lead to serious conflicts. In Belgium the 'royal question' – the debate about the political attitude of the King during the war – caused a polarization between left and right and between Dutch and French speakers which was only resolved in 1950. In Greece a terrible civil war broke out, while eastern European states were confronted by harsh Soviet repression. Daily life thus explains a great deal about the evolution of European states since 1945, which in turn deeply modified the daily lives of their populations.

Bibliography

1. Manuscript Sources

Belgium

Archives du Centre d'Études et Documentation Guerre et Sociétés Contemporaines
(CEGES) or *Studie- en Documentatiecentum Oorlog en Hedendaagse Maatschappij* (SOMA), Brussels
AB 316 and AA 1216, Enquête verplichte tewerkstelling (Diaries of forced workers in Germany).

Archives du Palais Royal
Kabinet Leopold III
168, JOC, 'Le service obligatoire pour les jeunes travailleurs', 15 Jan. 1943.
255, 'Ordonnance sur le travail', 31 Oct. 1942.

Archives de la Société Générale, Brussels

Czech Republic

Archives of the National Museum, Prague
Josef Kliment papers, Box 23.

Central State Archives, Prague
Reich Protector's office, Box 1802.

Denmark

Rigsarkivet, Copenhagen
Ankenævnet i henhold til lov nr. 260 af 1.6. 1945, nr. 241.
Justitsministeriet, 1. kontor, div. Journalsager 1940 and 1941, 160, 6/1945, 161,1–981/1942;161,1–986/1943; 161,1–1–1282/1944, 161,1–1972/1945–1951, 3514/1945, Q 2779/1941, Q 2483/1941.
Justitsministeriet, 3. kontor, 114 A/1945.

Socialministeriet, 3. kontor, 262/1944, 313/1941, 49/1943, 262/1944, 429/1944, 436/1944, 510/1944 and 511/1944.

Statsadvokaten for særlige Anliggender, AS 38–215, AS 34–23, AS 34–435, AS 0–7885, AS 0–7888, AS 0–7892, AS 0–8059, AS 0–2154.

Statsadvokaten for særlige Anliggender, månedlige indberetninger fra politikredsene 1940–44, Esbjerg, Feb. 1941, Ribe, April 1942.

Udenrigsministeriet, 21 D.8., 84.C.2.B./1940–45, 84.C.2.b., 13 Tys.1/8a/1940–45.

Landsarkivet for Sjælland, Copenhagen

Københavns Byret, afdeling 10 A, sag nr. 170/45 afsagt 4.9.1945.

Københavns opdagelsespoliti, protokol over anmeldte krigsforbrydelser og tabte sager 1945, j.nr. 2280–30.

Østre Landsrets arkiv, I. afd. sag nr. 304/45 afsagt 20.12.45.

France

Archives Nationales, Paris (AN)

F1a 3870, Préfecture régionale, Angers, 1944.

72 AJ 160, Archives of Comité d'Histoire de la Deuxième Guerre Mondiale.

Archives Départementales (AD)

Ille-et-Vilaine (I-et-V):

217W, Chambre civique de Loire-Atlantique, 1944–5.

Indre-et-Loire (I-et-L):

1305W 54, Comité de confiscation des profits illicites, 1945.

Loire-Atlantique (L-A):

132W 90/161, Commissaire de la République, Angers, 1944–5.

Maine-et-Loire (M-et-L):

74W 2, Comité interprofessionnel d'épuration dans les entreprises, 1945.

136W 3, Délégué départemental du ministère de l'information.

Moselle (M):

1W 6, Cultes et affaires scolaires, 1935–1944. Annexes: Amsblatt für das Schulwesen in Lothringen 1940–1941. Esprit public et mobilisation industrielle (rapports et notification du Parti nazi), 1936 –1944.

1W 211, Germanisation politique, expulsions, colonization, étrangers, rapports, inspections, 1941.

1W 754, Circulaires concernant l'organisation générale, les inscriptions, l'obligation scolaire, ouvrages prohibés, usage de l'allemand et les cours d'adultes, jumelages scolaires, 1940–1944.

1W 756, Affaires diverses: orphelinats et écoles maternelles, jeunesse hitlérienne, école Adolf Hitler, examens, congés, assurances, films. Inspections: rapports généraux et correspondances, 1941–1944.

311W 6–207: établissements scolaires.

J7110, Rapport sur la situation de la jeunesse en Moselle en 1945, sur les activités de la jeunesse hitlérienne et notes annexes émanant de la mission 'Jeunesse alsacienne et lorraine', bureau de Metz, 1945.

Archives Municipales (AM)

Nantes 38W 27, municipal administration, Nantes.

Metz 1Z6, Personnel enseignant, 1940–1944.

1Z32, Circulaires concernant l'enseignement, instructions de service, 1941–1944.

1Z48a,b, Organization de la jeunesse (Hitlerjugend), 1941–1944.

27Z19, Liste de 'Malgré-Nous'.

Germany

Bundesarchiv-Militärarchiv, Freiburg (BAMA)

M477/46781.

RH36/146, 511–12, Archives of Kommandantur, Nantes.

RW24/122, 126, Archives of Rüstungsinpektion, SW France.

RW 24/174, Archives of Rüstungskommando, Le Mans.

Great Britain

Public Record Office, Kew

Foreign Office (FO), FO 371, General Correspondence, Greece.

Italy

Ufficio Storico Stato Maggiore dell'Esercito Italiano (USSME)

N1–11, Diari Storici, M3b84.

Luxemburg

National Archives of the Grand Duchy of Luxemburg (ANGDL)

A2–2 123, Volks-und mittleres Schulwesen/Schulorganization der Stadt. Luxemburg: Leibeserziehung und Religionsunterricht, 1940–1941.

A 2–2 271, Volks- und mittleres Schulwesen/Lehrkräfte in Volksschulen, 1940–1942.

Netherlands

National Archive, The Hague, *Centraal Archief voor de Bijzondere Rechtspleging*
  (NA–CABR)
File H. Probsting.
File H.F.W. Küthe.

Netherlands Institute for War Documentation, Amsterdam (NIOD)
Archives 1–22, file 26 C
        61–76, file 3D
        77–85, files 27A, 36B, 129B
        207 file 731–265542.

United Nations

Archives of the United Nations Relief and Rehabilitation Administration (UNRRA)
  PAG 4/4.1:9, Memorandum of the Greek Government to the United Nations.

United States of America

National Archives and Records Administration, Washington, (NARA)
State Department Records
Decimal Files, 868.00, Greece – Political Affairs
        868.48, Greece – Calamities, Disasters

(Former) USSR

Tsentral'nyi Derzhavnyi arkhiv orhaniv vlady ta upravlinnia Ukrainy (Central State
  Archives of Civic Organizations of Ukraine) (TsDAHOU), Kiev
Fond 1 Central Committee of the Ukrainian Communist Party.
Fond 7 Central Committee of the Ukrainian Komsomol.

Rossiiskii gosudarstvennyi arkhiv sotsial'no-politicheskoi istorii (Russian State
  Archive for Socio-Political History) (RGASPI)
Fond M-1 Central Committee Komsomol.

Gosudarstvennyi Arkhiv Autonomnoi Respubliki Krym (GAARK)
Documents from the personal files of *Ostarbeiter* Returnees.

Newspapers

Biuletyn Informacyjny
Défense de la France
De Frie Danskere
De Telegraaf
Frit Danmark
Het Parool
Kolding Kirkeblad
Kontrast
Libération Morgenbladet
Nieuwe Rotterdamsche Courant
Vrij Nederland

2. Published Sources

Abrams, Bradley F., 'The Second World War and the East European Revolution', *East European Politics and Societies*, vol. 16, no. 3 (2002), pp. 623–44.

Aglan, Alya, *La Résistance sacrifiée. Le Mouvement 'Libération-Nord'* (Paris, Flammarion, 1999).

Amouroux, Henri, *La Grande Histoire des Français sous l'occupation* (8 vols, Paris, R. Laffont, 1976–88).

Anagnostopoulou, Margaret Polous, 'From Heroines to Hyenas: Women Partisans during the Greek Civil War', *Contemporary European History*, vol. 10, no. 3 (2001), pp. 481–501.

Anatolij, A., *Babi Yar. A Document in the Form of a Novel* (London, Cape, 1970).

Anderson, Truman, 'Incident at Baranivka: German Reprisals and the Soviet Partisan Movement in Ukraine, October–December 1941', *Journal of Modern History*, vol. 71, no. 3 (Sept. 1999), pp. 585–623.

Anderson, Truman, 'Germans, Ukrainians and Jews: Ethnic Politics in Heeresgebiet Sud, June–December 1941', *War in History*, vol. 7, no. 3 (2000), pp. 325–51.

Armia Krajowa w documentach 1939–1945 (Wroclaw, Ossolineum, 1990).

Atkin, Nicholas, *Church and Schools in Vichy France, 1940–1944* (New York and London, Garland, 1991).

Azéma, Jean-Pierre and Bédarida, François (eds), *La France des années noires* (Paris, Seuil, 1993).

Balace, F. (ed.), *Jours de Guerre, Jours de Lutte* (Brussels, Crédit Communal, 1992).

Barber, John and Harrison, Mark, *The Soviet Home Front, 1941–1945* (Harlow, Longman, 1991).

Bartoszewski, Władysław, *Warsaw Death Ring 1939–1944* (Warsaw, Interpress, 1968).

Bartoszewski, Władysław, *1859 dni Warszawy* (Kraków, Znak, 1984).

Baudhuin, Fernand, *L'Économie belge sous l'occupation 1940–1944* (Brussels, F. Bruylant, 1945).

Becker, Frank Grossbötting, T., Ozwar, A. and Schlögl, R. (eds), *Politische Gewalt in der Moderne* (Münster, Aschendorf, 2003).

Beevor, Antony, *Stalingrad* (London, 1998).

Beevor, Anthony, *Berlin. The Downfall* (London, Viking, 2003)

België 1940, *een maatschappij in crisis en oorlog, 1940. Belgique, une société en crise, un pays en guerre, 1940* (Brussels, Centre de recherches et d'études historiques de la seconde guerre mondiale, 1993).

Belot, Robert, *Aux Frontières de la liberté. Vichy, Madrid, Alger, Londres. S'évader de France sous l'occupation* (Paris, Fayard, 1998).

Beltran, A., Frank, R. and Rousso, H., *La Vie des Entreprises sous l'occupation. Une enquête à l'échelle locale* (Paris, Belin, 1994).

Benze, Rudolf, *Erziehung im grossdeutschen Reich. Eine Überschau über ihre Ziele, Wege und Einrichtungen* (Frankfurt-am-Main, Diesterweg, 1943).

Berends, H., *Woeste Hoeve 8 maart 1945* (Kampen, Kok Voorhoeve, 1995).

Bergerson, Andrew, *Ordinary Germans in Extraordinary Times. The Nazi Revolution in Hildesheim* (Bloomington, Indiana University Press, 2005).

Berkhoff, Karel C., *Harvest of Despair. Life and Death in Ukraine under Nazi Rule* (Cambridge, MA, Belknap Press of Harvard University Press, 2004).

Blom, J.C.H., 'Nederland onder Duitse bezetting 10 mei 1940–5 mei 1945', in *Nieuwe Algemene Geschiedenis der Nederlanden* 15 (Haarlem, Fibula Van Dishoeck, 1982), pp. 55–94.

Boom, Bart van der, *We leven nog. De stemming in bezet Nederland* (Amsterdam, Boom, 2003).

Bosák, František, *Česká škola v době nacistického útlaku* (České Budějovice, 1969).

Bosworth, Richard, *The Italian Dictatorship. Problems and Perspectives of the Interpretation of Mussolini and Fascism* (London, Arnold, 1998).

Bosworth, Richard, *Mussolini's Italy. Life under the Dictatorship* (London, Allen Lane, Penguin, 2005).

Bouman, Pieter J., *De April–mei-stakingen van 1943* (The Hague, Martinus Nijhoff, 1950).

Bouvier, Herma and Geraud, Claude, *NAPOLA. Les écoles d'élites du troisième Reich* (Paris, L'Harmattan, 2000).

Brandt, Karl, *Management of Agriculture and Food in the German-Occupied and Other Areas of Fortress Europe. A Study in Military Government* (Stanford, Stanford University Press, 1953).

Braudel, Fernand, *Afterthoughts on Material Civilisation and Capitalism* (Baltimore and London, Johns Hopkins University Press, 1977).

Braudel, Fernand, *Civilization and Capitalism, 15th–18th Century* (London, Collins, 1981–3).

Bräutigam, Harald, *Überblick über die besetzen Ostgebiete wärend des 2. Weltkriegs* (Tübingen, 1954).

Briais, Bernard, *Un Dossier noir de la Résistance. Le Maquis Le Coz* (Saint-Cyr-sur-Loire, Alan Sutton, 2002).

Broszat, Martin, Fröhlich, Elke and Grossmann, Anton (eds), *Bayern in der N–S Zeit* (Munich-Vienna, Oldenbourg, 1977–83).

Burleigh, Michael, *The Third Reich. A New History* (London, Macmillan, 2000).

Burnett, John and Oddy, Derek J. (eds), *The Origins and Development of Food Policies in Europe* (London, Leicester University Press, 1994).

Burrin, Philippe, *Living with Defeat. France under the German Occupation, 1940–1944* (London, Arnold, 1996).

Calvocoressi, Peter and Wint, Guy, *Total War, Causes and Consequences of the Second World War* (London, Allen Lane, 1972).

Cappelletto, Francesca, 'Memories of Nazi-Fascist Massacres in Two Central Italian Villages', *Sociologia Ruralis*, vol. 38, no. 1 (1998), pp. 69–85.

Cavanna, François, *Les Ruskoffs* (Paris, Club Français du Livre, 1979).

Certeau, Michel de, *The Practice of Everyday Life* (Berkeley and Los Angeles, University of California Press, 1984).

Chaumont, Jean-Michel, *La Concurrence des victimes. Génocide, identité, reconnaissance* (Paris, La Découverte, 2002).

Chiari, Bernhard, *Alltag hinter dem Front. Besatzung, Kollaboration und Widerstand in Weissrussland, 1941–1944* (Düsseldorf, Droste Verlag, 1998).

Chimbos, Peter D., 'Greek Resistance 1941–45: Organizations, achievements and contributions to Allied War Efforts against the Axis Powers', *International Journal of Comparative Sociology*, vol. 40, no. 2 (1999), pp. 251–69.

Christensen, Claus Bundgård, *Den Sørte Børs – fra besættelsen til efterkrigstid* (Forum, 2003), Copenhagen.

Christensen, Claus Bundgård, 'Food Consumption and the Black Market in Denmark, 1939–53', paper presented at the conference 'Food production and food consumption in Europe, 1914–1950', Centre for European Conflict and Identity History, Esbjerg, Denmark, 2–4 June 2004.

Christensen, Claus Bundgård Lund, Jaochim, Olesen, Niels Wium and Sørensen, Jakob, *Danmark Besat. Krig og Hverdag, 1940–45* (Copenhagen, Høst & Søn, 2005).

Chtěli nás vyhubit (They Wanted to Exterminate Us) (Prague, Naše vojsko, 1961).

Ciano, *Diary, 1939–1943* (London, Heinemann, 1947).

Cointet, Michèle, *L'Eglise sous Vichy, 1940–1945* (Paris, Perrin, 1998).

Conquest, Robert, *The Harvest of Sorrow. Soviet Collectivization and the Terror-Famine* (London, Hutchinson, 1986).

Corni, Gustavo, 'Terzo Reich e sfruttamento dell' Europa occupata. La politica alimentare tedesca nella seconda guerra mondiale', *Italia Contemporanea*, 209–10 (1997–8), pp. 5–37.

Crémieux-Brihac, Jean-Louis, 'La France libre et la radio', *Mélanges de l'Ecole française de Rome*, 108/1 (1996).

Czesław, Madajczyk, *Polityka III Rzeszy w okupowanej Polsce* (2 vols, Warsaw, Panstwowe Wydawnictwo Naukowe, 1970).

Dahl, Hans Fredrik, Hjeltnes, Guri, Nøkleby, Berit, Ringdal, Nils Johan and Sørensen, Øystein (eds), *Norsk Krigsleksikon 1940–45*. (Oslo, J.W. Cappelens Forlag, 1995).

Dahl, Hans Fredrik, *Quisling: A Study in Tyranny* (Cambridge, Cambridge University Press, 1999).

Dallin, Alexander, *German Rule in Russia, 1941–1945*. A Study in Occupation Politics (London, Macmillan, 1957).

Dard, Olivier, Daumas, Jean-Claude and Marcot, François (eds), *L'Occupation, l'Etat français et les entreprises*. (Paris, ADHE, 2000).

Davies, Norman, *Rising '44. The Battle for Warsaw* (London, Macmillan, 2003).

De Jong, L., *Het Koninkrijk der Nederlanden in de Tweede Wereldoorlog* (14 vols, The Hague, Martinus Nijhoff 1969–91).

De Vos, L., *De Tweede Wereldoorlog* (Leuven, Davidsfonds, 2004).

Deák, I., Gross, J.T., and Judt, T. (eds), *The Politics of Retribution in Europe. World War II and Its Aftermath* (Princeton, Princeton University Press 2000).

Dejonghe, Étienne, 'Le Nord et le Pas-de-Calais pendant la première année de l'Occupation, juin 1940–juin 1941' *Revue du Nord*, 51 (Oct. 1969), pp. 677–708.

Dejonghe, Étienne and Le Maner, Yves, *Le Nord dans la main allemande* (Lille, La Voix du Nord, 1999).

Desquesnes, Rémy, *'Atlantikwall et Sudwall'. La Défense allemande sur le littoral français, 1941–1942* (ANRT, Université de Lille III, 1987).

Diocèse de Tournai sous l'occupation allemande (Tournai, 1946).

De verplichte tewerkstelling in Duitsland/Le travail obligatoire en Allemagne, 1942–1945 (Brussels, Centre de recherches et d'études historiques de la seconde guerre mondiale, 1993).

Dolejší, Vojtěch, *Noviny a novináři* (Prague, 1963).

Doležal, Jiří, *Česká kultura za protektorátu Školstvi, písemnictví, kinematografie* (Prague, Národni filmový archiv, 1996).

Drolshagen, Ebba, *Det skal de ikke slippe godt fra* (Copenhagen, Det Schønbergske Forlag, 1999).

Droulia, L. and Fleischer, H. (eds), *Von Lidice bis Kalavryta. Widerstand und Besatzungsterror* (Berlin, Metropol, 1999).

Duméril, Edmond, *Journal d'un honnête homme pendant l'occupation, juin 1940–août 1944* (Thonon-les-Bains, L'Albaron, 1990).

Durand, Yves, *La Vie quotidienne des prisonniers de guerre dans les Stalags, les Oflags et les Kommandos, 1939–1945* (Paris, Hachette, 1987).

Dyson, Tom, 'British Policies toward Axis Reprisals in Occupied Greece: Whitehall vs. SOE', *Contemporary British History*, vol. 16, no. 1 (2002), pp. 11–28.

Editorial, *History Workshop. A Journal of Socialist Historians*, I (1976).

Eichholtz, Dietrich, *Geschichte der deutschen Kriegswirtschaft, 1939–1945* (Berlin, Akademie-Verlag, 1984).

Eilers, Rolf, *Die nationalsozialistische Schulpolitik. Eine Studie zur Funktion der Erziehung im totalitären Staat* (Cologne and Opladen, 1963).

Ellingsen, Dag, Björnsdottir, Inga Dora and Warring, Anette, *Kvinner krig og kjærlighet* (Oslo, Cappelen, 1995).

Erickson, John, *The Road to Berlin. Stalin's War with Germany* (2 vols, London, Phoenix Giants, 1996).

Ericsson, Kjersti and Simonsen, Eva (eds), *Children of World War II. The Hidden Enemy Legacy* (Oxford, Berg, 2005).

Eriksen, Knut Einar and Halvorsen, Terje, *Norge i krig. Frigjøring* (Oslo, Aschehoug, 1987).

Evrard, Jacques, *La Déportation des travailleurs français dans le IIIe Reich* (Paris, Fayard, 1972).

Fitzpatrick, Sheila, *Everyday Stalinism. Ordinary Life in Extraordinary Times: Soviet Russia in the 1930s* (New York and Oxford, Oxford University Press, 1999).

Flessau, Kurt-Ingo, Nyssen, Elke and Pätzold, Günter (eds), *Erziehung im Nationalsozialismus* (Cologne, Böhlen, 1987).

Foot, M.R.D., *SOE. The Special Operations Executive 1940–1946* (London, Mandarin, 1993).

Foot, M.R.D., *SOE in France. An Account of the Work of the British Special Operations Executive in France, 1940–1944* (London, Frank Cass, 2004).

Frijtag Drabbe Künzel, Geraldien von, *Het recht van de sterkste. Duitse strafrechtpleging in bezet Nederland* (Amsterdam, Bert Bakker, 1999).

Fürst, Juliane, 'Heroes, Lovers, Victims – Partisan Girls during the Great Fatherland War', *Minerva*, Vol. XVIII, Numbers 3–4, Fall/winter, (2000), pp. 38–75.

Garliński, Józef, 'The Polish Underground State', Journal of Contemporary History vol. 10, no. 2 (1975), pp. 219–59.

Garnier, Bernard and Quellien, Jean (eds), *La Main d'œuvre française exploitée par le IIIe Reich* (Caen, Centre de Recherche d'Histoire Quantitative, 2003).

Gerard, Emmanuel (ed.), *De Christelijke Arbeidersbeweging in België 1891–1991*, (2 vols, Leuven, Universitaire Pers, 1991).

Gérard-Libois, Jules and Gotovitch, José, *L'An 40. La Belgique occupée* (Brussels, CRISP, 1971).

Gerlach, Christian, *Krieg, Ernährung, Volkermord* (Hamburg, Hamburg Edition, 1998).

Gildea, Robert, *Marianne in Chains. In Search of the German Occupation, 1940–1945* (London, Macmillan, 2002).

Gildea, Robert, 'Resistance, Reprisals and Community in Occupied France', *Royal Historical Society*, 13 (2003), pp. 163–85.

Giltner, Phil, 'The Success of Collaboration: Denmark's Self-Assessment of Its Economic Position after Five Years of Nazi Occupation', *Journal of Contemporary History*, vol. 36, no. 3 (2001), pp. 485–506.

Glahn, Gerhard von, *The Occupation of Enemy Territory* (Minneapolis, University of Minnesota Press, 1957).

Gotovitch, José, *Du rouge au tricolore. Résistance et parti communiste. Les communistes belges de 1939 à 1944. Un aspect de l'histoire de la Résistance en Belgique* (Brussels, Labour, 1992).

Gotovitch, José (ed.), *La Belgique sous l'occupation allemande (1940–1944)* (Brussels, Complexe, 2002).

Greek Government Office of Information, *Ruins of Modern Greece 1941–1944. Cities and Villages of Greece Destroyed by Germans, Italians and Bulgars, 1941–1944* (Athens, n.d.).

Grootaers, Dominique, *Histoire de l'enseignement en Belgique* (CRISP, 1998).

Gross, Jan Tomasz, *Polish Society under German Occupation. The General-gouvernement, 1939–1944* (Princeton, Princeton University Press, 1979).

Gueslin, André, *Les Facs sous Vichy. Étudiants, universitaires et universités de France pendant la seconde guerre mondiale* (Clermont-Ferrand, Institut d'Études du Massif Central, Université Blaise-Pascal, 1994).

Gumz, Jonathan E., 'Wehrmacht Perceptions of Mass Violence in Croatia, 1941–1942', *Historical Journal*, vol. 44, no. 4 (2001), pp. 1015–38.

Hanson, Joanna K.M., *The Civilian Population and the Warsaw Uprising of 1944* (Cambridge, Cambridge University Press, 2004).

Hartmann, Grethe, *The Girls They Left Behind* (Copenhagen, Ejnar Munksgaard, 1946).

Havrehed, Henrik, *De tyske flygtninge i Danmark 1945–1949* (Odense: Odense Universitetsforlag, 1987).

Heiser, E., *La Tragédie lorraine* (3 vols, Sarreguemines, Pierron, 1978–83).

Helgesen, Kari '…f.t. siktet som tyskertøs', *Historisk Tidsskrift*, no. 3, 1990, pp. 285–310.

Heller, Michel and Nekrich, Aleksander, *Utopia in Power. A History of the USSR from 1917 to the Present* (London, Hutchinson, 1986).

Hemmerijckx, R., *Van Verzet tot Koude Oorlog 1940–1949. Machtsstrijd om het ABVV* (Brussels/Ghent, VUBPRESS/AMSAB, 2003).

Herbert, Ulrich, *Fremdarbeiter. Politik und Praxis des 'Ausländer–Einsatzes' in der Kriegswirtschaft des Dritten Reiches* (Berlin, JHW Dietz, 1985).

Herbert, Ulrich, *A History of Foreign Labour in Germany, 1880–1980* (Ann Arbor, University of Michigan Press, 1990).

Herbert, Ulrich (ed.), *Europa und der 'Reichseinsatz'. Ausländische Zivilarbeiter, Kriegsgefangene und KZ-Häftlinge in Deutschland 1938–1945* (Essen, Klartext, 1991).

Herbert, Ulrich, *Hitler's Foreign Workers Enforced Foreign Labour in Germany under the Third Reich* (Cambridge, Cambridge University Press, 1997).

Het Proces Christiansen (The Hague, Martinus Nijhoff, 1950).

Hiegel, H., 'L'enseignement en Moselle sous l'occupation allemande de 1940 à 1944', *Cahiers lorrains* (1983), pp. 227–48.

Higonnet, M.R., Jenson, J., Michel, S. and Weitz, M.C. (eds), *Behind the Lines. Gender and the Two World Wars* (New Haven and London: Yale University Press, 1987).

Hiegel, H., 'Les mesures anti-religieuses du national-socialisme en Moselle, 1940–1945', *Mémoires de l'Académie Nationale de Metz* (1982), pp, 70–108.

Hilberg, Raul, *The Politics of Memory. The Journey of a Holocaust* (Chicago, Dee, 1996).

Hill, Alexander, 'Popular Reactions to the German Occupation of North-Western Russia 1941–1944', Paper presented at the Annual Conference of the British Association of Slavonic and Eastern European Studies, Cambridge, April 1999.

Hill, Alexander, *The War Behind the Eastern Front. The Soviet Partisan Movement in North-West Russia, 1941–1944* (New York and London, Frank Cass, 2005).

Hjeltnes, Guri, *Norge i krig. Hverdagslivet i krig* (Oslo, Aschehoug, 1987).

Hjorth, Karen, Ilsøe, G. and Kragelund, M. (eds), *Kan, kan ikke. Vil, vil ikke. Kvindeliv i perspektiv* (Copenhagen, ARKI Varia, 1996).

Hochhuth, Rolf, *A German Love Story*, trans. John Brownjohn (London, Weidenfeld and Nicolson, 1980).

Homze, Edward L., *Foreign Labour in Nazi Germany* (Princeton, Princeton University Press, 1967).

Hondros, John L., *Occupation and Resistance. The Greek Agony 1941–44* (New York, Pella Pub. Corp., 1983).

Hong, N., *Sparks of Resistance. The Illegal Press in German-Occupied Denmark, April 1940–August 1943* (Odense, Odense University Press, 1996).

Horne, John and Kramer, Alan, *German Atrocities, 1914. A History of Denial* (New Haven and London, Yale University Press, 2001).

Hrabar, Roman, Tokarz, Sofia and Wilczur, Jacek E., *The Fate of Polish Children during the Last War* (Warsaw: Panstwowe Wydawnictwo Naukowe, 1970).

Iatrides, John O. (ed.), *Greece in the 1940s. A Nation in Crisis* (Hanover, NH and London, University Press of New England, 1981).

International Military Tribunal (IMT). *Trial of the Major War Criminals* (Nuremberg 1947–9).

Jäckel, Eberhard, *Frankreich in Hitlers Europa. Die deutsche Frankreichpolitik im Zweiten Weltkrieg* (Stuttgart, 1966).

Jacquemyns, Guillaume, *La Société belge sous l'occupation allemande, 1940–1944* (3 vols, Brussels, Nicolson & Watson, 1950).

Jansens, S., Frijtag Drabbe Künzel, G. von and Blum, J.C.H. (eds), *Een ruwe hand in het water. De gijzelingskampen Sint-Michielsgestel en Haaren* (Amsterdam, Het Spinhuis, 1993).

Jelineck, Y., *The Parish Republic. Hlinka's Slovak People's Party, 1939–1945* (Boulder and New York, Columbia University Press, 1976).

Kalken, Frans van, *Histoire des Universités belges* (Brussels, Brussels Office de Publicité, 1954).

Kaspi, André, *Les Juifs pendant l'occupation* (Paris, Le Seuil, 1991).

Keizer, Madelon de, Putten. *De razzia en de herinnering* (Amsterdam, Bert Bakker, 1998).

Keizer, Madelon de, H. Kleman, D. Luyten and P. Deloge (eds), *Thuisfront. Oorlog en economie in de twintigste eeuw* (Zutphen, Walbug Pers, 2003).

Kirchhoff, Hans, *Samarbejde og modstand under besættelsen* (Odense, Odense Universitetforlag, 2001).

Kirchhoff, Hans, Lauridsen, J.T. and Trommer, A. (eds), *Gads leksikon om dansk besættelsestid* (Copenhagen, Gads Forlag, 2002).

Kitson, Simon, *Vichy et la chasse aux espions nazis 1940–1942. Complexités de la politique de collaboration* (Paris, Autrement, 2004).

Klarsfeld, Serge, *Le Livre des otages. La politique des otages menée par les autorités allemandes d'occupation en France de 1941 à 1943* (Paris, Les Éditeurs réunis, 1979).

Klemann, H.A.M., *Nederland 1938–1948. Economie en samenleving in jaren van oorlog en bezetting* (Amsterdam, Boom, 2002).

Klessmann, Christophe, *Polnische Bergarbeiter im Ruhrgebiet, 1870–1945* (Göttingen, Vandenhoeck und Ruprecht, 1978).

Klinkhammer, Lutz, *L'occupazione tedesca in Italia, 1943–1945* (Turin, Bollati Boringhieri, 1996).

Knox, MacGregor, *Mussolini Unleashed, 1939–1941. Politics and Strategy in Fascist Italy's Last War* (Cambridge, Cambridge University Press, 1982).

Knudsen, Erik and Wivel, Ole (eds), *Kulturdebat 1944–48* (Copenhagen, Gyldendal, 1958).

Kobuszewskiego, B., Matusaka, P. and Rawskiego, T. (eds), *Polski ruch oporu 1939–1945* (Warsaw, Wydawnictwo Ministerstwa Obrony Narodowej, 1988).

Konieczny, Alfred and Szurgacz, Herbert, *Praca Przymusowa Polaków pod Panowaniem Hitlerowskin, 1939–1945. Documenta Occupationis*, X (Poznań, 1976).

Kraatz, Susanne (ed.), *Verschleppt und Vergessen. Schicksaale jugendlicher Ostarbeiterinnen von der Krim im Zweiten Weltkrieg und danach* (Heidelberg, S. Kraatz, 1995).

Krantz, Robert, *Luxemburgs Kinder unter dem Nazi–Regime 1940–1944. Ein Dokumentarbericht* (Luxemburg, Editions Saint-Paul, 1997).

Krasuski, Józef, *Tajne szkolnictwo polskie w okresie okupacji hitlerowskiej 1939–1945* (Warsaw, Państwowe Wydawnictwo Naukowe, 1977).

Kroener, B.R., Müller, R.-D. and Umbreit, H., *Das Deutsche Reich und der Zweite Weltkrieg*, Vol. 5/1 (Stuttgart, DVA, 1988).

Kroener, Bernhard R., Müller, Rolf-Dieter and Umbreit, Hans, *Organisation und Mobilisierung des Deutschen Machtbereichs* (Stuttgart, Deutsche Verlags-Anstalt, 1999).

Kroon, Ben, *In het land van de vijand. Mijn jaren van gedwongen arbeid 1943–1945*, (Amsterdam, Balans, 2004).

Laborie, Pierre, *Les Français des années troubles. De la guerre d'Espagne à la Libération* (Paris, Points-Seuil, 2003).

Lagrou, Pieter, 'Victims of Genocide and National Memory: Belgium, France and the Netherlands 1945–65', *Past & Present*, no. 154 (1997), pp. 181–222.

Lagrou, P., *The Legacy of Nazi Occupation. Patriotic Memory and National Recovery in Western Europe, 1945–1965* (Cambridge, Cambridge University Press, 2000).

Lagrou, P., 'The Politics of Memory. Resistance as a Collective Myth in Post-War France, Belgium and the Netherlands, 1945–1965', *European Review*, vol. 11, no. 4 (2003), pp. 527–49.

Langen, Ulrik (ed.), *Ritualernes magt* (Copenhagen, Roskilde Universitetsforlag, 2002).

Le Crom, Jean-Pierre, *Syndicats Nous Voilà! Vichy et le corporatisme* (Paris, Les Éditions de l'Atelier/Éditions ouvrières, 1995).

Le Marec, Gérard and Bernard, *Les Années Noires. La Moselle annexée par Hitler, documents et témoignages* (Metz, Editions Serpenoise, 1990).

League of Nations, *Food, Famine and Relief, 1940–1946* (Geneva, 1946).

Lefebvre, Henri, *Everyday Life in the Modern World* (New Brunswick and London, Transaction Books, 1984/1999).

Legnani, M., 'Il giner del general Roatta, le direttive della II Armata sulla repressione antipartigiana in Slovenia e Croazia', *Italia Contemporanea*, 209–10 (Dec. 1997–March 1998), pp. 156–74.

Lhote-Crée, Marie-Josèphe, *Claire à l'école allemande* (Sarreguemines, Pieron, 2003).

Liberman, Peter, *Does Conquest Pay? The Exploitation of Occupied Industrial Societies.* (Princeton, Princeton University Press, 1996).

Lierop, Pieter Van, *Kommunisten in bevrijd Zuid-Nederland. 'Voor één socialistische partij' (september 1944 – juli 1945)* (Amsterdam, Stichting Instituut voor Politiek en Sociaal Onderzoek, 1984).

Lilienthal, Georg, 'War Children in Nazi Race Policy', paper at the conference German–Norwegian War Children – An International Perspective, Oslo, 15–17 November 2002.

Lilienthal, Georg, *Der 'Lebensborn E.V.' – Ein Instrument nationalsozialistischer Rassenpolitik* (Frankfurt am Main, Akademie der Wissenschaften und der Literatur, 2003).

Lindenberger, Thomas and Wildt, Michael, 'Radical Plurality: History Workshops as a Practical Critique of Knowledge', *History Workshop*, 33 (1992), pp. 73–99.

'Lish' odinochki okazalis' izmennikami', *Istochnik*, 1996/2, pp. 52–66.

Lombard, Maurice, 'Les maquis et la libération de la Bourgogne', *Revue d'Histoire de la Seconde Guerre Mondiale*, no. 55 (July 1964), pp. 29–54.

Lommers, Suzanne, 'The Influence of War and Occupation on the Distribution of Industry Wages in Denmark and the Netherlands, 1938–1946' (MA thesis, Utrecht, 2003).

Lüdtke, Alf (ed.), *The History of Everyday Life. Reconstructing Social Experiences and Ways of Life* (Princeton, NJ, Princeton University Press, 1995).

Ludwik, Landau, *Kronika lat wojny I okupacji* (2 vols, Warsaw, Panstwowe Wydawnictwo Naukowe, 1970).

Lukas, Richard C., *Forgotten Holocaust. The Poles under German Occupation 1939–1944* (New York, Hippocrene Books, 1990).

Lund, Joachim, 'Den danske østindsats 1941–43. Østrumudvalget i den politiske og økonomiske kollaboration', *Historisk Tidsskrift*, 95/1 (1995), pp. 37–74.

Lund, Joachim, 'Denmark and the "European New Order", 1940–1942', *Contemporary European History*, vol. 13, no. 3 (August 2004), pp. 305–21.

Luyten, D., *Burgers boven elke verdenking? Vervolging van economische collabouratie in België na de Tweede Wereldoorlog* (Brussels, VUBPRESS, 1996).

Luyten, D., 'Prosecution, Society and Politics: the Penalization of Economic Collaboration in Belgium after the Second World War', *Crime, Histoire & Sociétés/ Crime, History & Societies*, II, 1998, pp. 111–33.

Luyten, Dirk, 'Over strafdossiers en sociale verhoudingen. De Schelde te Vlissingen in de Tweede Wereldoorlog', *Zeeland. Tijdschrift van het Koninklijk Zeeuwsch Genootschap der Wetenschappen*, XIII, 1, (2004), pp. 1–11.

Luyten, D and Hemmerijckx, R., 'Belgian Labour in World War II: Strategies of Survival, Organisations and Labour Relations', *European Review of History-Revue européenne d'histoire*, VII, (2000), pp. 207–27.

Luyten, D. and Vanthemsche, G. (eds), *Het Sociaal Pact van 1944. Oorsprong, betekenis, gevolgen* (Brussels, VUB-Press, 1995).

Mackenzie, William, *The Secret History of SOE. Special Operations Executive 1940–1945* (London, St Ermin's, 2002).

Madajczyk, Czesław, *Faszyzm i okupacje 1938–1945. Wykonywanie okupacji przez panstwa Osi w Europie* (2 vols, Poznań, Wydawnictwo Poznańskie, 1983–4).

Madajczyk, Czesław, *Okkupationspolitik Nazideutschlands in Polen 1939–1945* (Berlin, Akademie-Verlag, 1987).

Madajczyk, Czesław, *Dramat katynski* (Warsaw, Książka i Wiedza, 1989).

Maerten, F., *Du murmure au grondement. La Résistance politique et idéologique dans la province de Hainaut pendant la Seconde Guerre mondiale (mai 1940– septembre 1944)* (3 vols, Mons, Hannonia, 1999).

Marcot, François, 'La direction de Peugeot sous l'Occupation', *Le Mouvement social*, 189 (Oct.–Dec. 1999), pp. 27–46.

Margaritis, Giorgos, *Apo tin itta stin exegersi. Ellada: anoixi 1941–fthinoporo 1942* (Athens, O Politis, 1993).

Martin, Dirk, *De Rijksuniversiteit Gent tijdens de bezetting, 1940–1944. Levend met de vijand* (Ghent, 1985).

Mastny, Vojtech, *The Czechs under Nazi Rule. The Failure of National Resistance, 1939–1942* (New York and London, Columbia University Press, 1971).

Maun, Paul, *I apostoli mou stin katehomeni Ellada* (Athens, Metron 2000).

Mazower, Mark, *Inside Hitler's Greece. The Experience of Occupation, 1941–1944* (New Haven and London, Yale University Press, 1993).

Meihuizen, Joggli, *Noodzakelijk kwaad. De bestraffing van economische collaboratie in Nederland na de Tweede Wereldoorlog* (Amsterdam, Boom, 2003).

Messerschmidt, M., 'Völkerrecht and "Kriegsnotwendigkeit" in der deutschen militarischen Tradition', in W. Wette (ed.), *Was damals Recht war. NS-Militär- und Strafjustiz im Vernichtungskrieg* (Essen, Klartext, 1996).

Middelbeek, J. H., *Ik draag U op... Systeem en werk der Nederlandsche Binnenlandsche Strijdkrachten, getoetst aan de lotgevallen van lokale eenheden (Apeldoorn en omgeving)* (Apeldoorn, s.n., 1946).

Milward, Alan S., *The German Economy at War* (London, Athlone Press, 1965).

Milward, Alan S., *War, Economy and Society, 1939–1945* (Berkeley, University of California Press, 1979).

Moore, Bob (ed.), *Resistance in Western Europe* (Oxford, Berg, 2000).

Mulisch, Harry, *De Aanslag* (Amsterdam, Bezige Bij, 1982).

Mulligan, Timothy, *The Politics of Illusion and Empire. German Occupation Policy in the Soviet Union 1942–1943* (New York and London, Praeger, 1988).

Nabulsi, Karma, *Traditions of War. Occupation, Resistance and the Law* (Oxford, Oxford University Press, 1999).

Nefors, P., *Industriële collabouratie in België. De Galopindoctrine, de emissiebank en de Belgische industrie in de Tweede Wereldoorlog* (Leuven, Van Halewyck, 2000).

Ney-Krwawicz, Marek, *The Polish Resistance Home Army 1939–1945* (London, Studium Polski Podziemnej, 2001).

Niethammer, Lutz, *Lebensgeschichte und Sozialkultur im Ruhrgebiet, 1930–1960* (3 vols, Berlin–Bonn, Dietz, 1983–5).

1940–1945. Het dagelijkse leven in België (Brussels, CGER, 1984).

1940–1945. La vie quotidienne en Belgique (Brussels, CGER, 1984).

Nissen, Mogens R., 'Danish Food Production in the German War Economy', paper presented at the conference 'Food production and food consumption in Europe, c. 1914–1950', Centre for European Conflict and Identity History, Esbjerg, Denmark, 2–4 June 2004.

Noiriel, Gérard, *Longwy, immigrés et prolétaires, 1880–1980* (Paris, PUF, 1984).

Okupacja i ruch oporu w dzienniku Hansa Franka 1939–1945 (2 vols, Warsaw, Książka i Wiedza, 1972).

Øland, Arne, *Horeunger og helligdage* (Copenhagen, Det Schønbergske Forlag, 2001).

Olsen, Kaare, *Krigens barn. De norske krigsbarna og deres mødre* (Oslo, Forum Aschehoug, 1998).

Orlík, Josef, Opavsko a severní Morava za okupace. Z tajných zpráv okupačních úřadů z let 1940–1943 (Ostrava 1961).

Paape, A.H. (ed.), *Studies over Nederland in oorlogstijd*, 1 (The Hague, Martinus Nijhoff, 1992).

Parker, R.A.C., *Struggle for Survival. The History of the Second World War* (Oxford and New York, Oxford University Press, 1990).

Paul, G. and Mallmann, K.-M. (eds), *Die Gestapo. Mythos und Realität* (Darmstadt, Wissenschaftliche Buchgesellschaft, 1995).

Pavone, Claudio, *Una guerra civile. Saggio storico sulla moralità nella Resistenza* (Turin, Bollati Boringheri, 1991).

Pedersen, Bjorn Schreiber and Holm, Adam, 'Restraining Excesses: Resistance and Counter-Resistance in Nazi-Occupied Denmark 1940–1945', *Terrorism and Political Violence*, 10/1 (1998) pp. 60–89,

Perzekuce českého studentstva. Dokumenty (Persecution of Czech Students. Documents) (Prague, 1945).

Peukert, Detlev, *Inside Nazi Germany. Conformity, Opposition and Racism in Everyday Life* (London, Batsford, 1989).

Pfahlmann, Hans, *Fremdarbeier und Kriegsgefangene in der deutschen Kriegs-wirtschaft, 1939–1945* (Darmstadt, Wehr und Wissen Verlagsgesellschaft, 1968).

Pirotte, Jean (ed.), *Pour une histoire du monde catholique au XXème siècle, guide due chercheur* (Louvain-La-Neuve, 2003).

Pirotte, J., Zelis G., Groessens B. and Scaillet T., *Le monde catholique au 20e siècle. Wallonie-Bruxelles* (Louvain-La-Neuve, 2003).

Polski czyn zbrojny w II wojnie. Polski ruch oporu, 1939–1945 (Warsaw, Waydawnictwo Ministerstwa Obrony Narodowej, 1988).

Portelli, Alessandro, *The Battle of Valle Giulia. Oral History and the Art of Dialogue* (Madison, University of Wisconsin Press, 1997).

Raspin, Angela, *The Italian War Economy, 1940–1943. With Particular Reference to Italian Relations with Germany* (New York and London, Garland, 1986).

Retsopgøret med landssvigerne. Beretning til Justitsministeriet afgivet af det Statistiske Departement (Copenhagen, Statens Trykningskontor, 1958).

Rhodes, Anthony, *Louis Renault, a Biography* (London, Cassell, 1969).

Robertson, K.G. (ed.), *War, Resistance and Intelligence. Essays in Honour of M.R.D. Foot* (Barnsley, Leo Cooper, 1999).

de Rochebrune, Renaud and Hazera, Jean-Claude, *Les Patrons sous l'Occupation* (Paris, Odile Jacob, 1997).

Rochat, G., *Guerre italiane in Libia e in Etiopia* (Paese, Pagus, 1991).

Rochet, Bénédicte, *Les Universités belges pendant la Seconde Guerre mondiale. Le cas particulier de l'Université catholique de Louvain et de l'Université d'État de Gand* (Louvain-la-Neuve, Université Catholique de Louvain, 1998).

Rochet, Bénédicte, 'La vie quotidienne au Collège du Sacré-Coeur à Charleroi pendant la Seconde Guerre mondiale (mai 1940–1945),' *Actes du sixième congrès de l'association des cercles francophones d'histoire et d'archéologie de Belgique*, LIIIème Congrès de la Fédération (Mons, Sept. 2002), pp. 687–703.

Rodnick, David, *Post-war Germans. An Anthropologist's Account* (New Haven, Yale, 1948).

Rodogno, Davide, 'Italian soldiers in the Balkans: the Experience of the Occupation (1941–1943)', *Journal of Southern Europe and the Balkans*, vol. 6, no. 2 (August 2004), pp. 125–44.

Roest, F. and Scheren, J., *Oorlog in de stad Amsterdam 1939–1941* (Amsterdam, Van Gennep, 1998).

Rouquet, François and Voldman, Danièle (eds), *Identités féminines et violences politiques (1936–1946)* (Les Cahiers de l'IHTP, no. 31, 1995).

Samuel, Raphael, 'On the Methods of History Workshop: a Reply', *History Workshop* (1980), pp. 162–76.

Sanders, Paul, *Histoire du marché noir, 1940–1946* (Paris, Perrin, 2001).

Sauvy, Alfred, *La Vie économique des Français de 1939 à 1945* (Paris, Flammarion, 1978).

Schreiber, Jean-Philippe and Van Doorslaer, Rudy (eds), *Les Curateurs du Ghetto. L'association des Juifs en Belgique sous l'occupation nazie* (Brussels, 2004).

Schwartz, Paula, 'The Politics of Food and Gender in Occupied Paris', *Modern and Contemporary France*, vol. 7, no. 1 (1999), pp. 35–45.

Scott, James C., *Weapons of the Weak. Everyday Forms of Peasant Resistance* (New Haven and London, Yale University Press, 1985).

Sémelin, Jacques, *Unarmed against Hitler. Civilian Resistance in Europe, 1939–1943* (Westport, CT, Praeger, 1993).

Senje, Sigurd, *Dømte kvinner* (Oslo, Pax Forlag A/S, 1986).

Sfikas, Thanasis D., *The British Labour Government and the Greek Civil War. The Imperialism of 'Non-Intervention'* (Keele, Ryburn Pub., 1994).

Sidot, L., *L'Identité française dans la Lorraine annexée et nazifiée. Une Logique de l'être* (Mâcon, Gourdon, 1995).

Sijes, B.A., *De Februari-Staking* (The Hague, Martinus Nijhoff, 1954).

Sijes, B.A., *De arbeidsinzet. De gedwongen arbeid van Nederlanders in Duitsland, 1940–1945* (The Hague, Martinus Nijhoff, 1966).

Singleton, Fred, *A Short History of the Yugoslav Peoples* (Cambridge, Cambridge University Press, 1985).

Skodvin, Magne (ed.), *Norge i krig* (8 vols, Oslo, Aschehoug, 1984–7).

'Sovetskaia Molodezh' v Germanii: Dokumenty antifashistskogo soprotivleniiq 1943–1945gg', *Istoricheskii Arkhiv* (3), 1995, pp. 63–80.

Spoerer, Mark, *Zwangsarbeit unter dem Hakenkreuz* (Stuttgart-Munich, Deutsche Verlags-Anstalt, 2001).

Spoerer, M., 'Recent Findings on Forced Labour under the Nazi Regime and an Agenda for Future Research', *Annali dell'Istituto Storico Italo-Germanico in Trento*, XXVIII (2002), pp. 373–88.

Stargardt, Nicholas, *Witnesses of War. Children's Lives under the Nazis* (London, Jonathan Cape, 2005).

Steinbeck, John, *The Moon Is Down* (London, Heinemann, 1942).

Steinweis, Alan E., 'Ideology and Infrastructure: German Area Science and Planning for the Germanization of Eastern Europe 1939–1944', *East European Quarterly*, 28/3 (1994), pp. 335–47.

Struye, Paul and Jacquemyns, Guillaume, *La Belgique sous l'occupation allemande (1940–1944)* (Brussels, 1950).

Szarota, Tomasz, *Okupowanej Warszawy dzień powszedni* (Warsaw, Czytelnik, 1988).

Szarota, Tomasz, *Życie codzienne w stolicach okupowanej Europy* (Warsaw, Państwowy Instytut Wydawniczy, 1995).

Tamm, Ditlev, *Retsopgøret efter besættelsen* (Copenhagen, Jurist- og økonomforbundets Forlag, 1985).

Tandler, Nicolas, *L'Impossible Biographie de Georges Marchais* (Paris, Édition Albatross, 1980).

Tenfelde, Klaus, 'Forced Labour in the Second World War. German Experiences and European Comparisons', Paper given to the History of Work seminar at St Antony's College, Oxford, 18 Feb. 2005.

Texcier, Jean, *Conseils à l'occupé* (Paris, 1940).

Thalmann, Rita, *La Mise au Pas. Idéologie et Stratégie sécuritaire dans la France occupée* (Paris, Fayard, 1991).

Thomas, William and Znaniecki, Florian, *The Polish Peasant in Europe and America* (5 vols, Richard G. Badger, 1918–20).

Thompson, E.P., *Customs in Common* (London, Merlin Press, 1993).

Umbreit, Hans, *Der Militärbefehlshaber in Frankreich, 1940–1944* (Boppard-am-Rhein, Harald Boldt Verlag, 1968).

Uyttebrouck, André and Despy-Meyer, A., *Les 150 ans de l'ULB (1834–1984)*, (Brussels, Éditions de l'ULB, 1984).

Van den Wijngaert, Mark, *Schoollopen in oorlogstijd, het dagelijkse leven van middelbare scholieren tijdens de duiste besetting* (Brussels, 1988).

Van den Wijngaert, Mark, *Nood breekt wet economische collabouratie of accommodatie? Het beleid van Alexandre Galopin, gouverneur van de Société Générale tijdens de bezetting (1940–1944)* (Tielt, Lannoo, 1990).

Van Doorslaer, Rudi, *De kommunistische partij van België en het sovjet-duits niet-aanvalspakt* (Brussels, Masereelfonds, 1975).

Van Zanden, J.L., *Een klein land in de 20e eeuw. Economische geschiedenis van Nederland 1914–1995* (Utrecht, Het Spectrum, 1997).

Veillon, Dominique, *Vivre et survivre en France 1939–1947* (Paris, Payot, 1995).

Veillon, Dominique and Flonneau, Jean-Marie (ed.), *Le Temps des restrictions en France (1939–1949)*, Cahiers de l'IHTP, nos 32–3, May 1996.

Veld, N.K.C.A. in t, *De SS en Nederland. Documenten uit SS-archieven, 1933–1945* (Den Haag, Martinus Nijhoff, 1976).

Vergnon, Gilles, *Le Vercors. Histoire et mémoire d'un maquis* (Paris, Éditions de l'Atelier, 2002).

Verhoeyen, E., *België bezet 1940–1944* (Brussels, BRTN, 1993).

Virgili, Fabrice, *Shorn Women. Gender and Punishment in Liberation France* (Oxford, Berg, 2002).

Volder, K., *Werken in Duitsland, 1940–45* (Bedum, Profiel, 1990).

Vos, L. de, *De Tweede Wereldoorlog* (Leuven, Davidsfonds, 2004).

Walczak, Marian, *Nauczyciele wielkopolscy w latach wojny i okupacj, 1939–1945* (Poznań, Instytut Zachodni, 1974).

Warmbrunn, Werner, *The Dutch under German Occupation* (Stanford, Stanford University Press, 1963).

Warring, Anette, 'Køn, seksualitet og national identitet', *Historisk Tidsskrift*, no. 2 (1994), pp. 292–314.

Warring, Anette, *Tyskerpiger under besættelse og retsopgør* (Copenhagen, Gyldendal, 1994).

Warschau unter dem Hakenkreuz. Leben und Alltag in besetzten Warschau 1.10.1939 bis 31.7.1944 (Paderborn, Schöningh, 1985).

Weber, W., *Die innere Sicherheit im besetzten Belgien und Nordfrankreich 1940–1944* (Düsseldorf, Droste, 1978).

Weiner, A., *Making Sense of War. The Second World War and the Fate of the Bolshevik Revolution* (Princeton, Princeton University Press, 2001).

Wette, W. (ed.), *Was damals Recht war. NS-Militär-und-Strafjustiz im Vernichtungskrieg* (Essen, Klartext, 1996).

Wieviorka, Olivier, 'A la recherche de l'engagement', *Vingtième siècle, revue d'histoire*, no. 60 (Oct–Dec. 1998), pp. 58–70.

Windmuller, J.P. and de Galan, C., *Arbeidsverhoudingen in Nederland* (2 vols, Utrecht-Antwerpen, Het Spectrum, 1979).

Winters, M., *Herinneringen aan de Arbeitseinsatz, 1942–1945* (Leeuwarden, Perio, 1990).

Witte, E., Burgelman, J.C. and Stouthuysen, P. (eds), *Tussen restauratie en vernieuwing. Aspecten van de naoorlogse Belgische politiek* (Brussels, VUBPRESS, 1989).

Wright, Gordon, *The Ordeal of Total War, 1939–1945* (New York and London, Harper Torchbooks, 1968).

Wulf, Józef, *Lodz. Das letzte Ghetto auf polnischen Boden, Schriftenreihe der Bundeszentrale für Heimatdienst*, 59 (Bonn, 1962).

Xydis, Stephen G., *The Economy and Finances of Greece under Occupation* (New York, Greek Government Office of Information, n.d.)

Zee, H.A. van der, *The Hunger Winter. Occupied Holland 1944–45* (London, Jill Norman and Hobhouse, 1982).

'Znachitel'nye predpriiatiia vyvezheny polnost'in... (Dokumenty ob itogakh evakuatsii iz Belorussii) 1941, APRF, Staroe Ploshed', 1995, no. 2, pp. 115–66.

Zubkova, Elena, *Polsevoennoe sovetskoe obshchestvo. Politika in povsednevnost' 1945–1953gg* (Moscow, Rosspen, 2000).

Films and Television Documentaries

Molodaia gvardiia [The Young Guard] (1948). Screenplay Sergei Gerasimov, based on the story of the same name by Aleksandr Fadeev.

Op de drempel van het grote vergeten (2003). Director Thom Verheul. NCRV TV.

Interviews

Jacques Hervé, Joué-lès-Tours, 12 June 1997.

Websites

www.info.omroep.nl/ncrv
www.oorlogsmonumenten.nl
www.oktober44.nl
info.omroep.nl/ncrv

Index